THE ALL-NEW HOCKEY'S 100

also by Stan Fischler

Gordie Howe

Goal! My Life on Ice: Rod Gilbert's Story

Hockey! The Story of the World's Fastest Sport

Stan Mikita—The Turbulent Career of a Hockey Superstar

Bobby Orr and the Big, Bad Bruins

I've Got to Be Me, Derek Sanderson's Autobiography

Strange But True Hockey Stories

Hockey Stars of 1969

Hockey Stars of 1970

Hockey Stars of 1971

Hockey Stars of 1972

Hockey Stars of 1973

Hockey Stars of 1974

Hockey Stars of 1975

Hockey Stars of 1976

The Flying Frenchmen—Hockey's Greatest Dynasty (with Maurice "The Rocket" Richard)

Up From the Minor Leagues of Hockey (with Shirley Fischler)

Heroes of Hockey

Play the Man, Brad Park's Autobiography

The Burly Bruins

The Conquering Canadiens

The Roaring Rangers

Go, Leafs, Go!

Fire on Ice

Power Play, An Affectionate History of the Toronto Maple Leafs

The Fast Flying Wings

The Blazing North Stars

Saga of the St. Louis Blues

Chicago's Black Hawks

The Battling Bruins—Stanley Cup Champions

Slapshot

Phil Esposito

Ranger Fever (with Marv Albert)

Hockey's Greatest Teams

Gordie Howe and Sons

Hockey Action (with the editors of *Action Sports Hockey*)

Bobby Clarke and the Ferocious Flyers

The Philadelphia Flyers—Supermen of the Ice

The Buffalo Sabres—Swashbucklers of the Ice

New York Rangers—The Icemen Cometh

Hockey's Toughest Ten

Hockey's Greatest Rivalries

Slashing!

Fischler's Hockey Encyclopedia (with Shirley Fischler)

This Is Hockey (with photography by Dan Baliotti)

The Scoring Punch—Gilbert, Mahovlich, Apps, Dionne

Make Way for the Leafs—Toronto's Comeback

Speed and Style—The Montreal Canadiens

Those Were the Days

The Triumphant Islanders—Hockey's Newest Dynasty

Uptown, Downtown—A Trip Through Time on New York's Subways

Garry Unger and the Battling Blues

Power on Ice, Denis Potvin's Autobiography

Moving Millions: An Inside Look at Mass Transit

The Comeback Yankees (with Richard Friedman)

Showdown! Baseball's Ultimate Confrontations

The Hammer: Confessions of a Hockey Enforcer

Offside! Hockey from the Inside

The Hockey Encyclopedia (with Shirley Fischler)

Breakaway '86–'87—The Hockey Almanac (with Shirley Fischler)

Breakaway '87–'88—The Hockey Almanac (with Shirley Fischler)

Breakaway '88–'89—The Hockey Almanac (with Shirley Fischler)

A Personal Ranking of the Best Players in Hockey History

THE ALL-NEW HOCKEY'S 100

Completely Revised
and Updated!

STAN FISCHLER

Research Editor: Andrew Schneider

McGraw-Hill Ryerson Limited
Toronto Montreal

First published in 1988 by
McGraw-Hill Ryerson Limited
330 Progress Avenue
Scarborough, Ontario
Canada
M1P 2Z5

ISBN 0-07-549674-7

1 2 3 4 5 6 7 8 9 0 AP 7 6 5 4 3 2 1 0 9 8

Cover Design: Marc Mireault

Cover Photo Credits (clockwise from the top left): Bruce Bennett, Frank Prazak, Bruce Bennett, Denis Brodeur; (centre): Bruce Bennett

Frank Prazak photograph of Frank Mahovlich reproduced courtesy Hockey Hall of Fame, Toronto, Canada.

A complete list of photograph credits appears on page 382.

Printed and bound in Canada

Canadian Cataloguing in Publication Data

Fischler, Stan, date–
    The all-new hockey's 100

Completely rev. and updated.
ISBN 0-07-549674-7

1. Hockey players—Rating of.   2. Hockey—Records.
I. Schneider, Andrew.   II. Title.   III. Title:
Hockey's 100.

GV848.5.A1F585 1988   796.96'2'0922   C88-094937-6

To Munson Campbell, who for four decades has been to off-the-ice hockey greatness what Gordie Howe was to on-the-ice immortality.

by John Kieran

"I'll Take Hockey Any Time!"

I'm a fairly peaceful man, and an old-time baseball fan,
You can hear me yell when Heilman hits the ball;
And I howl when Ty Cobb stabs one, and I growl when Speaker grabs one,
And I roar when Babe Ruth's homer clears the wall.
But the diamond sport is quiet to that reeling rousing riot,
To a splashing game of hockey at its prime;
It's a shindig wild and gay; it's a battle served frappé;
Give me hockey, I'll take hockey any time!

Once, while crazy with the heat, I coughed up to buy a seat,
Just to watch a pair of robbers grab a purse.
It was clinch and stall and shove and "Please excuse my glove,"
Till I blessed them with a healthy Irish curse.
But for fighting, fast and free, grab your hat and come with me,
Sure the thing they call boxing is a crime,
And for ground and lofty whacking and enthusiastic smacking,
Give me hockey, I'll take hockey any time!

I've an ever-ready ear for a rousing football cheer,
And I love to see a halfback tackle low.
It's a really gorgeous sight when the boys begin to fight
With a touchdown only half a yard to go.
But take all the most exciting parts of football, baseball, fighting,
And then mix them up to make a game sublime,
Serve it up with lots of ice, you don't have to ask me twice,
Give me hockey, I'll take hockey any time!

Yes, for speed and pep and action, there is only one attraction,
You'll see the knockouts, they're a dozen for a dime,
When the bright steel blades are ringing and the shiny sticks are swinging,
Give me hockey, I'll take hockey any time!

Contents

Preface

One of the most popular ongoing contests in the National Hockey League never takes place on the ice but rather in living rooms across the continent. The participants are NHL fans and the competition can be categorized under the "Who's Better?" label.

In the mid-1950s, for example, when the Montreal Canadiens and Detroit Red Wings dominated big-league hockey, the prevailing question was "Who's better—Maurice Richard or Gordie Howe?" In the 1960s, the most debated question involved a pair of dynamic left wings, Bobby Hull and Frank Mahovlich.

Comparing superstars continues to be great fun, as any supporter of Wayne Gretzky and Mario Lemieux will freely admit. Even more enjoyable, as far as this long-time observer is concerned, is the business of determining the finest players of all time—in precise order.

The first time I undertook this challenge—in 1984—a number of readers were upset about the order of selection. Why, many asked, was Wayne Gretzky reduced to number ten status? Shouldn't the legendary Bobby Orr be listed higher than thirteen? Why is Eddie Shore number two on the all-time list?

In all cases, the answer is supplied by the book's subtitle—a *personal* ranking of the best players in hockey history. The opinions supplied herewith are unabashedly subjective. They are based on my personal viewing as much as possible. I began watching hockey in 1939 and, therefore, have had a first-hand look at the majority of players evaluated.

As for the players who skated in earlier seasons, I relied as much as possible on the word of those who were there and, in other cases, on the printed word. This was not an era that was taken lightly, which meant that considerable research was involved in appraising the likes of Eddie Shore, Frank Boucher, and their ilk.

Adjustments had to be made to suit the era. Significantly fewer games were played before World War II than in the postwar period, and goals were more difficult to come by in the epoch of defensive hockey that preceded the introduction of the center red line in 1944. When I was a youth, anyone who scored twenty goals in a season was considered the equivalent of a .300 hitter in baseball. Nowadays, an NHL sharpshooter would have to pot at least forty goals to be included in that category.

Another sticky point was the inclusion of goaltenders alongside forwards and defensemen on the list. The temptation was to list goalies separately, but that would have been too easy so I arbitrarily decided to place one goalie in every group of ten where feasible, while maintaining a balance between scorers and defenders throughout the book.

The biggest problem in the end was creating a standard that would apply to all eras despite the fact that the styles of play varied tremendously. To do so, a strict set of standards was established. This included longevity, championship teams, awards, records, impact on the game, character, the quality of hockey played at the time, and the quality of the team on which the player performed.

One reason for Bobby Orr's relatively low rating (for him) is the indisputable fact that he played during the NHL's first decade of expansion (1967–1977) when the game's quality was at an all-time low. By contrast, Doug Harvey, who in my estimation was a better defenseman than Orr, starred during the NHL's pre-expansion era when overall quality and competition were at their zenith.

When all is said and done, however, the bottom line is that this is a *personal* list and your disagreements and discussions are, as they were in the original edition, welcome.

Stan Fischler
New York City
May 1988

Acknowledgments

Like many authors who tend to exaggerate the importance of their works, I was under the impression that the original edition of *Hockey's 100* was a very special book, not to mention the first of its kind. Naturally, I believed that the positive reaction of the public underlined my point and that somewhere down the line a new and completely revised edition should be published.

But as any author who has been in the business a decade or more can attest, there's a considerable gap between an author's desires and the practical needs of a publisher. In short, it isn't that easy to find a book company willing to stick its neck out with a second edition of a tome that it didn't publish in the first place.

That, in a nutshell, is why I owe a significant debt of thanks to consulting publisher Dan Diamond of Toronto who linked yours truly with McGraw-Hill Ryerson. Once the publisher made its commitment, I then had the good fortune of working with a real pro, editor Glen Ellis. All of my colleagues in the writing business should be so lucky as to have a Glen Ellis to handle their books.

A book of this nature requires considerable behind-the-scenes legwork. Orchestrating the research was the indomitable Andrew Schneider, who performed Promethean feats without breaking a sweat. Without Andrew, this book would not have come to fruition.

Others who did nitty-gritty work and were, in effect, unsung heroes include Shirley Fischler, Kay Ohara, Kelly O'Reilly, Mickey Kramer, Steve Reilly, Gabe Price, Andrea Lehman, Jimmy Hopf, Dave Katz, and Keisha and Kell Ciabattari.

As always, the patience and inspiration of my top line, Shirley, Ben, and Simon, are appreciated beyond words.

Photo Acknowledgments

The author owes a debt of gratitude to several hockey sources who provided much-needed assistance in the gathering of photos for this book. John Halligan, who superbly orchestrates the New York Rangers public relations department, and his able lieutenants, Barry Watkins and Ginger Killian, unearthed a number of splendid pictures. Lefty Reid, curator of the Hockey Hall of Fame in Toronto, came through in the clutch as did Bill Galloway, who mans the National Archives of Canada in Ottawa. NHL Vice-President Steve Ryan was a vital catalyst, and the public relations directors of the NHL teams came through admirably. Special thanks to photographer Bruce Bennett, the pro's pro, and to Detroit Red Wings' publicist Bill Jamieson, the best at his trade in the business. Warm thanks are extended to all.

Introduction

The willingness of Stan Fischler to lay his hockey reputation on the line for all addicts of the game to dissect and analyze has produced a book that is stocked full of hockey lore, and at the same time as controversial as it is comprehensive. It is the hockey fanatic's history book and, as such, unlocks a wealth of heretofore little-known hockey facts and faces. The anecdotes, vignettes, and treasured memories of hockey wars past give us all a taste of the action through the game's formative eras—the pre-NHL years, the prewar years, the war years, preexpansion, postexpansion, and the WHA—right up to the game as it stands today.

From the perspective of a former Detroit Red Wings fan, I found nostalgia such as the recreation of Rocket Richard's playoff goals against the Wings to be particularly painful. The mental pictures and emotional strains evoked by Stan's description of such moments brought upon me the same empty feeling that I had as a fan when it actually happened. I would not be surprised if my fellow readers experienced similar flashes of *déja vu* in reading about a special moment in their own hockey lives. And, like myself, I am sure all readers will enjoy learning about some players and episodes of which we have never heard before.

But, above all, I believe that my fellow readers will derive the most enjoyment from this book in disagreeing with the rankings. For example, how could Bobby Orr not be rated in the top three? And how, incredibly, can Alex Delvecchio not be included in the top ten?

Stan, I am sure that with this work you have provided fuel for the Hot Stove League arguments for years to come. From one hockey fan to another, thanks for the hard work that produced just what we addicts needed: a volume chock-full of colorful stories about past and present ice heroes.

And, to your many readers, I pose one final question: When you prepare your own top 100, will you be as well researched as Mr. Fischler was in his listing? Whatever your reply, enjoy the road to your conclusions.

Thank you, Stan, for the honor of introducing this thoroughly delightful book.

National Hockey League
John A. Ziegler, Jr.
President

1

Gordie Howe
(1946–1980)

When the pseudonym *Mister Hockey* was coined, one did not require Sherlock Holmesian logic to deduce that there was one—and only one—performer who qualified for that distinction. Gordie Howe did it all.

The slope-shouldered native of Floral, Saskatchewan, was a star virtually from the moment he stepped onto a major league rink at the age of six. Miraculously, Howe remained a first-liner in the bigs forty-five years later.

In a moment of understated drollery, Aldo Guidolin, an opponent of Howe, once remarked, "Gordie plays the funny kind of game; he doesn't let anyone else touch the puck!"

A right wing possessed of extraordinary strength in a body measuring 6'1", 200 pounds, Howe's armament was the most formidable the game has known. "His shot was uncanny," said goalie Glenn Hall, a Hall of Famer, "because it would come at the net in so many different ways."

Unique among superstars, Howe was an ambidextrous stickhandler who would deliver a remarkably accurate shot with so fluid a motion that goalies frequently failed to see the puck leave Gordie's stick.

Howe's credentials said it all. He won the Hart Trophy as the NHL's most valuable player in 1952, 1953, 1957, 1958, 1960, and 1963. "He was not only the greatest hockey player I've ever seen," said defenseman Bill Gadsby, a Hall of Famer, "but also the greatest athlete."

Skating for the Detroit Red Wings, with whom he spent most of his professional career (1946–71), Gordie led the NHL in scoring in 1951, 1952, 1953, 1954, 1957, and 1963.

It has been said that hockey is a game of mistakes. And when one considers that players employ artificial feet (skates) and artificial arms (sticks) and maneuver on an artificial surface (ice), it is not surprising that errors are part of the game's fabric. Yet, Howe was the most flawless performer in a flawed and often brutal pastime.

Two episodes define the essential Howe. The first, which occurred on a night in March 1950, nearly ended his life at the age of twenty-two. The Red Wings had taken on their bitter rivals, the Toronto Maple Leafs, in the opening round of the Stanley Cup playoffs.

Ted "Teeder" Kennedy, the Leafs' captain and center, was carrying the puck toward the Wings' zone when Howe swerved diagonally across the ice to intercept his foe. A split second before Gordie connected, Kennedy pulled up and, according to the Red Wings, fouled Howe with his stick. Gordie was catapulted into the wooden sideboards and crumpled to the ice with a fractured skull. Removed to a hospital, Gordie was considered a goner. His parents were summoned from distant Saskatchewan and, at best, it was presumed that if he did manage to survive, Howe would never play professional hockey again. A year later, he was the league's scoring leader.

The second incident took place during a regular season game between the Wings and the New York Rangers. Howe had learned from the Kennedy affair that it was essential for survival in the ice jungle to hit first, keep the elbows high, and ask questions later. "Gordie," explained Islanders' general manager Bill Torrey, "would simply psych out his enemies."

Rangers' coach Phil Watson had assigned his behemoth left wing Eddie Shack the dubious task of checking Howe. At one point, the foes collided behind the Rangers' net whereupon Shack's teammate, Lou Fontinato, then regarded as the NHL's best fighter, pushed in and began flailing at Gordie. It was the worst move in Fontinato's career.

Referee Art Skov, who was a yard away from the battlers, describing the ensuing blows: "Howe began smashing him with lefts and rights, and then fired an uppercut that smashed Lou's nose. I just stood back and said, 'No way I'm going to break up this one.' Big George Hayes was the other linesman in the game, and he told me to stay out of it. Howe cleaned Fontinato like you've never seen."

It was a measure of Howe's absolute superiority over all challengers that he not only outperformed but outlasted the aces with whom he was most frequently compared. In the early 1950s, the standard argument was: "Who's better, Gordie Howe or Maurice Richard?" Yet, upon his retirement in 1960, Richard was the first to allow that Howe was the best of them all. "Gordie," said Richard, "could do *everything*."

Howe had already been an NHL star when Bobby Orr was born in 1948, and Gordie was still in the majors when Orr retired as an NHL defenseman in 1979. Neither Richard nor Orr, nor any skater for that matter, could compare with Howe when it came to surviving the test of time.

Ironically, Gordie suffered severe doubts about his ability to make a career out of hockey, although from the moment of his NHL debut, he had winner written all over him. Even after he led all scorers in the 1949 playoffs, Gordie wondered how he rated against the Richards and Kennedys. "I still wasn't so sure I was a star," Howe explained. "When I went home to Saskatchewan that summer, I started playing baseball again. One day, a kid came up for my autograph and while I signed it, he said, 'Mister Howe, what do you do in the winter?'"

In 1971, Gordie played his last game for the Red Wings and accepted what he later, sadly, discovered was an innocuous front office job. After two years of inactivity, Gordie executed one of the most astonishing comebacks in sports history. At age forty-five, he signed with the Houston Aeros of the World Hockey Association. His teammates were sons Mark and Marty. Slower perhaps but no less superb, Gordie orchestrated the Aeros the way Leonard Bernstein conducted the New York Philharmonic. Houston won the AVCO World Cup and the WHA title. That done, Gordie was selected to play for Team Canada against the Soviet All-Star team. Having shown the Russians the tricks of his trade, Howe returned to Houston and led the Aeros to another AVCO Cup in 1975.

Gordon Howe was born March 31, 1928, in Floral, Saskatchewan, near the city of Saskatoon. Gordie was the fourth of nine children of Catherine and Albert Howe. The Howes were a loving family, but, like so many others living through the Great Depression, they were poor.

"The only equipment I had was skates," Howe remembered, "and a stick. I took magazines and mail order catalogues, stuck 'em in my socks, and had shin pads. I tied 'em together with rubber bands from inner tubes. We played with tennis balls instead of a puck. The ball would get so hard from the cold (often thirty to forty degrees below zero Fahrenheit), we'd have to get new ones all the time. A woman next door used to warm them up in an oven for us."

Despite the hardship, Gordie recalled his youthful hockey years with affection. Long after he had established himself as the game's greatest star, he acknowledged that his most fervent wish was to skate on a line with his eldest sons, Mark and Marty. That wish came true on February 17, 1971.

"It was," said Howe, "the game I'll never forget."

It was an exhibition, charity match—the Detroit Red Wings against the Junior A Red Wings. Gordie skated alongside his kids, who then played for the Junior club. It was then that Gordie perceived what other hockey scouts later would realize—that Mark Howe had many of the same ice gifts possessed by his dad.

No matter where Howe skated, his trademark—effortless excellence—made an impression on critics. "Gordie had the ability and the knack for making the difficult plays look easy, routine," said Chicago Black Hawks' vice-president Tommy Ivan.

He was no less appreciated in Hartford, where he emigrated with his two boys in 1977 to play for the Whalers. When Hartford was admitted to the NHL in 1979, Gordie returned to his former hunting grounds and drew capacity crowds. They wanted to see whether the fifty-year-old grandfather could skate with young Turks like Bryan Trottier, Marcel Dionne, and Wayne Gretzky.

"Gordie proved that he could," said Whalers' president Howard Baldwin. "In our first year in the NHL we were the only former WHA team to make the playoffs. We can thank Gordie for that."

A year later, Howe retired at age fifty-one. The Whalers did not make the playoffs.

Over a period of thirty-two years, Gordie scored 975 goals, 1,383 assists, and 2,358 points. Most of these were obtained when the value of a goal in a defense-oriented game was considerably more than it is now. He was the most gifted forward, an accomplished defensive player, revered as a team man, and the only player to have dominated three different eras—postwar NHL, the Golden Era of the 1960s, and the Expansion Era.

"Hockey," Gordie liked to say, "is a man's game."

In that game Gordie Howe was *the* man.

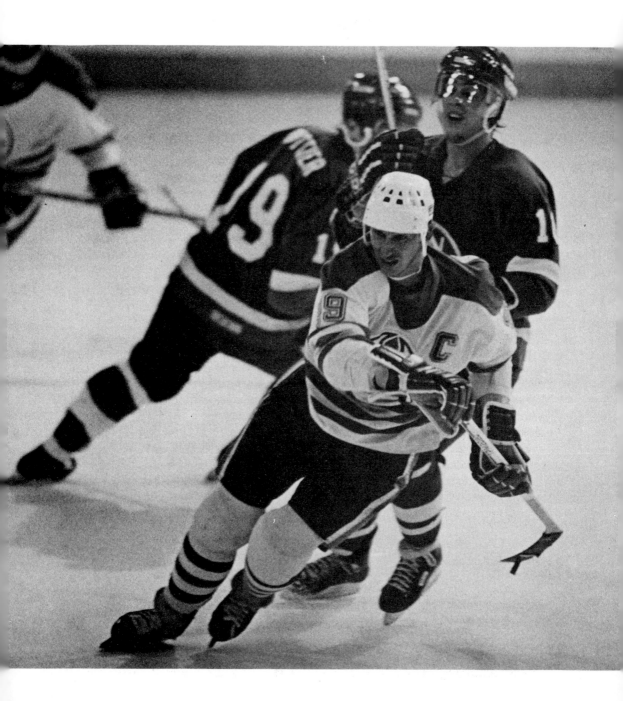

2

Wayne Gretzky
(1978–   )

There has never been anyone quite like the emperor of the Los Angeles Kings.

At age nine, he was commanding headlines across Canada. No one had ever scored goals with the ease and frequency of thimblelike Wayne Gretzky.

He was, of course, no one to be taken seriously. By the time he reached his teens, he would discover cars, girls, and beer. Hockey would be forgotten as it was with so many other high-scoring tykes before him.

But at age sixteen, Gretzky, who by now was built along the dimensions of a giant needle, was scoring at such a prolific pace that he was being pursued by every major league scout on the continent.

Still, few believed that he could ever cut it with the pros. He was too skinny, relatively slow, and with no disposition to bodycheck. Nevertheless, defying all odds, at age seventeen Gretzky signed a professional contract with Indianapolis of the World Hockey Association.

People in the know said he would last a month—if that long—under the bombardment of hockey's most notorious headhunters. Instead, he was an instant star and got better by the month. When the Racers of Indianapolis suffered an assortment of financial traumas, Gretzky was dealt to the Edmonton Oilers and continued his relentless improvement. And when the Oilers were admitted to the National Hockey League in 1979, a substantial number of doubters remained.

The WHA was easy, they scoffed. The NHL was the real thing. Gretzky, it was suggested, would wilt under the incessant pressure.

At age eighteen, *The Great One* made his NHL debut. The results were mind-boggling, to say the least. He finished tied for first in total scoring points with fifty-one goals in seventy-nine games, not to mention a league-leading eighty-six assists and a total of 137 points. He won the Hart Trophy as the league's most valuable player, was picked to the Second All-Star Team, and surely would have been designated the rookie of the year had he not been disqualified on a technicality (he had previously played in the WHA and therefore was deemed ineligible for the Calder Memorial Trophy). He also captured the Lady Byng Trophy for sportsmanship and excellence. "Right from the start," said St. Louis Blues' coach Red Berenson, "he just tore the league apart. It's scary to think what he might do before he's done."

Just as Berenson suggested, Gretzky increased his scoring dynamics with each passing year. As a sophomore in the NHL, *The Great One*—now nineteen years old— alternated between devastating and terrifying. This time he led the NHL in scoring (55 goals, 109 assists, and 164 points), won the Hart Trophy, made the First All-Star Team, and set NHL records for assists and points in a regular season.

"He has the greatest moves I've ever seen," said Henri Richard, a Hall of Famer who, as a center like Gretzky, was acclaimed for *his* moves.

Richard watched from a seat in Montreal's hallowed Forum in April 1981 as Gretzky choreographed one of the most uncanny upsets in Stanley Cup playoff annals. The Oilers, not merely underdogs but 200–1 longshots, routed the Canadiens in three straight games of the best-of-five series as *The Great One* mesmerized the foe.

Gordie Howe, who played against Gretzky and watched Wayne develop from his WHA debut on to NHL maturity, perceived *The Great One* another way: "Wayne's the only guy I've ever known who plays 70 percent of the game from the neck up."

By the time the 1981–82 season—Gretzky's third in the NHL—had begun, it had become evident that all previous adjectives would be inadequate to describe his performance. From the very first drop of the puck, he sprinted far ahead of his closest pursuers, and then an irony developed; Wayne had principally been renowned for his stickhandling and playmaking rather than his shot, but now he was popping goals at a breathtaking pace.

Only two players in NHL history had been able to score fifty goals in fifty games. Maurice Richard did it in 1944 and Mike Bossy equalled the mark in 1980–81. As stoppable as a runaway spaceship, *Gretzky scored his fiftieth goal in only his thirty-ninth game* and finished the 1981–82 campaign leaving the record book in shambles. He totaled ninety-two goals, exceeding the all-time record (76) previously set by Phil Esposito, collected 120 assists, topping his own mark, and amassed 212 points.

During the 1981 Stanley Cup quarterfinals between the Oilers and the defending Stanley Cup champion Islanders, Gretzky very nearly developed an even more monumental upset than the previous one over the Canadiens. Although the Islanders eventually prevailed, they were defeated twice, and even their respected general manager Bill Torrey was moved to verse to put Gretzky in perspective. Torrey sent the following poem to his pal, Lou Nanne, general manager of the Minnesota North Stars:

> *This epistle will be rather short*
> *and sweet*
> *I need time to figure a way to*
> *keep number 99 off the score*
> *sheet.*
> *It's scary to think disaster lurks*
> *due to some 20-year-old,*
> *But after looking at the tapes,*
> *Gretzky is something to behold.*

At the time these lines were penned, nobody could have imagined the heights to which Gretzky would ascend in the next seven years. Since then Gretzky has accomplished the following:

- Led Edmonton to four Stanley Cup championships
- Won eight Hart Trophies as the NHL's most valuable player
- Led the league in scoring from 1980–87, a total of eight consecutive seasons
- Set the NHL scoring record of 215 points (52+163=215) in 1984–85
- Set all-time goal, assist, and points records for one season—92 goals in 1981–82, 163 assists in 1985–86, and 215 points in 1985–86
- Was named to the First All-Star Team eight consecutive years

- Holds or shares forty-one NHL individual records
- Is third on the NHL all-time scoring list

These are only a handful of *The Great One*'s accomplishments. More experts have labeled him as the greatest active player than any other performer who has graced the NHL since expansion. He has not only proven himself in NHL play but also has excelled on the international front in Canada Cup tournaments, as well as *Rendez-Vous '87*.

Inquisitively, Gretzky's 1987–88 performance aroused the skeptics. For the first time since 1979, he failed to finish first in scoring, when Mario Lemieux easily topped him (168–149) in April 1988, revealing certain shortcomings in Gretzky's game. Wayne also proved vulnerable to injury for the first time, missing twenty-eight games and demonstrating that he could be even more susceptible to body work as he grows older and slower.

Gretzky seems to have lost his youthful enthusiasm, and during the summer of 1987, he freely talked of retirement in the next few years. Nevertheless, his ex-teammates insist that Wayne is still better than Lemieux. "He had a better point percentage than Lemieux," says Oilers' center Mark Messier. "He was the best player in the Canada Cup and his absence was the only reason we didn't get well over 100 points."

Gretzky has often been criticized for the fact that—unlike Bryan Trottier, Lemieux, and Messier—he has avoided the contact aspect of hockey. It was considered a major event during the 1988 Oilers-Jets playoff when Gretzky actually threw a bodycheck at Winnipeg defenseman Dave Ellett. It was so astonishing an event that he received an ovation from the crowd at Northlands Coliseum.

"The greatest thing ever to happen," pronounced Winnipeg Jets' general manager John Ferguson. "The hit," he said, "changes everything.

"Wayne Gretzky hit one of our players. Now there's no reason not to hit him back!"

Ferguson's sarcasm reveals that not everyone is enamored with Gretzky nor is there any certainty that he will be able to continue on his pace as a King. But there is no escaping the obvious. He has been the most prolific scorer the game has known—creative, insightful, and most of all, consistent on the highest level.

Wayne Gretzky was born January 26, 1961, in Brantford, Ontario. Almost from the moment his father, Walter, handed him a stick, Wayne was able to perform magic with the rubber. "He never had to skate well," his father pointed out, "because as a kid he could stay in the same place and beat a player three or four times."

He was seventeen years old and weighed only 161 pounds when he signed a four-year, $875,000 contract with the Indianapolis Racers. When the Racers tripped, Oilers' owner Peter Pocklington bought Gretzky's contract for $850,000 and moved him to Edmonton. It proved to be one of the most sagacious moves in the chronicles of any sport. From the moment he set skate in Edmonton's Northlands Coliseum, Gretzky guaranteed that all 17,300 seats would be filled—and they were. By January 1982, Gretzky had become so outstanding an attraction that scalpers were demanding $200-a-ticket for a regular-season Oilers–Maple Leafs game in Toronto because the fans wanted so desperately to see *The Great One*. "The NHL needs someone to hang its hat on, and Gretzky looks like a hat tree," said Gordie Howe.

Gretzky became more than a hat tree. In the decade 1978–1988, he became the most visible, appealing, and available superstar hockey has known, and, along with Howe, its most effective salesman. Which is not to suggest that Gretzky is "Mr. Perfection." Under pressure, he has been prone to become petulant, "like a spoiled child," as one reporter noted. "He's always complaining to officials," said Richard Brodeur, the veteran goalie.

Some opponents suggest that Gretzky could not maintain his peerless pace without the presence of goons like Kevin McClelland, Marty McSorley, and Steve Smith around him.

Whatever Gretzky's debits, his assets cannot be disputed. "Not since Bobby Orr came into the NHL in 1966 as an eighteen-year-old has anyone captured the imagination of hockey fans the way Gretzky has," wrote E.M. Swift in *Sports Illustrated*. "And no one has appealed to the general public like Gretzky since Bobby Hull appeared on the cover of *Time* in 1968."

Many shortsighted critics—usually of the youthful variety who never viewed Gordie Howe in his prime—have been prone to designate Gretzky as the greatest player of all time. This is absurd for several reasons. Firstly, Gordie Howe excelled for a much longer period; secondly, Howe dominated the NHL at a time when it was an intensely competitive six-team league with a much higher quality level than the diluted twenty-one-team circuit that Gretzky has conquered; and thirdly, even at his peak, Gretzky lacked the vital physical dimension that Howe brought to the game in abundance. Gretzky, however, has proven himself remarkable in so many facets of the game that he is a worthy runner-up to Howe at the top of the all-time list.

In August 1988, Gretzky was traded to Los Angeles in what was the greatest trade in sports history. If Wayne ever leads the Kings to a Stanley Cup, he might then be considered for the all-time top spot.

3

Eddie Shore
(1926–1940)

When the then all-Canadian National Hockey League decided to expand and embrace American cities in 1924, there was considerable doubt that spectators in New York, Boston, Detroit, and Chicago would accept the ice sport from north of the border.

"In order to succeed," said Frank Boucher, who starred for and later became manager of the New York Rangers, " the league needed a superstar of extraordinary dimensions."

Eddie Shore, alias *The Edmonton Express*, was the ace who, more than any, put professional hockey on the American map. Charismatic to a fault, Shore was a product of the Canadian frontier and carried the imprint of that upbringing to the NHL.

Absurdly fearless, totally talented, and dedicated to his profession like nobody before or since, Shore was a defenseman who was so extraordinary a skater that he instinctively became an intrepid puck-carrier and thus added a new dimension to the game—defender-on-the-attack—decades before another Boston skater, Bobby Orr, would copy his style.

During an era when hockey featured more woodchopping than the Canadian north-woods, Shore was virtually indestructible. Opponents understood that if they could neu-tralize the Boston Bruins' defenseman, the game would be theirs. A game involving the Montreal Maroons exemplified the brand of assaults inflicted upon Shore.

One of the Maroons tore open Eddie's cheek with his stick blade, and another sliced his chin. One after another, the Maroons belabored Shore. Late in the game, Shore was clobbered in the mouth. He fell to the ice minus several teeth and remained inert for four-teen minutes while doctors worked him over. When he was finally removed to the dress-ing room, medics discovered that he had suffered a broken nose, three broken teeth, two black eyes, a gashed cheekbone, and a two-inch cut over the left eye. The assortment of wounds would have been sufficient to sideline lesser athletes for more than a month. Shore donned a Bruins uniform for the very next game.

During the early 1920s, Shore's reputation carried across western Canada. He starred in the Pacific Coast League alternately playing for Regina, Edmonton, and Victoria, and soon, his reputation for consummate defensive play carried to the East, where the NHL was undertaking it most ambitious period of expansion.

Boston, already a center of amateur hockey, was selected as the first American NHL franchise. The Bruins' owner, millionaire grocery magnate Charles F. Adams, spent lib-erally to develop a winner, but the Bruins were militantly inadequate until the Pacific Coast League folded in 1926 and a number of superior players became available on the open market.

Adams opened his wallet and obtained a seven-man package including Shore, Frank Boucher, and Duke Keats—all future Hall of Famers. The tab was $50,000 for all seven, which made it one of the best bargains in sports. (By today's fiscal standards, the seven would have been worth $5,000,000.)

Shore arrived in Boston with suitable fuss and fanfare and on November 16, 1926, made his debut in a Bruins uniform. The Boston *Transcript* commented: "Eddie Shore caught the fancy of the fans. The new defenseman is tall, yet sturdily built. His speed is exceptional and he handles his body and stick well."

Within two years, Shore had guided the Bruins to their first Stanley Cup championship and had firmly established professional hockey as a major sport in Beantown. Fans who had never before seen a game were captivated by the iron-muscled defenseman who, at once, seemed to be blunting an enemy attack, wheeling with the puck, and then launching a counterattack against the opponent's goal.

"Shore's abnormally long stride built up a momentum that carried him down the ice with frightening speed," said writer-editor Ed Fitzgerald. "His chilling disregard for personal safety enabled him to maintain peak speed to a point well beyond the limit dared by lesser men. The result was that he came up consistently with plays that other stars were lucky to duplicate once in a lifetime."

From time to time, other enterprising NHL owners cast covetous eyes at Shore and hoped to lure him away from the Bruins but, of course, neither Adams nor manager Art Ross would part with their meal ticket. By far, the most absurd offer for Shore was generated by the New York Rangers.

Colonel John Hammond, president of Madison Square Garden, suggested to Lester Patrick, the Rangers' manager, that it would be to the Rangers' advantage if they obtained Shore. Patrick realized that Hammond was naive about hockey but had no choice except to listen to his boss. Colonel Hammond demanded that Patrick offer Myles Lane, a young, modestly talented defenseman to the Bruins for Shore.

Patrick obliged and, reluctantly, telegraphed the bid to Ross: Myles Lane for Eddie Shore. A day later Ross cabled back what has become a legendary squelch. The Bruins' cable read: LESTER: YOU ARE SO MANY MYLES FROM SHORE YOU NEED A LIFE PRESERVER.

Teamed with such stalwarts as Lionel Hitchman, Dit Clapper, and Cooney Weiland, Shore was named the NHL's most valuable player in 1933, 1935, 1936, and 1938. Not surprisingly, Eddie was voted to the First All-Star Team in 1931, 1932, 1933, 1935, 1936, 1938, and 1939.

Shore was no less galvanic nor capable at age thirty-seven, when the 1938–39 edition of the Bruins finished first with thirty-six wins, ten losses, and two ties—sixteen points ahead of the runner-up Rangers. The Broadway Blueshirts tested the Bruins to the limit in a best-of-seven series that ranks among the classics. During one interlude, Shore rammed Rangers' pesky center Phil Watson into the boards with such vigor that Watson's teammate Muzz Patrick felt obliged to come to the rescue. The robust Patrick, who once had been the amateur heavyweight champion of Canada, walloped Shore so hard that Eddie absorbed a broken nose and a black eye.

Significantly, though Patrick had won the battle, Shore helped win the war. Eddie had his wounds patched and then replied by steering his mates to a four-games-to-three win over the Rangers.

The Bruins next were challenged by the Toronto Maple Leafs who were powered by Harvey "Busher" Jackson, a future Hall of Famer. In the pivotal third game of the series,

Shore defused Jackson with a crunching bodycheck that dislocated the Toronto player's shoulder. The Bruins won the series four games to one and annexed the Stanley Cup.

Edward William Shore was born November 25, 1902, in Fort Qu'Appelle, Saskatchewan, and spent his early years working on the family farm. His youthful passion was breaking wild horses, and his interest in farming inspired him to enter the Manitoba Agricultural College in Winnipeg.

Shore's interest in hockey was tangential at best, and might never have been cultivated had it not been for his brother Aubrey who challenged Eddie to try out for the school team. Eddie accepted the challenge, and he mastered every aspect of the sport. When the Shore family suffered financial hardship, he quit college and began his professional hockey career. He had been steeled by the harsh Saskatchewan winter and imbued with the work ethic by his parents. Armed with these assets, Eddie was to continually startle the world with his extraordinary exploits. Nothing said it better about Shore than an incident that took place on the night of January 2, 1929.

Enroute to meet his teammates who were boarding a train that would take them to Montreal and a game with the Maroons, Shore got stuck in a traffic jam and missed the express train by a few moments. In those days, there was no airline service to Montreal and no further trains that night.

But Shore knew that the Bruins already had a defenseman on the injured list and his presence was needed. He was determined to reach Montreal. Unfortunately, a mid-winter blizzard was reaching its peak, and only the most hardy would even venture out into the streets of Boston.

Eddie contacted a wealthy friend, explained his predicament, and persuaded his pal to supply him with an automobile and a chauffeur. But after five miles of plowing through the storm, the driver told Eddie he would not continue at the wheel. Shore took over and headed for the Green Mountains and the perilous route to Canada. When snow gathered on the windshield, Eddie opened the top half of the glass and bore the brunt of the icy wind and storm. By the time they had reached the halfway point to Montreal, the car had slid off the road four times.

The auto reached the Quebec border at three in the afternoon, but soon fell into a deep ditch. Shore hiked a mile to a farmhouse and persuaded the farmer to hitch a team of horses to his car and put it back on the road. That done, Eddie resumed the drive, arriving at the team's quarters, the Windsor Hotel, at 6:00 p.m. Manager Art Ross was there when Shore arrived and recalled the sight of him:

"His eyes were bloodshot, his face was frostbitten, his fingers bent and set like claws after relentlessly gripping the steering wheel so long, and his unsteady gait showed that his leg was almost paralyzed from tramping on the foot brake."

Ross was reluctant to allow Shore to play that night, but Eddie would not be stopped. Except for a two-minute penalty he was assessed early in the game, *Shore played the entire sixty minutes*. He played one of the greatest games of anyone's career.

"On defense," Ross recalled, "he smacked the hard-driving Maroons left and center and the Bruins finally won the grueling game by a score of 1–0. I might add that Shore also found the energy to score that one goal!"

It is quite possible that had Shore entered the NHL at an earlier age—he was twenty-four when he joined the Bruins—he would have won even greater acclaim.

Nevertheless, he eminently qualifies for the number three position. The Midnight Ride to Montreal was only one of a hundred reasons why.

4

Red Kelly
(1947–1977)

As a long-time admirer of Leonard Patrick "Red" Kelly once noted: "Red's problem was that he never had a good press agent!"

One can only imagine how different Kelly's station in the hockey firmament might have been if there had been a tub-thumper to beat the drums for this most versatile of hockey players.

More than Gordie Howe, more than Eddie Shore, more than Bobby Orr, Red Kelly mastered every aspect of positional hockey, except goaltending. While Howe earned his spurs as a right wing, and Shore and Orr were defensemen par excellence, Kelly was one the of the best defensemen of all time *and* a truly superb center.

Curiously, the first half of Red's career was spent on defense for the Detroit Red Wings. Like Shore, Kelly was equally proficient at defending, as well as rushing the puck. It was Kelly who was the first of the modern backliners to carry the rubber deep into the enemy zone. Kelly was every bit as smooth a rushing defenseman as Orr and a much better defensive defenseman. What better proof than the fact that Red skated for eight championship squads and four Stanley Cup winners in Detroit. (By contrast, Orr played for only four first place teams and two Cup winners.) He won the Lady Byng Trophy for competence combined with gentlemanly play four times and was a First All-Star six times.

In 1959, the Red Wings' high command estimated that Kelly was washed up and dealt him to the Toronto Maple Leafs, who were being rejuvenated by general manager George "Punch" Imlach.

The turnabout, not to mention the events preceding it, proved to be most unusual for both Kelly and the NHL high command.

During the 1959–60 season, Red was approaching his thirteenth season as a Detroit defenseman and appeared a fixture in the Motor City because of his unwavering competence and devotion to the team. But Jack Adams, the Red Wings' aging and crusty manager, had become angry at Red because of a contract dispute they had had the previous summer.

Adams stewed over the dispute and midway in the season completed a trade with the Rangers. He dealt Kelly and forward Billy McNeill to New York for defenseman Bill Gadsby and forward Eddie Shack. "When I heard about the trade," said Kelly, "it didn't take me long to make up my mind about what I was going to do. I decided to retire rather than go to New York. So did McNeill."

Kelly didn't know it at the time, but his stance was the predecessor of free agentry. The NHL was rocked by his decision, and the Rangers, not surprisingly, cried foul. Adams had no choice but to call off the deal, and Gadsby and Shack returned to the Rangers.

NHL President Clarence Campbell advised Kelly that he had five days to report back to Detroit or go on the retirement list. "If I went on the retirement list," said Kelly, "I couldn't become active again if even one NHL club objected."

Kelly returned home and mulled over the matter for three days. He finally decided—reluctantly—to quit the game and concentrate on his bowling alley and tobacco farm. Two days remained before Campbell's deadline took force when King Clancy, assistant coach of the Maple Leafs, phoned. "Punch [Imlach] wants you on his hockey club," snapped Clancy. "Come to Toronto and the three of us will talk about it."

Unlike most of his contemporaries, Imlach believed that older, experienced hockey players were more useful in building a championship team than youngsters. He pointed out to Kelly how important he would be to the Maple Leafs' future even though he had turned thirty-two. Kelly was persuaded and agreed to play in Toronto providing that a deal could be worked out with Adams. Imlach phoned Detroit and offered Marc Reaume, a younger defenseman who was believed to be a potential ace.

Adams approved the trade, but there was still the league to contend with, particularly Rangers' general manager Muzz Patrick who was furious over Kelly's snub of New York. The deal was ultimately approved, but not before Kelly phoned his nemesis Adams. "I had to tell him I was reporting back to the Wings," said Red, "so he could reinstate me and trade me to the Leafs."

Had the trade not been consummated and Kelly retired as threatened, Red would have been remembered for what he was; one of the game's premier defensemen. But the night of February 10, 1960, proved to be a milestone in Red's life and in the life of the Maple Leafs. He donned the royal blue and white Toronto jersey and was presented with the same Number 4 jersey as he wore in Detroit.

Imlach, the innovator, was not precisely certain how he would exploit Kelly's talents, but he knew for sure that he would at least experiment with him at center, although Red had been a defenseman all his life. The Leafs' opponents that night were the Montreal Canadiens, already winners of four straight Stanley Cups and, perhaps, the greatest team of all time.

"I want you to go up against [Jean] Beliveau," said Imlach. The tall, majestic Beliveau was merely the best center in the league. Kelly skated to center ice, lined up opposite Beliveau, and waited for the referee to drop the puck for the opening face-off. "I was as nervous as a rookie," said Kelly. "I won the draw and sent the puck straight into the Montreal zone. The Canadiens' goalie, Jacques Plante, darted out to intercept the puck before I got there. I came right down like a shot and somehow got tangled up and went head over heels—into the net!"

Although the Leafs lost the game, 4–2, Imlach understood that his instincts were accurate; that Red would be more valuable to him as a center than as a defenseman. Never has the game known a more brilliant brainstorm. The next question was, with whom should Kelly play?

Imlach had a huge, brooding, young left wing named Frank "The Big M" Mahovlich who could skate like a zephyr and fired the puck with the fury of a howitzer. Somehow, *The Big M*'s power had not yet been harnessed, no doubt for want of a competent center.

The Leafs also possessed Bob Nevin, an unobtrusive right wing who excelled at all of a forward's basic skills. Imlach decided to unite Kelly with Mahovlich and Nevin.

From that point on the Maple Leafs' troubles were over. With Kelly ladling the passes to *The Big M* and Nevin, the Maple Leafs won four Stanley Cups in the seven-and-a-half years Red performed in Toronto. (Bill Gadsby, for whom Kelly was traded, played twenty years in the NHL and never skated for a Stanley Cup champion.)

Even more astonishing is the fact that Kelly was able to maintain his standard of playing excellence in Toronto while serving a term as a member of Canada's parliament.

Leonard Patrick Kelly was born July 9, 1927, in Simcoe, Ontario, and like so many youngsters determined to become professional hockey players, he enrolled at Toronto's St. Michael's College (a private high school by American standards) where he teamed with such future NHLers as Ted Lindsay and Jim Thomson.

"When I was ready to turn pro," Kelly recalled, "the scouts took a good look at me. The Leafs didn't want me because their scout said I wasn't good enough to last twenty games in the NHL. Detroit didn't see it that way, so the Red Wings signed me." Red was only seventeen when he launched his major league career in Detroit.

Low-key throughout his hockey and political careers, Kelly to this day remains the most underrated superstar to come down the pike, yet his dossier cannot be disputed. He was the balance wheel of champions as a defenseman in Detroit, and as a center, the most decisive factor in creating a dynasty in Toronto more than a decade later.

No other hockey player can make that statement, which is why Red Kelly deserves to be number four in *Hockey's 100*.

5

Frank Boucher
(1921–1944)

If a blue-ribbon panel of purists had ever been convened to select the one player who best epitomized clean, textbook hockey, the choice would have to be Frank Boucher.

The game has never known a center who parlayed style, selflessness, and sense of fair play like this native of Ottawa, Ontario. "I always recognized that hockey was a tough sport," said Boucher, "a rough one and one that can be played fairly. I was always a stickler on that. I got an exhilaration out of being able to avoid the checks in a violent game and tried to play it cleanly."

That was an understatement. Boucher won the Lady Byng Trophy exemplifying competence and clean play in 1928, 1929, 1930, 1931, 1933, 1934, and 1935—seven times in an eight-year stretch. At this point, Walter Gilhooly, a sportswriter for the Ottawa *Journal*, wrote an open letter in his column urging Lady Byng to give Boucher the trophy outright; and she did!

Boucher was more than a super-clean stickhandler. He was a creative genius who steered the New York Rangers to two division titles, three second place finishes, four appearances in the Stanley Cup finals, and two Stanley Cups. Finally, he was the pivotal force on what many observers regard as *the* most proficient line in NHL history— Boucher centering for Bill Cook on right wing and Bunny Cook on the left.

Among other plays, Boucher and the Cooks invented the drop-pass. Bill would steer a puck-carrier to Boucher who would hook the puck away. Bun raced down his wing, and Frank flipped the puck to him. "As soon as he crossed the other team's blue line," said Boucher, "he faked a shot, drawing a defenseman to him. Then he left the puck for me coming in fast behind him."

Frank and the Cooks were a part of the original Rangers team that made its NHL debut in 1926. Previously, he had played professionally with the Ottawa Senators and the Vancouver Maroons. When Madison Square Garden decided to add its own team to its original hockey tenant, the New York Americans, Conn Smythe, a Toronto sportsman, was asked to select the talent. Smythe spoke to Bill Cook who, in turn, recommended Boucher to Smythe.

Boucher only weighed 134 pounds when he met Smythe prior to training camp. Smythe anxiously eyed the seemingly frail athlete and then asked Frank how much he weighed. Boucher allowed that it was about 135 pounds.

"I paid fifteen thousand dollars for *you*," Smythe groaned. "Bill Cook must be crazy."

Smythe eventually signed Boucher to a contract, but he had a falling out with the Garden brass prior to training camp and was replaced as Rangers' boss by the courtly and

4362

insightful Lester Patrick. When the new club convened for training camp at Toronto's old Ravina Gardens, Patrick called Boucher to him and said, "I'm going to try you at center between Bill and Bunny Cook."

Patrick never had cause to change his mind. The unit remained intact in Rangers' uniforms for ten years. Unlike today's units who take the ice for three minute stretches and then are replaced, Boucher and the Cooks worked almost the entire game.

Frank Boucher was born October 7, 1901, in Ottawa, Ontario. He and his brothers George, Carroll, Billy, Joe, and Bobby learned to skate and play hockey on the snow-bordered Rideau River. "We played from dawn until dark," Frank recalled, "and in all kinds of weather, even forty degrees *below* zero. It was best after your toes froze; they turned numb and didn't bother you anymore—until later."

It was no accident that Boucher developed a meticulously clean style of play. His idol as a kid was Frank Nighbor, a star with the Ottawa Senators. "Nighbor," said Boucher, "was every young lad's hero in Ottawa in those days. He was a magnificent center who rarely lost his temper, who could hookcheck and pokecheck like nobody else." Nighbor's influence must have found its reflection in the years that followed.

Playing at a time when hockey was infinitely more rugged than today's game, Boucher engaged in only one fight in his ten-year NHL career, and that in his very first game at Madison Square Garden against the Maroons. He had been singled out by Bill Phillips, a square-set, rugged player who flattened Frank early in the game. In the third period, Phillips tangled again.

"I had simply had too much of him," said Boucher. "We threw aside our sticks and our gloves and went at each other. The crowd was standing and roaring, and he knocked me down, and I got up and knocked him down, and he got up and we grabbed each other and swung wearily. When the referee separated us, he sent us off with major penalties, five minutes each. It was as rough as I ever played.

"My philosophy always had been that fighting never solved anything—provided you didn't back down if you had to stand up. I was the one who swung on Phillips. I was the first Ranger ever to get a major penalty. Still, it was my last fight, too."

Boucher continued playing until 1938 when he accepted Lester Patrick's suggestion that he turn to coaching. Patrick gave him control of the New York Rovers, the Rangers' farm club in the Eastern Hockey League. Frank was an instant success as a coach after seventeen years as a player, four with the Vancouver Maroons, one with the Ottawa Senators, and twelve with the Rangers. He had led the Rangers in scoring in five seasons and was named to the NHL All-Star team three times.

After a year of steering the Rovers to a spectacularly successful campaign, Boucher was named coach of the Rangers, succeeding Patrick, who concentrated on managing the club. "The team Lester gave me," said Boucher, "was the best hockey team I ever saw."

In March 1940, Frank's rookie year as coach, the Rangers won their third Stanley Cup. It was the last time they annexed hockey's foremost prize.

Boucher's awesome Rangers' club was decimated by World War II and plunged to the bottom of the league. During the 1943–44 season at age forty-two, Frank brought himself out of retirement and played fifteen games. His legs obviously didn't have it, but the creative mind still functioned on the ice, and he managed to produce four goals and ten assists in fifteen games. Although he hadn't played a game in five years, Frank outscored *nineteen* other players the Rangers had tried that season.

It is unfortunate that only the genuine oldtimers had the good fortune to enjoy the skill of Boucher. One who did was Foster Hewitt, the dean of hockey announcers. Once during the Team Canada–Soviet All-Stars series of 1972, Hewitt was asked if he had ever seen anything to match the dazzling Russian skaters.

"There aren't many people around to remember," Hewitt told Canadian columnist Trent Frayne, "but the way the Russians play reminds me of the old Rangers, especially the line of Boucher and the Cooks. They were even better than the Russians. When Frank, Bill, and Bunny were on the ice, it always seemed to me they had the puck on a string."

Frank Boucher was the most completely beautiful hockey player ever to grace an arena and eminently qualifies for fifth place among the hundred best.

6

Maurice Richard

(1942–1960)

Frankie "Mister Zero" Brimsek, a Hall of Famer and one of the best goalies ever to don the pads, watched the galvanic Maurice "Rocket" Richard terrorize his ilk for almost a decade and finally concluded that no one in the hockey world could fire the puck like the Montreal Canadiens' right wing.

"He can shoot from any angle," said Brimsek. "You can play him for a shot to the upper corner and *The Rocket* wheels around and fires a backhander to the near, lower part of the net."

Brimsek's teammate, defenseman Murray Henderson, described what it was like trying to defuse *The Rocket* at the blue line. "When Richard breaks on one defenseman there's no telling what he'll do. If he get his body between you and the puck, you just can't get at it. He cradles the puck on the blade of his stick, steers it with one hand, and wards off his check with the other. Strong? That guy is like an ox, but he sure doesn't look it."

Or, take the word of Canadian author and television personality, Peter Gzowski. "Richard was the most exciting athlete I have ever seen. So much has been written about Richard that for me to offer a flood of new praise would be roughly equivalent to a Ph.D. candidate announcing he is going to prove *Hamlet* is an interesting play."

Mention *The Rocket* to anyone who played with or against him, or had the good fortune to watch him in the 1940s or 1950s, and a special glow instantly crosses the face. There was nobody quite like him before or since, nobody who generated such intensity, so much élan. If he had been a soldier, Richard would have been the genuine *poilu*.

Richard was the ultimate scorer. He burned with an intensity that put fear in the hearts of goaltenders because they could actually see the desire on Maurice's face. "When he skated in on the net," said Hall of Fame goalie Glenn Hall, "*The Rocket*'s eyes would shine like a pair of searchlights. It was awesome to see him coming at you."

The Rocket not only was a potent scorer but a clutch player of the highest order. His sudden-death overtime goals became legends, and his leadership and passion for the game helped make Les Canadiens the most revered dynasty in the NHL.

In March 1944, when The Flying Frenchmen won their first Stanley Cup with Richard on the right wing, the Toronto Maple Leafs assigned Bob Davidson, a rugged and intelligent left wing, to stymie Richard. *The Rocket* was held scoreless in the opener, but in the second game, on March 23, 1944, Maurice scored three goals in the second period, breaking a scoreless tie, and added two more in the third period. The final score was *Richard* 5, Toronto 1! The last time a player had scored five or more goals in a Stanley Cup match was in 1917 when Bernie Morris scored six against Les Canadiens for Seattle.

After disposing of Toronto, the Canadiens challenged Chicago and, once again, Richard dominated an entire game. The Montrealers defeated Chicago, 3–1, on April 6 in the second game of the final round, and Richard scored *all three goals*! Just to prove it was no fluke, Maurice practically single-handedly saved Montreal in the fourth and last game of the series after Chicago had mounted a 4–1 lead after two periods. *The Rocket*'s second goal of the game tied the match, 4–4, sending it into sudden-death overtime. Then his pass to Toe Blake set up the winning goal.

Every night that Richard took the ice during the 1944–45 season, it became apparent that he could not be stopped. Like nobody in the modern game, Richard blazed into the homestretch of the season maintaining a goal-a-game pace. In those days, the NHL played a fifty-game season. In Richard's forty-eighth game—on March 15—he scored his forty-ninth goal. In the next-to-last game, against the Black Hawks on Forum ice, Les Canadiens triumphed, but somehow Maurice was blanked. That left him with only one more match to make it fifty in fifty. The final game of the season was against the Bruins in Boston Garden. This time *The Rocket* came through in a 4–2 win, and he finished the season with fifty goals in fifty games, a modern hockey average that had not been equalled until 1980 when Mike Bossy of the New York Islanders matched Richard's mark.

Another who tried to torment Richard was "Terrible" Ted Lindsay, the truculent Detroit Red Wings' left wing. During the 1950–51 season, Detroit manager Jack Adams dispatched Lindsay to unnerve Richard. *The Rocket* wound up with a five-minute penalty, and Detroit rapidly scored two goals. "Perturbed by the turn of events," wrote author Vince Lunny, "rivers of anger scalded *The Rocket*'s brain. When he served his time he leaped from the bench like all hell breaking loose."

The Rocket pounced on the puck and drove it past the Detroit goaltender. He remained on the ice and seconds later, took a pass from his center, Elmer Lach, rounded the defense, and fired one of his patented backhanders into the twine. By now, Montreal coach Dick Irvin figured *The Rocket* was ready for a respite and called him to the bench. "Never mind," countered Richard, "I had my rest in the penalty box."

Lach won the next face-off and passed the puck to a teammate who relayed it to Richard. He skated straight into Lindsay, bowling him over, and then raced in for another goal. Montreal won the game, 3–2.

Maurice Richard was born on August 4, 1921, in Montreal's Bordeaux section. "Nearly everybody who lived there was French-Canadian," *The Rocket* remembered. "English was never spoken in our house."

Whenever he got a chance, young Maurice put on the skates. "Besides skating to school all the time," he remembered, "I used to skate on the frozen Black River near our house, or sometimes on our makeshift backyard rink or on the public rink run by the city."

In time, he gained a reputation as a quality amateur player and in the fall of 1942 was invited to the Canadiens' training camp. The Habitants were a mixture of French- and English-Canadian players who played harmoniously. Young Richard, however, could only say "yes" and "no" in English when he joined the team as a rookie. "I was deathly afraid to even try to say anything in English for fear of making a mistake and looking foolish. I'd just sit there silently."

Despite his promise as a scorer, Richard was also viewed as a brittle skater, prone to injury. He brooded about his seemingly endless series of wounds and doubted whether he would be kept on the Canadiens. "Fortunately," Richard recalled, "Dick Irvin wouldn't give up on me and I was invited back to training camp for the 1943–44 season.

From that point on until his retirement in 1960, *The Rocket*'s red goal glare was rarely snuffed out, and he emerged as the NHL's most exciting, if not complete, player. It had been said—with justification—that Richard was not as all-inclusive a player as Gordie Howe. *The Rocket*'s speciality was taking a pass from Lach—and later his brother, Henri—at or near the blue line and steaming relentlessly to the net for his shot on goal.

During a playoff game against the Bruins, *The Rocket* was viciously blindsided by Leo Labine, knocked unconscious, and carried from the ice, apparently finished for the series. Refusing to be hospitalized, Richard eventually returned to the bench as the teams battled to score the go-ahead goal in a bitterly played tie match.

Late in the game, Richard took the ice, charging along his right wing when the pass came his way. Bruins' defenseman Bill Quackenbush guarded *The Rocket* closely and appeared to have him boxed into the corner when, somehow, releasing his special quantity of pent-up energy, *The Rocket* whirled around Quackenbush and stuffed the puck behind goalie "Sugar" Jim Henry.

The 1951 playoff semifinals against Detroit was a vintage Richardian showcase. The first game of the series ended in a 2–2 tie after regulation time. Two sudden-death periods were played without a score. After midnight, the third overtime session began. At 1:10 a.m., Richard snared a loose puck like a leopard spotting an antelope. "He sped past the Detroit defense," said the *Canadian Press*, "with a blazing burst of speed. Alone in front of the net, he paused before lining a ten-footer past goalie Terry Sawchuk."

The second game of the series was a duplicate of the first, only this time it ended in a 0–0 tie after three periods. Again the teams struggled through two scoreless sudden-death periods. Early in the third overtime, Billy Reay of the Canadiens saw Richard zooming in from the left and slid him the puck. Richard's shot was so hard it nearly tore a hole in the goal mesh. "He is as great an opportunist as the game has ever known," said Baz O'Meara, sports editor of the Montreal *Star*.

Detroit rebounded to win the next two games, but it was *The Rocket* again in the fifth game scoring the winning goal in the third period as the Canadiens prevailed, 5–2. In the sixth and final game of the series, the game was tied 2–2, but *The Rocket* took over again, scored, and the Canadiens won the series.

In all, Richard played for eight Stanley Cup winners and eight first-place teams. He was a First All-Star eight times and six times a Second All-Star. More than that, Rocket Richard was the Babe Ruth of hockey.

Maurice Richard's name is synonymous with exciting hockey. Detroit *Times*' columnist Bob Murphy said it best: "*The Rocket* was made to watch and write about."

7

Howie Morenz
(1923–1937)

One of the major selling points of professional hockey is speed. It is called the "fastest game on earth." The essential pace of the game is what captured the hearts and minds of American fans when the NHL planted franchises in Boston, New York, Chicago, and Detroit, and one skater, more than any, epitomized the dynamic quality of the game—Howie Morenz.

Dubbed *The Stratford Streak*, Morenz seemed to be charged with lightning every time he took the ice for his beloved Montreal Canadiens. "He would challenge the opposing defenses by dazzling dash and deception rather than by shooting from longer range and following up for a rebound," said Montreal journalist Andy O'Brien, who covered Les Canadiens during the Morenz era.

Like Maurice Richard, who followed him, Morenz possessed the rare knack of producing the dramatic goal, the *chef d'oeuvre*. One such score won the 1931 Stanley Cup for the Canadiens. It was the fifth and last game of the best-of-five finals against the Chicago Black Hawks, and Morenz took the ice with this linemate Aurel Joliat.

As Joliat recalled, Morenz executed a near-impossible turnaround to deliver the goal. "Howie," said Joliat, "had rushed away from us with the puck down center and was checked at the Chicago defense. A Black Hawks forward picked up the loose puck at the gallop, but I checked him at mid-ice. I had taken only two strides when I heard 'Joliat!' screamed at me from right wing.

"It was incredible; even with the play going at top speed, Morenz raced back on my left wing, whirled around behind me, and had again picked up full speed down right wing. To catch him before he was offside at the blue line, I had to fire a shot rather than a pass. Howie picked up the puck as if he was using a lacrosse stick and without losing a stride.

"He was by the Chicago defense in a flash and in on goalie Chuck Gardiner before anybody really recognized the menace. His shot, fired with every last ounce from an exhausted body, hit an upper corner of the net. The Forum crowd gasped, then raised the roof in one earsplitting wave of cheering thunder."

From the moment he made his debut with the Montrealers, Morenz dazzled the enemy with his footwork. "The rookie Morenz was the fastest man on the ice," commented Toronto writers after Howie skated against the Toronto St. Pats in the fall of 1923. Morenz never stopped. He paced Les Canadiens to their first Stanley Cup in the seven-year history of the NHL. In a two-game total-goals Eastern playoff against Ottawa, Montreal won, 5–2. Howie scored three and assisted on a fourth goal.

Although Morenz was of Swiss descent and Maurice Richard was a French-Canadian, the two had many traits in common, especially their seething hatred of defeat. Elmer Ferguson, who was sports editor of the Montreal *Herald* during Morenz's halcyon years, remembered an episode from the 1928–29 season. The Canadiens visited Boston and dropped a pair of gripping 1–0 games to an excellent Bruins club. As usual, Morenz played a capable game.

"I was sleeping soundly when at six o'clock in the morning after the second game, there was a knock on my door," said Ferguson. "It was Morenz, face still drawn from the toll of fierce, close conflict the night before. He was dressed for the street. But he wasn't going out. He had just come in. He had tramped the winding, crooked streets of Boston all night, his mind still in a raging torrent of turmoil and conflict, through which the episodes of the battle were still running, 'I couldn't sleep,' he apologized, 'now I want to talk.'

"And so we talked, far towards noon. Play after play he ran through, analyzed, putting a finger on the spot where a different stride, another shift, might have meant the whole tide of battle…Other players had long since dismissed defeat and the game from their minds and were sleeping peacefully, but not for Morenz. He blamed only himself for the team's defeats."

During an era when low-scoring games were the norm and goals were hard to come by, Morenz totaled 270 in 546 regular season games, but his game was more comprehensive than most.

Howarth William "Howie" Morenz was born September 21, 1902, in Mitchell, Ontario, but moved with his parents to Stratford. By the time he had reached his early teens, he had created something of a sensation within his community but somehow failed to excite the Toronto St. Pats, the closest major league team.

Lou Marsh, sports editor of the Toronto *Daily Star*, who doubled as an NHL referee, went out of his way to catch a glimpse of Morenz. Marsh was so impressed he contacted Leo Dandurand, boss of the Canadiens, and urged him to sign the fleet forward. Dandurand dispatched his emissary Cecil Hart to the Morenz household. Hart spread $850 on the table and Howie signed with the Habitants.

It was one of the biggest bargains in sport. Morenz won the Hart Trophy as the NHL's most valuable player three times, thrice was a First All-Star, and twice won the league scoring championships. Still, it was less Howie's statistics and more his style that counted.

For years Morenz owned Montreal and then, almost as quickly, his legs began to go, and fans who once revered Number 7 now reviled him. At thirty-two years, Morenz still had plenty of good hockey in him and when the Black Hawks made an offer, Dandurand shipped Howie to the Windy City.

Howie couldn't summon his enthusiasm in foreign Chicago, and in the middle of the 1935–36 season he was dealt to the Rangers for Glenn Brydson. "HERE COMES HOWIE!" shouted a headline in *The New York Times*. His arrival was hailed as a major event in the city's sporting history but, once again, Morenz was a shadow of his former starry self.

During the summer of 1936, Cecil Hart was offered the job as coach of the Canadiens. He agreed, with one condition—that the Canadiens "bring back Morenz to where he belongs."

A trade was agreed upon and Howie once again donned the *bleu* (blue), *blanc* (white), *et rouge* (red) uniform of the Canadiens. The Forum fans took him to their hearts and during several moments he looked like the Morenz of old although he was thirty-four years old.

On the night of January 28, 1937, the Black Hawks came to town and Howie was playing a splendid game. At one point in the contest, he grabbed the puck and went one-on-one with crack defenseman Earl Seibert.

As Morenz executed his end run, Seibert crouched and managed to hurl Howie off balance with a clean check. Before he could regain his equilibrium, Morenz flew, legs first, into the boards. "The point of one skate embedded itself in the wood," said Andy O'Brien, "as the rest of Howie rolled over."

Witnesses instantly understood that this was an extraordinary accident. Linemates Joliat and Gagnon rushed to Howie's side as did members of the Black Hawks. Writhing in pain, Morenz had suffered a double fracture of his leg.

Under normal conditions, Morenz should have gradually recovered from the mishap, but conditions were not normal at Hospital Saint-Luc. Morenz received many visitors, but those who knew him best estimated that beneath the facade, Morenz was brooding over his declining career. On March 8, 1937, he died of cardiac failure.

Morenz's body lay in state at mid-ice in the Forum where thousands paid their last respects to *The Stratford Streak*. During the funeral service, 15,000 fans sat in complete silence with heads bowed while 200,000 Montrealers lined the streets as the cortege rolled on to Mount Royal Cemetery.

"Howie Morenz," Andy O'Brien concluded, "will be recalled as the *beau sabreur* of hockey—*sans peur, sans reproche*."

It was a brilliant career; not quite as long as Howe's, Richard's, or Kelly's but certainly worthy of seventh on the honor roll.

8

Jean Beliveau
(1951–1971)

In French-speaking Quebec City, where Jean Beliveau originally carved a niche in hockey's annals, they called him *"Le Gros Bill"* (Big Bill). As the majestic center progressed through senior ranks and finally the National Hockey League, his stature as a player grew to Bunyanesque proportions.

Articulate, diffident, and the supreme team player, Beliveau was captain and major ace on a Montreal Canadiens dynasty that annexed ten Stanley Cups during his extraordinary reign. He was twice voted the Hart Trophy as the NHL's most valuable player and was a First All-Star in 1955, 1956, 1957, 1959, 1960, and 1961.

Versatile in the extreme, Beliveau's passing was matched only by his radar-accurate shot. He was NHL scoring champion in 1956 and won the Conn Smythe Trophy as the most valuable playoff performer in 1965.

One hard-bitten hockey journalist who had covered the game for over three decades remarked that Beliveau was the only superstar to span twenty years of active performing "literally above criticism."

Beliveau's teammates shared that view. "It's hard to put into words how we felt about Jean," said Ralph Backstrom, who teamed with Beliveau on several championship clubs. "It's just that...well, we were so damned proud to have him as our captain."

Although he made his mark as an offensive threat, Beliveau could play a sound defensive game and, when necessary, could play a rough—if not dirty—brand of hockey. However, it was not his nature to trespass beyond the realm of fair play.

"It's practically impossible for anyone who knew him well to have any ill feelings toward Jean," said Toronto Maple Leaf's manager Punch Imlach, who coached Beliveau as a junior. "He would go on the ice, play one heckuva game, change, and leave without saying much. He was one player all the fellows liked."

Playing alongside such boisterous performers as Bernie Geoffrion and Maurice Richard, Beliveau might have been rendered obscure were it not for his stylish efforts on the ice. To put Jean in a baseball perspective, he was to Rocket Richard what Lou Gehrig was to Babe Ruth.

"It was his quiet dignity," said ex-teammate Dick Duff. "He was so unassuming for a guy of his stature. He had great moves—that great range—and anybody playing on a line with him was certain to wind up with a lot of goals. If you got there, the puck would be there."

At the height of his career, in the late 1950s and through the 1960s, Beliveau was the toast of Canadian sport. The late Leonard Shecter, one of America's most perceptive

journalists, made this observation: "Jean Beliveau is like Mickey Mantle and Joe DiMaggio in the United States. When Beliveau walks down the street in Quebec the women smile, the men shake his hand, and the little boys follow him."

With Beliveau wearing the captain's "C" on his jersey, the Canadiens dominated hockey through the 1960s and, in the fans' eyes, big Jean could do no wrong—even when he suffered through a horrendous slump.

During the 1966–67 season, he went through the first fourteen games with nary a goal. The municipality of Montreal shared the Canadiens depression, and by the time the Habitants were scheduled to play the Chicago Black Hawks on December 3, 1966, Beliveau wondered whether he'd ever see the red goal light go on again.

Jean did virtually nothing in the first period. During the subsequent intermission, Beliveau made a television appearance with the Canadian Prime Minister Lester Pearson, himself a hockey fan. The two exchanged pleasantries, and then Pearson asked about Beliveau's scoring drought. "I have a feeling," said the PM, "that you'll score tonight." Jean said he would do his best to oblige.

In the second period, Beliveau powered his way through the Chicago defense and fired a wrist shot at Black Hawks' goalie Denis DeJordy. The initial drive was blocked, but DeJordy gave up a rebound and Beliveau lifted the puck over the fallen netminder.

The exultant crowd toasted Jean with a four-minute ovation and littered the ice with everything from overshoes to fedoras. Teammates hugged him and Beliveau blushed as the tribute continued. Later, Beliveau would say, "That goal was my biggest thrill—imagine the fans sticking with me like they did."

Jean Marc Beliveau was born August 31, 1931, in Trois Rivières (Three Rivers), Quebec. He began capturing headlines during the 1947–48 season when he made his debut as an amateur with a team in Victoriaville, Quebec. By 1949–50, he had moved up to the strong Quebec Citadelles in the Quebec Junior League. Big Jean so thoroughly dominated the Junior circuit that a new and larger rink was needed to handle the hordes of fans who wanted to see him play. Thus, *Le Colisée* (The Coliseum) was erected and colloquially called "Chateau Beliveau."

In those days, an amateur player was allowed to play five "trial" games with the professionals without losing his amateur status. So, while Beliveau was still nineteen, Les Canadiens invited him for a couple of NHL games. After watching *Le Gros Bill* in one turn on the ice, coach Dick Irvin of the Canadiens compared Beliveau to the legendary Lester Patrick, which was tantamount to linking the kid with God.

The Canadiens dearly wanted Beliveau to sign with them, but he was deeply attached to the fans of Quebec City and snubbed Montreal in favor of a contract with the Quebec Aces, a professional team in the fast Quebec Senior League. Crowds who had filled *Le Colisée* to watch him star with the Citadelles now became *aficionados* of the Aces.

"The NHL must certainly know by now that my boy rates only with Gordie Howe and Rocket Richard in their league," chirped Aces' coach Punch Imlach.

Needless to say, the Canadiens' manager Frank Selke was more determined than ever to wrest Beliveau from the Aces, but it would not be easy. Big Jean was being well paid in Quebec, and he savored the ambiance of the quaint city where he had so many friends.

But several factors worked in the Canadiens' favor. Although the Aces paid him well, the Canadiens were willing to open their vault for him. In addition, there was a matter of professional pride. In the Quebec Senior League, Jean was a big fish in a small pond. Professional pride demanded that he ultimately show how well he could play in the bigs. His advisor, Emile Couture, also influenced Beliveau's decision to sign with Montreal.

"I told Jean," said Couture, "that if he really loved to play hockey, there was only one league in which to play and one team with which to play. Again, his idol had always been Rocket Richard and the thought of being a teammate intrigued Jean."

By the time Beliveau signed with Montreal in 1953, he had become the most widely acclaimed young player ever to step onto an NHL rink. Not surprisingly, Beliveau succumbed to the pressure and won less than total raves in his rookie season in the NHL.

His gentlemanly play invited every low-salaried skater from New York to Chicago to get a piece of *Le Gros Bill*, and many of them did. He suffered a cracked fibula after being heavily checked in Chicago and was sidelined a total of twenty-six games.

A year later, Beliveau began asserting himself, and his tormentors began to disappear. From that point on, there was no stopping him. "The playing of Beliveau," commented Canadian novelist Hugh MacLennan, "is poetry in action."

Skating side by side with *The Rocket*, Beliveau propelled the Canadiens to new heights of excellence and, naturally, promoted comparisons between his style and that of the inimitable Richard. "Big Jean," said coach Toe Blake, "doesn't have the desire to score that Maurice has."

It was a perceptive comment. With his abundance of skills, Beliveau nevertheless seemed too mechanical in a sport that relies more than most on human desire.

"The difference between the two best players in the game today is simply this: Beliveau is a perfectionist, Richard on the other hand is an opportunist," added Blake.

Richard and Beliveau comprised two-fifths of the most devastating power play in hockey. Doug Harvey and Bernie Geoffrion were stationed at the left and right points near the blue line. Beliveau, Richard, and tenacious left wing Bert Olmstead played up front. The Habs' power play became so overwhelming that the NHL had to legislate against it. At the time, a penalized player was compelled to serve the full two minutes of a minor penalty. When that happened, the Canadiens would often score as many as three goals. The NHL decreed that the player could return to the ice if a goal was scored during a power play.

Long after Richard retired, Beliveau maintained his high standard of excellence. He scored one of the most spectacular goals of his career during the 1971 playoff upset of Bobby Orr and the Big Bad Bruins, and then he decided to call it a career. His timing, as always, was exquisite. He packed it in and became an executive with the Canadiens, still remaining very visible and very likeable.

Yet, it is a fact of life that Beliveau never obtained the intensity of acclaim accorded Gordie Howe, Rocket Richard, and Eddie Shore. He simply could not fulfill the enormous buildup he received as a junior and senior player in Quebec.

"People would come to the rinks," Beliveau concluded, "and want to see me score two, three, or four goals in a game. If I would score only once, the people would be unhappy."

Nevertheless, *Le Gros Bill* created an enormous number of happy moments for Canadiens' fans and is well-suited for the number eight position.

9

Doug Harvey
(1947–1969)

If ever there was a hockey player whose style could be described as eminently laconic, it was that of Doug Harvey who appeared never to panic in more than two decades of defense play that, modestly speaking, was marvelous to behold.

Others were more emphatic about the crew-cut Montrealer who always seemed to wear a whimsical grin. "Doug Harvey was the greatest defenseman who ever played hockey—bar none," said Toe Blake, who coached Harvey and the Canadiens for six years. "Usually, a defenseman specializes in one thing and builds a reputation on that, but Doug could do everything well."

When Harvey played out his career during the 1968–69 season, Bobby Orr had emerged as the new defensive phenomenom and, in years to come, inexperienced journalists, who did not have the good fortune to view Harvey in his prime, labeled Orr the best ever.

Orr, clearly, was not and, unlike Harvey, never did stand the test of time. Harvey, even in his declining years, was a better defensive defenseman than Orr.

The Harvey dossier is filled with superlatives. He won the Norris Trophy as the NHL's best defenseman (remember it wasn't awarded until 1953, six years after Harvey became a Canadien) in 1955, 1956, 1957, 1958, 1960, 1961, and 1962. Doug was a First All-Star in 1952, 1953, 1954, 1955, 1956, 1957, 1958, 1960, 1961, and 1962.

Thanks to Harvey's uncannily accurate passes, the Canadiens were able to create a style all their own called "Firewagon Hockey." Always, the Montrealers appeared to be in a grand rush to get the puck out of their zone and into enemy territory with Harvey orchestrating the attack.

Harvey often exhibited a touch of the Harpo Marx spirit, which was a vital ingredient in the Canadiens' makeup. "Doug," recalled the often somber Maurice Richard, "had a terrific sense of humor and he'd relax us with a gag whenever we were tense."

Doug was not all laughs. Although he was neither as consummately tough nor as hard-hitting as Eddie Shore (an important distinction between the two), Harvey's nice-guy facade could be penetrated by an enemy's indiscretion. He played the game clean, but woe to the foe who played him dirty.

Harvey-watchers agree that Doug's aplomb was lost in the extreme during a game against the Rangers in November 1956. It had been Harvey's contention that Red Sullivan, never lauded for his lily-white play, had developed an obnoxious, not to mention dangerous, habit of "kicking skates." When Harvey and Sullivan would pursue the puck into a corner of the rink, Sullivan would kick Harvey's skates out from under him, making it very easy for Doug to fall on his head.

Several warnings failed to impress Sullivan so Harvey decided to escalate the war. During the fateful game in question, Harvey and Sullivan once again appeared to be on a collision course when Harvey planted the pointed blade of his stick in Sullivan's gut. The Rangers' center was taken to the hospital with a ruptured spleen.

For a time, Sullivan's condition was so grave he was given the last rites of the Catholic church. Fortunately, Sullivan recovered and resumed his playing career. When Harvey was traded by the Canadiens to the Rangers in 1961, Doug immediately became player-coach, and one of his centers was none other than Sullivan. They maintained a reasonably amicable relationship, at least superficially, but insiders believed that the mutual loathing remained.

At the time that Harvey was dealt to New York, the Broadway sextet had been in the "slough of despond." Few critics expected Harvey to turn them around—especially in his dual role. He fooled them, not only turning the Rangers into a playoff club but winning the Norris Trophy and a nomination to the First All-Stars to boot.

The Rangers relationship didn't last long, mostly because of Doug's desire to remain one of the boys and not a martinet coach. "When I was coach," he explained, "I couldn't be one of the boys. This way, if I want a beer with 'em, I get a beer."

Harvey hooked on briefly with the Detroit Red Wings but when the NHL expanded from six to twelve teams in 1967, he was signed by Lynn Patrick, manager of the St. Louis Blues. For Doug, it was like old times. His buddy from Canadiens days, Dickie Moore, was making a comeback in St. Louis, and another old crony, Jacques Plante, would soon arrive.

Harvey's excellence surfaced during the 1968 divisional playoffs when the Blues met the favored Philadelphia Flyers. St. Louis won the series in seven games and made it to the Stanley Cup finals in the club's first year of existence.

Douglas Norman Harvey was born on December 19, 1924, in Montreal, and like many of his future teammates such as Dickie Moore and Rocket Richard perfected his game on the city's outdoor rinks.

Those who remember the young Harvey believe that he could have become a major league baseball star. He played two summers in the Border Baseball League at Ottawa, once leading all hitters with an average of .351. When the Boston Braves (then in the National League) tried to persuade him to forsake hockey for baseball, he refused and concentrated on the ice game.

Doug's apprenticeship was served with the Montreal Royals of the high-grade Quebec Senior Hockey League. In 1947, he was promoted once and for all to Les Canadiens. During his blue line stewardship, the Montreal sextet finished first five times and won the Stanley Cup a remarkable six times.

Based on his performance, Harvey deserved to be inducted into the Hockey Hall of Fame shortly after his retirement in 1969, but fourteen years went by before the NHL nabobs got around to inducting Doug. The reason—to anyone familiar with Harvey's habits—was obvious. He had always been an antimanagement maverick who liked nothing better than twitting the establishment. By letting Harvey twist in the wind before they got around to installing him in the Hall, the hockey barons got their revenge.

But Doug got the last laugh. When the rival World Hockey Association made its professional debut in 1972, a bitter scramble for talent ensued. One of the prize prospects was Mark Howe, son of the immortal Gordie Howe. The NHL bosses expected that Mark would sign with one of their teams, either Boston or more appropriately Detroit.

Harvey, who had been named assistant manager of the WHA's Houston Aeros, persuaded the Texas-based hockey club to sign both Mark and his older brother, Marty. The Aeros agreed and included Gordie in the package thereby completing one of the most astonishing coups in sports.

Unfortunately, Harvey's liaison with hockey was less pleasant after that. The affiliation with the Aeros was short-lived and, according to friends, Doug fell upon less pleasant times, although he rebounded and went to work for the Canadiens.

Those who felt a kinship with Doug preferred recalling his golden years with the Canadiens, especially when he was the linchpin of their power play, the defenseman at the point when they won an unparalleled five Stanley Cups in succession and finished in first place in six out of seven years.

As the ultimate defenseman, he was surpassed only by Shore, who could deliver the more robust bodychecks. Doug earned his way into the select circle.

10

Glenn Hall
(1952–1971)

When Chuck Rayner played goal for an embattled New York Rangers team during the late 1940s, somebody asked him what he would do if his son announced he was going to enter the goaltending profession. Rayner wasted little time telling the other that he'd grab the goalie stick out of his hand and hit him over the head with it. Goaltending was the toughest job in sports, according to Rayner, particularly in those primitive days when goalies never dreamed of wearing a mask to protect their oft-stitched faces. Any goaltender who could survive 100 straight games without missing a contest was considered extraordinary. How, then, can one describe Glenn Henry Hall, who tenaciously guarded the twine for 552 straight games without a mask and with an artistry rarely matched for his position? They can simply call him *Mr. Goalie*, the moniker he earned for nineteen seasons in the NHL as the epitome of the professional goaltender.

Hall broke in with the Detroit Red Wings in 1955, displacing the great Terry Sawchuk as the Wings' regular goalie. He wasted no time making his mark in the NHL, skating off with the Calder Trophy as the league's rookie of the year. After two campaigns in Detroit, Hall was traded to Chicago where he captured the Vezina Trophy in 1963 and 1967 (shared with Denis DeJordy). In 1961, Hall led the Black Hawks to their first Stanley Cup since 1938, performing spectacularly as Chicago eliminated, ironically, the Red Wings in the final round. With the coming of expansion, Hall was drafted by the St. Louis Blues with whom he won his third Vezina in 1969 (shared with Jacques Plante), and the Conn Smythe Trophy in 1968. Hall also was an eleven-time All-Star; his seven First-Team berths a record for NHL goaltenders.

More indicative, however, of the intensity of Hall's play than any number of awards could ever be is an incident that occurred during a game between the Red Wings and Boston Bruins in the semifinal round of the 1957 playoffs. Minding the net for Detroit, all of a sudden Hall found himself the only Red Wing around and, as such, the target of a straight-on rush by Boston's Vic Stasiuk. Stasiuk roared in on the young goalie and shot a bullet that caught Hall on his unprotected face. He dropped to the cold ice, blood flowing from his mouth. The crowd buzzed and one writer noted that Hall, lying in a heap in his goal crease, "looked dead."

Taken from the ice on a stretcher, Hall regained consciousness in the trainer's room. Hardly impressed by the severity of his injury, Hall's first words upon awakening were, "C'mon, doc, let's get this thing over with." The physician then proceeded to weave twenty-three stitches into Hall's upper lip and mouth, which the puck had ripped open.

A half-hour later, Hall emerged, skating onto the ice, his eyes black, his face swollen and covered with bandages. As he took up his position in front of the goal, a Bruins player remarked, "I don't believe it. How do you stop this guy?" By that time the answer was clear: you didn't.

Resistant to change in his refusal to don a protective mask until late in his career, Hall was an innovator nonetheless. He is credited with being the forerunner in the development of the "butterfly" style of goaltending, the fanning out of the pads toward the goalposts while dropping to the knees to block shots. Hall's technique, originally scoffed at as a perversion of the traditional stand-up goaltending style, eventually became the standard for goalkeepers from the late 1960s to the present.

Glenn Hall, a native of Humboldt, Saskatchewan, was born in 1931, the son of a railroad engineer. As a boy, he played center and captained his public school hockey team. When he was ten, the club's goalie quit. "I picked someone to replace him but he refused," Hall said. "So did the next ten guys. As captain, I had no choice but to put on the pads myself. After a few years I actually got to like it."

So treacherous did Hall find his work that he became unique in his pregame preparations. "Before every game, and sometimes between periods, I'd get sick to my stomach; I'd have to throw up. Sometimes it happened during a game and I'd have to fight it off until the whistle blew. I tried drinking tea between periods and that seemed to help. But I didn't worry about it. Nervousness is part of the game. It helps keep me sharp." It was Hall's love-hate relationship with his profession that made his iron-man streak that much more remarkable.

Far from the madding sounds of the hockey rink, Hall now spends most of his time on his farm, although he is listed as a goaltending coach for the Calgary Flames. The old master of puck-stopping is hardly impressed with the direction of today's game and harks back to the good, old days when defense was not yet against the law. "We're seeing darn little defense and I don't particularly like what I'm seeing," *Mr. Goalie* remarked.

From the beginning of his career, Glenn Hall was a defensive gem amidst a conglomerate of offensive specialists such as Howe and Delvecchio in Detroit and Hull and Mikita in Chicago. Nonetheless, Hall retired with a shining 2.51 GA average to go with eighty-four shutouts in 906 career contests. He was inducted into the Hall of Fame in 1975.

Coiled in readiness in front of his cage, Hall's hair-trigger reflexes consistently kept him ahead of the most dangerous shooters in the NHL for close to two decades. For valiant service under fire with a steadiness unmatched by any other puck-stopper, Glenn Hall is hereby awarded his distinguished place among *Hockey's 100*.

11

Syl Apps
(1936–1948)

With all deference to Frank Boucher and Howie Morenz, there has never been a hockey player who filled the role of a Frank Merriwether on ice better than Syl Apps. When his lilting style began gracing NHL rinks in 1936, he was hailed as the All-Canadian boy. And for good reason.

To begin with, his virtues were beyond reproach. He played the game with infinite finesse, yet with a courage and vigor that inspired every hockey-loving father to tell his son that *that* was the way he wanted his kid to do it.

Most youngsters didn't have to be told. The Toronto Maple Leafs' center was tall, handsome, lithe, and lively. "He is," said Canadian author Vincent Lunny, "a Rembrandt on the ice, a Nijinsky at the goal mouth. He plays with such grace and precision you get the impression that every move is the execution of a mental image conceived long before he goes through the motions."

Apps inspired the Maple Leafs to the single most astonishing comeback hockey—and maybe all professional sports—has known when Toronto lost the first three games of the 1942 Stanley Cup finals and then regrouped and took the next four straight and the Cup.

After serving in the Canadian Army, Apps returned to the NHL and captained the Maple Leafs to two consecutive Stanley Cups in 1947 and 1948. He was thirty-three years old at the time and seemed capable, thanks to his fluid skating and superb condition, of at least two to five more years of superlative play. But he shocked the hockey world with the announcement of his retirement.

Apps won the Calder Trophy as NHL rookie of the year in 1937 and the Lady Byng Trophy in 1942. He was First All-Star center in 1939 and 1942, although there were other times when he was unaccountably overlooked by the voters.

Jack Adams, the irascible Detroit Red Wings' manager who considered the Maple Leafs his most loathed enemy, could not ignore the quality of Apps's play. "Apps," said Adams, "is the greatest center I have ever seen."

Although Apps produced many a melodramatic moment, most of his fans consider his exploits in the homestretch of the 1947–48 season his finest hour. It was a magnificent race, with Toronto neck-and-neck with Detroit in the run for first place while Apps was shooting for his 200th goal; at the time, a remarkable achievement. When the final buzzer had sounded, Apps had completed a three-goal "hat trick" and finished the season with 201 goals.

As dramatic as Apps's goal-scoring was, his adherence to a special code of honor won him even more applause. "He was the cleanest athlete I've ever known," said his coach

Hap Day. "I used to figure I came pretty close to that myself. I didn't drink and didn't smoke but I used to do my share of swearing. That's where Apps had me beaten. He didn't smoke. He never bent his elbow except to twist his stick over an opponent's wrist. The strongest language he ever used was 'By Hum' and 'Jiminy Christmas'."

Apps's code of honor was so comprehensive that he once suggested to his boss, Conn Smythe, that he was being overpaid. "It was the only time that ever happened to me," Smythe recalled. "Syl had crashed into a goal post, shattered his leg, and missed half the games of the 1942–43 season.

"I was paying him $6,000 that year and he came to me and said: 'Conn, I'm making more money than I deserve. I want to give you this check for $1,000.' When I heard that I almost died of heart failure. I refused the check. I figured anyone who thought in such terms was bound to square off what he thought was a debt the next season."

Joseph Sylvanus Apps was born in Paris, Ontario, on January 18, 1915, and by the time he had become a teenager exhibited superior ability in both team and individual sports. At the age of seventeen, he entered McMaster University in Hamilton, Ontario, and turned out for the track team. His speciality was pole-vaulting, and he became so adept at it that in 1934 he was invited to represent Canada at the British Empire Games in London, England. He later became captain of the McMaster football team and played for the college hockey squad as well.

While playing hockey for the collegians, he was discovered by Smythe's friend, Bill Marsden. Smythe actually refused to scout Apps but Marsden changed Smythe's mind. He signed with the Maple Leafs but only after appearing in the 1936 Olympiad where before 100,000 spectators he vaulted to a sixth-place tie for Canada.

In his rookie NHL season, Apps finished second in scoring to Dave "Sweeney" Schriner of the New York Americans and polled seventy-nine out of a possible eighty-one points for the Calder (best rookie) Trophy.

Apps quickly established that he would brook no nonsense from the bullies. His most persuasive performance occurred when Bill "Flash" Hollett, a persnickety Boston Bruins defenseman, jammed his stick in Apps's mouth, removing two teeth.

"By hum!" snapped Apps. "This has gone far enough." He then belabored Hollett with a series of jabs and hooks that reminded onlookers of heavyweight champion Joe Louis. It was a lesson that Syl would be obliged to repeat from time to time; that he could handle his dukes as well as he could deliver goals, or help create them for a teammate.

"Syl was a terrific skater," said a critic, "stickhandler, and had speed to burn at all times on the ice. He possessed the faculty of breaking fast from a standing stop, which left his opposition flatfooted. He took great pride in having one of his linemates score from a play set up by him. In fact, I think that he enjoyed that better than if he had bulged the twine himself. Every time Apps touched the puck, the crowds would let out a deafening roar, because they sensed something spectacular, and in most cases he did not disappoint them."

Watching Apps in action was a wonderful experience right down to the final games of his career. In the spring of 1948, after the Leafs finished first, the Toronto sextet met the Boston Bruins in the opening playoff round.

Underdogs though they were, the Bruins led the Maple Leafs 4–2 with only eight minutes remaining in the opening game. But Syl rallied his club, scored a goal and Jim Thomson followed to tie the count, whereupon the Leafs won in overtime. They eliminated the Bruins in five games and then swept the Red Wings in four straight to retain the Cup.

When the triumphant champions stepped off the train from Detroit, they were hailed by tens of thousands of Toronto fans. At City Hall another 10,000 fans cheered as captain Apps was introduced. It was the last time Syl would be seen as a Maple Leaf, although his teammates urged him to reconsider.

"If Syl would only come back for one more season," said center Max Bentley, "we would be a cinch to repeat next year."

Apps, as always, was a man of his word. He retired—prematurely of course—but as a champion, just as he was when he entered the NHL.

The All-Canadian boy had become the All-Canadian man. His comprehensive excellence guaranteed him an exalted position among *Hockey's 100.*

12

Denis Potvin
(1973–1988)

It was early in the 1987–88 season at Nassau Coliseum. The Islanders needed a win over the Los Angeles Kings to maintain the delightful early-season momentum they had established.

The Kings—especially goalie Glenn Healy—had sufficiently muffled the local skaters to suggest that an Islanders' win was not in the cards that night.

Then, it happened. A break, the tying goal for Terry Simpson's skaters. Oh, well, the crowd figured, a tie under these circumstances would not be bad. Or, maybe a win in overtime.

But sudden death was unnecessary. From the Islanders' zone, the bulky sweater with the Number 5 fluttered in its self-made breeze as Denis Potvin careened over the Los Angeles blue line.

"It looked like he was going too wide to do any damage," recalled Kelly Hrudey.

Few in the audience expected any good to come of the foray. Denis swerved wide to the left as if hellbent on an end run. The vigilant Healy slid a trifle out of his reach to the right.

"The shot," remembers Bob Nystrom, "took a lot of people by surprise."

The rubber skimmed across the ice, past Healy's left pad, off the right goal post, and into the net. A goal, the winning goal. Vintage Denis Potvin.

In his Channel-5 studio, sportscaster Bill Mazer picked up the phone and urged a friend: "Tell Denis *not* to retire."

A few minutes later, I was standing in the corridor outside the jubilant Islanders' dressing room, waiting to do my *SportsChannel* post-game interview. Potvin ambled over, wiped the perspiration from his face, and stared that inquisitive stare of his when he wasn't sure of the opening question.

"Your friend Bill Mazer asked me to suggest that you reconsider your retirement declaration," I said.

The winning grin broke across Potvin's face.

"That's very nice of him," he said, "but I'm not about to change my mind."

There were many occasions during Potvin's glorious final season when fans hoped that he would, in fact, decide to give it one more last shot in 1988–89. But his decision had been locked into place and was irrevocable.

Potvin retired in April 1988 secure in the knowledge that he was one of the NHL's most significant players. Whether he was better than Bobby Orr has been a matter of considerable debate.

It was Denis Potvin's misfortune, even before he set foot in the National Hockey League, to be labeled "the next Bobby Orr." At the time the comparison was made, in the early 1970s, Orr was the king of hockey and believed by many to have been the greatest defenseman of all time.

"I didn't like being compared with Orr," said Potvin, "because we were different personalities with different playing styles, skating for different teams. The only thing we had in common was that we both played defense. What these statements about me and Orr do is make my job that much harder; but I accept it as part of the business."

Remarkably, Potvin then proceeded to justify the lofty comparisons. He emerged as one of the brightest young players on the hockey horizon, winning the Calder Trophy as rookie of the year in 1974. He was named to the First All-Star Team in 1975, 1976, 1978, 1979, and 1981 and to the Second Team in 1977. In addition, he was voted the Norris Trophy winner as the NHL's best defenseman in 1976, 1978, and 1979.

Potvin could score and create attacking opportunities in the Orr manner, but he added a dimension to his game that never was part of the Orr repertoire; he could deliver crushing bodychecks behind the blue line—and often did.

It has been fashionable to cite Bobby Orr as the best defenseman since expansion, but it has also been an error of judgment.

Potvin was the cornerstone of a New York Islanders team that won Stanley Cup championships in 1980, 1981, 1982, and 1983. But, perhaps even more important, it was Potvin who helped establish the Islanders at a time when they were struggling at birth into one of the league's most robust franchises.

The arrival of Denis on Long Island in 1973 meant the club had its first legitimate superstar. The Isles' graph, which had been at a solemnly low point, began a relentless upward climb, culminating with captain Potvin hoisting Stanley Cups four straight years; a record for an American team.

Planting Denis' skates at Nassau Coliseum was more than a difficult chore for Isles' president-general manager Bill Torrey. In the spring of 1973, when Potvin graduated from junior hockey, the World Hockey Association was making strenuous efforts to lure young players away from the NHL. This was a major problem for Torrey.

Three WHA teams, the New York Raiders, the Chicago Cougars, and the Ottawa Nationals, had contacted Potvin's representative with offers. This was not surprising considering the impact Denis had already made on Canadian amateur hockey.

Once, when Denis and his Ottawa 67s played a game against the Toronto Marlboros at Maple Leaf Gardens, an unofficial record number of scouts were in attendance. "There were more elbowing infractions [among the scouts] around the coffee urn than there were out on the rink," wrote Jim Proudfoot of *The Toronto Star*. They were there, of course, to scout Potvin.

Another time, an all-star team from the Ontario Hockey Association (all teenagers) played a powerful touring squad from the Soviet Union. Potvin scored a goal in the 6–3 upset of the Russians. Once again, Denis got rave reviews.

"The poise and skill which Potvin displayed impressed the large number of NHL scouts on hand," wrote Frank Orr of *The Toronto Star*. "They knew he could go against boys, but wanted to see him against men. He didn't disappoint them."

Bill Torrey was acutely aware of the notices and equally certain that Potvin would be a winner on the Island—that is, if Torrey could land him.

D (for draft) Day took place in June 1973, at The Queen Elizabeth Hotel in Montreal.

Although the WHA teams were still flexing their wallets, Denis had decided once and for all that the *real* challenge would be in the NHL. He arrived at The Queen Elizabeth in a conservative business suit ("I wanted to look like anything but a hockey player," said Potvin) to witness firsthand the decision on his fate.

It was rumored before the draft had even begun that the Montreal Canadiens had offered the Islanders four good players in exchange for Potvin.

Torrey, whose club had finished last the previous season, enjoyed first pick. But before NHL President Clarence Campbell signalled the Islanders' leader for his choice, Sam Pollock, the boss of the Canadiens, requested a time-out. Pollock walked over to Torrey and the two began whispering. It appeared as if Pollock was making an eleventh hour attempt to obtain Potvin.

When the secret conference had ended, the audience waited breathlessly as Campbell ordered Torrey to, at last, make his move. "The New York Islanders," said Torrey, "wish to draft as their first choice—DENIS POTVIN!"

Denis, who privately told friends that he did not want to play for Montreal, was the most relieved person in the building. "It was," Potvin said, "a marvelous moment for me."

It was to be the harbinger of many marvelous moments for the Islanders.

Decorated with a Fu Manchu mustache, Denis arrived at the Islanders' training camp in September 1973, determined to fulfill his advance notices, which were considerable.

From the very start in the NHL, Denis was "tested" by this foes. In Pittsburgh, long-time needler Bryan "Bugsy" Watson lured him into a fight. Potvin took the decision, opening cuts above and below Watson's left eye. "He's a strong kid," Bugsy allowed.

He was strong on defense as well as offense. From the opening face-off, it was evident that Denis Potvin was a winner.

It was also evident that Denis had a special quality that pleased coach Al Arbour.

On February 14, 1974, Denis cracked a bone on his left ankle in a game at St. Louis. Other athletes would have begged off, but Denis continued playing. He wore a plastic cast on the ankle that severely limited his skating, but he played nonetheless.

Playing against the Canucks in Vancouver, he escaped serious injury when a blazing shot by defenseman Jocelyn Guevremont smashed into his helmet above the right eye.

Denis bounced back from all of the hits, bumps, pokes, and other annoyances with commendable resiliency. He was nominated to play in the 1974 All-Star Game at Chicago Stadium. Skating with *la crème de la crème* of the NHL, he scored a goal and was toasted by coach Scotty Bowman.

Potvin's excellence was apparent right down to the homestretch and in the final game of the season, against the Minnesota North Stars at Nassau Coliseum, Potvin demonstrated that the future could only be bright for the home club.

He assisted on Billy Harris's three goals and then personally sewed up the contest by scoring the tie-breaker with only five minutes left in the game.

And when the final arithmetic was completed, the leading scorer on the Islanders was a defenseman, Denis Potvin.

That spring of 1974, Denis was awarded the Calder Trophy as rookie of the year.

Since then, Potvin's accomplishments were staggering, to say the least. He finished his career with 310 regular season goals and 742 assists for 1,052 points. He thus became the highest scoring backliner in history. He guided the Islanders to four Stanley Cups and proved himself to be equally effective on defense. Because of his longevity (fourteen years compared to Orr's twelve), Stanley Cup superiority (four Cups to Orr's two), and more total defense-offense game, he is selected ahead of Orr, whether Bobby's supporters like it or not.

"I've always found it one of the highest honors I could get when someone—Denis or some other young star—comes around and sizes himself up to me. But you'll never get a definitive answer from me. Those judgments should be left to those on the outside," says Orr.

Potvin has been world class as a competitor and controversial as a character. His instincts always were impeccable, even when it came to his decision to retire in the spring of 1988, after leading his Islanders to first place in the Patrick Division.

13

Bobby Orr
(1966–1979)

Had Bobby Orr been blessed with a pair of unassailably healthy knees, his ranking most certainly would have been at least five levels higher than this position. Threatened with wobbly wheels almost from his National Hockey League debut, Orr managed to play only eight full seasons and, in the end, failed to pass the test of time, even though he was at his prime during the diluted expansion era.

A physically fit Orr would still have been playing through the early 1980s. He was an effortless skater (when the knees were right), and an intuitively brilliant tactician who was so idolized by friend and foe alike that he rarely was challenged by the NHL's wood-choppers. He was second to Eddie Shore as the ultimate Boston Bruin.

In his prime, Orr was evaluated as the "Perfect Hockey Player." He played defense well enough to have won the Norris Trophy in 1968, 1969, 1970, 1971, 1972, 1973, 1974, and 1975. Offensively, Orr was no less awesome, and although he was, technically, listed as a backliner, he won the Art Ross Trophy for the league scoring championship in 1970 and 1975.

Orr's legion of admirers would cite chapter and verse to underline his position among hockey's definitive leaders. Harry Sinden, who coached Orr when the Bruins won the Stanley Cup in 1970, perceived aspects of Orr's play that were superior to those of Gordie Howe.

"Howe could do everything but not at top speed," said Sinden. "Hull went at top speed but couldn't do everything. Orr would do everything, and do it at top speed."

That was true only during those precious few years when Orr was not under the knife or recuperating from knee surgery. After two NHL seasons, he underwent two operations.

By the time Orr retired in 1979, he had amassed an impressive collection of silverware. Apart from the Norris and Ross trophies, he had won the Calder Trophy as rookie of the year in 1967; the Hart Trophy as the NHL's most valuable player in 1970, 1971, and 1972; and the Conn Smythe Trophy as the most valuable player in the Stanley Cup playoffs in 1970 and 1972.

Still, there were several chinks in Orr's armor. He betrayed numerous defensive weak-nesses and rarely threw a damaging bodycheck. He won the Norris Trophy not because of defensive ability but rather because he amassed points on offense. Additionally, Orr, for all his abilities, played on only two Stanley Cup-winning teams—in 1970 and 1972. (By contrast, Doug Harvey skated for six Cup-winners.) And in some ways, Orr was a selfish hockey player. During the 1974 Stanley Cup finals in which the Philadelphia Flyers up

set the Bruins, the Bruins were defeated because Orr insisted on carrying the puck rather than pass off to teammates.

Yet, Orr had a quality that only a few have brought to the game: charisma. His blond hair flowing in the breeze he created by skating upwards of twenty-seven miles per hour gave the illusion of a Mercury on skates. Orr was a dashing figure and seemingly capable of coming up with the big play at the appropriate time.

Robert Gordon Orr was born in Parry Sound, Ontario, on March 20, 1948. His all-inclusive talents were detected by big-league scouts before he reached his teens, but it was the Boston Bruins who made the decisive move in gaining a lock on his services after watching him as a twelve-year-old playing in Gananoque, Ontario. In those days, a professional team could gain control of a twelve-year-old simply by putting his name on a protected list. That done, the Bruins patiently waited for Orr to mature.

His ripening as a hockey star was faster than anyone could imagine. By the time he was sixteen, he had become the talk of Canada, and the Bruins, then a last-place club, began the usual ritual of touting a teenager who had never played a professional game as the eventual Messiah who would save the franchise.

The NHL establishment then became shaken by the kid from Parry Sound because he did what neither Gordie Howe nor Rocket Richard had done when they were invited to the bigs: Bobby brought an agent with him. His representative, Toronto attorney R. Alan Eagleson, stunned Bruins' manager Hap Emms with the declaration that Orr would not come to Boston unless he was rewarded with a contract commensurate with his ability. At the time, it was an outrageous demand, particularly in view of the fact that Orr had yet to play a single game as a professional. Emms objected to Eagleson's presence but Orr replied, in effect, no Eagleson, no Orr.

The result was a two-year $150,000 contract that caused reverberations throughout the league. Although nobody knew it at the time, Orr was helping to organize and perpetuate an NHL Players' Association with Eagleson at the helm.

Orr's salary ballooned as his value increased. When he became a Bruin, they were at the bottom of the league. Within three years they were at the top, and Orr became the biggest drawing card in the game. "Bobby," said Eagleson, "is the only player capable of filling every rink in the NHL."

The "Orr Effect," as his style came to be known to analysts, had, and continued to have, a profound impact on the manner in which hockey was played. Before Bobby donned a Bruins uniform, defensemen, as a rule, concentrated on defense. While there were rushing backliners of note in the past—Eddie Shore and Red Kelly being the most prominent—none of them influenced a major change in the mode of play. But Orr did.

Bobby's idea of playing defense was to poke the puck away from the foe and then carry it the length of the rink for either a shot on goal or a pass to a teammate, usually center Phil Esposito. In no time at all, every Canadian kid wanted to be another Bobby Orr.

In a sense, the NHL became too dependent on Orr. When his knees began crumbling in the late 1970s so, too, did the NHL. It lost a network television contract and suffered at the gate. There simply was no successor to the golden boy—at least none who could sell the game so effectively.

Yet, Orr's rainbow evaporated almost as quickly as it appeared on the hockey horizon. After Boston's 1972 Stanley Cup win, Bobby was never the same, literally, figuratively, and physically. He betrayed his weaknesses during the 1973 playoffs when, without his teammate Esposito, who had been injured, he could not lift the Bruins past the opening round, and they were upset by the Rangers. Again, in 1974, he was stymied by Fred

Shero and the Flyers. He never again played on a Cup-winner and soon became embroiled in an intense and prolonged contract dispute with the Bruins' owners.

If the NHL had become too dependent upon Orr, so, too, did Bobby become too dependent upon Eagleson. Had Orr been left to his own devices, it is likely that he would have remained a Bruin until he was compelled to hang up his skates. But Eagleson was calling the shots, and Bobby did what nobody familiar with the NHL scene had ever believed possible: he left the Bruins and wound up signing with the Chicago Black Hawks in 1976.

In some ways, the declining days of Orr were reminiscent of those of Babe Ruth who will always be associated with the New York Yankees. Ruth's final season was spent playing for the Boston Braves. Orr did his thing in the Windy City. For both, it was terribly anticlimactic.

On the few occasions when the knees were not causing him excruciating pain, Orr displayed signs of the glorious past. But the flashes of finesse were insufficient for the Black Hawks, the fans, and most of all, Bobby himself.

He announced his retirement in 1979 and, like Ruth, seemed out of place on the sidelines. His long-term friendship with Eagleson ended abruptly and bitterly for both sides.

In 1979, amid much pomp and circumstance, Orr was named a special assistant to NHL President John Ziegler but, again, the marriage was not binding. Less than two years later Orr, complaining that he was not more than a figurehead, said he would no longer work with the league.

Returning to his beloved Boston, Orr maintained his income by doing endorsements, and, in 1981, he became the unofficial advisor (agent) to Bobby Carpenter, the teen-aged wonder from Massachussetts who was selected first in the NHL draft by the Washington Capitals.

It was a rather depressing denouement for a delightful athlete who at one point could claim that the sky was his limit. In truth, one can only say that Orr's career can be summed up by what might have been.

He was a great one but, because of his limbs, not the greatest.

14

Bobby Hull
(1957–1980)

It is rather symbolic that Bobby Hull, *The Golden Jet* of the ice lanes, should be selected for fourteenth position in *Hockey's 100*. Despite the luster that characterized his career, it ended amid a tragic divorce scenario, followed by a new romance that was tortured by a horrible automobile accident but, finally, a happier Hull emerged in the late 1980s.

These unfortunate events seemed patently unfair to a glamorous performer who brought nothing but guts, goals, and glamour to his profession. He did so as a member of a colorful Chicago Black Hawks team in the late 1950s and 1960s, and then did it again with the Winnipeg Jets of the World Hockey Association.

Adulation for Hull was generated by veteran journalists such as Jim Proudfoot of *The Toronto Star* as well as newcomers to the game like Dwight Chapin of the *Los Angeles Times*. Chapin watched *The Golden Jet* and offered the following critique: "Hull did everything. He scored twice. He added two assists. He was in on power plays. He killed penalties. He talked to his team, and argued moderately with officials."

Hull's impact on the contemporary game was manifold. He popularized the slapshot to such an extent that players who never before had tried the golf-type blast were adding it to their repertoire. He was easily the most magnetic player of the early 1960s and, more than any other player, popularized the game and inspired the NHL to expand from six to twelve teams in 1967.

In terms of his impact on the course of hockey history, Hull was pivotal in the creation of the World Hockey Association and the fact that the upstart league was able to survive and challenge the NHL for six years.

"One reason for that," commented Proudfoot, "was that Bobby was a pro. And he always had plenty of time for the fans."

Like Gordie Howe, Hull was an utterly courageous athlete. Once, during a playoff game against the Red Wings, Hull's nose was smashed by the stick of Detroit's Bruce MacGregor. Doctors said it was futile for Hull to dress again for the series. But a few hours before the match, Hull left the hospital, dashed to the airport, and caught a plane to Detroit. Although his face was covered almost completely by a plaster mask and he could hardly breathe, *The Golden Jet* scored a hat trick.

Hull won the Art Ross Trophy as the NHL's leading scorer in 1960, 1962, and 1966 and the Lady Byng Trophy for skill and gentlemanly play in 1966. He was a First Team All-Star left wing in 1960, 1962, 1964, 1965, 1966, 1967, 1968, 1969, and 1972.

Perhaps the most meaningful goal in Hull's career was scored on March 12, 1966, against the New York Rangers. *The Golden Jet* had scored his fiftieth goal earlier, tying

the mark set by Maurice Richard, Bernie Geoffrion, and himself. But no one ever had levitated above the fifty-goal level during the regular season.

Earlier in the 1965–66 campaign, Hull had missed five games because of torn knee ligaments, but he managed to regain his form and scored his fiftieth goal in his fifty-seventh game. Now the entire hockey world had its eyes on Hull.

He failed to flash the red goal light in Game 58, Game 59, and Game 60. The site of Game 61 was cavernous Chicago Stadium, which was overflowing with 21,000 spectators—4,000 above the listed seating capacity.

The Rangers scored twice in the second period to take a 2–0 lead, while Hull was manacled by the New York checking corps. Early in the third period, Bobby broke free and skimmed a pass to teammate Chico Maki who converted it for the Black Hawks first score. Shortly thereafter, New York defenseman Harry Howell was tagged with a two-minute slashing penalty.

Black Hawks' coach Billy Reay fingered Hull to take the ice as point man on the Chicago power play. For more than a minute, the Rangers defused the Black Hawks' attack, but Hull and teammates Eric Nesterenko, Lou Angotti, and Bill Hay regrouped for another assault. Angotti headmanned the rubber to Hull who loped across the New York blue line. He had decelerated to three-quarter time as his mates moved into position. Nesterenko swerved in front of the Rangers net where stringbean goalie Cesare Maniago had his eyes riveted on Hull's stick.

Instead of relying on his potent slapshot, Hull flicked his mighty wrists, and the puck blurred its way toward Maniago. The Rangers' goalie prepared for the blast but was momentarily distracted as Angotti tipped his stick. Before Maniago could regain his composure, the puck plopped into the twine and Chicago Stadium turned into a cacophony of screaming, hoarse voices. *The Golden Jet* had scored his fifty-first goal at 5:34 of the third period. As the decibel count rose, Bobby skated to the section where his wife was sitting and whispered to her through the protective glass, "Well, I did it."

He finished the season with a total of fifty-four goals. During the 1968–69 season, he scored fifty-eight goals and in 1971–72, his last NHL year before his remarkable "jump" to the WHA, he reached fifty goals once more.

Hull's contract was up for renewal and his popularity had reached an all-time high in the Windy City. Few doubted that he would wear the Indian-crested Black Hawks' jersey when the 1972–73 season began. But the WHA had arrived, promising bundles of cash to NHL superstars who would dare leave the established league for the uncharted future of the new circuit.

When it was learned that Hull was having difficulty agreeing on a new pact with the tightwad Black Hawks, the WHA zeroed in on him and began what would become a long romance. The Winnipeg Jets, owned by rotund Ben Hatskin, had drawn Hull's name in a draft of NHL flesh. Hatskin offered Hull a then astronomical $1,000,000 for five years.

When Hull balked, the WHA raised the ante to $2,000,000. Meanwhile, the Black Hawks' high command failed to impress Hull with their salary offerings or their sincerity. On June 27, 1972, Hull rode a Rolls-Royce through St. Paul, Minnesota, to autograph the WHA portion of his contract. Then the motorcade headed for the airport where a chartered airliner waited to take Hull and family, Hatskin, and their entourage to Winnipeg where he signed the Jets contract.

Robert Marvin Hull was born on January 3, 1939, in Point Anne, Ontario. When he was a fourteen-year-old skating for a Woodstock, Ontario, Junior B team, Black Hawks' scout Bob Wilson discovered Bobby and lined him up for a future contract much in the manner that the Bruins landed Bobby Orr.

Bobby made his NHL debut in 1957–58, and despite his powerful strides and Promethean strength, he was less than prolific. The turnabout for Hull, oddly enough, was a postseason European junket involving the Black Hawks and the Rangers. "Bobby got a lot of ice time," said Muzz Patrick, then manager of the Rangers, "and he seemed to gain confidence with each shift. He was a different player after that."

Within three seasons, Hull had traumatized goalies with what was officially regarded as the hardest shot ever to be hurled netward. Its speed was variously estimated at between 110 and 120 miles per hour. "When the puck left his stick," recalled former Pittsburgh Penguins' goalie Les Binkley, "it looked like a sweet pea. Then as it picked up speed it looked smaller and smaller. Then you didn't see it anymore."

Bobby led the league in goals (39) and points (81) in 1959–60 and repeated two years later with fifty goals and eighty-four points. In 1961, he figured prominently in the Black Hawks' first Stanley Cup triumph since 1938 and only one since then.

Hull's shot was only one feature of his armament. His mighty legs and equally powerful arms enabled Bobby to withstand bodychecks that would have demoralized lesser players. With such raw power at his disposal, Hull could have been a menacing player but—to his everlasting credit—he chose to play clean hockey. Hull suffered as a result and was goaded into numerous *embroglios* by "shadows" like Bryan Watson and John Ferguson. One evening Ferguson broke Hull's jaw. A few weeks later, Bobby returned to combat wearing a massive guard around his injured mouth. Before the night was up, Ferguson had provoked Hull into another fight, completely oblivious to *The Golden Jet*'s wound.

Hull's positive attitude toward the WHA, its fans, and its administrators did much to perpetuate the league's existence long after its projected life expectancy. He was a First Team All-Star left wing in 1974 and 1975. During the 1974–75 season, he scored seventy-seven goals in seventy-eight games, although the opposition was not up to NHL standards. Nevertheless, in his advanced years Hull seemed like a colt, skating on a line with two creative Swedes, Anders Hedberg and Ulf Nilsson.

When Hedberg and Nilsson jumped to the NHL's New York Rangers, it marked the beginning of the end for Hull. Family problems began to affect his play, and Hull "retired" until the NHL and WHA finally merged. *The Golden Jet* had hoped that Winnipeg would swing a deal with the Black Hawks so that he could complete his career in Chicago. But neither Jets' general manager John Ferguson nor his Black Hawks' counterpart, Bob Pulford, could agree on a deal, so Hull unwillingly returned to Winnipeg and played eighteen games for the Jets as an NHLer once more.

In February 1980, he was traded to Hartford where he teamed with Gordie Howe, another distinguished senior citizen. Hull had played nine games when his lady friend was involved in a near-fatal automobile accident. Rather than continue playing, Hull visited the hospital as often as possible and decided against finishing the season.

And that, sadly, is how Bobby Hull ended his hockey career. It was an anticlimactic last act to an otherwise glorious pair of decades and does not in any way detract from Hull's accomplishments on and off the ice. He merits fourteenth position in every way.

15

Bryan Trottier
(1975–   )

It is a measure of Bryan Trottier's durability and excellence that he continues to be a major factor for the New York Islanders after Stanley Cup-winning aces such as Mike Bossy and Denis Potvin have packed up their gear for keeps. Trottier remains a workhorse of the highest order, even after surpassing the thirty-year-old plateau.

"He never ceases to amaze me," said coach Terry Simpson. "He'll go out and play the power play, kill penalties, do extra face-off work, and take his regular turn, and never for a minute will he complain or play less than his best."

Trottier's career has embraced three phases. In the first, he became an astonishingly productive forward, although he entered the league with few advance notices. In the second phase, he emerged as one of the NHL's foremost centers and key to the Islanders' 1980–83 dynastic run.

Leading scorer in the 1980 Stanley Cup playoffs, Trottier paced the Islanders to Stanley Cup triumphs in 1980, 1981, 1982, and 1983. He won the Calder Trophy as the NHL's rookie of the year in 1976; was First All-Star center twice; won the Hart Trophy as the league's most valuable player in 1979, the same year that he led the NHL in scoring; and was voted the Conn Smythe Trophy as the most valuable player in the playoffs in 1980.

There is a fluidity about his play that suggests Gordie Howe. "He's rugged like Howe," explained former teammate Eddie Westfall. "Gordie liked to play a physical game and so does Bryan."

At times Trottier appears more concerned with bodychecking than scoring, although his statistics indicate otherwise. Beginning in 1978, he scored more than 100 points in a season five years running and was as responsible as anyone for turning the Islanders into the powerhouse of the 1980s.

Watching Trottier in action, one senses that the game is fun for him. "I'd think nothing of playing twice in one day, if I could," said Trottier. "That's how much I love this game."

Trottier has not only made hockey fun for himself. He was an intrinsic factor in the development of teammate Mike Bossy's scoring prowess. A right wing, Bossy played alongside Trottier starting in 1977 and concluding a decade later. Together, they had been two of the most productive linemates in history. "It was instinct," said Bossy. "There weren't any little signals. The thing between us was the communication we had. We weren't afraid to tell each other that we should have done this, or we should have done that. As much as Bryan helped me, I helped him."

In the third phase of his career, after Bossy retired, Trottier remains productive. With an assortment of linemates, he managed to score thirty goals and fifty-two assists for eighty-two points in 1987–88.

Unselfish to a fault, Trottier cruises around the rink seemingly unemotional and unaware of the abrupt changes in the ebb and flow of play. Yet, he invariably is the first one where the puck happens to be and, though he masks his feelings, plays with an intensity rare among his colleagues or foes.

Trottier's shot is not especially hard nor is he as fast as Gretzky. "Bryan doesn't stand out in any one area," said Bruins' general manager Harry Sinden. "He's deceptive. When he's in close, he can find an opening and he has tremendous patience and poise. He is able to control the puck and keep it away from the opposition until he's good and ready to shoot."

If there is one shortcoming to Trottier's game, it is his playoff failings in his earlier years in the NHL. He had scored but five goals in his first forty-two playoff games before he finally exploded in the 1980 Stanley Cup rounds. "When I was holding the Cup," Bryan recalled of his first Stanley Cup triumph, "I could feel all the names. My senses peaked. I could hear everyone. The crowd was incredible, one continuous roar."

Bryan John Trottier was born July 17, 1956, in Val Marie, Saskatchewan, in the heart of Canada's wheat country. By the time Bryan was in his mid-teens, he had been more than casually scouted by several NHL teams. Bill Torrey, architect of the Islanders' juggernaut, was in Swift Current, Saskatchewan, to watch the teenaged Trottier in action. "One night," said Torrey, "it was so cold the wind-chill factor was about eighty-three degrees below. Trottier got two or three goals, two or three assists, and he had the puck the whole night. The first thing you noticed was instinct. Things happened."

Torrey and coach Al Arbour remembered, and when draft time came and there was a choice between Trottier and Tiger Williams, Bryan's teammate at Swift Current, the question was settled when Arbour asked which one was the better player. That's how Trottier became an Islander.

When the solidly built, baby-faced kid turned up at the Islanders' training camp in September 1975, there were those who believed he was at least two or three years away from making it in the NHL. But each time a training camp roster cut was made Trottier survived, and he was in the lineup when the Islanders opened their home season at Nassau Coliseum. He responded with three goals, two assists, tying a team record with five points.

"Bryan is a tremendous skater who controls the puck extremely well," said Clark Gillies, who frequently played on a line with Trottier. "His main strength is that he's always coming up with the puck in the corners. He's also good at causing the other team to make a mistake. He anticipates so well that he's often able to intercept passes. But he rarely makes mistakes himself."

What is most remarkable about Trottier is his ability to log so much ice time while playing a physically punishing game and maintaining a high skill level. Although Wayne Gretzky will finish his career with more goals and assists than Trottier, *The Great One* will have finished far behind his Islander counterpart in the area of physical play. Hall of Famer Bill Chadwick, the former ref, once described Trottier as "the greatest player of all time." Perhaps it was an exaggeration born of an emotional accomplishment for the Islanders, but in his exaggeration Chadwick made the point that Trottier ranks alongside Gretzky, Jean Beliveau, Syl Apps, and Marcel Dionne as one of the greatest centers of all time.

16

Bill Cook
(1926–1937)

Before Maurice Richard, Gordie Howe, and Andy Bathgate redefined the role of a right-winger there was Bill Cook, the original New York Ranger who combined lyricism with true grit. Since Cook's era spanned the 1920s and 1930s, preceding the time of the high-speed game, it is not quite fair to compare him with the moderns. But some who played with and against Cook and who watched the moderns insist that Bill was in his own class.

"He's my choice as the best right-winger hockey ever knew," said Frank Boucher, who opposed Cook and later teamed with him in New York. "He was better than *The Rocket* [Richard] and, in my estimation, better than Gordie Howe as well."

Well-proportioned, the glint-eyed Cook took the game every bit as seriously as Richard and fought his foe as grimly as Howe. "He was," said Boucher, "the finest all-around player in Ranger history."

The pity of it all is that Cook did not make his National Hockey League debut until the age of thirty, a time when other players were retiring. He won the NHL scoring championship in his rookie year and repeated again in 1933 at the age of thirty-seven!

A series of unavoidable circumstances delayed Cook's ascent to the NHL clouds. A farm boy from Kingston, Ontario, his hockey skills were sufficient to earn him a professional invitation by the time he was twenty, but duty came first. With the outbreak of World War I, Bill enlisted in the Canadian army and was assigned to a field artillery unit overseas.

His reward, upon returning home, was a soldier's allotment of land in Saskatchewan. But the life of an agriculturalist was not stimulating enough for him so Cook resumed his hockey career in 1922 with Saskatoon of the Western League. It was fast company—Eddie Shore and Frank Boucher were among other top-flight opponents—and Cook established himself among the best. When Madison Square Garden moguls decided to organize the Rangers and asked Conn Smythe to do the recruiting, Bill and his brother Bun Cook were the first choices.

Cook wasted no time establishing his credentials. Skating against the champion Montreal Maroons, the Rangers held them to a scoreless tie until Bill and Bunny broke away against Clint Benedict, the Montreal goalie. Bun took the first shot but Benedict made the save. He retrieved the rebound and tapped the puck to Bill who flicked the rubber over the fallen goalie.

As the red light glowed, Benedict crumpled to the ice momentarily stunned by his crash into the goal post. A short delay was necessary for the netminder to be repaired.

"During this lull," Boucher remembered, "the crowd stayed on its feet, cheering and clapping for the Cooks and refusing to sit until Benedict returned to finish the period."

Bill had scored the winning goal in a match that tickled the fancy of New York hockey fans and instantly gave the Rangers credibility along with their rivals, the New York Americans. The Rangers had one advantage and that was the Cooks-Boucher line, which combined like perfectly meshed gears.

Although Boucher and Bunny were critical to the line's success, Bill had the commanding personality and gave the unit a Pattonesque leadership.

"When the three of us got together to discuss strategy," said Boucher, "Bill would give the orders. Once, he said, 'When I want that puck I'll yell for it, and you get that damn puck to me when I yell.' On the ice, Bill's cry was the most amazing half-grunt, half-moan, half-yell that I ever heard. He'd let this weird sound out of him, meaning that he was in the clear."

Cook, who was a superior player to brother Bunny, was named to the NHL First All-Star Team in 1931, 1932, and 1933. In any debating over the best forward line in hockey history, the Cooks-Boucher line at the very worst would rank among the top three and certainly would obtain innumerable votes as *the* best. Both Bunny and Boucher were good shooters, but Bill's shot was more potent than his linemates'.

"Bill didn't have a bullet shot," Boucher explained, "or at least not a *long* bullet shot like the golf-style slapshot Bobby Hull perfected. But he had a very hard wrist shot from close in and could score equally well backhand or forehand."

Over eleven seasons—at a time when the NHL played a short schedule—Bill scored 229 goals and was a conspicuous contributor to the Rangers' Stanley Cup wins in 1928 and 1933. The most striking similarity between Cook's play and Gordie Howe's was in their aggressive play. Some journalists referred to the right wing as "Bad Bill" and had enough episodes to support the nickname.

By far the most sinister episode involved Cook and Nels Crutchfield, a Montreal Canadiens rookie who had made the jump from McGill University to the NHL. Their fateful collision took place during a playoff game in 1935 after Crutchfield—according to Cook—had committed several fouls without being penalized.

"Crutchfield was interfering with me throughout the game and the referee wouldn't do anything about it," said Cook. "So I finally caught Crutchfield with the butt end of my stick. Then he hit me right on the bean with his stick. The next thing I saw was a million stars."

Cook might have been killed by the two blows delivered by Crutchfield, but he avoided catastrophe by instinctively deflecting each clout with his arm. "When I finally came around," said Bill, "all I saw was the stockings of the players who were scrapping. I never saw so many people getting belted on the ice."

What Bill didn't see was his brother, Bunny, leading the charge of Rangers over the boards. Bun carried his stick over his shoulder racing toward Crutchfield who didn't see him coming. Boucher sensed that Bunny wanted to murder Crutchfield and rather subtly stuck his skate out and tripped Bun a few feet short of his intended victim. "Frank told me," said Bill, "that he had to stop my brother or he would have killed Crutchfield."

After eight stitches had been embroidered in Bill's wounds, he returned to the bench. "I was kind of groggy," he admitted, "but I wanted to finish the game."

The Rangers' doctor outfitted him with a makeshift helmet, and Bill finally took his position on the right side of Boucher. Late in the game, he gained control of the puck and bobbed and weaved his way through the Canadiens' defense to score the game-winning goal. Bill maintained that it ranked among his two greatest thrills in hockey—the other being the winning goal he scored against Toronto in 1933 to provide the Rangers with their second Stanley Cup title.

The Cooks and Boucher had become popular heroes alongside Babe Ruth and Lou Gehrig in the well-publicized New York sports fraternity. Writing in the New York *Sun*, journalist Harold C. Burr composed this ditty.

> *Old adages live because they are true;*
> *If they weren't they wouldn't survive.*
> *But once in a while there are a few*
> *That shouldn't be kept alive.*
> *In hockey, where speed and grit hold forth,*
> *Some sayings sound awfully funny.*
> *'Too many cooks spoil the broth.'*
> *Did you ever meet Bill and Bunny?*

William Osser Cook was born October 9, 1896, in Brantford, Ontario, and learned the essential hockey skills on the frozen outdoor rinks near the family home. The rugged farm life helped steel him for the ice wars ahead and accounted, in part, for Cook's longevity as a professional. He played regularly for the Rangers until 1937 when he was forty-one and was named player-assistant to Lester Patrick.

When a coaching job became available with the Cleveland Barons of the American Hockey League, Bill left the Rangers. In 1951, his old pal Boucher, who had become Rangers' manager, asked Bill to coach the slumping New York sextet. Rangers' president General John Reed Kilpatrick hoped that Bill could revive the Rangers, but he couldn't. He was fired in 1953 on Kilpatrick's orders. Bill blamed Boucher, and for three years they wouldn't talk until they met one night at a banquet. Bill threw his arms around Boucher's shoulders and said: "What the hell, Frankie, it's been too many years. Let's forget the whole thing."

Nobody should forget that Bill Cook was one of the definitive NHL right wings.

17

Max Bentley
(1940–1954)

I saw my first hockey game in 1939 and have watched thousands since then everywhere from Pittsburgh to Prague. If I had to pick one player above all who I'd like to view in action just once—or maybe a hundred times—more, there is no hesitation on my part in coming up with an answer.

Max Bentley.

It isn't even close. Maurice Richard was electrifying and Gordie Howe was disarmingly smooth. Bobby Orr offered supersonic dimensions and Bobby Hull's speed with both skates and shots were irresistible to the eye.

But Max Bentley delivered something more to this viewer. Even at a time when the National Hockey League was not peopled by behemoths, Bentley looked fragile. He measured 5'8½", 150 pounds, which made him susceptible to the crunching bodycheck. But as many a defenseman noted, you can't hit what you can't see.

What set Max apart from other artists was the manner in which he combined his amalgam of talents. For starters, he was the best and fastest stickhandler I have ever seen. It wasn't simply a matter of keeping the puck from the foe, which Howe did to perfection, but rather the magical series of jiggling maneuvers (all without ever having his eyes on the puck) in front of him, to the sides, and, sometimes, behind his back.

Jean Beliveau executed many of these tricks with a liquid motion that was impressive but not exciting. Bentley's motions had something more deliciously frenzied. He was aptly described by one writer as stickhandling like a scared jackrabbit.

Max's stickhandling was complemented by his rapid acceleration and deceleration. His movements were reminiscent of the crazy electric bumping cars at amusement parks. If Max were one of the cars, he would have zigzagged through the maze without being bumped. Finally, there was the wrist shot; again the speediest, most accurate in my memory.

As a center, Max could deliver a pass as deftly as he could fire a puck, and for many years the recipient of his passes was his older brother Doug who was built along the same lighthorse dimensions as Max. It was mistakenly believed by some skeptics that Max could not excel without Doug on his wing, but this theory was obliterated in the second half of his career when Max wrote himself into the records as a one-of-a-kind center who helped create several Stanley Cup champions.

Bentley twice (1946 and 1947) led the NHL in scoring and won the Hart Trophy as the league's most valuable player in 1946 and the Lady Byng Trophy for excellence and clean play in 1943. He was voted First All-Star center in 1946 and skated for three Stanley Cup winners.

Apart from his obvious skills, Max had something likeable about him. There was never any doubt in the minds of spectators or opponents that this man was interested, above all, in playing the game—not in maiming or taunting or intimidating.

Max remained in the bigs for fourteen years and in that time one vignette said more about Bentley, his style, and his clutch ability than any other—and it wasn't a goal he scored either.

It was the fifth game of the 1951 Stanley Cup between Bentley's Toronto Maple Leafs and the Montreal Canadiens paced by Maurice Richard. Toronto led the series three games to one, but the Canadiens were coming on strong. They led 2–1 with little more than a half-minute to play and appeared strong enough to take the game and eventually the series.

Leafs' coach Joe Primeau removed his goalie Al Rollins and dispatched Bentley to the right point as the sixth skater along with Ted Kennedy, Sid Smith, Tod Sloan, Harry Watson, and Gus Mortson. Kennedy won the face-off deep in the Canadiens' zone and sent the puck back to Bentley.

Ed Fitkin, who was the Maple Leafs' publicist at the time, remembered Max's moves: "In a thrilling and artistic display of stickhandling, Bentley fought his way across the front of the Montreal net and then fired. The puck hit a defender's leg and bounced out to Smith. He shot and hit the goal post but the rebound fell at Sloan's feet and Tod promptly blazed it home."

The Leafs won the game and the Cup in sudden-death overtime. "That game," said Bentley, "was one of my greatest thrills."

Maxwell Herbert Lloyd Bentley was born March 1, 1920, in Delisle, Saskatchewan. His grandfather came from Yorkshire, England, and originally settled in Pembina, North Dakota. His father had a livery barn there and would have remained an American were it not for Prohibition in North Dakota in the 1880s.

Bill and Mathilda Bentley had thirteen children, including seven daughters who, in their own right, were remarkable hockey players; but Doug was the first Bentley to reach the top. He broke in with the Chicago Black Hawks in 1939 and kept telling management that he had a kid brother playing in Saskatoon who was even better.

There was no disputing Max's ability but his health was questionable. In 1938, he was told by physicians to quit hockey because of a serious heart condition, but Max returned to the ice with no ill effects and in 1940 joined Doug on the Black Hawks. By the 1941–42 season, the Bentleys had become the sensations of State Street. Although they looked like they would crumble on contact, each possessed a damaging shot. When right wing Bill Mosienko, another lightweight, was welcomed to the Black Hawks' varsity, The Pony Line of Mosienko and the Bentleys was formed.

Along with The Punch Line, The Kid Line, and The Production Line, the Bentleys-Mosienko unit proved one of the most fetching trios the game has known. The pity of it all was that they had little substance behind them, and the Black Hawks rarely were contenders.

At the end of World War II, most of the NHL teams were bolstered by the return of prewar stars who had been in the armed forces, but the Black Hawks remained inept except for The Pony Line. The club's most marketable player was Max Bentley, who was at the top of his game. Rumors that Max would be traded surfaced for several weeks during the start of the 1947–48 season, but there were a number of considerations raised.

Could Max retain his edge without Doug? What would the Black Hawks demand in return? How would Chicago fans handle the departure of Max?

On November 4, 1947, the biggest trade in hockey history was consummated. The Maple Leafs sent an entire first team (less a goaltender) to the Black Hawks for Max. Included in the package was a complete (and rather good) forward line called *The Flying Forts* comprising Gaye Stewart, Bud Poile, and Gus Bodnar, as well as a pair of defensemen, Bob Goldham and Ernie Dickens.

Max was heartbroken at the news for it meant splitting with Doug. "It makes me feel," said Max, "like I lost my right arm."

For a time, it seemed that Maple Leafs' mogul Conn Smythe had goofed in making the trade. Max went ten straight games without a goal while coach Hap Day sought appropriate linemates for him. He finally settled on Nick Metz and Joe Klukay and, soon, Bentley regained his form. When Metz retired, Ray Timgren was added to the line and Max was better than ever.

Max, Ted Kennedy, and Syl Apps were centers on that 1947–48 club, which finished first and won the Stanley Cup. No hockey team ever boasted more awesome strength down the middle. When Apps retired in 1948, more pressure was applied to Bentley to take up the slack and, again, he proved his worth. The Leafs won the Stanley Cup again and almost repeated in 1950 when the Detroit Red Wings topped them in a seven-game series. A year later, Toronto regained the championship, and Max was the most popular Maple Leaf.

Throughout his career, Max was notorious as the NHL's foremost hypochondriac. But once he passed the thirty-year-old milestone, he was assailed by both real and imagined injuries. Rather than embarrass himself before the Toronto fans, he advised Smythe that he would retire and did so in 1953. He decided to return to Saskatchewan and play hockey with Doug who had become player-coach of the Saskatoon Quakers, a New York Rangers' farm team. It was then that Rangers' manager Frank Boucher got a brainstorm; why not reunite the Bentleys on a line with his club? He obtained permission from the Maple Leafs and Black Hawks to negotiate with them, and Max finally agreed to sign.

Doug was hesitant and ultimately chose to start the season in Saskatoon. Boucher employed Max as a point man on the Rangers' power play and in spot duty. A bit slower, perhaps, Bentley still had the touch of the poet and made Boucher look good. Early in January, the Rangers' manager convinced Doug to sign with the Rangers. This time he agreed and on January 21, 1954, one of hockey's most magnificent moments took place as the Bentleys were reunited.

Moving, as one reporter described them, "like a pair of black-haired waterbugs on the ice, darting, gliding, driving," the Bentleys worked with another oldtimer, Edgar Laprade, and they bewitched the Boston Bruins to the tune of 8–3. The 13,463 fans gave them a standing ovation at game's end and in the dressing room Max wept openly.

"He's crying for happiness," said Doug. "He's tickled because we finally played together again...and so am I."

It was a uniquely magnificent moment that caused many in the crowd to shed a tear because they knew they would never see anything like it again. "We recognized," said Boucher, "that we had sat in on something very rare, not to be turned on like a recording or an instant replay."

The charm and skill of Max Bentley has never been duplicated and, I am certain, never will be because he was the only one of his kind.

18

Georges Vezina
(1917–1926)

"The Vezina!"

"How often we have equated the name with goaltending excellence. The Vezina Trophy, since 1927, has been awarded to the netminders who have delivered the lowest goals against average each season.

More than any National Hockey League prize, this one has the deepest meaning because Georges Vezina, after whom the trophy is named, was a nonpareil athlete whose ability was matched only by his infinite sportsmanship.

A gangling six-footer, Vezina guarded the Montreal Canadiens' nets when the team played in the National Hockey Association and later for the Habitants when the National Hockey League was organized.

In each milieu, he excelled. The Canadiens won the NHA championship twice with Vezina between the pipes and won three NHL championships and two Stanley Cups. He played a total of 373 consecutive games for Les Canadiens in an era when goaltenders' masks were unheard of and was nicknamed *The Chicoutimi Cucumber* for his birthplace and his cool under fire.

Vezina starred for the Canadiens for fifteen years, from 1910 to 1925, and no doubt would have remained the master of his trade for several more seasons had he not been fatally stricken with tuberculosis. A quiet man, Vezina continued to play although he was aware that his life was doomed.

On November 28, 1925, his body wracked with pain, Vezina skated out onto the ice of Mount Royal Arena to face the visiting Pittsburgh sextet. "No one knew," wrote author Ron McAllister, "that the great goaltender had struggled to the arena despite a temperature of 105 degrees.

"A deathlike chill settled over him; but with Pittsburgh forcing the play from the face-off, Vezina functioned throughout the first period with his usual dextrous ease, deflecting shot after shot. In the dressing room, he suffered a severe arterial hemorrhage, but the opening of the second period found him at his accustomed place in goal."

Fighting desperately against the fatigue and fever that completely throttled his body, the great Vezina could no longer see the puck as it skimmed from one side of the rink to the other. Suddenly a collective gasp engulfed the arena. Vezina had collapsed in the goal crease. "In the stricken arena," said one observer, "all was silent as the limp form of the greatest of goalies was carried slowly from the ice."

It was the end of the trail for Georges and he knew it. At his request, he was taken home to his native Chicoutimi where doctors diagnosed his case as advanced tuberculosis.

On March 24, 1926, he passed away. An enormous funeral, held in the old cathedral at Chicoutimi, saw players and fans from all parts of the country deliver their final tribute to the gallant goaltender. A year later the Canadiens' owners donated a trophy in his honor.

Georges Vezina was born in January 1887 in Chicoutimi, Quebec, a city that sits on the edge of the dark Saguenay River and flows into the blue St. Lawrence at historic Tadoussac.

Although young Vezina established himself as a class-A goalie even as a youth in Chicoutimi, he had developed a habit of playing without skates. For some peculiar reason, he found the idea of wearing skates a bother, and it wasn't until two years before he graduated to Les Canadiens that he actually learned to wear skates while tending goal.

Conceivably, the Montrealers would never have discovered Vezina were it not for a chance exhibition game between the Canadiens and the local Chicoutimi club on February 23, 1910. The match between the awesome professionals from Montreal and the patchwork amateur outfit figured to be so one-sided that only a handful of fans turned out for it.

Chicoutimi hardly looked like a formidable foe except for the six-foot goalie, wearing a red-and-white *Habitant toque* on his head. Leaning against the goal post, the tall, lanky Vezina appeared almost too bored for words. But once the overpowering Canadiens sliced through the fragile Chicoutimi defense, Vezina suddenly responded with a peripatetic style that thoroughly dumfounded the pros. Try as they might, the Canadiens could not score. Chicoutimi won the game, 2-0.

That was all the Canadiens' high command had to know. They invited Vezina to Montreal and he made his debut on December 31, 1910. Curiously, Georges never signed a contract with the Montrealers. He preferred a gentleman's handshake with his managers, first Joe Cattarinich and later Leo Dandurand.

The father of twenty-two children, Vezina was virtually impregnable once he took his position in the goal crease. Once, during a game at Hamilton, Bert Corbeau smashed into him with such force that the goaltender's head was cut open and his nose broken. Vezina continued playing despite the wounds, his ability undiminished by pain.

According to hockey historians, Vezina was the author of several hockey classics, including the 1916 Stanley Cup final between Les Canadiens and the Pacific Coast Hockey Association's Portland Rosebuds. The best-of-five series went the limit; the final game being played on March 30, 1916. With the score tied, 1–1, Vezina defused the most explosive Portland offensives until Goldie Prodgers scored the winner for Montreal. Vezina and each of his Stanley Cup-winning teammates received $238 for taking the championship.

In the Roaring Twenties Vezina was better than ever. During the 1923–24 season, he allowed only forty-eight goals in twenty-four games, including three shutouts for a 2.00 goals against average. He then blanked Ottawa, 1–0, in the NHL playoff opener and sparkled as Montreal swept the series. Montreal went on to rout Calgary and Vancouver for the Stanley Cup. Vezina's Stanley Cup record was six goals in six games—an even 1.00 average.

By this time, Vezina's body was afflicted with the early symptoms of tuberculosis. "Beads of perspiration formed on his forehead for no apparent reason," said Ron McAllister. "An expression of pain flitted momentarily across his face, but the Great Vezina invariably settled down to the business at hand, turning in his usual matchless performance."

During the 1924–25 season, despite the ailment, he came up with a 1.9 goals against average, easily the best in the league. But when he arrived at the Canadiens' training camp in the fall of 1925, he seemed unusually fatigued.

It has been said that not even those in his own family realized that Vezina was fighting for his life as he prepared for the 1925–26 season. This would be a particularly fascinating year for the worldly Vezina. The NHL was expanding into the United States more than ever. It had embraced a Boston franchise a year earlier, and now New York and Pittsburgh had been added, as well as a second Montreal team, the Maroons, who would provide an English-speaking team as natural rivals for the Canadiens. Needless to say, the outstanding attraction in the American cities among the Montreal players was the redoubtable Vezina.

Sadly, *The Chicoutimi Cucumber* donned the *bleu*, *blanc*, *et rouge* uniform for the last time in the season opener of the 1925–26 season. There were 6,000 spectators in the stands on that rainy night who had come to see the great Vezina.

Few realized as he left the ice after a scoreless first period that he was bleeding from the mouth. But they began to perceive his pain in the second period when he fell to the ice for the last time.

Georges Vezina was the personification of courage and capability. When someone in hockey says "The Vezina," they need say no more.

19

King Clancy
(1921–1937)

In the final game of the 1923 Stanley Cup series between Ottawa and Edmonton, a goal by Punch Broadbent of Ottawa won the game, 1–0, and the championship for the skaters from Canada's capital.

Yet it was neither Broadbent's score nor the triumph by the Senators that proved so extraordinary. On that night, manager Tommy Gorman of Ottawa had five stars sidelined with injuries and was able to dress only eight skaters for the climactic game. What was so astonishing was that one of those eight stalwarts, defenseman King Clancy, came to Gorman's rescue and *played every position on the team, including goal.*

"He had taken turns on defense, at center and had filled in on both wings," Gorman recalled. "In the last ten minutes of the game our goalie, Clint Benedict, drew a penalty. In those days, a goalie actually had to serve his sentence in the penalty box, himself, and any substitution occurred in the net, and not in the box.

"Clancy volunteered to take over Benedict's goaling job and I let him do it. Not only did he stop Edmonton but he almost scored on them while he was playing goal. King had made a save and saw a loose puck in front of his cage. He dashed out, got his stick on the puck, wiggled past an Edmonton attacker and started to rush down the rink."

Gorman kept yelling at Clancy to get back in his net, but the King paid his boss no heed and moved in on the enemy defense. "He pulled one of Edmonton's defensemen out of position," said Gorman, "and then fired a shot. Then, grinning happily, he scooted back to his own end of the rink to resume business as a goalie."

Such was the manner of Clancy, a man of infinite humor, ability, and guts. At a time when defensemen such as Eddie Shore and other Goliaths of the rink would as soon carve their initials in an opponent's brow as score a goal, the lilliputian Clancy backed away from no one and also emerged as the definitive backliner who was twice a First All-Star and played on three Stanley Cup winners.

More than Shore, Doug Harvey, Red Kelly, or Bobby Orr, Clancy offered an exuberance to the game that had a more positive touch than Maurice Richard's almost sinister pursuit of the almighty goal. There was an "I love life—I love hockey" aura about the King that was infectious on any team that had Clancy playing defense.

Perhaps it was imperative that King adopt such a philosophy. When he tried out for Gorman's Ottawa Senators in 1921, *he weighed in at 125 pounds.* And this was a defenseman. Gorman was appropriately flabbergasted but figured he'd go along with the gag so he invited young Clancy to lace on the skates and have his audition with the big-leaguers. "If you make the team," said Gorman, "I'll sign you for three years at $800 per season."

Gorman, whose team was Stanley Cup champion in two of the past two seasons, did not expect Clancy to come close to making it; not when aces such as Frank Nighbor, Eddie Gerard, and Sprague Cleghorn were on the team. Clancy was militantly unimpressed by his surroundings. "Everyone who watched his debut marveled at the confidence of the Irish lad as he sailed into the Stanley Cuppers as though they were all kids together playing shinny on a local rink," commented one reporter.

Gorman had no choice but to sign the lad, although the manager suffered doubts about Clancy's size. "We'll put fifty pounds of rock salt in your shirt," said Gorman, "to weigh you down."

Clancy played on four Stanley Cup winners in Ottawa and appeared to be a fixture in the capital city. Then the Great Depression cast a black cloud over the continent and the Senators' attendance dropped at an alarming rate. The team needed money to survive and a decision was made to sell the Senators' most marketable player. Thus King Clancy became the centerpiece in professional hockey's biggest trade up until that time.

The Toronto Maple Leafs, operated by the flamboyant Conn Smythe, wanted Clancy, as did the New York Rangers and Chicago Black Hawks. Both the Rangers and Hawks seemed to have the edge because of their bigger bankrolls. But Smythe had a colt named Rare Jewel entered at Toronto's Woodbine Racetrack. The odds were 100–1 against Rare Jewel, but Smythe put his bankroll on the colt. It obliged by coming in first and filling its owner's pocket with enough cash to bid for Clancy. He offered Ottawa $35,000 cash, as well as two players—Art Smith and Eric Pettinger—worth a total of $15,000. Clancy cost Smythe $50,000 (today $1 million would be a low figure) and was worth every penny of it.

Clancy realized early on that he was not going to prevail on his strength, so he compensated in other ways. Toronto *Telegram* sports columnist Ted Reeve observed Clancy as a rookie with Ottawa in 1921 to his final game with the Maple Leafs in 1937 and had this to say about King's style:

"His main forte was his ability to break fast, to come leaping off the blue line as though it were a springboard, with the loose puck tossed out in front. He could pass on the dead tear, though not a graceful skater [he was almost running on his blades at times], and he had a wicked shot.

"It was that indefinable something—the competitive spirit—that made Clancy so valuable to the Leafs. And the God-given gift of fun in him that would bring them out of the doldrums with a whoop and a holler. That high-pitched sort of husky voice, his piping exclamations and infectious grin."

Francis Michael Clancy was born February 25, 1903, in Ottawa, Ontario. His father, Thomas Clancy, pushed him into sports despite his size. Tom Clancy was the original "King" in the family. An accomplished football player, he was known as *The King of Heelers* because of his ability to get the ball into play from scrimmage in the manner of that day.

The second King developed into an even better athlete than the original. Teaming up with the likes of Hap Day, Charlie Conacher, Harold Cotton, and Ace Bailey, Clancy reveled in his role with what became The Gashouse Gang of hockey. "We didn't win the Cup every year," said Clancy, "but winter after winter we won the world's championship for assorted pranks and jokes in Pullman cars and hotels."

What is so remarkable about Clancy's career is that it just seemed to begin after he finally began losing his edge with the Leafs. On November 24, 1936, he realized that it was time to pack it in. He walked into the dressing room and addressed his buddies. "Fellows," said King, "I just want to say a few words..." Tears welled in his eyes and he lifted a hand in farewell. The Clancy era had ended in Toronto.

When Clancy retired, the NHL came through and made him a referee. He was to become one of the most beloved referees in the game. For the most part, Clancy employed the laissez-faire philosophy of officiating. And he had a rather unusual manner of giving penalties for offenses that he didn't see. "If Clancy caught a player swiping another with his stick," said one NHLer of the Clancy refereeing era, "he'd give 'em *both* two minutes. He figured that the other guy must have started it; and, usually, King was right."

Clancy refereed from 1937 to 1949. From 1953 to 1956, he coached the Maple Leafs, again employing the same easygoing style that succeeded as a player and referee. Although he didn't win any Stanley Cups, Clancy was able to get more out of his players than most coaches. He later became an invaluable aide-de-camp to Maple Leafs' general manager-coach Punch Imlach and club president Harold Ballard.

The ubiquitous Clancy rarely missed a Maple Leafs road game with Ballard at his side well into the 1980s, and he seemed to have lost none of the enthusiasm that he brought to the Ottawa training camp in 1921.

When Conn Smythe stepped down as boss of the Maple Leafs, he turned to Clancy and said, "You're the biggest name of any we've got."

He was one of the biggest—and most uplifting—names hockey ever had. Frank Clancy's nickname was more than apt; he was truly a King.

20

Mario Lemieux
(1984–)

It had to happen. Wayne Gretzky could not remain the undisputed king of hockey forever. Sooner or later there had to be a legitimate challenger, and in the late 1980s, a big man burst onto the scene to test Gretzky as never before. The young rival, Mario Lemieux, not only matched *The Great One* in terms of total quality of play but also outpointed Gretzky in production. Two specific episodes provided telling examples of the 1987–88 Lemieux challenge.

The first was his performance in the 1987 Canada Cup tournament. In the curtain-closer, Lemieux scored the game-winning goal with 1:24 left in Game 3. (He also set a tournament record with eleven goals.) The second unfolded at the 1988 NHL All-Star Game in St. Louis when Mario scored a record six points including a hat trick. That splendid performance earned him the most valuable player award, a truck, and a lot of respect.

"He's so good," said Mats Naslund, the Swede who earned a record five assists skating alongside Lemieux. "I don't think that it would be embarrassing my Montreal teammates to say he's the best player I've ever played with."

Perhaps most telling of all is the fact that Lemieux ousted Gretzky for the first time in eight years as the NHL's scoring champion during the 1987–88 season. Although he was saddled with a non-playoff Pittsburgh team, Lemieux compiled an extraordinary seventy goals and ninety-eight assists for 168 points.

"Mario is very much like [Jean] Beliveau," said Max McNab, executive vice-president of the New Jersey Devils. "The tall lanky players have a way of looking casual and slow, but nobody seems to catch them. Lemieux is skating harder than he looks out there. You never see anybody hit him head on. He's very elusive."

However, the debit on Lemieux's ledger could not be erased through four seasons in the league—Mario, despite all his assets, could not steer the Penguins into the playoffs. Nevertheless, he has fulfilled his assignment as franchise-saviour as proven by the record number of sellouts during the 1987–88 season.

"He did just about everything for us," said former Penguins' general manager Eddie Johnston. "The way he played down the stretch proved that he's one of the great players in history."

Mario's marks in the 1987–88 season read like a chapter out of the *NHL Guide and Record Book*. He led the league in points (168), goals (70), shorthanded goals (10), and shots (382). He also had nineteen multiple-goal games, including five hat tricks and thirty-three games with three or more points.

Gretzky makes no bones about Lemieux's talent. "He deserves everything he gets. He won it (the scoring race) fair and square. I don't make any excuses. Mario is a great, great hockey player."

Lemieux was able to showcase his immense talent alongside *The Great One* during the 1987 Canada Cup tournament. For the first time since turning pro with the Penguins in 1984, Lemieux not only matched the great Gretzky in terms of excellence but surpassed him in some respects.

At least one Soviet hockey expert suggested that, talent for talent, Lemieux was his choice over Gretzky. And when it came to high intensity drama, once again it was Lemieux who got the nod over Gretzky, as the Penguin's young star scored the pivotal goal that ruined the Russians.

This does not for a minute diminish Gretzky's ultra-high level of play. In fact, having Gretzky alongside Lemieux during the Canada Cup showdown is like staging a dance duet with Baryshnikov and Nureyev side by side on the stage.

"Wayne and I clicked right away," Lemieux remembered, "because we both handle the puck well and we know how to read a situation. The Soviets couldn't stop us because Wayne could always keep the puck an extra second so I could get free, and I could do the same for him."

The result was some of the best offensive hockey between Moscow and Moose Jaw. However, once the 1987 tourney was over, a meaningful question was raised: What could Mario do for an encore?

Despite an unavoidable letdown after the Canada Cup, Lemieux returned to Pittsburgh and played some of the best hockey imaginable for one of the NHL's mediocre teams.

"Playing in the Canada Cup gave me a lot of confidence," Lemieux recalled. "I learned a lot, especially practicing with guys like Wayne and Paul [Coffey]. We had very high-intensity practices. And I learned a lot about what to say in the dressing room, like if you're two or three goals down between periods. I listened to guys who've played on Cup-winners."

Lemieux's assets cover skating, shooting, play making, leadership, and scoring in critical situations. *Montreal Gazette* reporter Jack Todd offered this portrait of Lemieux: "Everything seems to slow down when Lemieux has the puck; in a game of swirling, blinding action, he's the still point, the eye of the hurricane. It's as if he can run the play in front of his own eyes in slow motion until he finds an opening.

"Where physical play is concerned, Mario can hold his own. Lemieux is often an aggressor. He can be downright nasty and, quite simply, dominates with his body. Knocking him off the puck can be almost impossible because of his unusual balance, size, and leverage with the stick; you won't knock Lemieux off the puck or on his pants."

What remains to be seen is how long Lemieux can play consistently high-level hockey. Checkers are giving him more and more grief, and Mario must decide whether he'll risk retaliation or discipline himself in the Gretzky manner. This much is certain: Lemieux has developed into a player who will rival *The Great One* for control of the game of hockey. As Mario gains more experience and plays with and against the elite of the league, he will ascend to the Hall-of-Fame level. He has already earned a position in *Hockey's 100*.

21

Nels Stewart
(1925–1940)

There was a time in the 1950s when the only names on the minds of hockey fans were Nels Stewart and Maurice Richard.

Nicknamed *Ole Poison* for his inevitable sting around the enemy net, Stewart reigned for more than a decade as the National Hockey League's all-time goal scoring titlist. Stewart's career record of 324 was pursued and finally surpassed by Richard but not until the race finally focused attention on the oft-overlooked and occasionally maligned center with the radar stick.

One reason why Stewart got a bum rap was his mobility, or rather, lack of it. He displayed none of the dash of a Howie Morenz or fluidity of an Eddie Shore.

"Nels was slow," said Myles Lane, a New York Rangers defenseman when Stewart skated for the Montreal Maroons. "But he made up for his lack of speed with his stick. He was tremendous around the net."

Husky and handsome with a wide grin, Stewart broke in with the Maroons during the 1925–26 season, playing both center and defense. He won the scoring championship with thirty-four goals and also annexed the Hart Trophy as the NHL's most valuable player.

Stewart's scoring ability inspired the Maroons' high command to play him exclusively at center where he pivoted *The Big S Line* with Babe Siebert and Hooley Smith. The line was less than discreet in handling the opposition and earned notoriety as the roughest trio in the league.

It was not uncommon for Stewart to chew a wad of tobacco, produce juice, and then spit it unerringly in the eyes of a goalie as he shot the puck.

Cooper Smeaton, who refereed when Stewart was in his heyday, regarded *Ole Poison* as a vastly underrated talent. "In today's game," said Smeaton, "Nels would have scored 100 goals. He was terrific in front of the net, a big strong fellow who had moves like a cat. Stewart never seemed to be paying attention to where the puck was and, if you were checking him, he'd even hold little conversations with you; but the minute he'd see the puck coming his way he'd bump you, take the puck, and go off and score."

In his rookie season, Stewart spearheaded the Maroons to the NHL playoff championship, qualifying them to meet Victoria for the Stanley Cup. *Ole Poison* scored six goals in four games for the Maroons as they carried the Cup back to the Montreal Forum.

Stewart's laser shot often inflicted serious damage to members of the Goaltenders' Union. The most devastating injury from *Ole Poison*'s shot was inflicted upon Rangers' goalie Lorne Chabot during the 1928 playoffs.

"The shot," recalled Rangers' center Frank Boucher, "struck Chabot squarely on the left eyeball, causing a hemorrhage. Lorne didn't play again for the rest of the series."

In 1930, when he finished second in scoring in the NHL's Canadian Division with three fewer points than the leader Hec Kilrea, Stewart nevertheless was voted the Hart Trophy for the second time.

Such accomplishments failed to still his detractors, one of whom was referee Bobby Hewitson, who doubled as sports editor of the Toronto *Telegram.*

"I always felt that Stewart had an exaggerated reputation," said Hewitson. "I never thought he was such a great player. Nels was big and tall but awfully lazy. He wouldn't backcheck and he'd just stand around the net waiting for the centering pass, then flip the puck in. That much he could do. We used to say that Nels stood in one spot all the time."

Similar charges have, from time to time, been leveled against other superstars. Stewart was deceptive, not lazy. Nobody who scored 324 goals during an era when red lights were at a premium could legitimately be labeled lazy. In fact, *Ole Poison* was an ardent competitor who, like Gordie Howe in a later period, would resort to any technique for victory.

Stewart gave the Maroons seven solid years of service before being traded to the Boston Bruins where he centered a line with Dit Clapper and Red Beattie. Just as effective, Nels scored his 200th career goal as a Bruin and remained a boisterous attacker. In 1935, after he had been suspended for fighting, Stewart was traded to the New York Americans with whom he played until his retirement in 1938.

The truculent scoring champion from Montreal, Quebec, was born December 29, 1902, so it was rather natural for him to eventually sign up with the Maroons in his home town. A true professional, Stewart played as efficiently in Boston and New York as he did in Montreal.

Stewart saved one of his finest performances for the 1938 playoffs. The Americans, who had played second fiddle to the Rangers for more than a decade, finished second in the Canadian Division while the Rangers were runnerup in the American Division. The rivals, who shared Madison Square Garden, met in a best-of-three playoff round.

Coached by Red Dutton who had once been a Montreal Maroons teammate of Stewart, the Americans won the opener 2–1, lost the second game 4–3, and appeared doomed in the finale.

A capacity crowd of 16,340 watched the Rangers jump into a 2–0 lead but Lorne Carr scored for the Americans as the game bristled with tension. It was then that *Ole Poison* came through with the tying goal, sending the match into sudden-death overtime. After three extra periods the Americans scored and moved into the next round against the Chicago Black Hawks.

By this time, Stewart was showing the effects of his age and his labored skating style. He was thirty-six years old, and too often to suit him, the Black Hawks were tying up his wings. In the second game, with the Americans leading one game to none, the score tied 1–1 in the third period, *Ole Poison* tried one of his patented plays.

"Nels shouldered his way between a couple of players who were scrapping for possession of the puck, " recalled Clarence Campbell, who refereed the game. "He nabbed it and passed it back to Tommy Anderson, his wing, who was just inside the Chicago blue line. Then, as fast as he could, Nels ambled over to a side edge of the goal crease—home sweet home to him."

Instead of passing, Anderson took a shot. At that moment, Stewart whacked Chicago goalie Mike Karakas over the shins so hard that the goalie fell to the ice. Meanwhile, the puck sailed into the net for what could have been the game-winner for the Americans.

"I disallowed the goal for interference," said Campbell.

A bitter argument ensued between the Americans, led by Stewart, and referee Campbell. Stewart and cohorts were finally becalmed, and the game continued in a deadlock until Chicago won it in overtime to tie the series. The Black Hawks also won the decisive third game and eliminated the Americans.

Stewart remained one of Dutton's stalwarts until he retired in 1940. A few critics have been tough on *Ole Poison,* but none can take away his Hart Trophies, the fact that he led the league in scoring, played on a Stanley Cup winner, and was deservedly inducted into the Hockey Hall of Fame in 1962.

If you want to know how good Nels Stewart was, ask anyone who scored 324 goals. Maurice Richard would be delighted to tell you.

22

Mike Bossy
(1977–1988)

They come once in a decade; sometimes not even that often. They are so superior in their craftsmanship that it is not at all unreasonable to call them inimitable.

In the 1930s, it was Howie Morenz, *The Stratford Streak*. In the 1940s, Maurice Richard, *The Rocket*. In the 1950s, Gordie Howe, *Mister Hockey*. In the 1960s, Bobby Hull, *The Golden Jet*. In 1977, another brilliant ray appeared on the hockey horizon— Mike Bossy, *The Goal Machine*.

The genius of Bossy was evident from his rookie season, but it was not fully realized until he equaled Rocket Richard's accomplishment of scoring fifty goals in fifty games in the 1980–81 season. Bossy had made it clear that his goal was to break *The Rocket*'s record. Tradition demanded that Bossy keep his intentions to himself. But Mike is not a traditionalist. "Nobody sets out to break records," said Bossy. "You just play, you score, and they happen. But the fifty in fifty, that's one I want. Having my name next to Richard would not be too shabby."

The Bossy-Richard connection was not a figment of his imagination. Often without Bossy's knowledge, the legendary Richard watched young Mike mature as a kid player on assorted Montreal rinks. In 1968, Bossy was the proud recipient of an award from *The Rocket* himself. The Richard-Bossy link was forged early.

Michael Bossy was born in Montreal, Quebec, on January 22, 1957. The streets of the Canadiens' home town were the early stages for young Bossy's hockey antics. And with the legend of *The Rocket* everywhere around the Forum, it is easy to understand Bossy's obsession with the fifty-in-fifty record.

Early in the 1980–81 season, it had become apparent that Bossy was carrying an unusually hot stick. (This had happened to extraordinary athletes before, and inevitably, they would be struck down by injury or slump.) Mike underlined the point by stating that obtaining fifty in fifty would be his deepest personal achievement. That done, the media responded to his clarion call.

Occasionally, Bossy broke stride and fell behind the goal-a-game pace, but in mid-January he came on strong, scoring seven goals in two games. After his forty-seventh game Bossy had forty-eight points!

The Calgary Flames, Detroit Red Wings, and Quebec Nordiques would form the final blockade in Games 48, 49, and 50.

"It's a challenge," said Bossy before Game 48 (against Calgary at the Nassau Coliseum). "I think that I owe it to everybody to get the record now because I sort of announced it and I owe it to myself too."

The Flames blockade was flawless. They double- and sometimes triple-teamed the Islanders' gifted right wing. New York was able to score (the final was 5–0 for the Islanders) but Bossy was manacled at every turn, especially when tenacious Eric Vail shadowed him.

Two nights later, Bossy took the ice at Joe Louis Arena against the Red Wings. "We're going to do everything we can to see that Mike gets it," said teammate Denis Potvin, "and he's going to get it. I'll be surprised if he doesn't do it against Detroit. But I'll guarantee that he's going to get it."

The captain's guarantee looked fragile after the Detroit match. Once again Bossy had been stymied. The final score of Game 49 was 3–0. Mike had zip.

"If I didn't get the record," Bossy allowed, "it would have been embarrassing because I had made it such a big thing."

Game 50 was at Nassau Coliseum. Now he needed not one but two goals to tie the mark, yet he had been unable to scrape up even one goal in the past two games.

Nordiques' coach Michel Bergeron knew Bossy from junior hockey days. He did not subdue his admiration for the Islanders' ace and said straight out that he would not try any dirty tricks.

"Calgary and Detroit both lost their games by zeroing in on Mike," said Bergeron. "I'd rather win our game and see him score a pair of goals. He'll get no special attention."

Bergeron's words had a hollow ring once the puck was dropped. Although the Nordiques did not assign one special shadow to follow Bossy, they were no less attentive than the Flames or Red Wings; and for most of the game, Mike was no more productive than he had been in the two previous games.

After two periods of play in which Bossy seemed almost invisible, he had nothing to show for it but the look of an anxious young man. "I had never been so frustrated in all my hockey career," he admitted later. "I couldn't do anything right. I felt as if my hands were bound with tape and my stomach was tied in knots."

Still, there were twenty minutes of hockey left on his itinerary so he took the ice and gave it a good Bossy try. At first, he seemed to be on a treadmill to nowhere, but by mid-period some of Mike's magic became evident, although he still had a goose egg for his efforts.

More than anything Mike needed a break, and then, almost miraculously, it happened. With a little more than five minutes left in the game, Quebec was hit with a minor penalty. Bossy was dispatched to the scene for the Islanders' power play.

For forty seconds the pattern of futility continued. The clock relentlessly ticked away "4:15...4:14...4:13..." Suddenly, the puck was cradled on Bossy's stick. "4:12...4:11." He released a backhander in the direction of the crouched goalie Ron Grahame. "4:10." The red light flashed behind the Nordiques' net.

With a little more than four minutes remaining, Bossy was now back in the chase. Could he translate forty-nine into fifty? If cheers could help, the 15,000 faithful supported Mike with lung power, but with three minutes remaining, and then two, he was still stuck at forty-nine goals.

Early that afternoon, Charlie Simmer of the Los Angeles Kings also had taken aim at the fifty-in-fifty mark. Simmer came up short by one, although he had scored a hat trick against the Boston Bruins. Unlike Bossy, Simmer had a minimum of pressure. He never was as candid as Mike about his desire to equal *The Rocket*'s record.

"The pressure Mike put on himself to score amazes me," Simmer had said.

That pressure had never been more intense than in the final minute-and-a-half of the Quebec game. Once again, coach Al Arbour signaled Mike to the ice.

The Bossy-watchers wondered what Mike would do if he got the puck in scoring position. Some recalled what he had said about his shot: "About 90 percent of the time I don't aim: I just try to get my shot away as quick as possible as a surprise element. I just try to get the puck on the net."

Again the clock was working against him. "1:36...1:35...1:34...1:33...1:32...1:31." The puck came to Bossy. He was camped near the left face-off circle. Goalie Grahame prepared for the shot. Mike cracked his wrist and the puck arched goalward. Grahame never touched the rubber. It hit the twine with 1:29 remaining, and the Coliseum reverberated with a noise rarely heard in an arena.

Mike Bossy had challenged himself and triumphed.

Nobody said it better than *Newsday*'s Joe Gergen about Mike Bossy, his accomplishment, and his future.

"This particular challenge is ended. There will be others. For Mike Bossy, it is not enough to play the game; he must excel."

Bossy's existence was recorded on the scoring lists. He scored fifty or more goals in no less than nine consecutive seasons, a record that even Gretzky cannot match. Unfortunately, during the 1986–87 campaign, he was so severely afflicted with back problems that he could only play sixty-three games. His goal scoring was limited to thirty-eight. Even worse was the medical outlook. Mike's chronic back problem became so debilitating that he finally announced that he had become unable to play. He told a press conference in September 1987, that he would take a season off in the hopes that a cure could be found. When none was forthcoming, Bossy called it a career. However, his name has already become institutionalized. It is not unusual to tell a potential goal scorer to "shoot the puck like Mike Bossy."

The Bossy that his admirers choose to remember was the one who had reached his peak in 1981–82, when he led the champion Islanders in scoring with sixty-four goals, eighty-three assists, and 147 points. Despite a debilitating leg injury that clearly cramped his style, he choreographed the Islanders to their third consecutive Stanley Cup championship in May 1982, and was awarded the Conn Smythe Trophy as the most valuable player in the playoffs. He also was voted to the First All-Star Team at right wing, garnering 309 points out of a possible 315.

He was no less effective in 1982–83, when the Islanders won their fourth consecutive Stanley Cup. It also should be noted that Bossy, throughout his career, remained a champion of clean hockey and frequently went public with his proclamation that the goon game belongs in the sewer. It is to his credit that Bossy always backed up his words with an admirably clean brand of play, always fortified by his excellence.

23

Lester Patrick
(1905–1928)

If anyone did more to advance the game of hockey than Lester Patrick, he must be hiding somewhere. And that is precisely why *The Silver Fox* and his contributions as a player have been overlooked by many talent appraisers.

Lester and his brother Frank were responsible for more innovations, more positive rule changes, and more miscellaneous improvements in the game than any other personalities. Most of these alterations were accomplished while Lester was either a coach, manager, or club owner and thereby overshadowed his role as a player of note.

Most relevant is the fact that Lester was the very first defenseman ever to make a practice of lugging the puck out of his zone and deep into enemy territory. It happened in 1902, when Patrick played for a team in Brandon, Manitoba. Lester could never comprehend why forwards and only forwards were the puck-carriers and, conversely, why defensemen did nothing but engage the enemy attackers.

"Instinct and temperament proved too strong for Lester," said Elmer Ferguson of the Montreal *Herald*. "He felt that a defenseman should do more than defend, so he rushed the puck as well."

When his coach demanded an explanation, Lester replied: "Why not let defensemen rush if it works—and if the fans like it?" His logic was impeccable and reinforced when he scored a goal.

That was just the first of innumerable Patrick innovations. He thought it rather foolish for defensemen to stand in front of each other like the point and cover-point players in lacrosse. "That doesn't make sense," said Patrick. "It would be wiser to have the defensemen line up abreast." And once again the Patrick imprint was indelibly etched in hockey strategy.

Frank graduated from Brandon to the powerful Montreal Wanderers in 1903. It was a time when organized hockey was dominated by the Ottawa Silver Seven, a club that captured the Stanley Cup in 1903, 1904, and 1905.

The Wanderers finally dethroned the Silver Seven in the 1906 two-game total-goal series, 12–10. Patrick scored the eleventh and twelfth goals for Montreal.

Imperial-looking—many fans said he reminded them of the distinguished actor John Barrymore—Patrick stood six-feet tall, was slim but solidly built, and had a crown of thick curly hair. (When the mane grew gray, he was dubbed *The Silver Fox*.) Lester had an inimitable knack of striking dramatic poses, tossing his head back, and staring archly.

He was, actually, one of the first of the high-priced athletes because he knew the value of a buck and, more important, the value of Lester Patrick.

While Lester was starring for the Wanderers, a wealthy group of businessmen in Renfrew, Ontario, decided to organize a major league team and pursued Lester. He eventually signed with them for what, at the time, was regarded as an absurdly high fee for a hockey player—$3,000 for twelve games.

It was a honey of a deal, but Patrick only stayed a season, and then abruptly moved west to British Columbia with his family when his father established a lumber business in the Canadian northwest. While logging the giant trees of the Fraser Valley, Lester and Frank came up with an ambitious plan to run their own hockey league along the Pacific coast. The only problem was that there was no natural ice and no rinks.

Undaunted, Lester borrowed $300,000 from his father and with Frank's assistance built a chain of rinks that gave birth to the Pacific Hockey League, including Victoria, Vancouver, Seattle, Edmonton, Calgary, Regina, and Saskatoon. Lester operated the Victoria team while Frank operated Vancouver.

"The Patricks," said Ferguson, "took hockey into an area where no hockey existed, built magnificent rinks, and made a major sport of it. They were the greatest personal factors in twentieth-century hockey."

Lester never gave up his skates for the executive suite. He was a one-man gang, who owned, managed, coached, and played for his club. Patrick did wonders for the Cougars but never more than in 1925 when Victoria met the Montreal Canadiens in the Stanley Cup finals.

"All the sportswriters had conceded the series to Montreal," said Frank Frederickson, a Hall of Famer who played for Victoria. "But they didn't bargain for Lester's analytical mind and we wound up beating the Canadiens."

The triumph added another ribbon on Patrick's uniform, but it soon was dwarfed by his unexpected performance in the 1928 playoffs when he was forty-four years old and had retired as an active defenseman. It was then that Lester startled the hockey world by actually going into the nets and *playing goal* for the New York Rangers against the Montreal Maroons.

"This dramatic moment," wrote Toronto *Sun* columnist Trent Frayne, "has become a part of the lore of sport, as legendary in hockey as the World Series home run Babe Ruth hit off Charley Root of the Chicago Cubs when he pointed to the distant center field bleachers and then laced the ball there."

Patrick was manager of the Rangers at the time and his regular goalie, Lorne Chabot, was nearly blinded by a shot from the stick of Montreal Maroons' ace Nels Stewart. The Rangers had no spare goaltender so Lester agreed to put on the pads.

John Barrymore couldn't have played the part better had the playoff been staged by Hollywood. "Lester struck poses in the net," one of his players recalled. "He would shout to us, 'Let them shoot!' He was an inspiration to the rest of us."

Patrick had a shutout going—the Rangers scored once—until late in the third period when Nels Stewart finally beat him. The game went into overtime and Lester foiled the Maroons until Frank Boucher scored the winner for New York. At that moment, Lester Patrick became immortalized.

He was half-dragged, half-carried off the ice by his players while he received a tumultuous ovation from the crowd. It was Lester's final curtain as a player.

Lester Patrick was born December 30, 1883, in Drummondville, Quebec, not far from Montreal. Although hockey was his forte, Lester was equally gifted at rugby, lacrosse, and cricket. He enrolled in McGill University when he was seventeen but quit after a year to devote his energies to hockey. His first raves were received in Brandon where he led the

Manitoba sextet to the provincial championship, and then to the Stanley Cup round where they almost beat the mighty Ottawa Silver Seven. When he became captain of the Montreal Wanderers, they won the Stanley Cup in 1906 and 1907.

"Lester was a classical player in every phase of the game," said Cyclone Taylor, who teamed with Patrick on the Renfrew Millionaires.

It is fascinating to note that a number of Patrick's most glorious moments as a player occurred at a time when most observers figured him for washed-up. He had decided to retire and concentrate on front office duties in Victoria in 1921, but a year later two defensemen on his Cougars' club were seriously injured so Lester retrieved his skates and took his position on right defense.

"From the start," one of his opponents commented, "he was a sensation."

The Cougars, who had not won a game in seven starts, won 19–5 and Patrick was never better. He personally won two games, scoring a goal to win an overtime game against the Saskatoon Sheiks and scored the only goal in a 1–0 win over the Vancouver Maroons.

Patrick's facile mind already had wrought permanent changes in the game. After watching a soccer game in England, Lester and Frank introduced the penalty shot to hockey. To this day, it remains one of the most exciting aspects of the game. Lester and Frank were the first to put numbers on the players' jerseys. "It was a Patrick innovation," said Elmer Ferguson, "pure and simple. And has been universally adopted by all major sports."

The Patricks were the first to adopt forward passing and to legalize puck-kicking in certain areas as a means to sustain play. They invented the assist in hockey, and they broadened the rules governing goalies. Under the older rules, the goalie could not legally make a stop while in any other position but a vertical one. The Patricks said a goalie could fall to the ice. Today, that's all they ever seem to do when blocking the rubber.

"The Patricks," said Ferguson, "legislated hockey into modernism."

More than that, Lester and his brother brought the professional hockey establishment to its knees. They fought the National League, raided it, took a whole champion team away on one of their forays, and forced the National League to terms. They organized, reorganized, and then broke up a whole league on the Pacific coast. When it became obvious that the Pacific League could no longer compete with the NHL, he sold his Victoria team to a Detroit group for $250,000.

Lester became manager and coach of the Rangers at the start of the 1926–27 season. He continued to display his tactical brilliance. With the inception of All-Star Teams in 1930–31, Lester dominated the voting as outstanding coach in seven of the first eight seasons, from 1930 through 1938. He missed only the 1936–37 season.

The Rangers have won three Stanley Cups since the club's inception, all of them with Lester Patrick as manager. "Lester," said Babe Pratt, who starred on defense for him as a Ranger, "was to hockey what John McGraw was to baseball."

That is true. But one can interchange the names of Babe Ruth, Connie Mack, and Christy Mathewson for McGraw and still not be doing enough justice to *The Silver Fox* of hockey.

24

Marcel Pronovost
(1950–1970)

When Marcel Pronovost was a lad of seven years, he experienced a common childhood accident: he fell off his bicycle. But where other kids might fall and scrape their knee or bruise their elbow, Marcel broke his nose. Although not obvious at the time, that particular mishap was an omen of things to come for Pronovost during his NHL career in which he stood as one of the premier defensemen in the league for the better part of two decades. Pronovost, through his days with the Detroit Red Wings and Toronto Maple Leafs, accumulated his fair share of awards and recognition for his on-ice accomplishments. But the one title to which he holds sole possession was not awarded by the NHL and doubtless never will be: Marcel Pronovost—The Most Injured Man in Hockey.

Pronovost's dubious distinction makes his career accomplishments that much more remarkable. It is a rare athlete indeed who can suffer just about every injury in the medical dictionary and overcome each one and return to perform at his previous level of excellence. But Marcel Pronovost took all that in stride.

Pronovost first laced up and donned a Red Wings sweater in 1950 when an injury to Gordie Howe forced the Wings to move defenseman Red Kelly to the forward line and bring up the youngster from the Omaha Knights to fill the gap on the backline. With the nineteen-year-old Pronovost playing the brand of hockey that earned him the U.S. Rookie of the Year in Omaha, the Wings captured their first Cup since 1943, defeating the Rangers in a hotly contested final series. Pronovost, with less than a season of NHL experience behind him, played with the composure of a hardened veteran and became one of the youngest players to have his name inscribed on the Stanley Cup. He went on to play on seven championship teams in Detroit including Cup-winning teams in 1952 and 1954.

When Marcel arrived in training camp in 1951, he fully expected to crash the Detroit varsity. Instead, he was blasted right out of the NHL. On a patented Pronovost rush, he tried bisecting the defense of ironmen Leo Reise and Bob Goldham. When the three fell to the ice, Goldham's stick creased Marcel's face. His noble charge cost him a fractured cheekbone and a ticket to Indianapolis. But after thirty-four injury-free games in the minors, he was recalled and from that time on he became a fixture on the Detroit blue line.

Stitches, bruises, fractures, and separations have all spent time in one spot or another on Pronovost's 6'1", 175-pound body, but none were able to penetrate the determination that was his armor. No injury, it seemed, could discourage Pronovost from playing his position with nothing short of reckless abandon.

Dancing with danger never fazed Pronovost, and he dismissed the perils of the rink as just another fact of life. "Making a dangerous play on the ice didn't make me any more nervous than crossing the street might make someone else. He doesn't worry about getting hit by a car and I don't worry about getting hurt on the ice. If I did, I'd probably go crazy."

Pronovost's kamikaze approach to the game may not have taken its toll on his nerves, but it had a significant effect upon him physically. As a young horse in his early NHL days, Pronovost was known as one of the finer rushing defensemen of his time, sometimes compared to the likes of Ken Reardon before him and Bobby Orr after him. But those rink-long dashes were not only glorious but grueling as well. As the injuries mounted, Marcel mellowed into a graceful puck-carrier and a solid two-way defenseman.

Overshadowed by the brighter stars of the powerful Red Wing teams of the 1950s, Pronovost emerged as a bona fide star himself when Red Kelly was traded from Detroit to Toronto in 1959. Along with recognition by his team as the anchor of its blue line corps, Pronovost began to gain more notoriety league-wide and was thusly named to the First Team All-Stars in 1960 and 1961.

Rene Marcel Pronovost was born on June 5, 1930, in Lac la Tortue, Quebec. At the age of fifteen, Marcel was "stolen" out of the French-Canadian province by Detroit scout Marcel Cote, who first eyed the youngster in action playing juvenile hockey in Shawinigan Falls.

During his NHL career, which ran from 1950 to 1970, Marcel Pronovost played 1,206 games, netting eighty-eight goals and adding 257 assists. He also was engaged in 134 playoff contests, scoring eight goals and twenty-three assists and played in eleven All-Star games. His personal high for offensive production was thirty-four points for the 1954–55 season.

Pronovost worked for the Detroit club for fifteen seasons until, at the age of thirty-four, he was traded to Toronto as part of an eight-player swap. Prior to the trade, Pronovost was second only to Gordie Howe in length of service with the Red Wings. With the Maple Leafs, Pronovost played five more seasons and drank from the Stanley Cup one more time, in 1967, before retiring in 1970.

When hockey historians grasp for comparisons to measure Marcel Pronovost against, they will be hard pressed to find any. To add a new twist to an old cliché, it could be said that if they hadn't broken the mold after they made him, he probably would have broken it himself. He did, after all, manage to break everything else.

In the contemporary game, where players are motivated by incentive clauses, the likes of Pronovost's pure dedication to the game are simply nonexistent. One scenario, which took place during the 1961 Stanley Cup finals, fully illustrates the intensity that typified Marcel Pronovost. With the Red Wings matched against the Chicago Black Hawks, Pronovost played four games on a badly cracked ankle. He would arrive at the arena on crutches, play the game, and then put his leg back in a cast. A teammate who watched him suffer through each tortuous turn on the ice put it simply: "He played on guts alone, nothing else."

25

Paul Coffey
(1980–   )

It was one of the most important hockey games of the decade, and certainly one of the most vital to the 23,000,000 citizens of the Dominion of Canada.

"Our reputation as the kings of hockey is on the line," said former NHL coach Don Cherry. "If we lose to the Russians, we're has-beens."

Plain and simple, on September 13, 1984, the capitalists were waging a war with the commies on Calgary Saddledome ice. This was the decisive contest in the 1984 Canada Cup tourney. On one side was the mighty Soviet All-Star squad, gold medal winners at Sarajevo and, arguably, the best in the world. Well, maybe the best. On the other side skated *la crème de la crème* of the NHL—Team Canada—loaded with stars such as Wayne Gretzky, Mike Bossy, and Larry Robinson.

The plot couldn't have been better scripted by Alfred Hitchcock. After sixty minutes of regulation time, the score was tied, 2–2. After twelve minutes of pulsating, sudden-death overtime, the Canadian Heart Association should have sent out letters to the 16,762 on-lookers with the message: *WARNING: Watching this game can be injurious to your health.*

Then, the worst possible scenario unfolded. Twelve minutes into overtime, Soviet forwards Vladimir Kovin and Mikhail Varnakov sprinted toward the Canadian end of the rink, orchestrating a classic two-on-one break. Only one player stood between the Russians and goalie Pete Peeters—Paul Coffey, a twenty-four-year-old backliner whose defensive shortcomings once were so extensive that even in home town Edmonton the Oilers' defenseman was reviled as PAUL COFF-UP.

With textbook precision Kovin waited for the perfect moment and then skimmed what appeared to be an ideal pass to his comrade, but it never reached its destination.

Coffey dropped to his knees, jabbed his stick at the puck with the speed of a frog nab-bing a fly with its tongue, and intercepted the prize. Then, defying all the laws of gravity and physics, Coffey instantly rebounded on his skates and, in the same motion, rushed in full flight toward the Soviet net.

"It was the greatest defensive play in international or any other kind of hockey," said former Boston Bruin Ted Green, who had logged nineteen years as a big-league defense-man.

Coffey flicked the puck into the Russian zone and then accepted a quick pass from John Tonelli. Before anyone could say Mikhail Gorbachev, he delivered a shot that Mike Bossy tipped in for the winning marker.

"No one could teach Paul Coffey to make that play," added Calgary Flames' coach Terry Crisp. "It was inside him on the day he was born."

Compressed within ten seconds, Coffey had executed the quintessential defensive *and* offensive play and had become a national hero.

In that precious give-and-take, Coffey revealed to millions of television viewers what *he* had known all along—that he could stop plays as well as he could start them *and* score goals.

"It takes a single play sometimes," says Coffey, "to change a person's opinion."

Others agreed.

"They said he was no good defensively," chortled Cherry, "and now the baloney goes down the pipe. Just because of that one play."

And that one play, more than any other, demonstrates why Coffey evolved into the *total* defenseman of the 1980s. His speed, shooting, and playmaking sense were never a question. But on that fateful night in Calgary, the 6'1", 205 pound native of Weston, Ontario, lifted himself above the Ray Bourques, Mark Howes, and James Patricks of the hockey world.

By 1988, the raven-haired Coffey had three Stanley Cup rings, two Norris Trophys (best defenseman), two First All-Star Team nominations, and enough records to fill a paperback. Some of these include:

- Most goals by a defenseman in the playoffs—twelve
- Most points by a defenseman in one game—six
- Most points by a defenseman in the playoffs—thirty-seven in eighteen games

And yet Coffey, after seven years as an Edmonton Oiler, was dispatched to the Pittsburgh Penguins in 1987. The traumatic move took place in the autumn of 1987, all because Coffey lacked a sense of fiscal discretion. During the summer of 1987, he quarreled with Oilers' general manager–coach Glen Sather over contract revisions and ultimately walked out on the team in protest against Sather.

"Coffey's trade wasn't easy—but it certainly was necessary," said Sather. "Before he was traded it was difficult because I always had—and still have—a lot of respect for him."

When all attempts at mediation had failed, Sather traded Coffey along with Wayne Van Dorp and Dave Hunter to Pittsburgh in one of hockey's biggest deals ever.

In exchange, the Oilers obtained Dave Hannan, Moe Mantha, Craig Simpson, and Chris Joseph. "I don't care who won the deal," Coffey said. "I don't know who got the best of it. That's not my concern. More than anything, I just want to play."

Critics wondered whether Coffey would flourish without Wayne Gretzky at his side. Others wondered how well Coffey could weave his silken passes through the fabric of Mario Lemieux's magnificent maneuvering. Unfortunately, an asterisk was required after the 1987–88 season, mostly because Coffey was almost immediately sidelined with an injury that would eventually halt his quest for a third Norris Trophy.

Interestingly, there was little to suggest that a Norris Trophy was on the distant horizon when four-year-old Paul Coffey took his first tentative steps on a rink in Malton, Ontario, a working-class neighborhood near Toronto. At his side was his father, Jack, an executive with the McDonnell Douglas aircraft company, and his mother, Betty. Jack had his son playing center, just like Paul's idol, Dave Keon, the Toronto Maple Leafs' former ace. But when Paul turned eight, his hockey coach moved him back to defense. At first, Paul rebelled. Then, his father explained the facts of hockey life.

"Paul, how many defensemen are there on your team?"

"Four."

"Paul, how many forwards are there on your team?"

"Nine."

"Paul, four against nine means one thing: *More ice time!*"

Paul got the point.

Jack Coffey applied the gentle but firm push that his son needed. "We used to have a rink in the schoolyard right behind our house," explains Paul, "and he'd always say, 'Don't come home unless you've got sore groins.' If I didn't, I hadn't been skating enough.

"When I was a kid I always knew where my dad sat in the stands at games and I'd look up at him. If he made a certain sign with his hands, I knew I had to get my legs going. My family gave me a lot of support. They used to travel everywhere when I played junior hockey (Sault Ste. Marie and Kitchener). Times are tough when you're away from home. You appreciate having your parents there to help. They didn't care if I had a bad game, they were still behind me."

Coffey needed all the support he could get during his rookie season with the Oilers. Plucked in the first round of the 1980 Entry Draft, Paul traveled to Alberta with great expectations. But somewhere between Toronto and Edmonton, Coffey lost his confidence and damn near lost a job. Luckily, coach Glen Sather was willing to be patient, and soon Coffey found himself.

His ascent as an Edmonton star paralleled that of Mark Messier. The two were untamed stallions in the early 1980s but matured under Sather's guidance. The difference was that Messier communicated more easily with the boss. Ultimately, Coffey rebelled one time too many and the rupture never healed. But even as a Penguin, Coffey is unique and has enough ability for one more Norris Trophy down the line. But whether he makes it or not, he has already demonstrated that he belongs among hockey's superior backliners.

Joe Blake

26

Toe Blake
(1934–1948)

In any discussion of the outstanding five forward units of professional hockey, the Montreal Canadiens' *Punch Line* of Maurice Richard, Hector "Toe" Blake, and Elmer Lach invariably is included.

Reaching their apex during the mid-1940s, *The Punch Line* featured Richard, the inimitable Rocket, at right wing; Elmer Lach at center; and Blake on the port side. "It was," said Canadian hockey historian William Roche, "one of the best-balanced arrays seen in hockey in many a day."

Because of his élan and flamboyant goal-scoring, Richard inevitably obtained the most attention but, as Roche has noted, Blake made the line tick. "He was the line's sparkplug," said Roche, "and anchor. The line suffered an irreparable loss when Blake broke a leg and retired in the 1947–48 season."

What is, perhaps, most surprising—if not ironic—about Blake's career is that despite his truculence and affinity for rough play, he won the Lady Byng Trophy for good sportsmanship combined with ability in 1946.

From the moment he entered the bigs as a rookie with the now defunct Montreal Maroons in 1935, he established himself as a fighter. "Reckless," "truculent," and "boisterous," were some of the terms employed to describe Blake, the rookie. At the time, he often appeared too busy fighting his own battles to be effective to the Maroons.

The Maroons, in what proved to be a classic blunder of a dying franchise, failed to realize Blake's potential and soon traded him to the Canadiens. No less impudent, Blake proceeded to get himself into a mess of trouble.

Playing against the Detroit Red Wings, he attempted to hit Detroit's Ebbie Goodfellow with his stick. Before the blow could be struck, Toe's stick was deflected by another Detroit player. Several Red Wings immediately jumped Blake and pummeled him on the ice. "They really went amok," remembered Jack Adams, who was the Red Wings' coach at the time. "But Blake never backed away from any of them. He was a helluva competitor."

His zeal for combat was matched only by his ability to score goals, and by the start of the 1940s Blake had been nicknamed *The Old Lamplighter*, as in red goal lamp. In thirteen years of NHL play, he scored 235 goals and 292 assists, skating for three Stanley Cup-winning teams and five first-place clubs.

In 1939, Blake was voted Canada's outstanding athlete and had become, as one observer put it, "as gentlemanly as a hockey player can afford to be." The metamorphosis from pugnacious brawler to mature hockey player added to Blake's effectiveness and, according to *Sports Illustrated*, contributed to the devastating success of the Canadiens from 1943 to 1947.

At the start of the 1940s, Toe was used on a unit with Johnny Quilty and Joe Benoit, a pair of effective but unspectacular linemates. During the summer of 1943, Montreal's astute coach Dick Irvin realized that his young right wing, Maurice Richard, was capable of spectacular production if aligned with the proper linemates.

Irvin had theorized that hard-nosed Elmer Lach was the ideal center for Richard, but he wasn't so sure about left wing. He finally decided that Blake would be worthy of an experiment on the unit and in no time the line was made—for keeps.

Originally nicknamed *The Mad Dog Line*, Blake's trio was more appropriately renamed *The Punch Line*, as they dominated the NHL during its most offense-minded era. The trio finished one–two–three (Lach, Blake, Richard) in scoring on the team.

"Being on a line with Toe," said Richard, "was probably the greatest thrill I had experienced up until then."

Richard and Blake were kindred spirits and soon developed what would become a lifelong affection for each other. Professionally speaking, it would work to the advantage of both of them, particularly for Blake when he turned coach of the Canadiens and Richard continued to excel as a player. As captain, Blake inspired the Montrealers to first place and the Stanley Cup in 1944 and another Stanley Cup in 1946.

Hector Blake was born August 21, 1912, in Victoria Mines, a smelting and mining community in northern Ontario. Unlike many Hall of Famers, Blake was discouraged from playing hockey by his mother. Her goal for her son was a "nice and steady" job in the mines.

At the age of twelve, Blake was hired by a milk company to hitch the horses before they embarked on their day's journey. Until then, Toe had been a goaltender—without skates. With his newly acquired wealth, he bought a pair of skates and passionately involved himself with hockey and more hockey.

His diligent pursuit of the puck eventually won him starting assignments with an assortment of amateur teams in Canada. Ultimately, he made his way to a club in Sudbury, Ontario, which happened to be scrutinized by some major league scouts. Sudbury's best prospect was a lad named Nakina Smith. Sam Rothschild, who was scouting for the NHL Maroons, watched the Sudbury sextet and then wired Maroons' coach Eddie Gerard: "FORGET SMITH. BLAKE'S THE ONE."

And he was. Smith had an undistinguished big league career whereas Blake became the cornerstone of the Canadiens' rebuilding program at the start of the 1940s.

Blake certainly would have gone much further as a scorer had he not suffered a shattered ankle as a result of a bodycheck on the night of January 10, 1948. The blow was to end Toe's playing career, but it was to launch one of the most successful coaching experiences in all of sports.

Before the 1948–49 season had ended, Frank Selke, Sr., managing director of the Canadiens, signed Blake as coach of the Houston club in the old United States Hockey League. When Houston promptly won the league championship, Toe was promoted to coach of the Buffalo sextet in the still faster American Hockey League. A disagreement— "They said I was too easygoing," said Blake—with the front office forced Toe to quit, but then he signed on as coach of the Valleyfield Braves of the Quebec Senior Hockey League.

When an opening as coach of the Canadiens developed in the spring of 1955, a number of promising candidates bid for the job, but Selke sided with Blake who proceeded to coach the Canadiens to eight Stanley Cup championships, including an unprecedented five in a row. His teams finished first nine times.

Blake retired from coaching after his club had won the Cup in 1968, but he was retained by the Canadiens in a number of advisory capacities after that.

As magnificent as Blake was as a player, his coaching proved so extraordinary that many critics revere him more as a coach than a player, although he was one of the most severe taskmasters in the business. "It's the way I am," Blake would say by way of explanation. "It's the only way I know how to get there."

He *got* there; both on the ice and behind the bench. Few have made more meaningful contributions to the game than the man from Victoria Mines.

Best Wishes
Bernie Geoffrion

27

Bernie Geoffrion
(1950–1968)

He was nicknamed *Boom Boom*, and there was more than a metaphor in that. Bernie Geoffrion caused reverberations throughout the hockey world from the moment he stepped onto a National Hockey League rink in 1950 to the day of his retirement eighteen years later.

His galvanic personality was a match for his dynamic shot; one that set a new standard for offense in the professional ranks. It was *The Boomer*, as he was often called, working the right point on the Montreal Canadiens' power play, who popularized the fearsome slapshot that soon would be copied by Andy Bathgate of the New York Rangers and Bobby Hull of the Chicago Black Hawks.

Zooming at speeds of upwards of 100 miles per hour, the Geoffrion slapper put fear in the hearts of enemy goaltenders as never before. *The Boomer*'s shot, blended with his effervescent play and unquenchable desire to win, enabled him to win the Calder Trophy as rookie of the year in 1952 and the Hart Trophy as the NHL's most valuable player in 1961. He twice led the league in scoring (1955 and 1961) and was named to the First All-Star Team in 1961 and the Second Team in 1955 and 1960.

Geoffrion played on six Canadiens' Stanley Cup-winning teams and no less than seven first-place clubs. His contributions in both cases were substantial. Yet for a very good reason, Geoffrion never attained the accolades that should have come his way. It was *The Boomer's* misfortune to be a right wing during an era when both Gordie Howe and Maurice Richard dominated that position.

At the time of his retirement, *The Boomer* had totaled 393 goals, which then placed him fifth on the NHL's all-time goal-scoring list behind Gordie Howe, Maurice Richard, Bobby Hull, and Jean Beliveau.

He teamed with Richard and Beliveau, often working on a line with the masterful Beliveau at center and the tenacious Bert Olmstead on left wing. It was one of the best-balanced units the game has known.

Nicknamed *Boom Boom* because of the reverberation of his stick hitting the puck and the puck hitting the end boards (although it often went directly into the net), Geoffrion had many of the incendiary qualities of Richard.

But the Geoffrion character had one ingredient that was missing in the Richard psyche, a flamboyant sense of humor. He began delighting teammates late in the 1950–51 season after scoring 103 goals in fifty-seven Montreal Junior League games. Geoffrion was under great pressure to turn pro with Les Canadiens, and he resisted until there were only eighteen games remaining in the 1950–51 schedule. He realized that the Calder Trophy for rookie of the year was given to players who had skated in twenty or more games. By waiting until there were fewer than twenty games in the 1950–51 schedule, he thus became eligible to win it the following season.

When approached by Selke, Geoffrion laid the facts on the line: "I'll lose my chance for the Calder. It's too late in the season to catch up with the other guys."

The Boomer was no fool. He opened the 1951–52 season with two goals, including the winner, against Chicago in a 4–2 Montreal victory and immediately established himself as the newest Canadiens' hero. For Geoffrion, it was relatively easy. Not only was he an excellent young prospect, but he had recently married Marlene Morenz, the attractive blonde daughter of the late Howie Morenz.

Not long after Geoffrion's opening scoring burst, Les Canadiens visited New York, and Geoffrion was interviewed by New York *Daily News* sports columnist Jimmy Powers. The writer observed that the NHL had a prize crop of rookies and wondered just who *The Boomer* thought would win the prize.

"Me," said Geoffrion, in as candid a reply as Powers could hope for.

As he had so candidly predicted, Geoffrion had become the foremost rookie-of-the-year candidate, but it was more the manner in which he was scoring that was meaningful than merely the fact that he was scoring at an amazing clip. Geoffrion, although he may not have realized it at the time, had become a hockey revolutionary. Instead of using the traditional forehand wrist shot or the backhand shot for his tries at the goal, Geoffrion would draw his stick back like a golfer and slap the puck. The result was the "slapshot" that would eventually be adopted by most of the leading scorers in the NHL and would dramatically change the face of the game.

Bernard Geoffrion was born in Montreal on February 14, 1931, and learned his hockey on the many neighborhood outdoor rinks sprinkled throughout the city. He originally made his mark with the St. Francis Xavier school team and then moved up the teenaged ranks until he was discovered by ex-Canadiens' defenseman Sylvio Mantha. *The Boomer* played Junior "A" hockey for Mantha on the Montreal Nationales and continually improved his shot with endless workouts.

By the mid-1950s, Geoffrion was regarded as one of the most magnetic personalities in the game and a major cog in the dynastic Canadiens' machine.

Yet, as glittering as *The Boomer*'s career may have seemed on the surface, it nevertheless concealed the fact that for most of those seasons he skated with a double burden: he was the son-in-law of the Canadiens' superstar Howie Morenz, and he was manacled by a succession of injuries that would certainly have defeated a less persevering individual. Geoffrion's ability to ignore pain during hockey crises was one of the primary reasons why he was a cut above the normal star, and no episode illustrates this better than one that occurred during the 1961 championship round between the Canadiens and Black Hawks.

Bernard "Boom Boom" Geoffrion sat brooding in his compartment as the train sped the Montreal Canadiens to Chicago for the sixth game of the Stanley Cup playoffs. Although Boom Boom had won the NHL scoring championship, tied Maurice Richard's fifty-goal record, and led the Canadiens to first place, the breaks once again were going against him.

He studied the heavy plaster cast imprisoning his injured knee, then called captain Doug Harvey. "Look, Doug," he said in his deep, rich voice, "one more loss and we're out. Let's cut the cast."

Harvey borrowed a knife, and they slipped into the washroom where they delicately removed the hard plaster. Geoffrion's knee was blotched with red. "It hurt so much I couldn't sleep," *The Boomer* recalled. "But I wanted to play. Next morning I asked coach Toe Blake to let me take a turn."

At game time, Boom Boom's leg was frozen with pain-killer. On his first turn, Bobby Hull and Reg Fleming of Chicago crashed him into the ice; he tried to get up but collapsed as if his knee was stuffed with cardboard. Later he attempted again to play, but the knee was useless. Without Geoffrion, Montreal lost the game and missed the Stanley Cup finals for the first time in eleven years.

After his retirement from the Canadiens in 1964, Geoffrion began coaching but returned to the NHL as a player with the Rangers in 1966 and remained active until 1968. In the Rangers' second game of the opening playoff round against the Black Hawks, Geoffrion set up a goal by Harry Howell. It was *The Boomer*'s 822nd—and last—NHL point.

Geoffrion tried his hand at coaching several times—with the Atlanta Flames, New York Rangers, and Montreal Canadiens—but each attempt ended disastrously.

It was an unfortunate denouement but could in no way dim the luster of a superbly exciting career.

28

Henri Richard
(1955–1975)

When Henri Richard turned up at the Montreal Canadiens' training camp in September 1955, his appearance was interpreted by the media as a publicity stunt. Henri was nineteen at the time and, as all the experts surmised, there was no room on the talent-laden Canadiens for a kid with no professional experience.

But he *was* the brother of Maurice "The Rocket" Richard and therein was the essence of the gimmick. It was assumed that Henri would be placed on Maurice's line, photos would be taken, the customary interviews would be held following the workout, and then the kid brother would be dispatched to a suitable minor league team for his one- or two-year apprenticeship.

Henri obviously didn't read the script. Centering a line with Maurice and galvanic left wing Dickie Moore, the kid brother orchestrated play from the moment he obtained the puck to the moment a line change was made. He did it again and again until it became clear that here was a very special young man. More than that, his appearance proved a tonic to thirty-five-year-old Maurice while Moore complemented the line with his tough checking and superb shooting.

Clearly, Henri's appearance was no stunt. Nicknamed *The Pocket Rocket*, he would not be dropped from the varsity. "He's a little small yet," said coach Toe Blake, "but with his speed we keep telling him not to try to go through the big opposition defensemen, just go around them."

Henri accepted the advice and ripened into one of the NHL's most creative centers during his two decades of major league play. He was voted to the First All-Star Team in 1958 and the Second Team in 1959, 1961, and 1963. More important, *The Pocket Rocket* provided essential ingredients—leadership, goal-scoring, play-making—of the highest quality for no less than eleven Stanley Cup championship teams.

Vintage Henri was an episode in the sixth and what proved to be final game of the 1966 Stanley Cup finals between the Canadiens and Detroit Red Wings. Montreal led the series three games to two and had held the Red Wings to a 2–2 tie in regulation time of Game 6. But now, it was sudden-death overtime and a goal for the Canadiens would mean the Stanley Cup.

With a little more than two minutes gone in overtime, the Canadiens launched a counterattack against the Red Wings' defense. Montreal defenseman Jean-Guy Talbot skimmed the puck to left wing Dave Balon who, in turn, lifted a pass over Red Wings' defenseman Gary Bergman. At that moment, *The Pocket Rocket*, skating at more than twenty miles per hour, lunged to deflect the puck just as defenseman Gary Bergman threw his body at Richard.

As the foes collided, Richard slid head first toward goalie Roger Crozier. The puck nestled just under the upper portion of Richard's right arm. The momentum carried the stomach-down Richard just past the left goal post while the puck slid into the far left corner of the net. The rubber had been deflected into the net by Henri's body, giving Montreal another world's championship.

Henri Richard surmounted the most challenging demand of all: playing in the shadow of his uniquely gifted brother Maurice, and then maintaining his stardom after *The Rocket* retired in 1960.

There was some question about the long-term durability of the Dickie Moore-Richards line, especially because Maurice was en route to his thirty-sixth birthday. Despite *The Rocket*'s age, he managed to keep pace with his younger cronies, although one afternoon he nearly regretted it. The Canadiens were in the midst of a workout when Henri rounded the net at full speed from one side and Maurice approached on the same track from the other direction. They collided violently and both fell to the ice unconscious. When they were finally revived, both were escorted to the first-aid room where Maurice needed twelve stitches to close his wound and his kid brother, six stitches.

Then, in a masterful understatement, Maurice intoned: "You'd better watch yourself, Henri. You might get hurt."

Henri and Maurice Richard began drifting apart as the kid brother came into his own around the league. *The Rocket* was like the maternal lioness, watching over her cub at first but leaving it to fight for its place in the world once it reached maturity. For Henri, maturity came fast. He fought on even terms with his tormentors. He would not be run out of the league, and he would be a very accomplished hockey player, although never the electrifying personality that *The Rocket* was.

In contrast, *The Pocket* was determined but not explosive, strong but not over-powering. If *The Rocket* was the home-run hitter, *The Pocket* was more the base stealer and opposite-field hitter. He also had *The Rocket*'s touch of the brooder in him.

The Pocket Rocket was an essential cog in managing director Frank Selke's rebuilding plan, and he was an asset to Pollock, too, in Sam's first years in Montreal. Les Canadiens finished first in 1965–66, breezed past Toronto in the first round of the playoffs with four straight wins, and appeared capable of disposing of the Detroit Red Wings at will in the Cup finals, especially since the series opened with two games at the Forum. But Detroit's hot hand goalie, Roger Crozier, was sizzling, and the Red Wings upset Les Canadiens in the first two games.

It was then that *The Pocket Rocket* rallied the troops and capped the adventure by scoring the Cup-winning goal in the sixth game on enemy ice.

But no matter how many major goals he scored, Henri could never fulfill the demands of fans who wanted him to be a clone of his tempestuous brother Maurice. Exasperated to the core, Henri once complained: "What do they expect from me? I am *me*, not my brother. Maurice is the best hockey player of all time. I do not try to imitate him. I just try to do my best. All I can say is that I try to play my best."

To the purist, Maurice never was the best in such skills as stickhandling and playmaking, but others believed that Henri came close to perfection.

"*The Pocket*," said Canadiens' coach Toe Blake, "became a better *all-around* player than *Rocket* was. But it's asking an awful lot of any man to be the scorer that Rocket was. He was the greatest scorer under pressure that I've ever seen."

Henri had exceptional powers of self-insight. He perceived that he never could be the athlete that Maurice had been. "My brother's biggest thrills," said Henri, "came when he scored many goals. I am most satisfied when I play in a close game and do not have any goals scored against me. Sometimes people have asked me whether it helped or hurt having Maurice as an older brother. It was not easy, because many people expected me to be as spectacular as Maurice. But I believe it also helped me as well as hurt me. Don't forget, Maurice was a great scorer, and he could get goals that many other players could not get. That helped my passing because I knew that he would always be near the net waiting for a shot. But Maurice never gave me any advice. I never asked him for it and he never offered it."

The Pocket Rocket finally packed it in following the 1974–75 campaign and concentrated on his *brasserie*, which he had opened in Montreal. His twenty NHL years were consistently superior and memorable. They would have been even more so had he not been Maurice Richard's kid brother.

29

Dickie Moore
(1951–1968)

"Dickie Moore is one of the kids making the customers forget Maurice Richard."—Jim Vipond, *The Toronto Globe and Mail.*

Such a testimonial is roughly equivalent to suggesting that a promising playwright is capable of making literary critics forget William Shakespeare.

But such was the promise of Montreal-bred Moore that only the most lavish praise was adequate for his contribution to the Canadiens. Dickie played left wing for a dozen years in Montreal, won two scoring championships, was twice the First All-Star, and played for six Stanley Cup winners and six first-place teams.

It was a measure of Moore, the competitor, that he limited his battles to the tougher members of the opposition. He was absolutely unsparing in the manner in which he sacrificed his body for the cause of victory, and, eventually, such grit would take its toll on his body.

During the 1958–59 season, Moore set a standard for courage that rarely has been matched in professional sport. His left wrist, which had been broken two years earlier, had not mended properly and required regular reinforcement. His right wrist had suffered a chipped bone and, by all rights, Dickie should have been recuperating in a hospital. But he would not miss a game.

"Sure, my wrist hurts when I shoot," Moore said, "but the only time I'll stop playing is when it breaks off."

He was true to his word. Although the wrist is the essential transmission behind a hockey shot, Moore endured the agony and when the 1958–59 season had ended he had scored ninety-six points (forty-one goals and fifty-five assists) to break the NHL scoring record during the six-team league, winning his second straight scoring title.

Moore blended his scoring prowess with a special brand of truculence and was constantly embroiled in one fight or another. One of his first feuds was with Ted Lindsay, who was then with the Detroit Red Wings and later of the Chicago Black Hawks. Picking on the Lindsay of that era was like walking unarmed into a den of tigers.

Lindsay soon discovered that Moore was tough too. Threats couldn't stop Dickie, but a string of crippling injuries did; they almost forced him to retire. First, he suffered three shoulder separations. Then he had recurring knee trouble, after that, broken right knuckles. All required operations.

Hobbled by injuries, Moore remained a disappointment until the 1955–56 season, when he scored fifty points. More importantly, he played a full seventy-game schedule for the first time, which seemed to be just the psychological tonic he needed. From then on, he zoomed off like a space rocket and hit his own personal moon when he won the scoring title in 1958.

Typically, Dickie had to clear some cumbersome hurdles to win that title. Moore, Andy Bathgate of the Rangers, and Montreal's Henri Richard were locked in a tight race for the scoring lead with three months left. Then, Dickie broke his left wrist. The Canadiens' management feared he would be lost for the season, but Moore had other ideas. "How about putting a cast on my arm?" he suggested. "Let me take care of the rest."

Sure enough, when the Canadiens faced-off in their next game, there was Moore on the ice, handcuffed with a bulky plaster cast on his left arm. Gone was the freedom to stick-handle and the possibility of flicking a wrist shot, but nothing dampened Dickie's spirit. He played in every game and scored thirty-six goals—tops in the league—with forty-eight assists for a total of eighty-four points. And Dickie had spent most of the season playing right wing—an unfamiliar position for him.

In the 1958–59 season, without any consequential injuries, Moore, now back at left wing, won his second scoring title, beating Gordie Howe's 1952–53 scoring record of ninety-five by one point.

Dickie's talent was all-inclusive. He shot hard and accurately, stickhandled and passed well, played right or left wing, worked easily with all players, and, at 5'11", 170 pounds, played rugged and smart defense.

While there were a few egomaniacs on the championship Canadiens' clubs, Moore conspicuously was not one of them. He was unselfish to a fault. In 1958–59, for instance, when Geoffrion jumped into an early scoring lead, Moore said honestly, "I'd like to see *The Boomer* win it and I'd like to finish second." Later Geoffrion was sidelined and Moore and Jean Beliveau outraced Andy Bathgate to finish first and second in scoring.

Richard Winston Moore was born on January 6, 1931, in Montreal and grew up in an intensely hockey-oriented environment. Dickie played for the Canadien Juniors and Montreal Senior Royals before being called up to the Canadiens. He alternated the next two seasons among Buffalo, the Montreal Royals, and the Canadiens. He came up to stay in 1954–55 and scored thirty-six points in sixty-seven games, while playing with a trick shoulder that popped out of place almost every third game. The condition was bad enough for Frank Selke to put Moore on the trading block. Failing to make a deal, the Canadiens decided to see how Dickie would respond to an operation. It was successful and so too was Moore from then on.

Although Moore's wrists plagued him during the apex of his career, it would be his gimpy legs that would prove to be his undoing in later years. His final season as a Canadien was 1962–63. Dickie decided to hang up his skates and went into business, but the lure of the rinks proved too much and when he was invited to make a comeback by general manager Punch Imlach of the Toronto Maple Leafs in 1964 he accepted. The comeback lasted for a season and, again, Dickie returned to the business world, seemingly for keeps.

When the NHL expanded from six to twelve teams in the 1967–68 season, the St. Louis Blues made a policy of signing over-the-hill veterans who had starred elsewhere. Dickie and his old pal, Doug Harvey, provided the leadership the Blues required and took them to an upset victory over the Philadelphia Flyers in the seven-game opening round of the playoffs. Moore played spectacularly as the Blues reached the final round against the Canadiens before being eliminated in four games. Dickie's totals were seven goals and seven assists for fourteen points in eighteen games. He missed tying for the scoring lead by a point.

Cut from the same cloth as Rocket Richard and Howie Morenz, Moore desperately wanted to continue—and the Blues would have welcomed him again—but this time his legs delivered an emphatic rejection of still another season in the bigs.

Dickie Moore never did make the customers forget Maurice Richard, but he did make a very large name for himself on a team filled with giants such as Richard, Jean Beliveau, Doug Harvey, and Jacques Plante.

After retirement, Moore became as successful in business as he had been on the ice. He may not have possessed Richard's goal-scoring flare, but he was a big winner and as courageous a player as the ice game has ever known.

30

Joe Primeau
(1928–1936)

The career of Joe Primeau has been so thoroughly intertwined with that of his partners on the Toronto Maple Leafs' *Kid Line*—Busher Jackson and Charlie Conacher—that his virtuoso performances as a center have been ignored by too many hockey critics.

Yet, there was little that the skater known as *Gentleman Joe* could do about his position as centerpiece on one of the National Hockey League's most accomplished trios. When respected hockey people such as Frank Selke, Sr., discuss the mighty Maple Leafs of the early 1930s, Primeau invariably is lumped together with his linemates.

Although Primeau's trophy collection was less bountiful than some of his contemporaries, it was only because he was the quintessential team player who thought of his own accomplishments as secondary to that of the club. Primeau did, however, play on three first-place teams and one Stanley Cup winner. And in 1932, he won the Lady Byng Trophy for his impeccably clean play combined with a high level of proficiency.

Joe's instincts and insights into the game were well above average. An example was the manner in which *The Kid Line* profited by a rule change permitting forward passing in the enemy's zone. Primeau mastered the new form by skating over the opposition's blue line and luring the defensemen toward him, while Conacher and Jackson outflanked the foe. At the last possible second, Primeau would skim a pass to one of his mates, who would have an unimpeded shot on goal.

The Kid Line jelled to perfection in 1932 when the Maple Leafs won the Stanley Cup, although they had originally been melded as a unit during the 1928–29 season.

Whether Primeau would have been accorded more attention had he been a flamboyant sort like many of his teammates is a moot point. He was never once picked as the First All-Star center. Twice he finished second in the scoring race, trailing Jackson the first time and Conacher the second. He was voted to the Second All-Star Team for the 1933–34 season.

There is no mention of it in the NHL record book, but Primeau was the only player ever to have scored a goal at each end of the rink on successive plays. It happened in a game against the Boston Bruins. Joe happened to be near the Maple Leafs' goal when a Boston player took a hard shot at his goalie, George Hainsworth. As Joe tried to deflect the shot, the puck caromed off his stick and sailed into the Toronto net.

Primeau was so angry—and determined—that on the ensuing face-off he captured the puck, sped straight toward the Bruins' goal, faked a pass that fooled the Boston defense, skated in on goalie Tiny Thompson, faked *him*, and slid the rubber into the open net.

Joe's admirers have often cited a match with the Montreal Maroons during the 1932–33 season as one of his most arresting performances. The Montreal club was leading 2–0 after the first period, when Maple Leafs' manager Conn Smythe roared into the dressing room in a fit of pique. "He walked around the room," said Primeau, "and told each of us personally just what he thought of us. We went out of that room fighting mad. Everyone felt like showing that so-and-so Smythe what we could do. I just happened to get lucky."

Primeau scored a goal in the second period and another early in the third to tie the score. Then, Toronto moved ahead 3–2, but the Maroons kept threatening to knot the count again. Suddenly, Primeau stole the puck from Montreal's ace defender Lionel Conacher, raced in to score his third goal, and clinched the decision.

Joseph Primeau was born in Lindsay, Ontario, January 29, 1906. His relatively fragile-looking physique seemed to militate against his professional hockey aspirations, but young Primeau excelled wherever he played.

Frank Selke, Sr., who had managed an amateur club on which Primeau played, told Conn Smythe that Joe was a comer. Smythe took the advice and *Gentleman Joe* never looked back.

Perhaps the most startling aspect to Primeau's career was his decision to retire at the end of the 1936 season. He was only thirty years old at the time and believed to be good for several more years. But Joe had made up his mind.

Joe's departure from the Maple Leafs marked the beginning of the end of a marvelously colorful era in Toronto hockey. Along with Jackson, Conacher, and such amusing teammates as Hap Day, Hal Cotton, and King Clancy, the Maple Leafs of that era were to hockey what the St. Louis Cardinals were to baseball.

Upon his retirement from the Maple Leafs, Primeau became a successful businessman in Toronto. But he never could resist the lure of the rinks and soon returned to coaching where he achieved a "first." Joe became the only coach ever to lead a team to the Memorial Cup, emblematic of junior hockey supremacy; the Allan Cup, senior hockey's major trophy; and the Stanley Cup.

Gentleman Joe was a superior professional on the ice and behind the bench. He qualifies for a high rank in *Hockey's 100*.

31

Frank Mahovlich
(1956–1974)

There was a time, a little more than two decades ago, when the most pursued target in hockey was Maurice "Rocket" Richard's accomplishments of fifty goals in a regular season.

The Rocket set his mark during the 1944–45 season and while many, such as Gordie Howe of the Detroit Red Wings, came close to reaching the Richardian plateau, the fifty-goal mark remained inviolate through the 1950s.

It was during the 1960–61 campaign that the most serious threat to *The Rocket*'s hallowed "fifty" was delivered. Frank Mahovlich, a Toronto Maple Leafs left wing with mighty strides and a dynamite shot to match them, was beating enemy goaltenders at better than a-goal-a-game pace by the middle of the 1960–61 season.

Skating on a line with the veteran center Red Kelly and workmanlike right wing Bob Nevin, the diffident Mahovlich emerged as the most exciting shooter of his day and was assailed by newsmen in the manner of Roger Maris at the time that the New York Yankees' outfielder was challenging Babe Ruth's sixty home run record.

Unlike Maris, Mahovlich never did break the record, although he ultimately did quite well by himself and his assorted teams. He won the Calder Trophy as rookie of the year in 1958 and was a First All-Star left wing in 1961, 1963, and 1973. He made the Second Team in 1962, 1964, 1965, 1966, 1969, and 1970. Frank played on no less than five Stanley Cup champions, four with the Maple Leafs and one with the Montreal Canadiens.

The statistics suggest that Mahovlich luxuriated through a lengthy career sprinkled with laughs and coated with dollars. In fact, Mahovlich was plagued with trauma and tribulation ever since 1960–61.

"Life was never the same after that," Frank smiled. "I wound up with 48 goals that year, so everybody figured that next year I would do better. And the season after that would be greater than the other two."

Mahovlich can afford to laugh now. He has been knighted by hockey's Hall of Fame, owns a travel agency in Toronto, and is graced by a charming wife, Marie, and devoted kids.

But the scars remain.

Like Hall of Famer Jean Beliveau before him, Mahovlich was truly superb, but never superb enough.

"They expected too much from me," he says. "The year of the 48 goals, I had scored 38 in thirty-five games. I was on a roll, heading for *The Rocket*'s record but that was expecting too much.

"We didn't have depth on that club. All of a sudden four of our guys got injured and our balance was gone. So, the opposition began zeroing in on me and I was neutralized."

Unfortunately for Frank, neither the Toronto Maple Leafs nor general manager-coach Punch Imlach were neutralized.

The abrasive Punch had his own way with hockey players and he nettled *The Big M*. He mispronounced his name, calling him Mahallovich, and he often would treat Frank—and others—as if they were invisible.

One of the favorite tortures in the Imlach concentration camp was inflicted after a losing weekend of hockey for the Leafs. They would often play at home on Saturday night and travel as far as Chicago or Boston for a Sunday night game. Explained Mahovlich:

"We'd catch a plane back to Toronto on Monday morning, and then he would take us directly from the airport to the rink for a practice. If that were the case, why didn't he practice us on the ice right after the game?

"After a while I began to wonder how long I could take this kind of thing. A day off from hockey does a man a lot of good, but we never seemed to get a day off with Imlach."

Then there were the demands from the supposedly sophisticated Toronto fans. If Frank scored forty-eight goals when he was twenty-three years old, they reasoned, he should score at least fifty goals a year later. On top of that, Chicago owner Jim Norris allegedly had offered $1 million for Mahovlich, but the Leafs had turned him down. When Frank slipped to thirty-three goals in 1961–62, a few local purists in Maple Leaf Gardens began what was to be a chronic chorus of boos whenever *The Big M* played a mediocre game. Soon the hoots began grating on his nerves, not to mention those of other stars around the league.

Mahovlich couldn't conceal his anxiety. He became introverted and distant. "I played with Frank for eleven years," said teammate Bob Baun, "and didn't say twenty-two words to the guy."

In Toronto, hockey is by far the most popular sport. The city has three English-language dailies that carry by-lined stories about the Leafs every day from September through the end of the playoffs in April. Mahovlich began to feel hounded by some of the reporters, and he burrowed even deeper into his shell.

Mahovlich succumbed to his first breakdown on November 12, 1964. He was suffering from what doctors later described as "deep depression and tension," but the exact diagnosis wasn't made public at the time.

While Torontonians indulged in the usual wild speculation about *The Big M*'s condition, Frank remained in seclusion for a couple of weeks before returning to the Leaf lineup. He remained secretive about his ailment, and he became exceptionally confidential about his interviews with reporters.

Once, a season later, Paul Rimstead asked to talk with him. "Okay," said Frank, "but not on the team bus. I'll see you later sometime."

They eventually held their rendezvous at a Montreal hotel, where Mahovlich allowed that his relationship with Imlach was worsening. *The Big M* pointed out that his doctor advised him to ignore Punch whenever possible. "He told me to pull an imaginary curtain around myself whenever Punch was around," Frank said. "I've been doing it, and feel a lot better."

But the boos from the crowds became more frequent and more annoying. In the middle of the 1967–68 season Mahovlich played superbly and the Leafs routed the Montreal Canadiens 5–0 at Maple Leaf Gardens. Frank scored a goal and two important assists. Even his arch-critic, Imlach, described Frank's game as "outstanding."

Mahovlich was named the second of three stars, which were picked after every home game by broadcaster Foster Hewitt. Normally a "star" is greeted with cheers or, at worst mild applause when he skates out on the ice to acknowledge the selection. When Frank planted his blades on the ice he heard some applause, but there was no mistaking the boos that were uttered by some spectators.

Mahovlich completed the home-game ritual and returned to the dressing room. He showered and changed into street clothes and later headed for the team's sleeping car, which would carry the Leafs to Detroit for their next game. *The Big M* boarded the sleeper and prepared to go to bed, but he couldn't shake the memory of the catcalls, and he couldn't go to sleep.

Torn by his anxiety, Mahovlich finally walked off the sleeper at about 4:00 a.m. He contacted a club doctor and was escorted to a hospital. This time his ailment was no secret. Dr. Hugh Smythe disclosed that *The Big M* was suffering from "deep depression and tension" and was in the care of Dr. Allen Walters, a psychiatrist.

The Maple Leafs' brass had begun thinking about dealing Frank to another team, but they couldn't make a move until he returned to the lineup and proved to the satisfaction of prospective buyers that he was capable of playing big-league hockey again. The sabbatical proved beneficial to both Mahovlich and the Leafs, and he once again rejoined the club after a few weeks rest.

Early in March 1968, Imlach finally concluded a deal with Detroit. The Leafs would receive Norm Ullman, Floyd Smith, and Paul Henderson in return for Mahovlich, Pete Stemkowski, and Garry Unger, all forwards.

In addition, the Leafs would receive the right to obtain ace defenseman Carl Brewer, who had quit pro hockey but might be induced to return.

The deal was one of the most spectacular trades ever negotiated in the NHL. Mahovlich, of course, was delighted to be free of Imlach's shackles. For years, the Red Wings were renowned as a relaxed team with an obvious joie de vivre. During playoff time, manager Abel would take his men to the racetrack rather than seclude them in some distant hideaway. Frank was aware of this, but he wasn't quite sure how the Detroit players would react to him.

The Big M was restored to life in Detroit and played with similar enthusiasm after being traded to the Montreal Canadiens. At last, he seemed to have been rewarded with the happiness and relaxation that had eluded him during the halcyon days in Toronto.

Francis William Mahovlich was born January 10, 1938, in Timmins, Ontario. The son of a Croatian immigrant, Frank was scouted as a teenager by the Maple Leafs and several other NHL clubs. His father was persuaded by Leafs' scout Bob Davidson to send Frank to a Catholic high school in Toronto from where he could eventually graduate to the pro ranks.

The Big M's all-time NHL totals were 533 goals and 570 assists for 1,103 points in 1,182 games. He ended his career in the World Hockey Association and then retired to devote time to his travel agency in Toronto. When he was inducted into hockey's Hall of Fame in 1981, someone asked Frank if he missed the limelight. No, he insisted, he didn't miss it a bit. "You see," smiled Frank, "I'm content and happy. I don't have to play hockey anymore!"

32

Milt Schmidt
(1937–1955)

A case could be made for Milt Schmidt as the greatest center in National Hockey League history. It is made by those who have played against the hard-bitten Boston Bruin and not by those who live by statistics and awards alone. They swear by his creativity, his endurance, his strength, but most of all, by his soldierly fearlessness that somehow enabled him to accomplish more in the heat of battle than his contemporaries.

Not that Schmidt was a slouch when it came to production. He led the NHL in scoring in 1940, was picked to the First All-Star Team three times, and was voted the Hart Trophy as the league's most valuable player in 1951, all as a member of the Bruins.

Schmidt's career, unfortunately, was shortened by World War II. Milt, along with his *Kraut Line* buddies, Woody Dumart and Bobby Bauer, enlisted in the Royal Canadian Air Force at the very height of his career and, thus, "lost" the best three years of playing time. Nevertheless, he played for four first-place teams and two Stanley Cup winners.

Apart from his own personal achievements, Schmidt was the pivot on a remarkable forward line whose roots could be traced to the city of Kitchener, Ontario. Milt and his boyhood pals, Bobby Bauer and Woody Dumart, originally gained recognition on a local team known as The Greenshirts.

Dumart and Bauer, the oldest of the trio, were signed by the Bruins and assigned to their farm team, the Boston Cubs. When Bauer and Dumart arrived at Boston Garden, they immediately made an appointment with Bruins' general manager Art Ross. They insisted that their center, Schmidt, was as good if not better than they were as professional prospects.

Ross did not want a seventeen-year-old in Boston and rebuffed the lads, but they persisted and Ross finally mailed a letter to Kitchener inviting Schmidt to the Bruins' training camp in the autumn of 1936.

A week later, Ross received a letter from Schmidt, accepting the invitation and promising that he "would work all summer to save the money needed to report in Boston and would pay his train fare and board."

Schmidt made his NHL debut late in the 1936–37 season, and even though he scored two goals, he nurtured doubts about his future. He mailed his first paycheck home to his mother with a note saying, "Better bank this for me, mom; it may be the last I'll get."

Once the trio got the feel of big-league hockey, they became a dominant factor for the Bruins and a hit with the fans. They were alternately known as *The Kraut Line*, *The Sauerkraut Line*, and *The Kitchener Kids*.

The Krauts not only played together, traveled together, and relaxed together but they also presented a united front when it came to contract-signing time. "We felt if we went in together, asked for exactly the same salary for each, and took a stand in our dealings we'd be better off," said Schmidt.

So close were The Krauts that when Schmidt married Marie Peterson in 1946, Dumart and Bauer had to toss a coin to decide which one would be best man. When Bauer married, Schmidt and Dumart had also tossed. When, in January 1948, Schmidt became the father of a daughter, Nancy, he announced that Dumart and Bauer were *both* godfathers!

This closeness was often reflected in the scoring statistics. During the 1939–40 season, when the Bruins finished first, Schmidt led the league in scoring with fifty-two points while his linemates were tied for second with forty-three points apiece.

Not surprisingly, *The Kraut Line* enlisted as a unit in the Royal Canadian Air Force and played from time to time against other service teams. While stationed in England, where Schmidt played as often as possible when not performing his duties as flying officer, he was as popular as ever.

Milton Conrad Schmidt was born March 5, 1918, in Kitchener, Ontario, a German-Canadian community, which had originally been named Berlin until the outbreak of World War I. The youngest in a family of six, Milt attended King Edward Public School and began playing hockey almost as soon as he was able to walk.

It was young Schmidt's good fortune to meet Montreal Canadiens' goalie George Hainsworth, who had grown up in Kitchener, at a trophy presentation in King Edward School. Hainsworth gave the dark-haired Schmidt words of encouragement that remained with him through his lengthy career.

The hallmark of Milt's play, both as a youth and later as an NHL star, was a muted ruggedness. "Schmidt," said one longtime admirer, "was a gentleman's hockey player—until someone started pushing his teammates around."

It had been feared that Schmidt, like so many other NHL stars returned from the war, would have lost his touch, but Milt regained his form and in 1946–47 enjoyed the best productivity—twenty-seven goals, thirty-five assists, sixty-two points—of his entire career. Even the retirement of Bobby Bauer failed to put the brakes on Schmidt, and in 1950–51, still teaming with Dumart, he produced twenty-two goals and thirty-nine assists for sixty-one points. It was enough to win him the Hart Trophy.

On March 18, 1952, the Bruins held a "Schmidt-Dumart Night" and talked Bobby Bauer out of retirement for that one game. After elaborate pregame ceremonies, The Krauts got down to the business of winning a hockey game against the Chicago Black Hawks. Boston won the game, 4–0, clinching a playoff berth in the process, and Bauer went back into retirement.

Schmidt remained an active player until 1955 when he was given the coaching reins of a struggling Boston hockey club. He stayed on until 1962–63 when Phil Watson was called in to take charge. But Watson could not rejuvenate the Bruins and Schmidt took over again in the middle of the 1962–63 season. He remained at the helm of the Bruins as general manager from 1966 until 1973 and enjoyed two Stanley Cup triumphs, in 1970 and 1972, with the help of trades he had engineered.

Easily the greatest accomplishment of Schmidt, the manager, was a deal he made with the Chicago Black Hawks. He sent goalie Jack Norris, defenseman Gilles Marotte, and center Pit Martin to Chicago in return for forwards Phil Esposito, Fred Stanfield, and Ken Hodge.

In the view of some experts, it was the most one-sided deal in NHL annals and was directly responsible for the Cup victories in 1970 and 1972.

Milt left Boston in 1974 to become the first general manager of the new Washington Capitals franchise, but it was a move that generated nothing but woe. The Caps, under his administration, never became competitive and Schmidt eventually left the disaster scene, returning to Boston where he went to work for the Bruins in the ticket-selling department and more recently ran the Boston Garden Club.

He was embittered by the Washington experience and lamented the fact that none of the other twenty NHL teams saw fit to utilize his talent and experience.

Nevertheless, the debacle with the Caps couldn't obscure Schmidt's handsome playing career nor his exceptional victories as a manager. That is enough to qualify him for a finish at number thirty-two in *Hockey's 100*

33

Ted Kennedy
(1942–1956)

"I was dumbfounded by his mature observations on the game as it progressed. I remember telling sportswriter Ed Fitkin that I thought we might have acquired a superstar."

The speaker was Frank Selke, Sr., acting manager of the Toronto Maple Leafs. The subject was Ted "Teeder" Kennedy, the seventeen-year-old Maple Leafs' center who had been injured and was sitting next to Selke during the 1943 Stanley Cup playoffs.

Selke's radar, in this case, was extraordinarily accurate. Kennedy would be orchestrating a Stanley Cup championship for the Maple Leafs before he was even twenty years old and ultimately would skate for no less than five Cup winners of which he captained two.

Perhaps the most difficult of all, from a personal standpoint, was Kennedy's ascendancy to the Maple Leafs' captaincy. From the start of the 1940s through the spring of 1948, Syl Apps had been the captain and acknowledged leader of the Leafs. More than that, Apps had been the most revered athlete in Canada during his time, which meant that when Apps retired at the end of the 1947–48 season, his successor, Kennedy, would be in a position roughly equivalent to Mickey Mantle following Joe Di Maggio in center field at Yankee Stadium.

At a city hall ceremony honoring the Stanley Cup champions in April 1948, it was felt by many of the thousands of spectators that they were witnessing the swan song of the Maple Leaf hockey club. Apps officially announced his resignation and Kennedy, at age twenty-three, accepted the captaincy.

Apps's heir apparent did not—at least superficially—suggest a dominating hockey player. Whereas Syl had been an exceptionally strong and fluid skater, young Ted seemed to agonize through every stride. But despite his plodding style, he managed to get from point A to point B as well as any and better than most.

From the moment he skated out on the ice wearing the "C" on his royal blue and white jersey, Kennedy demonstrated that he was no less a leader than Apps and, in some ways, even more forceful. The Maple Leafs, in the first three years of Kennedy's leadership, won two Stanley Cups.

The captain, himself, never was dazzling enough nor productive enough to win scoring prizes. He was twice voted to the Second All-Star Team and in 1955 captured the Hart Trophy as the NHL's most valuable player.

At Maple Leaf Gardens, Kennedy became a folk hero in the same mold as Apps. John Arnott, a service station operator, especially deified Kennedy with a periodic yell during a lull in the action that soon became a trademark of every Toronto game in which Kennedy played.

Several years earlier, Arnott had delivered a regular cheer for Peter Langelle, a Toronto hero who went off to the wars and never played again for the Leafs. The cheer was a penetrating "C'monnnnn PETER!" Now it was altered.

Just as a face-off was about to take place, a booming voice could be heard across Maple Leaf Gardens. "C'monnnn, TEEDER!" Somehow it sounded just as good as the cheer for the retired Langelle.

Although Kennedy had been well-schooled in hockey basics by his mentor, Nels Stewart, Teeder was weak in one department: skating. His strides were labored, almost painful to watch, and he often seemed to be moving like an express train with one set of brakes locked into its wheels. He finished his freshman season with twenty-six goals and twenty-three assists for forty-nine points in a year in which inept goaltending made high scoring relatively simple.

It was, of course, no fluke. Kennedy would emerge as a consistently productive pointmaker, much in the style of a solid .300 hitter who invariably comes through in the clutch. During the 1946–47 season, in which he scored twenty-eight goals and thirty-two assists in sixty games, Teeder was placed at center between two equally eager youngsters, Howie Meeker on right wing and Vic Lynn on the left.

The trio was christened *The New Kid Line*, a reference to the Maple Leafs' original *Kid Line* of the 1930s featuring Charlie Conacher, Joe Primeau, and Busher Jackson.

Once again, an ideal blend had been devised. In the 1947 Stanley Cup finals between the Maple Leafs and the Canadiens, the Montrealers were heavily favored, but the effervescent *Kid Line* defused Montreal's big guns and the Maple Leafs won the Stanley Cup in six games.

Maple Leafs' president Conn Smythe regarded Kennedy as one of the most valuable acquisitions the team had ever made, and Teeder received acclaim throughout the NHL— except in the city of Detroit where he was permanently painted as a villain. To this day there is question whether or not Kennedy was the culprit in one of the most controversial episodes in hockey history: the accident that nearly killed the Red Wings' young ace, Gordie Howe.

The incident took place during the first game of the Stanley Cup semifinal round between Detroit and Toronto on March 28, 1950, at Olympia Stadium. By the middle of the third period, Toronto had a 4–0 lead in what already had become a bitter series.

The Toronto-Detroit rivalry was extraordinarily bitter so it was not surprising that the tempers remained taut in the dying minutes of the game as the Leafs' captain launched a counterattack for the visitors.

Kennedy was six feet from the left boards as he reached center ice. Behind him in hot pursuit was Wings' defensman Jack Stewart. Sweeping in from the right side was Howe, who attempted to crash Kennedy amidships. Howe was skating a trifle too slow to hit Kennedy with full force, and it appeared that the best he might do would be to graze the Leaf and throw him off balance. But he missed even that opportunity, and as Kennedy stopped short, and then pressed forward, Howe tumbled, face first, into the thick wooden sideboards. Seconds later he was lying unconscious on the ice, his face covered with blood. As 13,569 fans sat horrorstruck, Gordie Howe, the young favorite, was carried off the ice on a stretcher and removed to Harper Hospital.

For several hours there was some doubt that he would survive. A call was put through to Saskatoon, Saskatchewan, to urge Gordie's mother to take the first plane to Detroit so that she could be at her son's bedside.

Gordie pulled through. But as far as Detroit's press and public were concerned, Gordie had been lethally assaulted and somebody would have to pay for it. Toronto naturally denied responsibility, and the argument raged like a forest fire with sportswriters, coaches, and fans from both sides pouring verbal gasoline on it to keep it going.

Detroit's theory was that Teeder Kennedy had deliberately speared Howe. Kennedy offered to take an oath that he had not caused the injury. "I saw Howe lying on the ice with his face covered with blood," said the Leaf captain, "and I couldn't help thinking what a great player he was and how I hoped he wasn't badly hurt. Then Detroit players started saying I did it with my stick. I knew I hadn't, and as I've always regarded Coach Tommy Ivan as a sensible, levelheaded man, I went over to the Detroit bench and told him I was sorry Howe was hurt but that I wasn't responsible."

Leaf defenseman Garth Boesch suggested that Howe was hurt accidentally by his own teammate Jack Stewart, an opinion that was shared by other members of the team. Al Nickelson, who covered the game for *The Globe and Mail*, wrote: "It appeared to this observer that Kennedy, in stopping short, had raised his elbow as a protective gesture and that Howe had struck it, before smashing into the boards with his face as he fell."

Sportswriter Red Burnett, of the Toronto *Daily Star*, added: "Referee George Gravel saw the mishap to Howe, didn't call a penalty, and that proves, as far as we are concerned, that Kennedy did not hit Howe."

But Paul Chandler, who covered the Red Wings for the Detroit *News*, was not to be soothed by such unheated reporting. "The *Telegram*," he wrote, "has made Kennedy a martyr, an innocent man put to torture by a cruel conspiracy between the Detroit sportswriters and the Detroit Red Wings. Kennedy Cleared, screamed the *Telegram* page one of its news section the day after Howe was injured. Cleared of what?"

It didn't take long for the antagonists to find a common enemy in NHL President Clarence Campbell, whom they blamed for his failure to prevent the brutality and violence that both preceded and followed Howe's injury.

Despite the charge of vacillation, Campbell quickly took a stand on the Howe case and exonerated Kennedy. "Kennedy," said Campbell, "as a right-handed player, had the butt part of his stick right to the fence as he was going up the ice. He was being checked from his right. The injuries to Howe were on the right side of the head. Kennedy had stopped to avoid the check, and Howe went in front of him."

The Toronto player was further exonerated when referee Gravel submitted a report. It read: "Jack Stewart carried the puck in the Toronto end and was checked by Kennedy, who carried the puck into the center zone right close to the fence on the players' bench side. I turned to follow the play, and Stewart was trying to check Kennedy and was right close to him. Just as Kennedy crossed the Toronto blue line, I saw Howe cut across toward Kennedy, skating very fast. Just before Howe got to Kennedy, Kennedy passed backhanded and stopped suddenly. Howe just brushed him slightly and crashed into the fence and fell to the ice. Stewart fell on top of him. Play carried on for a few seconds as Toronto had possession."

Even the mayor of Toronto, the Honorable Hiram McCallum, squeezed into the act and dispatched a message to Kennedy: "The people of Toronto know that absolutely no blame in any way can be attached to you for the accident to Gordie Howe. They are 100 percent behind you all the way and know you will go on and continue to play wonderful hockey and lead the team to the Cup. We regret very much the injury to Howe as he is a great player, but at the same time we know that he was the aggressor in attempting to crash you on the boards."

Although Kennedy was ultimately exonerated in all quarters but Detroit, the Red Wings never forgave him and pinpointed Teeder for all manner of vicious assault in the remainder of the playoffs and for years to come.

Theodore Kennedy was born December 12, 1925, in Humberstone, Ontario. Once Ted had shown that he had special hockey talents, he caught the attention of Hall of Famer Nels "Old Poison" Stewart who took the lad under his wing. "I've been around he NHL for fourteen years," counseled Stewart. "You'll do all right. Just take this advice: keep your head up when you're near the goal. Just take your time—and pick that corner!"

Early in 1942, Stewart conferred with coach Hap Day of the Maple Leafs. "If I were in your shoes," said Stewart, "I'd trade away twelve players to get young Kennedy."

The Maple Leafs' high command took Stewart's advice—although not literally—and signed Kennedy to a contract late in the 1942–43 season. Teeder scored fifty-five goals in his first two full seasons in the NHL, underlining the faith Stewart had in the young man.

He remained a Maple Leaf until his retirement after the 1955–56 season. Although he was only thirty years old at the time, his legs were gone and there was little that his enormous heart could do to keep him in the bigs.

Kennedy was equally successful and respected off the ice. He became an official of the Ontario Racing Association and still is a familiar figure at the annual Hockey Hall of Fame banquet in Toronto. He paid his dues to get into *Hockey's 100*.

34

Mark Messier
(1979–)

Edmonton Oilers' boss Glen Sather would never publicly admit it as long as Wayne Gretzky was on his team, but those close to Sather insist that his favorite player of all-time is Mark Messier, whom he nurtured as an awkward Oiler in 1979. Like Sather, Messier has unflinchingly played a tough game. Unlike Sather, the Edmonton native has emerged as one of the most gifted shooters of the 1980s and, arguably, the best clutch player of his era.

Granted, these are fighting words, sure to evoke steamy protest from Edmonton to Los Angeles, but they are based on fact, observation, consultation, and the most compelling reason of all: the realization that the fragile Gretzky as a Los Angeles King could be crumpled to oblivion at any time. On the other hand, Messier, the extremely mobile medium tank, can't wait to sink his armor into his next foe.

"When I compare Messier and Gretzky," noted career coach Herb Brooks, "I have to wonder whether Gretzky is on a fast-forward burnout cycle. Based on some of his retirement talk in the last two years, you start questioning Wayne's NHL longevity from here on in; which is not something you do with Messier."

"Mark seems to have that unbeatable spirit," says Sather. "Mark reminds me of a galloping thoroughbred in the wind. He gets that look in his eye; it's a look that I've only seen once before in a great hockey player, and that was Maurice Richard. But Mark has it even more. At critical times in the playoffs he'll give everyone that look in the dressing room and away we go!"

While Gretzky gets the ink, Messier does as much—if not more—when it comes to scoring critical goals. Twice Mark saved the Edmonton franchise from disaster when critics wondered whether the Oilers should be labeled the "Choke Team of the Decade."

The first incident occurred in the 1984 Stanley Cup final when Edmonton upset the Islanders in the opener at Nassau Coliseum but got clobbered in Game 2. The series then switched to Edmonton's Northlands Coliseum, where New York was expected to zip through the next three games for their fifth straight Cup.

"We had 'em on their heels early in that third game," recalled retired Islander Denis Potvin, "and we had Gretzky tied up pretty good. But Messier killed us."

Had Edmonton lost Game 3, the Oilers likely would have been blown out of the series, as they had been the previous spring. And if that had happened, massive trades would have brought about a change in the team. "We couldn't keep going without winning a Stanley Cup," said veteran Oilers' defenseman Kevin Lowe. "There was a lot of concern."

Messier quickly eliminated that. "Before the game," Lowe recalled, "Mark told me that he was going to go out there and lead the team; that he'd get some goals."

Messier made good on his word at a critical point in the game. With Edmonton trailing by a goal, Messier stormed the Islanders' zone, skating one-on-one with New York defenseman Gord Dineen. He faked the Islander into a knot and then delivered a mighty shot that handcuffed goalie Billy Smith. It was a one-two punch that few players could produce.

"The shot he got off after he cut toward the net was just a blur," Sather remembered. "I don't think that any goalie could have stopped it."

The goal ignited an Oilers rally that sent them to a 5–2 victory. "Thanks to Mark," added Lowe, "the Islanders couldn't touch us after that."

Edmonton won the Stanley Cup and Messier (not Gretzky, mind you) won the Conn Smythe Trophy as the playoffs' most valuable player. The Oilers then won a second straight Cup in 1985 and seemed destined to be a dynasty until the Calgary Flames pulled off a second-round playoff upset in 1986. "It was no secret," said Lowe, "that we had to come back and regain the Cup [in '87]—or else." And, thanks to Messier, they did.

Until 1988, Gretzky had gotten the nod as the NHL's best player principally because of a combination of arithmetic, availability, and articulation. It's difficult to argue against a legend who has won eight consecutive Hart (MVP) Trophies and seven scoring titles. Gretzky had accomplished everything and, to his credit, established himself as the most easily accessible superstar in contemporary sports. The media gravitates to Gretzky like a nail to a magnet and Gretzky, in turn, will dissect the game until the writers' pens run dry, particularly now that he's playing for Los Angeles.

Less communicative than Gretzky, Messier has been left floating in a media backwater. Less *numerically* productive than Gretzky, Messier left the impression that he wasn't in *The Great One*'s class, but the professionals knew differently.

"Numbers don't tell you everything you have to know about a hockey player," said former U.S. Olympic coach Lou Vairo, author of an in-depth hockey manual. "There are intangibles that can be seen and felt but can't be calculated with a computer."

The intangibles, combined with existing stats, give Messier a certain edge over Gretzky. The intangibles include:

- Energy
- Toughness
- Checking ability
- Fighting ability
- Desire

Messier is stronger than Gretzky and ranks with the most feared skaters in history. "Messier," added former Flames' coach Bob Johnson, "is to hockey what Jimmy Brown once was to pro football. He's a bull—with finesse." Gretzky doesn't come close to matching Messier as a checker, and in a game that still features fighting, *The Great One* admits, "I'm not a fighter." Messier can duke it with the best of them if anybody dares challenge him. "He's a mean hombre," adds Johnson.

No doubt it has to do with his genes. Born in Edmonton, Alberta, on January 18, 1961, Mark was five years old when his father presented him with skates, a hockey stick, and a puck. The family lived in Portland, Oregon, where Messier's father, Doug, played for the Buckeroos of the old, tough Western Hockey League. When Doug's career as a defenseman ended, he returned home to Edmonton and guided his son up the traditional hockey ladder from Peewee to Bantam to Junior. "He was good when he was young," says Doug, "but he always played the game for fun, not because he wanted a pro career."

Mark explained: "I took to it naturally. I got a lot of hockey knowledge watching my dad play, and being around hockey all my life helped. He knew what it took for me to play pro. Not that he pushed me. He more or less let me make my own decisions about playing hockey. When I made that decision, he helped me tremendously. I gave a lot of sports a try, but hockey was the sport I wanted to make my career."

Messier was a highly-visible attacker during Edmonton's 1988 Stanley Cup march. He intimidated the Winnipeg Jets and Calgary Flames in the first two rounds and was decisive in the Campbell Conference championship series against Detroit. "When Mark gets going," said Red Wings' coach Jacques Demers, "it's impossible to stop that man."

Nor could the Boston Bruins manacle him in the 1988 finals as the Oilers swept to their fourth Cup in five years.

It has been a most successful decade for the Oilers—with even more good things to come, thanks in large part to Mark Messier, particularly now that he must fill the gap left by Gretzky's departure.

35

Charlie Conacher
(1929–1941)

"The trouble with Big Charlie," a friend once said, "is that he thinks he's a truck, so he takes on the other team in a personal, hand-to-hand battle!"

Most of the time Charlie Conacher came out on top, whether he was challenging an enemy defenseman or shooting at the opposition goaltender.

During an era when the wrist shot prevailed and such high-velocity scorers as Babe Dye, Cooney Weiland, and Nels Stewart dominated the game, Conacher's shot was regarded as the hardest of all. The Bunyanesque right wing could crack a two-inch plank with the fury of his shot.

Although Conacher skated for an assortment of NHL clubs, including the Detroit Red Wings and New York Americans, his niche as a superstar was carved during his seven-year tenure on the Toronto Maple Leafs' renowned *Kid Line* along with Busher Jackson and Joe Primeau.

In the seven years they were together from the 1929–30 season until Primeau retired at the end of the 1935–36 season, the unit amassed a total of 792 points in regular league play and an additional seventy-one points in playoff competition for a grand total of 863 points. Significantly, that was twenty points more then New York's famed line of Frank Boucher, Bill, and Bun Cook collected during the same seven-year span.

Conacher's importance to *The Kid Line* was reflected in the stats. Over the seven-year era he scored 204 goals and 122 assists for 326 points. Jackson collected 153 goals and 119 assists for 272 points, while Primeau's mark was seventy-one goals and 194 assists for 265 points.

Charlie won the scoring championship in 1934 and 1935, was a First Team All-Star in 1934, 1935, and 1936, and made the Second Team in 1932 and 1933.

Among Conacher's finest hours was a match in April 1936, when the Maple Leafs were fighting elimination in the second game of a two-game total goal series against the Boston Bruins. The Bruins had taken the first game on their home ice, 3–0, and scored another goal in the second game to lead the round, 4–0.

With his team still down 0–4 in the second period, Conacher rallied his troops. First, he set up King Clancy with Toronto's first goal. Then, Charlie scored to make it 2–4. Red Horner scored for Toronto, reducing the deficit to one, whereupon Conacher scored his second goal of the night, tying the count. Next, Charlie set up Jackson who put Toronto ahead, 5–4, and Buzz Boll made it 6–4 for the Leafs. Conacher then capped the glorious evening with his third goal of the game, thereby eliminating the Bruins.

"The grateful crowd," noted one report of the game, "waited in pouring rain on Carlton Street and cheered the Big Bomber to the echo."

Charles William Conacher was born December 10, 1909, in Toronto, within shouting distance of a hockey rink, and it was inevitable that the gifted youngster would be discovered by professional birddogs.

Scouting Conacher was easy. Charlie learned his hockey on Toronto's venerated Jesse Ketchum Public School rink, and he learned all other sports from his older brother, Lionel, who was to be voted Canada's athlete of the half-century. Charlie broke in as a hockey player guarding the goal, but soon he moved to the front line.

Conacher eventually became captain of Selke's Marlboros in 1926, a club that won the Memorial Cup for Canada's Junior championship. Conacher's smoking shot was his forte, but his skating still left something to be desired. Thus, when Smythe announced that Charlie had made the team for 1929–30, straight out of the juniors, there was considerable surprise.

Charlie made his NHL debut on November 14, 1929, at Mutual Street Arena. Chicago's Black Hawks, with the redoubtable Charlie Gardiner in goal, were the opponents, and the fans filling the old Toronto ice palace were frankly skeptical of Conacher's ability to skate and shoot with the pros, especially since he had never had basic hockey training in the minor leagues.

The game was close, but Charlie was never out of place. At one point, the puck came to him as he skated over the blue line. Conacher caught it on the blade of his stick and in the same motion flung the rubber in Gardiner's direction. Before the Chicago goalie could move, the red light had flashed, and Charlie Conacher was a Leaf to stay.

At first, Smythe used Conacher on a line with Primeau at center and Harold Cotton on left wing; but despite Conacher's instant success, Primeau still failed to click. Just before Christmas, 1929, Smythe made the move that would alter hockey history. He pulled Cotton off the line and inserted Busher Jackson in his place on right wing. Hockey's first and most renowned *Kid Line* was born. Success was as dramatic as a volcanic eruption. Toronto defeated the Black Hawks, the Canadiens, and the Maroons right after Christmas and went undefeated until January 23 of the new year.

Off the ice, Conacher was something else. Like other members of the Maple Leafs, hockey's Gashouse Gang, Conacher was an inveterate prankster.

A legendary Toronto gag involved Conacher and his teammates King Clancy and Hap Day. It occurred not long after Cotton's gripping performance at the Hotel Lincoln. The Leafs had moved on to Boston for a game against the Bruins, and Clancy and Day were rooming together. On such trips the players usually convened for their pregame meal in the afternoon and then retired to their rooms to rest.

In those days, Bruins games started at 8:30 p.m., so it was customary for Clancy to get up about 6:30 p.m., enabling him to get to the rink about an hour before game time. Conacher and Day huddled after the pregame meal and agreed that it was time for another joke on Clancy.

When King and Hap retired to their room, Clancy set his alarm and soon fell into a deep sleep. Day remained awake, and when he saw that Clancy was well into slumberland, Hap tiptoed out of the room, met Conacher in the hall, and the two of them took the elevator to the lobby. With the secrecy of an espionage plot, the pair persuaded the room clerk to ring Clancy' room in a few minutes. The hotel employee was advised to inform Clancy that he was working for Boston Garden, it was game time, and the two teams were on the ice ready for the opening face-off.

The culprits returned to their floor and huddled outside Clancy's room. They listened as the phone rang and King screamed in horror. A moment later, Clancy ran out the door, dashed downstairs, and sprinted for the nearest taxicab. He found one and advised the astonished driver that he was King Clancy of the Maple Leafs and was late for his hockey game. The driver happened to be hockey fan and knew very well that the Bruins match wouldn't start for more than two hours. He asked what Clancy's rush was all about since the time was only 6:00 p.m.

The truth dawned on King, and he ordered the cab stopped. He slowly climbed out and walked back to the hotel, where Day and Conacher were waiting for him in the lobby. There is no official record of what Clancy said to them, but it probably could not be printed here anyway.

When The Gashouse Gang began to disintegrate in the late 1930s, Conn Smythe decided to reshape the Maple Leafs as a younger team. Conacher was dealt to the Detroit Red Wings in 1938 and then to the New York Americans in 1939. He finished his career on Broadway in 1941.

Charlie stayed close to the hockey scene and in 1948 was named coach of the Chicago Black Hawks. At the time, the Windy City sextet was a shambles and Charlie did little to restore the club to life. He had an unfortunate run-in with Detroit *Times* sportswriter Lew Walter and gave up coaching in 1950.

Beloved by Torontonians, Charlie remained a hero in his birthplace. He died on December 30, 1967, but his name remains one of the most venerated in the sport.

36

Bobby Clarke
(1969–1984)

What Pete Rose has meant to any baseball team with which he has been affiliated, Bobby Clarke has been to the Philadelphia Flyers. Since 1969, when he made his National Hockey League debut, the gap-toothed center has been the Charlie Hustle of hockey.

"Clarke," said Dave Schultz, who teamed with him on the 1974 and 1975 Stanley Cup-winning Flyers teams, "was the heart and soul of our club."

Like Rose, Clarke displayed a fervor for his pastime that never diminished with age. In 1982, at the age of thirty-two, he was clawing for position with greater zeal than rookies fourteen years his junior.

Bobby's contributions were duly recorded. He was voted the Hart Trophy as the NHL's most valuable player in 1973, 1975, and 1976. He was First All-Star center in 1975 and 1976 and Second Team All-Star in 1973 and 1974. He starred for Team Canada in the eight-game series against the Soviet All-Stars in 1972 and played for the NHL All-Stars against the Soviet Selects in the 1979 Challenge Cup.

It has always been less than easy for Clarke. A diabetic, he lacked the smooth skating skills of a Bobby Orr or Guy Lafleur. His shot was never particularly potent, but he made the most of what he had. "Guts is what he had in abundance," said ex-Flyer Larry Zeidel. "Not everybody saw his qualities at first but, after a while, they realized that he was a winner."

If anyone suggested to Philadelphia Flyers' boss Ed Snider that the seventeenth player claimed in the 1969 amateur draft would, in May 1973, be selected for the Hart Trophy as the NHL player adjudged the most valuable to his team, it is quite possible that Snider would have tumbled from his chair laughing.

Yet, in September 1969, while the Flyers' first-year men were working out at Le Colisée in Quebec City, someone detected that rare quality of utter superiority in just such a man.

"Within three years," said Bud Poile, then general manager of the Flyers, "that twenty-year-old boy will be the best in the league. And if he's not the best I'll guarantee you that he will be in the top three."

Poile was talking to his heir apparent, Keith Allan, about a rather awkward center named Bobby Clarke. Precisely what it was about Clarke that inspired Poile's raves was somewhat of a mystery. But as the 1972–73 season wound down to a playoff conclusion, it was evident that Poile either knew what he was talking about or had made an awfully good guess.

By the time the Flyers went up against the Montreal Canadiens in April 1973, Bobby had irrevocably become Mister Hockey in Philadelphia. Such veterans as Ed Van Impe, an original Flyer, knew it as well as the man in the street. Players such as forward Terry Crisp, who was new to the team, sensed it immediately.

Robert Earle Clarke was born August 13, 1949, in the mining town of Flin Flon in northern Manitoba. Bobby played for the local junior team, the Flin Flon Bombers, in a frontier atmosphere that was rife with brawling and intimidation.

He survived the battles and seemed destined for professional hockey when word of his diabetic condition circulated through the NHL scouting grapevine. Fortunately for Clarke, his coach, Paddy Ginnell, was determined to see that his crack center got a fair chance to reach the top.

Ginnell arranged for Clarke to visit the famed Mayo Clinic in Rochester, Minnesota. His coach personally escorted him before the 1968–69 season. Following a battery of tests, the doctors agreed that there was absolutely no reason why Bobby could not play pro hockey, provided he took good care of himself. "What's more, the doctors put it in writing," said Ginnell.

"That was all I needed," Ginnell said. "We went home and when the scouts came around the following season I showed them the letter. I wanted everyone from any NHL team who came to Flin Flon to know about Bobby exactly what the doctors at Mayo Clinic knew."

Skeptical though they were, the Flyers gambled on Clarke, picking him seventeenth overall in the 1969 amateur draft. He made the team on his first try and by the 1972–73 season had exceeded the 100-point mark.

His modesty notwithstanding, Clarke could not deny his accomplishments, which were immense during the 1972–73 season. For example, during a game against the Montreal Canadiens at the Forum, Philadelphia came away with a 7–6 victory. Bobby scored a hat trick; the winning goal achieved with only 3:39 remaining in the game. Even partisan Montrealers agreed that the kid from Flin Flon was Hart Trophy (most valuable player) material, and Flyers' manager Keith Allan was not disinclined to agree.

"In Philadelphia," Allan observed, "there's nobody but Clarke to consider. Rick MacLeish had has a remarkable year, but I'd hate to think where the Flyers would be without Clarke." Together with his diabetes, Bobby also had a little difficulty with his eyesight, which is 200–100 myopic. "That means," he explains, "trouble seeing far away. I never wore lenses in junior hockey. If I'm on top of the play, I'm okay. It's when the puck is in the air that I have trouble judging it."

Yet Clarke would still be the All-Canadian Boy, except for one factor: the company he was keeping. By the middle of the 1972–73 season, the Broad Street Bullies had established themselves as the riotous swashbucklers of the NHL. Their scorn for the rule book was notorious from Flin Flon to Toronto and a cause for alarm at NHL headquarters in Montreal.

Inevitably, Clarke would be affected by the brawlers around him. For like Gordie Howe who once defended hockey violence by asserting that "It is a man's game," Clarke too was aware.

By playoff time, 1973, Bobby Clarke had fulfilled the promise of his September press clippings when he surprised everyone in the Team Canada camp. He finished second in the scoring race behind perennial leader Phil Esposito with thirty-seven goals and sixty-seven assists for 104 points in seventy-eight games.

In 1974–75 and 1975–76, he led the NHL in assists with eighty-nine each time. He also led in playoff assists in both years with twelve and fourteen, respectively. But by the late 1970s, the wear and tear was taking its toll, and Bobby's point production began a downward spiral—ninety, eighty-nine, seventy-three, sixty-nine, and sixty-five in the 1980–81 season.

The Flyers attempted to relieve him by making Clarke an assistant coach and limiting his playing time, but his will to play was overwhelming, and in 1981–82 he helped re-generate the Flyers' rebuilding process with a gallant show of energy.

Clarke retired in May 1984, and in a natural progression became the Flyers' general manager. Although he seemed to be a novice at the demanding job, he turned the Flyers into a powerhouse. They reached the Stanley Cup finals in 1985 and again in 1987. The kid from Flin Flon demonstrated that hard work pays off on all levels.

37

Jacques Plante
(1952–1975)

That Jacques Plante was the third-best goalie of all time is an assertion that few could challenge. That Plante was the best goalie ever is a statement that could be supported in some quarters although not this one. However, Plante's enormity in his field is certainly without question. He may not have been the iron man that Glenn Hall was with the Chicago Black Hawks or the implacably perfect puck-stopper that Georges Vezina had been during an earlier era with the Montreal Canadiens, but Plante *was* stupendous in his own right.

He was a winner. He was expert. He was creative, and he was durable. He won the Hart Trophy as the National Hockey League's most valuable player in 1962 and won the Vezina Trophy as the top goalie from 1956 through 1960 and again in 1962 and finally, sharing it with Glenn Hall, in 1969. He was named to the First All-Star Team in 1956, 1959, and 1962 and to the Second Team in 1957, 1958, 1960, and 1971.

Unlike Terry Sawchuk, whose skills eroded with time, Plante was in mint condition at the age of forty when he starred for the St. Louis Blues. Plante played for six Stanley Cup-winning teams and eight clubs that finished in first place. And, more than Sawchuk, Plante was the most innovative of the modern goaltenders. In fact, it would be safe to say that Jacques did more to revolutionize the modus operandi of puck-stopping than anyone in the past thirty years. On top of that, Plante, plainly and simply, was a very interesting character.

In his spare time, Plante, alias *Jake the Snake*, had a hobby of knitting toques, the French-Canadian wool caps worn by his ancestors. He was confident to the point of being cocky and betrayed a bizarre goaltending style that would soon be copied by other netminders around the league. It was Plante's idea that he would be aiding his defensemen by roaming out of his cage, formerly a strict taboo, and behind the net when the pucks were caromed off the boards and skidded in behind his cage. By doing so, Plante was able to control the puck and pass it off to a teammate, while scrambling back to his goal crease before any shots were taken. This style was introduced when the Canadiens, coached by Dick Irvin, were engaged in a thrilling semifinal against the Chicago Black Hawks in 1953.

All this was well and good and terribly fascinating, but for the adventurous and unconventional Plante to experiment with the Canadiens in the playoffs and on the brink of elimination was something else! But Irvin had made a commitment, and Plante was his goalie. Jacques the Roamer immediately went into the cage and stopped the Black Hawks cold. He foiled a breakaway early in the fifth game, and with that impetus Les

Canadiens won two straight games and captured the first round. Plante won himself a job and helped the Canadiens to the Stanley Cup. By the late 1950s, Montreal had the most formidable club of the decade—if not all time—with the defense of Doug Harvey and Tom Johnson available to thwart attackers. Toe Blake had replaced Irvin as coach and a coolness eventually developed between the explosive coach and his enigmatic goalkeeper.

Still the best in the league, *Jake the Snake* occasionally enraged spectators with his scrambles behind the net for the puck. Once, the play backfired on him. He missed the disk; an opponent retrieved it and shoved the rubber into the yawning cage before Plante could return to guard it. In November 1958, Plante's goals against average began climbing, matched by Blake's temper.

The Blake-Plante repartee was, perhaps, even more ominous than it sounded. Severe to a fault, the coach was down on his goaltender and was to become more and more disenchanted with Plante's behavior as the seasons progressed.

It was ironic that the Plante-Blake rift widened at the precise point when Jacques executed one of his most courageous acts. The date was November 2, 1959. Plante was in the Canadiens' net facing the Rangers at Madison Square Garden. Right wing Andy Bathgate of the Rangers, one of the league's hardest shooters, released a quick shot that struck Plante squarely on the nose and sent him bloodied to the ice. His face looking like a mashed potato laden with ketchup, Plante was helped to the dressing room where seven stitches were sewn into his pulverized proboscis.

Until then, Plante had been experimenting during practice sessions with a mask that was molded to his facial contours. Blake, an old school hardliner, was irrevocably opposed to Jacques using the face piece in a regular game, but, this time, the Canadiens had no spare goalie and Plante would not go back onto the ice without a mask. Blake had no choice but to oblige and, on that night, history was made. Plante wore the mask, won the game, and vowed to continue wearing the device as long as he played. Blake was not the least enamored with the idea, although he publicly asserted that, as long as it helped Plante keep the pucks out of the net, it would be all right. For 1959–60, the mask proved effective enough to enable Plante to win the Vezina Trophy.

But Blake was a hard man and his grievances against Plante—anger that transcended the mask issue—simmered within him and, often without. The breaking point came in 1963 when he was dealt to the Rangers. Blake would have preferred it if Plante had displayed an uncompromising attitude toward the game; the kind that marked other Canadiens, most notably Maurice Richard. This, however, was not Plante's way. He pursued his unorthodoxy with the Rangers, then the St. Louis Blues, Toronto Maple Leafs, and Boston Bruins.

Jacques Plante was born January 17, 1929, in Shawinigan Falls, Quebec, and like many a French-Canadian youngster, played his hockey on the outdoor rinks of *La Belle Province*. His goaltending excellence was unquestioned in the early 1950s, yet he was not given a serious thought as a potential goalie for the Canadiens because they had a relatively young and efficient Gerry McNeil guarding the twines for them. But Dick Irvin took a dramatic gamble in 1953, and Plante rewarded him with a memorable clutch effort.

Plante concluded his NHL career with the Boston Bruins in April 1973, then became general manager-coach of the Quebec Nordiques in the World Hockey Association. It was another case of a superstar being unable to orchestrate from the sidelines as well as he had on the ice. A season later, at the age of forty-five, he returned to the nets, this time with the WHA's Edmonton Oilers. He played commendably for the Oilers but finally retired for good at the conclusion of the campaign and became a part-time goaltending coach for the Philadelphia Flyers; a position he retained through the early 1980s.

Through the years Plante rubbed several people the wrong way, and many have never forgotten what they intrepreted as his abrasive manner. But no follower with a sense of hockey history will ever forget the comprehensive contributions made by Plante or his consummate skill at blocking a puck.

There was nobody like him before and there will not be anyone like him again. An original. A craftsman.

38

Aurel Joliat
(1922–1938)

They called him *The Little Giant.* Aurel Joliat weighed in at 140 pounds (on a heavy day) and appeared only slightly taller than a fireplug. But size was no more a debit to the French-Canadian left wing than it was to the likes of King Clancy and Frank Boucher.

"Aurel was as slippery as Howie Morenz was swift," said Boucher.

Despite his size, Joliat played sixteen seasons in the NHL, all with the Montreal Canadiens. He scored 270 goals—the same number as Morenz—and was voted the Hart Trophy as the league's most valuable player in 1934. He made the First All-Star Team in 1931 and the Second Team in 1932, 1934, and 1935. Joliat played on three Stanley Cup championship teams.

Both teammates and foes were intrigued and often amused by Joliat and his idiosyncracies. "Aurel always wore a black cap," Boucher recalled. "He wore it on the ice whenever he played. It was a baseball cap and he positively would not chase the puck if it were knocked from his head."

Joliat's forte was stickhandling. He could pass with the best of them, and many old-timers insist that he was similar in style with Gil Perreault, the one-time Buffalo Sabres center.

One of the Canadiens' finest lines comprised Joliat, Howie Morenz, and Johnny "Black Cat" Gagnon. "Aurel always used to get the puck and pass it to me," Gagnon remembered, "and then I'd pass it to him. We had pretty much the same stickhandling style and I always knew what kind of moves he'd make. For instance, as soon as he'd hit the blue line he'd throw me a pass behind his back. Morenz wasn't as good a playmaker so I'd play more with Aurel."

The Joliat-Gagnon connection was primarily responsible for the Canadiens' Stanley Cup victory over the Chicago Blacks Hawks in the 1931 finals. The series was tied at two games apiece in a best-of-five round. In the final match, Joliat dispatched a perfect pass to put Gagnon in the clear, giving Montreal a 1–0 lead. Gagnon scored again late in the game and Montreal triumphed 2–0.

"Morenz may have been 'the Babe Ruth of Hockey' but Joliat was more of an artist, a stickhandler," said Gagnon. "Aurel always made beautiful passes. He wasn't as fast as Morenz but he could move when he wanted to."

Joliat was paid almost $10,000 in his prime and returned the favor by leading the Canadiens in scoring in 1933 and 1934. It was to be the apex of his career not because his abilities diminished but because of the decline and fall of Morenz and, therefore, the Joliat-Morenz-Gagnon line.

Morenz was traded to Chicago during the 1934–35 season, but his replacements on the Joliat-Gagnon line proved inadequate and the Canadiens slipped to last place in the 1935–36 campaign.

Joliat yearned for his old pal, Howie, and then in a surprise move, the Canadiens reobtained Morenz for the 1936–37 season. The line was reunited and while it lacked the *élan* of earlier years, it still provided the old thrill for Montreal fans. But the leg fracture suffered by Morenz on January 28, 1937, ruined the line, broke Joliat's spirits, and, of course, spelled *finis* for the great Morenz.

Writing about Joliat in his book, *Hockey's Hall of Fame*, author Tim Moriarty noted that Morenz's death had a debilitating effect on Joliat's career. "The fierce spark in Joliat seemed to die, too," wrote Moriarty. "Age and injuries were catching up to the tiny French-Canadian. He was thirty-six and had suffered six shoulder separations, three broken ribs, five nose fractures, plus an assortment of routine injuries."

Joliat played two more seasons, scoring seventeen goals and six goals respectively, before retiring after the 1937–38 season. "He was," noted Moriarty, "one of hockey's greatest left wingers."

Aurel Joliat was born August 29, 1901, in Ottawa and, like Hall of Famers King Clancy and Frank Boucher, learned to play the game on the frozen Rideau Canal. Joliat and Boucher were the same age and enjoyed the *joie de vivre* of kids hockey in the crisp outdoors.

Joliat and Boucher grew up together on the rinks and fields of Ottawa but took different routes to the NHL. A superb football player, Aurel went west to play professionally in Regina, Saskatchewan. He suffered a broken ankle but stayed in Saskatchewan. When his injury was mended he signed on as a left wing with the Saskatoon Sheiks hockey club.

Frank Boucher's brother, Billy, also a chum of Joliat's, watched Joliat mature with the Sheiks and urged Canadiens' owner Leo Dandurand to obtain Aurel for Les Canadiens. Dandurand obliged by unloading his aging Newsy Lalonde for the young left wing.

Aurel weighed 140 pounds, at his heaviest, but his size never bothered him. It apparently motivated him to compensate with a vast repertoire of stickhandling maneuvers and pirouettes.

Joliat teamed up with Morenz in the 1923–24 season. The pair jelled perfectly right from the start, although Aurel was to prove that season that he could excel with or without Morenz at his side. The Canadiens had gone up against Calgary in the playoffs, and Morenz's shoulder was broken after he intercepted an enemy pass and circled his own net to gain momentum.

Joliat was a constant source of annoyance to his larger opponents. Once, after Aurel had thoroughly confounded Toronto's huge Babe Dye with a series of fakes, the distressed Dye skated over to Dandurand and said: "I'm tired of chasing that shadow of yours, that Frenchman, Joliat. Move him to center, Leo, hold a mirror to each side of him, and you'll have the fastest line in hockey." Later, Howie Morenz told a reporter, "If it wasn't for Joliat, you wouldn't be writing about me so much."

Goal-wise, Joliat's best season was 1924–25 when he produced twenty-nine red lights in twenty-four games. Morenz had twenty-seven and Billy Boucher, who now was his teammate, had eighteen. When the Canadiens finished first in 1927–28, Joliat and Morenz were the talk of the hockey world and were partly responsible for propagating the game in American cities such as New York, Chicago, Detroit, and Boston.

The boundless energy that was a hallmark of Joliat's play remained an essential part of his makeup long after he retired, and little Aurel was frequently welcomed at hockey functions both in Canada and the United States.

One of his most memorable appearances took place at the old Madison Square Garden in New York at ceremonies prior to the final hockey game played there in 1968 before the opening of the new Garden.

The host New York Rangers invited every living member of hockey's Hall of Fame including the boyhood pals, Joliat and Frank Boucher. The well-orchestrated program featured individual introductions of each Hall of Famer whereupon the personality would skate on the ice in his original team jersey.

Maurice Richard, Eddie Shore, Babe Pratt, Bill Cook, and Ching Johnson were among the luminaries who were toasted by the crowd as they modestly made their appearance; and sometimes immodestly as in Richard's case.

Tim Moriarty, who reported the game for his newspaper, Long Island *Newsday*, remembered the Joliat appearance. "Aurel stole the show. Wearing the same tiny peaked cap that was his trademark as a player, Joliat skated the entire length of the ice, turned, and then cut several figure-eights on the way back. As the crowd roared its approval, Joliat did a series of pirouettes, bowed, and tipped his cap. It was a remarkable performance."

Especially remarkable, considering that Joliat was sixty-seven years old.

Joliat made his home in Ottawa where he held a job as a railway passenger ticket agent and later enjoyed a quiet retirement. He enjoyed life—especially his life on ice—to the hilt and leaves a legacy of spectacular plays and heroism for a little man that may never be matched. *The Little Giant* is a big man in *Hockey's 100.*

39

Marcel Dionne
(1971–   )

It always will be the bane of Marcel Dionne's professional athletic life that he never will *really* know how good he could have been as a major-leaguer. From the very moment when he stepped onto National Hockey League rinks as a well-trumpeted rookie in 1971, Dionne has been burdened with mediocre teammates and subpar teams. This, however, has not prevented him from achieving bountiful goals and an assortment of prizes.

He twice won the Lady Byng Trophy for good sportsmanship and high-quality play. He twice was voted to the First All-Star Team at center and twice was Second Team center. In 1980, he led the NHL in scoring.

Yet, Dionne's biggest challenge, lifting a team to a first-place finish or the Stanley Cup, eluded him in more than a decade of NHL play. Time and again, Marcel would fail in the playoffs, and the Kings would make a hasty exit in postseason action. Nevertheless, until the advent of Wayne Gretzky at the start of the 1980s, Dionne was the single most productive center in the league and had been a luminary ever since he made his debut at the beginning of the 1970s.

Marcel completed his rookie season with twenty-eight goals and forty-nine assists for seventy-seven points, a new NHL record for points in a season by a rookie. Thus, it was hardly surprising that he received a veteran's responsibility.

For inexplicable reasons, Dionne finished a distant third in the voting for the Calder Trophy, given to the NHL's outstanding rookie. Marcel placed behind Buffalo's Richard Martin, who scored forty-four goals, and Montreal's goalie-lawyer Ken Dryden. The rejection of Dionne inspired a hail of protest, especially in Detroit.

As a second year man, Dionne enjoyed an outstanding offensive year, with forty goals and fifty assists for ninety points. In Marcel's third season, irascible Ted Garvin took over as head coach, and instantly there was a personality clash. Garvin accused the young center of loafing, and Dionne responded by demanding to be traded.

By now the troubles were having a telling effect. Dionne slumped off to a disappointing twenty-four-goal year.

The 1974–75 season, Dionne's fourth in the majors, brought yet another head coach, this time former Detroit superstar Alex Delvecchio. But more importantly, it was Marcel's option year—by not signing a new contract, Dionne would be free to go to the team of his choice at the end of the campaign. Knowing this, the Red Wings attempted to make Marcel happy by giving him more responsibility. In a shocking move, Dionne was named team captain.

Playing like the Dionne of old, Marcel had his finest season as a Red Wing, amassing forty-seven goals and seventy-four assists for 121 points, placing him behind only Phil Esposito and Bobby Orr in the NHL scoring race.

But the productive campaign failed to erase the scars of bygone years and, once the season ended, his agent informed Delvecchio that Dionne would be taking his services elsewhere.

"We offered him a four-year contract for a million—$250,00 per year," said Delvecchio. "But he thinks he can get more money somewhere else. He said he didn't want to play in Detroit anymore. He said 'the name of the game is money' and he thinks he can get more money somewhere else. Personally, I think Dionne is a pretty selfish individual. Now it looks as though what he did for the Red Wings last year was all for himself." And so the big question: who would sign Marcel for 1975–76?

Six teams were in the early running—the Montreal Canadiens, St. Louis Blues, Buffalo Sabres, Toronto Maple Leafs, Los Angeles Kings, and Edmonton Oilers (of the WHA). Dionne's demands were high, as were the Red Wings', who were entitled to compensation from the team that signed Marcel. Ultimately, the Kings, whose owner Jack Kent Cooke had just acquired Kareem Abdul-Jabbar for his basketball Lakers, offered the most money.

The Kings won the bidding war and surrendered veteran defenseman Terry Harper and rugged forward Dan Maloney to Detroit. Cooke signed Marcel to a five-year, $1.5 million pact.

Although Dionne and Cooke danced cartwheels of joy, Kings' coach Bob Pulford unhappily muttered that the deal was not in the best interests of the club. Under Pulford's disciplined defensive style, the Kings previously had enjoyed an extremely successful season. Los Angeles had the fourth best won-lost record in the league, and only the Stanley Cup champion Philadelphia Flyers allowed fewer goals. Terry Harper had been the captain of the squad and the leader on defense. Maloney, a muscular winger, could score goals and tend to checking. In Dionne, the Kings were adding a freewheeling player whose style appeared conspicuously out of place in the Kings' system. Coach Pulford worried that Dionne might disrupt his previously sound club, both on and off the ice.

Marcel Elphege Dionne was born on August 3, 1951, in Drummondville, Quebec. He required only two years before he began skating on a makeshift rink in his backyard. His parents encouraged young Marcel to play hockey, aware that if he didn't make a career of hockey, he inevitably would spend his life working in the steel mills, like his father.

As a result, the Dionnes saw to it that their son's hockey thirst was always quenched.

When Marcel was fifteen, he had established himself as a professional prospect, and he had outgrown Drummondville. It was time for him to move on to the big time and play for the Montreal Junior Canadiens, one of the strongest amateur teams in Canada.

The move to Montreal was also part of the price of wanting to make it to the pros. Dionne played spectacularly for his new club, and after his rookie season he received an invitation to play for the St. Catharines Ontario Junior A team, a club that had developed and sent such stars as Bobby Hull and Stan Mikita to the majors. Dionne accepted the offer although St. Catharines was in Ontario, where only English was spoken. Since Marcel could only speak French, he had catapulted himself into a very awkward situation.

During his three-year pro apprenticeship at St. Catharines, Marcel established a career Ontario Hockey Association scoring record of 375 points. He attracted attention throughout Canada, and NHL clubs scouted the mighty little scoring machine as if they had found a gold mine of goals. In fact, Dionne was so highly regarded that he was selected second in the 1971 NHL amateur draft by the Detroit Red Wings; only Guy Lafleur of the Canadiens was chosen before Dionne. Desperate for help, the Red Wings expected instant miracles from Marcel. Detroit general manager Ned Harkness sought a replacement for the legendary Gordie Howe, who had quit the Wings following the 1970–71 season. Dionne hired super-attorney Alan Eagleson to negotiate his contract, and the result was a pact that Eagleson labeled "the best I've ever negotiated for a rookie...better even than the original one I negotiated for Bobby Orr with the Boston Bruins."

Along with big money, Dionne received unprecedented attention from the Detroit press and the fans, who expected the kind of results that a six-figure contract suggests.

Consequently, Dionne found himself in a pressure-cooker atmosphere before he even put on a Red Wings uniform. He scored a paltry two goals, and the press promptly needled him.

"It was more difficult in the NHL than I imagined," Dionne says. "There was such a big difference in the style of play; it's so much faster in the majors. I had scoring chances as a rookie, but I just couldn't connect. My teammates told me not to miss on those kind of chances in this league. They are so much quicker and the checking is quicker, and then there is the pressure because here you are playing for money: big money."

Red Wings' coach Doug Barkley defended and shielded his prize twenty-year-old rookie. "I'm not disappointed with Marcel," Barkley said at the time, "He's improving with each game. He can skate. He can shoot. He has all the moves. But he must learn the difference between the NHL and junior hockey. And, mark my words, he will!"

Marcel did. His arithmetic is among the best in all NHL history. At the conclusion of the 1981–82 season, he again led the Kings with fifty goals, sixty-seven assists, and 117 points. "It's very impressive," said an NHL scout who remembered Dionne as a rookie. "But it would have been even more impressive if he had managed to skate for a champion."

Dionne remained with the Kings until the 1986–87 season when he was traded to the New York Rangers. By this time, he had become the second leading pointgetter in NHL history, behind Gordie Howe. Despite hints of retirement, Dionne was still a Ranger in 1988–89.

40

Terry Sawchuk
(1950–1970)

No less an authority than Emile Francis, a professional goaltender for more than twenty years, regards Terry Sawchuk as the greatest goalie of all time.

Were it not for a series of debilitating injuries and some erratic behavior rooted in personal problems, Sawchuk could be regarded as number one. But he lacked Glenn Hall's extraordinary durability, strength, and even temper. At times, Sawchuk was his own worst enemy in a career marked by extreme peaks and valleys.

His glory days—and the ones which helped mold his image of immortality—were spent with the dynastic Detroit Red Wings of the early 1950s. He was named rookie of the year in 1951 and won the Vezina Trophy in 1952, 1953, and 1955. As a Toronto Maple Leaf, he shared the Vezina honors with Johnny Bower and fully earned his half of the prize.

Creator of the crouch-style of netminding, Sawchuk was named to the First All-Star Team in 1951, 1952, and 1953 and was a Second Team choice in 1954, 1955, 1959, and 1963. He played for four Stanley Cup winners and four first-place teams.

In Detroit, Sawchuk was fronted by an exceptionally gifted crew including Gordie Howe, Ted Lindsay, Red Kelly, Marcel Pronovost, and Alex Delvecchio, but he was as responsible as any for the club's success. He was an innovator and his ability to cope with screened shots by use of the crouch was considered a great advance in goaltending technique in its day.

Sawchuk was the product of the Red Wings' farm system, which developed a remarkable string of Hall of Famers, starting with Harry Lumley and also including Glenn Hall. Lumley had starred on the Detroit 1950 Stanley Cup winner while Sawchuk was in the wings, playing superbly on the Indianapolis farm team.

In a terrific gamble, Red Wings' manager Jack Adams dealt Lumley to Chicago and elected Sawchuk as his number one netminder. The results were obvious from the start. Lumley was quickly forgotten and by springtime Sawchuk was the talk of the ice world. The Red Wings annexed the Stanley Cup in eight games during which Terry allowed but five goals for a 0.62 goals against average.

Nothing speaks more eloquently about Sawchuk's first five NHL seasons than his goals against average, which never rose higher than 1.98. Yet, despite the triumphs, there always was a shadow of gloom surrounding him. His right elbow, which had been dislocated in a childhood football accident, continued to bedevil him and he underwent operations in the summers of 1950 and 1951 for removal of pieces of bone that had chipped off in the elbow.

The operations were unsuccessful, and surgery was ordered again in 1952 whereupon the surgeon removed sixty pieces of bone. Sawchuk believed his troubles were over; for the first time in ten years he had almost compete movement in his right arm.

But the cumulative effect of all the hospitalization seemed to have a boomerang effect on Sawchuk psychically, not to mention physically. His weight, which had consistently been around 205 pounds, dropped during the 1952–53 season to 168. Sawchuk was given exhaustive medical tests.

Less than a month later he was hospitalized for an appendectomy. Even Terry, himself, found humor in his woes. When a reporter asked him what he did during the off-season, he chortled: "I spend my summers in the hospital."

He wasn't kidding. He returned to the hospital in 1954 after an auto accident resulted in severe chest injuries. Once again, he recovered to play more than competently for the Red Wings but now—irony of ironies—Sawchuk's threat was the Detroit farm system. Jack Adams now had another whiz goalie in Indianapolis named Glenn Hall, who could not be kept in the minors.

Once again, the Red Wings' boss packed a major deal involving his goalkeeper, this time sending Sawchuk to the Boston Bruins. What few skeptics there were questioned Terry's ability to play superior goal for a relatively weak team such as the Bruins, but his high standard of performance delighted Boston Garden fans and, for one season at least, the deal looked good.

But his second year in Beantown was a disaster. He was stricken with infectious mononucleosis and spent twelve days in the hospital. When he returned to the ice—perhaps prematurely—he seemed almost skeptical and a shade of the Sawchuk who once had starred for Detroit.

He lost four of his next eight games and the Boston press turned on him. His weight was now 166 pounds and, at age twenty-seven, he felt he had had it. To the astonishment of teammates and foes alike, he announced that he was retiring. "I told them I thought it best to quit since my nerves were really shot."

It was suggested that much more was being concealed than reached print. Sawchuk, some noted, never did take to the Boston scene and yearned for his old digs in Detroit.

Sawchuk's "retirement" lasted until the beginning of the next season when Adams sweet-talked the Bruins into giving him the rights to Sawchuk "because he's too good a goalie to remain out of hockey." That done, Adams dealt Hall to Chicago and Sawchuk played seven more years for the Red Wings, often displaying his pre-illness form.

Following the 1963–64 season, the Red Wings' high command figured that Terry was washed-up. Toronto Maple Leafs' general manager Punch Imlach, always one to give a veteran a chance, signed Sawchuk and Terry demonstrated that, yes, there was still some good goaltending left in him. The Leafs won the Stanley Cup, defeating Chicago and Montreal, and Sawchuk won six of Toronto's eight victories.

While one might have expected Terry to be a joyful man in Toronto, where he was receiving unanimous raves, the fact remained that he seemed to be an unhappy man. "He reminded you of a prisoner in a wartime concentration camp," said Toronto journalist Jim Hunt.

Nevertheless, the Toronto experience was one that also provided some inner peace and satisfaction, particularly the Cup-winning effort. "I'd like to leave hockey like that," said Sawchuk. "In style."

He didn't, of course. When the NHL expanded from six to twelve teams in 1967, Terry was obtained by the new Los Angeles Kings, played one season on the West coast and then returned to the Red Wings in 1968–69. A year later he was signed by the Rangers, playing for Emile Francis, the man who had admired him so much.

It was clear that Sawchuk no longer considered the game anything more than a way of making a dollar, but every so often he would betray the beauty part of his game; the one that once moved Jack Adams to drop a superstar just to put Terry on his roster.

Terrence Gordon Sawchuk was born December 28, 1929, in Winnipeg, Manitoba, and, from all indications, was physically unfit to be a goaltender before he reached his teens.

An endless series of physical mishaps did not stop his climb to the top, and one can only wonder what Sawchuk's fate might have been had he not reported to the Red Wings' camp one season weighing a roly-poly 229 pounds. Adams was furious and ordered Terry to go on a strict diet.

Week by week, Sawchuk's weight dropped until he had lost forty pounds. But now he couldn't stop the weight loss, and management got worried. He was ordered to a doctor. The weight loss finally was stemmed, but Terry was never able to put any of it back.

It has been theorized—and correctly so—that the pressure of his grueling job had also gotten to him. From that point on, his emotional graph described a downward turn that bottomed out in Boston. He had left his wife and children back home in Detroit and lived in a rooming house.

And while he did recover, it was always difficult for Terry to enjoy even the most intense moments of glee. One that should have brought him happiness was the Stanley Cup finale in 1967 when he and another veteran, Johnny Bower, guided the Leafs to the championship. While teammates exulted in the dressing room, sipping champagne, the goalies, as Jim Hunt observed, "sat in a corner by themselves, dragging deeply on cigarettes and grappling silently with the frayed nerves and many physical ailments that are an inescapable part of life for aging men."

He played his last professional game on April 9, 1970, against a mighty Boston Bruins' team in the Stanley Cup playoffs. The Rangers were beaten 5–3 and soon were eliminated from the Cup round.

Conceivably, Emile Francis might have invited Sawchuk back to the Rangers for the 1970–71 season as a goaltending coach and possible second goaltender. But three weeks after the Rangers were eliminated, Sawchuk, who shared a room in suburban Long Island with teammate Ron Stewart, had a row with his pal. The precise details never have been fully pieced together, but Sawchuk was taken to the hosptial for treatment of intestinal injuries.

At first, it seemed just a matter of weeks until he would be released, but Terry's condition worsened dramatically and, finally, he was moved to a more sophisticated Manhattan hospital where emergency surgery was performed.

It was all in vain. Sawchuk died of a pulmonary embolism on May 31, 1970. His was one of the most tragic of hockey careers but also one of the most glorious. He was a definitive goaltender—just short of being the greatest.

41

Ted Lindsay
(1944–1960) (1964–1965)

Although he was one of the highest paid players of his time, Ted Lindsay often said that he would play the game for nothing. That is a measure of both his love for the game and the seething, combative spirit that he displayed every time he skated out onto the ice.

Lindsay was an intrinsic part of the intimidating Detroit Red Wings' dynasty of the early 1950s. It was Lindsay, Gordie Howe, and Sid Abel who made up the famous *Production Line*. During his thirteen seasons with the Red Wings, Ted played on eight first place teams and played on four Stanley Cup championship winners.

Lindsay's blazing competitive spirit made him one of the toughest and most feared skaters in the NHL. He was one of the best left wingers of his generation and one of the meanest of all time.

More than that, Lindsay was a courageous rebel. He was one of the first organizers of the Player's Association. For this act, he was duly punished by the Lords of Hockey, and like fellow organizers—Jim Thomson and Doug Harvey—he was traded to a lower team, in Lindsay's case, the hapless Chicago Black Hawks.

To say that he was rowdy and rambunctious would be putting it mildly. Ted accumulated over 760 stitches on his person, all mementos from the various battles he waged on the ice. The stitches earned him the moniker *Scarface*. He had many other nicknames that attested to his style of aggressive play—names such as *Terrible Ted* and *Tempestuous Ted*.

Ted was a little guy (5'8", 163 pounds), and he resented players who thought they might take advantage of his small stature. He would not be intimidated. "Okay, so I was cocky," he admitted, reflecting back on his career, "I had the idea that I had to beat up everyone in the league, and I'm still not convinced it wasn't a good idea. Probably I'd do it the same way if I did it over again. That's the way I am."

Once during a game between the Red Wings and the Toronto Maple Leafs, Ted battled Gus Mortson all night. The peculiarity of this situation was that Gus had been Ted's friend since boyhood, a teammate of his at St. Michael's College, and also was in partnership with him in a gold mine they owned near Kirkland Lake. "I don't know anybody when a hockey game starts," Ted explained.

In Ted's seventeen-year career, he played in 1,068 games. Lindsay scored 379 goals and added 472 assists for a total of 851 points. He had also spent 1,808 minutes in the penalty box, ranking him high on the All-Time Penalty Leaders list.

In 133 playoff games, Lindsay scored forty-seven goals and forty-nine assists for ninety-six points and spent 194 minutes in the penalty box.

Lindsay also made the First All-Star Team eight times, first making it during the 1947–48 season, and then from 1949–50 to 1953–54. He again made it during the 1955–56 and 1956–57 seasons. Ted made the Second All-Star Team in 1948–49.

In 1949–50, while playing in sixty-one games, Ted scored twenty-three goals and had fifty-five assists for seventy-eight points. It was in this year that he won the Art Ross Trophy, emblematic of the player who leads the league in scoring points at the end of the regular season.

As was typical of his aggressive style of play, while playing for the Black Hawks in 1958–59, Ted led the league in penalties, spending 184 minutes in the penalty box.

Robert Blake Theodore Lindsay was born in Renfrew, Ontario, on July 29, 1925. Ted was the youngest of six brothers, coming from a large family that also included three daughters. His dad, Bert, was also a fine hockey player, being the star goalie for the Renfrew Millionaires in the early 1900s.

He tried goaltending in an attempt to follow in his dad's footsteps, "But I soon discovered I'd rather shoot than be shot at, so I gave up goaltending," he remarked.

The war had broken out, and in 1940, the five older Lindsay boys joined the armed forces. With no more family practices to participate in, Ted tried out—and made—the Holy Name Juveniles. He played with them for four years, during which time they won the Ontario championship.

By the 1943–44 season, Ted was considered an up-and-coming player. He had accepted an invitation to join St. Michael's College. He played well the second half of the season, after a poor start. St. Mikes was eliminated that year, but while on a trip to Hamilton in the spring of 1944, Carson Cooper, the chief scout for the Detroit Red Wings, spotted him.

The Red Wings' general manager Jack Adams signed him at once. Lindsay was drafted as a wartime replacement by the Oshawa Generals to help them win the Memorial Cup. With Ted scoring several goals, Oshawa did win the Cup.

It was in the fall of 1944–45 that Ted was invited to Detroit's training camp. Lindsay was only nineteen years old. Sixty-three rookies tried out—only two of them made the club. Ted was one of them.

Lindsay appeared in forty-five games for the Red Wings and had seventeen goals and six assists. The next season was disappointing—only seven goals and ten assists.

In 1946, Jack Adams decided to take a risk with the young man from Renfrew. With only one year of junior hockey behind Ted, Adams placed him on the line with a farm boy from Saskatchewan—Gordie Howe, and the veteran center Sid Abel. That was the start of Detroit's immortal *Production Line*, which became one of the greatest lines in hockey history.

To illustrate how powerful a team they were, Detroit won the Prince of Wales Trophy from 1948–49 to 1954–55, and again in 1956–57. At that time, the trophy was presented each year to the team finishing with the most points (the league championship) at the end of the regular season.

That superior Detroit Red Wing team is also in the record books for having the longest winning record, including playoff games. They won fifteen straight games from February 27, 1955 to April 5, 1955, which included nine regular season games and six playoff games.

In 1948–49, the Red Wings finished in first place for the first of seven straight years on top (spanning from 1948–49 to 1954–55). During this incredible dynasty, they won the Stanley Cup four times, in 1949–50, 1951–52, 1953–54, and 1954–55.

The Red Wings were hot again in 1956–57. Ted had produced his greatest season—eighty-five points on thirty goals and fifty-five assists—but it was also the season that Adams decided to break up the Red Wings' famous line. He traded Ted, along with goaltender Glenn Hall, to the Chicago Black Hawks for four players and cash.

Lindsay was now reunited with Tommy Ivan, who had coached him ten out of his thirteen seasons with the Red Wings. But the Black Hawks were a pathetic team; they had finished last in each of the previous four years.

Ted scored fifteen goals in his first season with the Black Hawks. He scored twenty-two goals the next season, and in his third season with Chicago, only seven. Then he retired at the age of thirty-four in 1960. "I guess my heart wasn't in it at Chicago," Ted revealed. "They treated me well, but my home and business was in Detroit. I'm a Detroit guy."

For the next four years, Lindsay spent most of his time tending to his automotive plastics firm in Detroit. He would occasionally engage in workouts with the Red Wings.

In 1964, Ted applied for the job as color commentator for the Detroit Red Wings. Sid Abel, then the Wings' general manager, asked Ted if he would like to join Detroit again. After careful thought, Ted decided to report to training camp to give it a shot. He made the team, and when the Red Wings opened their 1964–65 season (ironically against Ted's most hated adversary, Toronto), Ted was playing left wing. The Olympia fans gave him a standing ovation. It marked his 1000th NHL game.

Reunited with Howe, the Wings finished in first place (after finishing fourth the previous year). Ted scored fourteen goals, had fourteen assists, and proving that nothing had changed since he left hockey, spent 173 minutes in the penalty box. Even his long-time foe, Clarence Campbell, had to admit that the comeback after four years away from the game was "…one of the most amazing feats in professional sport."

Ted retired after that one season to the broadcast booth. When asked why he chose to play one final season, he answered, "I thought it would be nice to finish my career as a Red Wing."

In 1966, in honor of his illustrious career, Ted Lindsay was elected to hockey's Hall of Fame.

Ted was named general manager of the ailing Detroit Red Wings in 1977, and held that job until 1980, when he was fired.

His aggressive style did not erode with time. In the 1981 oldtimers game in which he participated, he was so aggressive that the other players urged that he not be invited back again.

Old Scarface had as many detractors as boosters. Some intimates swear by him, and others cursed him to the core. But there was no disputing his essential talent and the contributions he made to the superior Red Wings' club. Like him or not, you can't keep Ted Lindsay off *Hockey's 100*.

42

Phil Esposito
(1963–1981)

Who was the highest paid garbage collector in the United States? Well, you wouldn't have him working for any sanitation department, but during the last two decades he did his fair share of cleaning up—in the National Hockey League, that is. Phil Esposito, one of the finest scorers ever to lace up a pair of skates, was not particularly artistic. But when you shovel in 700 NHL goals, you don't have to be.

With his Northland magic wand in hand, Esposito kindled more goal lamps than all but one of his competitors—that being the incomparable Gordie Howe. Espo swept 717 pucks behind the men in the cages during his eighteen-and-a-half-year career. He turned goaltender's garbage into his "G–O–A–L–D," and the Midas touch of his quick wrists earned him one MVP award, four scoring titles, two Stanley Cup championships, and a sea of ink in the NHL record books.

Throughout his career, Esposito was overshadowed by this teammates—the golden namesakes of ice hockey—in Chicago it was *The Golden Jet*, Bobby Hull, and in Boston, *The Golden Boy*, Bobby Orr. As a result, people were skeptical about Espo's true ability. He was accused of being a selfish glory seeker who scored goals by hanging out in front of the net and depositing rebounds. But Esposito counters his critics by saying, "Then why don't others do the same?"

Phil admits that he would love to score classic goals with the finesse of Orr or the power of Hull, "But I haven't got that hard shot," he said. "I could shoot from sixty feet out all season and not get a goal. A player must do what he does best." Thus, Phil does it his way.

What way is that? Chip Magnus, a reporter for the Chicago *Sun-Times* captured it best when he wrote, "We see Phil move into the slot, waiting, just off the right corner of the net. Keith Magnuson belts him back into the net post and Phil recovers. Jerry Korab traps Esposito's stick with his own, digs with an elbow, spins Phil around.

"Stan Mikita moves in and rocks Phil with a hip check as he swings past. Magnuson returns, sending a shoulder into Esposito's spine…Phil is once more bounced by Magnuson, but he regains his balance, gets the puck and scores."

Esposito began his NHL career in 1963 with the Chicago Black Hawks. Following a quiet rookie season, he returned to the Hawks as the center for Chico Maki and Bobby Hull. Phil averaged twenty-three goals per season over the next three years, but more importantly, Espo helped Bobby Hull lead the league in goals scored over this duration.

Esposito, however, was not to remain a permanent fixture in Chicago. Coach Billy Reay and manager Tommy Ivan were disenchanted with Espo's playoff performance and decided to trade him. In May 1967, the Black Hawks and Bruins concluded a six-player deal. Esposito, center Fred Stanfield, and winger Ken Hodge were sent to Beantown in return for defenseman Gilles Marotte, crafty center Pit Martin, and goalie Jack Norris. Hockey columnists regarded this deal as "the most one sided trade in modern hockey history." Time would prove them prophetic.

The trade didn't surprise Esposito, but the thought of joining a team full of guys that he'd grown to hate bothered him. Espo said, "to me, guys like Ted Green and Bobby Orr have been the villains. I don't know how I'll adjust to playing alongside of them." But the Bruins were understanding. They gave Espo the confidence he needed by immediately naming him the team's alternative captain.

Phil led the NHL with forty-three assists in his first season with Boston and, by adding thirty-five goals to his totals, emerged as a substantial offensive threat.

Bobby Hull commented on the progress of his former linemate by saying, "The difference is that when Phil was with the Black Hawks he had to give me the puck all the time. Now, he can keep it for himself. He's gone from being the little toad in the big pond, to being the big toad in the little pond that turned out to be the big pond. Boston thought that Bobby Orr would lead them out of the wilderness. But Bobby couldn't do it alone. Orr and Esposito; they complemented each other."

The following season coach Harry Sinden placed Espo and Ken Hodge on the same line and finished off the trio by adding Ron Murphy. The threesome decimated opposing defenses and established a line-scoring record of 263 points. Phil was TNT offsensively, feeding his teammates for an NHL record of seventy-seven assists and 126 points, also a record. Never before had a player topped the 100 point plateau; Espo accomplished it with plenty of points to spare.

Judging by Esposito's accomplishments a case could be made for him as a one of the finest centers of all time. He was a First Team All-Star in 1969, 1970, 1971, 1972, 1973, 1974, and 1975. Both in 1969 and 1974, he was voted the Hart Trophy as the NHL's most valuable player. He led the league in scoring in 1969, 1971, 1972, 1973, and 1974. He wears a pair of Bruins' Stanley Cup rings—from 1970 and 1972. In addition, Esposito was considered the pivotal factor for Team Canada in its four-games-to-three (one tie) victory over the Soviet National Team in September 1972.

Yet, there were those who found a flaw in Esposito's armament. His critics charged that he was a selfish hockey player, who lacked the ability to combine defensive aspects with his offensive game. Despite his many accomplishments, Esposito was traded— along with Carol Vadnais—from the Bruins to the New York Rangers on November 7, 1975, for Brad Park, Jean Ratelle, and Joe Zanussi.

The adjustment was extremely difficult for Phil, who at first complained about conditions in Manhattan. But he gradually came around and, although he never regained his Stanley Cup form of the early 1970s, he won the hearts of New York fans.

In the midst of the 1980–81 season, Phil startled the hockey world by announcing his retirement—then and there—and moving behind the bench as an assistant coach.

Philip Anthony Esposito was born February 20, 1942, in Sault Ste. Marie, Ontario. He was not very highly regarded as a youthful skater, but the Chicago Black Hawks thought enough of him to place him with their St. Louis farm team in the early 1960s. It was there that he learned to employ his size and quick shot to his advantage.

The season following his retirement, Esposito was named color commentator for the New York Rangers, although many believed his future in hockey was in the executive suite as the general manager of a major league club. Sure enough, Phil soon found himself running the Rangers from the G.M.'s suite. As a player, Esposito was expert and prolific. Whatever his faults, he more than qualifies for *Hockey's 100*.

43

Doug Bentley
(1939–1954)

When Doug Bentley arrived at the Chicago Black Hawks' training camp in the fall of 1939, coach Paul Thompson introduced him to club president Bill Tobin. Tobin courteously shook hands with the recruit and wished him luck. Later Tobin said to Thompson: "Is *he* one of our new prospects?"

Thompson nodded, while the players skated at the Hibbing, Minnesota base.

Tobin shook his head, "I didn't know things were *that* tough," he sighed. "What did you say his name was?"

"Doug Bentley," Thompson replied.

"Doug Bentley, eh?" Tobin mused. "He's the first walking ghost I've ever seen."

Tobin returned to Chicago and a few days later Thompson contacted his boss. "He's not a walking ghost," said Thompson, "he's a skating ghost. The kid's terrific!"

Bentley was signed to a major league contract that included a minor league clause. It was a clause that in fifteen years neither the Black Hawks nor the New York Rangers had an occasion to utilize. Doug Bentley, for all his apparent fragility, was a big-leaguer through and through.

He led the National Hockey League in scoring once and was a First Team All-Star left wing twice and once a Second Team All-Star. More than that, Bentley was the essential fiber of the Black Hawks through both good and bad years, although his younger brother, Max, reaped more of the headlines.

Doug had already established himself as a Black Hawk when he was summoned to Tobin's office and given a bonus. "Gee, Mr. Tobin," said Doug, "that's wonderful and I really appreciate it. But if you think I'm good, you should see my brother, Max. He's twice as good."

Unaware that there was still another Bentley with a surplus of hockey gifts, Tobin looked quizzically at Doug. "Is that so?" said the Black Hawks' boss. "Well, in that case, maybe we'd better grab him, too."

Max Bentley became a Black Hawks regular a year after Doug. Max was the more sensational of the two and tended to obscure his older brother, but those who knew the nuances of the game realized that Doug, in his own unobtrusive way, was a splendid stickhandler in his own right and, of course, proved it in years to come.

Playing alongside Max, Doug was able to engineer the give-and-take plays that the brothers learned on the outdoor rinks of their native Saskatchewan. They took Chicago by storm and seemed an inseparable team until Max was to join the Canadian army during World War II. This would be a particularly severe test for Doug, since there were some who believed that he couldn't play capably without Max at center. But Doug was better than ever. With thirty-eight goals and thirty-nine assists for seventy-seven points in fifty games, he finished runner-up to scoring leader Herbie Cain of the Boston Bruins during the 1943–44 season. In the playoffs, he was no less superb with eight goals and four assists in nine playoff games.

When Max returned to the Black Hawks for the 1945–46 campaign, he was aligned with Doug on left wing and another smallish but speedy player on the right side, Bill Mosienko. Rarely have three skaters better complemented each other than the Bentleys and Mosienko. The trio was appropriately christened *The Pony Line* and added a dimension of vitality to the attack that rarely has been seen in the National Hockey League.

Sadly, however, there was little else on the Chicago roster beyond the Bentleys and Mosienko. Because the Black Hawks were so shockingly bereft of depth, the enemy was able to zero in on *The Pony Line* and often battered them without retaliation.

Despite the endless assaults, the Bentleys and Mosienko scored plentifully, but one line simply could not carry a club that was woefully deficient on defense, in goal, and on its second and third lines. The Black Hawks missed the playoffs in 1947 and were struggling again during the early part of the 1947–48 season when Bill Tobin decided that the only move—drastic as it was—had to be a trade and his most tradeable commodity was Max Bentley.

Curiously, when Tobin broached the subject of a *possible* deal involving Max, Doug, crushed as he was, suggested that it might be better for all concerned. "It might be the best thing for the two of us," said Doug.

Max was traded to the Maple Leafs and played brilliantly for one of the strongest sextets the league has known. Doug was not as fortunate. Despite Doug's game efforts along with those of Mosienko, the Chicago club remained essentially inept, and Doug was never to skate for another playoff team.

Douglas Wagner Bentley was born on September 3, 1916, in Delisle, Saskatchewan. Before reaching the NHL, he played on a team with four other Bentley brothers in Drumheller, Alberta. There were thirteen Bentley kids in all and their dad, Bill, had bought them all skates. They would skate on a backyard rink that Bill Bentley flooded behind the family farm.

The deal that sent Max to the Maple Leafs broke Bill Bentley's heart, and both brothers wondered if they would ever skate together on the same team. It seemed unlikely, especially after Doug retired in 1952. But a miracle of sorts happened during the 1953–54 season when New York Rangers' manager Frank Boucher persuaded the brothers to come out of retirement and skate for the Broadway Blueshirts. Boucher made his pitch to them during the summer of 1953.

The Bentleys were a sensation at their reunion. Before a crowd of more than 13,000 at Madison Square Garden, they teamed with Edgar Laprade to defeat the Boston Bruins and thrust the Rangers right into the playoff race. They continued to play well together down the homestretch, but the Rangers, like Black Hawks' teams of the past, were simply too weak and faltered at the end, missing the playoffs by a scant margin.

That season marked *finis* for both Bentleys in the NHL, although they continued to play organized hockey. Doug went back to coaching Saskatoon the next year, and Max joined him in 1954. Incredibly, Doug made a brief comeback in 1962 with the Los Angeles Blades of the Western Hockey League and then retired for good. He returned to his native Saskatchewan and died on November 24, 1972. He was elected to the Hockey Hall of Fame in 1964.

44

Frank Frederickson
(1926–1931)

Frank Frederickson's glorious hockey career nearly ended in the Mediterranean Sea.

Frederickson was being transferred from Egypt to Italy during World War I, when the transport on which he was a passenger was hit by a German torpedo. Frederickson, who was a member of the Royal Flying Corps (later the Royal Air Force), searched for an empty lifeboat but found none.

"Suddenly, I realized that I had left my violin in my bunk," Frederickson remembered. "My violin was very important to me. So, I ran back, got hold of it and gave it to one of the captains of another lifeboat and told him to take good care of it."

Before the ship went down Frederickson found a space on another lifeboat and, ultimately, was carried to safety. In time, he returned to Canada and resumed his hockey career.

Frank captained the Winnipeg Falcons team that won the Gold Medal in the 1920 Winter Olympics at Antwerp and later enjoyed a short but illustrious career as a professional.

He was a stylish center who scored forty-one goals in thirty games for Victoria during the 1922–23 season and helped that club win the Stanley Cup two years later. There have been better centers, to be sure, but not many with Frederickson's grace both on and off the ice.

Frank Frederickson was born in Winnipeg, Manitoba, in 1895. His parents came from Iceland and spoke only Icelandic in the house. Frank couldn't speak a word of English until he was six years old. Yet, when I interviewed him in 1968 his English was perfect.

At the time of Frederickson's youth, the Icelanders in Winnipeg were treated as a second-class minority group, and Frank found himself the target of insults when he would return home from school. During our interview, he recalled how he was able to find a safety valve in sports.

"My best outlet was hockey. I got my first pair of skates when I was five and had a great time learning to play. School came easy for me. After finishing grade eight I decided I ought to earn a living and got a job as an office boy in a law firm. This turned out to be an excellent move since the firms all sponsored hockey teams then so naturally we had one too. It was a seven-man team because in those days a rover was the seventh player, in addition to three forwards, two defensemen, and a goalkeeper.

"I played well and captured the attention of two of our attorneys. They took a great deal of personal interest in me, not just as a hockey player, and urged me to go back to

school. So in 1914 I enrolled at the University of Manitoba, took liberal arts courses, and a year later was named captain of the hockey team."

Not long after the outbreak of World War I, Frank enlisted in the 223rd Scandinavian Battalion, but when he got to England he switched to the Royal Flying Corps and remained an airman—miraculously surviving several close calls—until the end of the conflict.

Once, during an interview in his Vancouver living room, he told me this tale: "It took a year from the time the war ended before I could get back to Winnipeg. When I returned in 1919, a bunch of us led by Mike Goodman, the speed-skating champion of North America, and Slim Halter, a great big, gangling six-footer who was a beautiful stickhandler, organized the Falcon hockey team and applied for admission to the senior league.

"The leaders of that league wouldn't let us in because they claimed we weren't good enough to compete with teams like the Monarchs and Winnipegs. So we did the next best thing and organized our own league composed of such teams as Selkirk, which had "Bullet" Joe Simpson as captain. We later found out the reason we couldn't get in the senior league was because the players there were from well-to-do families and wanted no part of us. But they couldn't quite get away from us that easily. We finished in first place, then played the winners of the big league in a two-game series. In a terrific upset, we beat them in two games straight 14–2. We then defeated Lake-of-the-Woods, Head-of-the-Lakes, and Fort William, and went on to Toronto where we won the Allan Cup for the senior championship of Canada, beating the famed University of Toronto.

"That was quite a triumph because it qualified us to represent Canada in the 1920 Winter Olympics at Antwerp, Belgium—the first time ice hockey was ever included on the Olympics program.

"Winning the Olympic championship was quite a feather in our cap and gave us all a lot of publicity. I had the world at my feet but instead of returning immediately to Canada I was asked by the Icelandic government to go there to do some experimental flying. As it turned out, I became the first pilot of Icelandic extraction to fly in Iceland.

"I flew from May to September and had to give it up at that time because they couldn't get petrol supplies. Then I went to England to try and get some of the English concerns interested in flying to Iceland but I failed in that and returned to Canada, making a stop in Toronto.

"When I got there, Mayor Church entertained me and asked, 'Now that you're back, Frank, what do you want to do?' I told him I wanted to join the Canadian air force but didn't think I could get in because there were many senior officers ahead of me. Church was a wonderful guy and a very influential man; when I got home to Winnipeg there was a telegram advising me to report to camp for duty. So, in 1920 I joined the Canadian air force.

"For all intents and purposes it appeared that my career was set for years to come. Life is funny though and out of the blue I received a letter from Lester Patrick, the *Old Silver Fox* of hockey, who was in Victoria, British Columbia, where he had a team in the old Pacific Coast League. It was top-notch hockey and Lester offered me what was a substantial contract in those days—$2,500 for twenty-four games. I call it substantial because the rest of the boys were playing for $800 and $900. I couldn't resist the offer and so found myself right back in the middle of hockey again."

Although Frederickson did not play in the NHL as long as other members of the Hockey Hall of Fame, he was an eminent center in the years he played for Detroit, Boston, and Pittsburgh.

Following the conclusion of his playing career, he coached and managed Pittsburgh in 1930–31 and later returned to his home in Vancouver.

"I learned one important thing from hockey," said Frank, "and that is from cooperation and joint effort you can do an awful lot more than when you're just by yourself."

Frank remained a vigorous citizen even in retirement and followed the modern game of hockey with great interest. He died on May 28, 1979, a splendid human being and a worthy member of *Hockey's 100*.

45

Bill Durnan
(1943–1950)

During the latter part of the World War II years, and through 1947, you could not find a hockey expert who believed there was a better goaltender playing then Bill Durnan.

Canadian sportswriter Vincent Lunny expressed the prevailing sentiment in 1948, when he wrote the following appraisal: "It would be superfluous to say that Bill Durnan is the greatest netminder of the last twenty years and probably the greatest of all time. We'll accept that as an established fact."

What prevents Durnan from attaining a higher listing in *Hockey's 100* is his relatively brief big-league career. He came up the hard way, and was discovered late. Durnan played for the superb Canadiens during the 40s with Rocket Richard. He joined the Canadiens in 1943 and, stricken with a nervous ailment, tearfully retired in the spring of 1950, although he had again won the Vezina Trophy. But during his seven seasons with the Canadiens, he set new standards for goalkeeping excellence.

Guarding the Montreal net, Bill won the Vezina Trophy in 1944, 1945, 1946, 1947, 1949, and 1950. He was named to the First All-Star Team those same seasons.

During his tenure in Montreal, the Canadiens finished first four times and twice won the Stanley Cup, in the years 1943–44 and 1945–46.

The ability that made Durnan unique among goaltenders was the fact that he was ambidextrous. It was Steve Faulkner, who coached him at Westmoreland United who taught Bill that trick, which helped him become the best goaltender in the league. Faulkner showed Bill how to use his hands instead of relying solely on his stick and pads to block shots. Bill's switch was so deceptively quick that it fooled the opposing forwards.

Durnan became known as hockey's greatest "holler guy." With his deep voice booming, he advised, urged, and roared whenever the play was torrid around the Canadiens' end of the rink.

Big Bill (6'2", 200 pounds) had big hands and lightning reflexes. Few players scored hat tricks against Durnan. His keen analytical mind simply soaked up hockey intelligence, although he made no conscious effort to study the styles of opposing forwards.

Durnan was one of the most popular Canadiens among his teammates, as is evidenced by the fact that his forwards were often willing to sacrifice their opportunities to score to help him. His teammates often thought of him and his bids for records when they might not have given another goaltender a thought. If they were leading by three or four goals late in the third period, one of the players would often say to coach Dick Irvin: "We've got enough goals to win now, Skipper. Is it all right if we just backcheck and help Bill with his shutout?"

Bill was also a great team player. Irvin gave him the responsibility very few goal-tenders ever had, by naming him captain of the Montreal Canadiens.

Durnan broke into the NHL in 1943, and despite his short career, he established many records. He won the Vezina Trophy in 1944, becoming the first rookie ever to win it. In the process, he also became the first player to win it four consecutive years, spanning 1944–47.

Turk Broda of the Toronto Maple Leafs won it the following season in 1948, but Durnan won it again the next two seasons before his sudden retirement.

In 1944–45, the Montreal Canadiens placed five players on the First Team All-Stars. It was the first time that had ever happened. The team consisted of Emile Bouchard on defense; Elmer Lach, center; Maurice Richard, right wing; Toe Blake, left wing; and Bill Durnan as goaltender. Dick Irvin was named coach.

It was during the 1948–49 season that Bill set the NHL modern record for the longest shutout sequence by holding his opponents scoreless for 309 minutes and 21 seconds with four consecutive shutouts. That was the longest shutout sequence in eighteen years.

Durnan had ten shutouts in the 1948–49 season in sixty games, and it was in 1949 that he was the runner-up to Sid Abel (Detroit Red Wings) in the voting for the Hart Trophy, awarded to the most valuable player in the league.

During his entire career, which spanned 383 regular season games, he registered thirty-four shutouts and had a 2.35 goals against average. In forty-five playoff games, he shut out the opposition in two games and his goals against average was 2.20.

William Durnan was born opposite a city dump in Toronto on January 22, 1915, the younger of two brothers. Bill was nine when he tried out for a hockey team of the West-moreland United Church. The boys were grouped according to weight. Bill was a big kid, and it was felt he was too heavy to compete with the fellows on the forward line, so he was moved into the nets. Westmoreland won five city championships in the six years that Durnan played in the nets for them.

In 1930–31, Bill joined the North Toronto Juniors, a farm club for the Junior Marl-boros, which was a farm team for the Maple Leafs. Red Burnett, a hockey writer for *The Toronto Daily Star* recommended Bill to the coach of the Sudbury Ontario Junior team. They invited him to play on their team the following year.

Durnan was considered a hot prospect while he was playing in Sudbury, as he helped them win the Memorial Cup in 1931. The Leafs were impressed and signed an agreement with him. He was only twenty years old.

Before the start of the 1932 season, Bill and a friend were wrestling on Wasaga Beach and Bill twisted a knee. This sidelined him for a season, and it was then that the Leafs dropped him as a prospect. It was at this point that Bill vowed he'd play pro hockey.

His pride was really hurt by Toronto's treatment of him. "I was disillusioned and fig-ured if that was the kind of treatment I was to get, then hell, I didn't want any part of it."

During the 1934–35 season, Bill ended up playing in the T and Y Mercantile League in Toronto.

In 1936, Bill took a job as a millwright in a gold mining mill in Kirkland Lake in northern Ontario. Between shifts, he played with the Kirkland Lake Blue Devils. For four seasons, Bill played for the Blue Devils. In 1940, the Blue Devils won the Allan Cup, emblematic of the Senior championship of Canada, with Bill as their goaltender.

After the success of the 1940 season, Bill moved to Montreal to tend goal for the Montreal Royals, the top amateur club in the Quebec Senior League, a Canadien farm operation. At this point, he had no plans of becoming a professional hockey player, as he was still smarting from the snub he received from Toronto.

Bill was a man of few illusions, and he would have been satisfied if he spent the rest of his career with the Royals. He was earning a comfortable living with his part-time job in the accounting department of the Canadian Car and Foundry. However, his boss was Len Peto, who was also a director of the Montreal Canadiens.

Peto pressured him into turning professional. Durnan said no, the incident with Toronto still burned in his mind. He did not want to play pro hockey. Peto insisted. Bill asked for the then huge sum of $4200. Surprisingly enough to Bill, the Canadiens' management agreed.

Bill tried out for the Canadiens in the autumn of 1943. He was scheduled to be the goaltender in a preseason exhibition game. The average rookie would have been estatic to receive an opportunity such as this. However, Durnan was not your average rookie. He was twenty-nine years old, and it didn't matter to him whether or not he played pro hockey.

His Montreal team was in the provincial softball finals, and Bill was their star pitcher. He turned down the net assignment, unconcerned that it might endanger his NHL career. At his own expense, Bill instead went back to Montreal and pitched his team to the Quebec championship.

Coach Irvin persuaded Durnan that his place was in goal. In 1943, his first season with the Flying Frenchmen, remembering the advice of Faulkner, he used his hands in his goaltending and seldom let a rebound escape. He emerged as the premier goaltender that year and won the Vezina Trophy. In the process, he helped his team beat the Chicago Black Hawks in four straight games to win the Stanley Cup.

However, Bill had trouble with the fans in Montreal. The Canadiens were in a slump in 1947 and the Forum crowd began chanting: "We want Bibeault!" (Paul Bibeault, the Canadiens' goaltender before Durnan.) "They booed me and made me feel six inches high," he said. All this despite the fact that he had won the Vezina Trophy.

Hockey started to get rough for him toward the end of the 40s. Durnan had broken his hand earlier, and even though it had mended, his entire arm would ache whenever he caught the puck. He was going to be thirty-five years old in an era where the goalie played the entire season without an alternate and with no mask for protection.

The 1949–50 season was the turning point for Bill Durnan. It was the beginning of the end for him. There was little fun left for him in the game. A lot of his friends were leaving—or had already gone. The old camaraderie was missing.

In January of 1950, he told Dick Irvin he would be retiring at the end of the season. He felt that his reflexes were slow. Although he had won the Vezina Trophy five times and heard countless writers proclaim him the best goaltender ever, the most he had ever made in a season was $10,500. He wasn't educated and he had two girls to raise. He began to worry.

The end came quickly. In March 1950, the Canadiens would be playing the Rangers in the first round of the playoffs. Montreal had finished second, and the Rangers had finished fourth. Naturally, the Canadiens were favored. Quickly the Rangers won three games in a row from the Canadiens.

The nerves and pressures began building up. It was then he decided to retire.

Before the fourth game, Irvin asked him to go in and tell the players it was Bill's decision to quit, not Irvin's. In a poignant scene in the dressing room, a tearful Bill Durnan handed young Gerry McNeil his stick. McNeil, the successor, took the stick from the master, crying also. It was a very emotional scene.

The Canadiens with Gerry McNeil in goal went out and won the fourth game. The Rangers won the fifth game and took the series. "A lot of people thought it was a nervous breakdown," Bill said, "but it wasn't. To this day, people won't believe me. What the hell, I'm quitting and this is as good a time as any. If the kid goes in and wins, well great, it's a terrific start for him."

Durnan ended his professional career in the middle of the 1950 playoffs, a victim of frayed nerves. Although he played but seven seasons, his outstanding play was remembered and rewarded, as he was inducted into the Hockey Hall of Fame in 1964.

On October 31, 1972 in Toronto at the age of fifty-seven, Bill Durnan died in North York General Hospital. He had been in ill health for some time, having been afflicted with arthritis for years. He left his wife, a son, and two daughters.

Durnan could pass for the greatest goaltender of all time had he endured the test of time and played more seasons. Although he played only seven seasons, he raised the art of goaltending to new heights and in doing so, he more than earned his berth in *Hockey's 100*.

46

Brad Park
(1968–1985)

There has been only one missing link in Brad Park's glorious hockey necklace—a Stanley Cup ring.

The consummate contemporary defenseman, Park was the master of the hip check, as well as an exceptionally accurate shooter who could develop an attack and then retreat in time to intercept an enemy counterthrust.

His game was embellished by a fluid skating style that often underplayed his speed, as well as a storehouse of power that proved deceptive because of his relatively modest size.

It was Park's misfortune never to have skated for a genuine powerhouse. He was the ice general and captain of a modestly successful New York Rangers team in the late 1960s and early 1970s but never tasted the Stanley Cup champagne. After his trade to the Boston Bruins, he played for a team already reporting a decline, but the team remained competitive because of Park's combative play.

Because he played in the shadow of some of the all-time great backliners, Park may not have received the media attention he merited, but the experts took due note of his excellence. Brad was voted to the First All-Star Team in 1970, 1972, 1974, 1976, and 1978. He made the Second Team in 1971 and 1973.

More than anything, Park was a refreshing player to watch and, in some ways, a throwback to an earlier more robust era of defense play.

"One of the glorious aspects of sports," said author Roger Kahn, "is having your spirits renewed by Brad Park."

Park's own spirits occasionally have been deflated by Bobby Orr's presence in the same league. A defenseman like Park, Orr is regarded by many as the most-holy-blessed-be-he in hockey since the invention of the puck. Playing second-fiddle to a superstar like Orr can't be the easiest thing in the world, but Park made the adjustment.

"If I have to be number two," Brad explained, "I might as well be number two to a super player like Orr."

Park had been super, or close to it, ever since he became a Ranger in 1968–69. An instant regular, he learned the ropes, took punches in the chops, and scored goals almost immediately. His career almost came to an end with similar suddenness.

The Rangers were playing the Red Wings, and dangerous Gordie Howe was still playing for the Detroit sextet. Park was guarding Howe, notorious for his great strength, durability, and viciousness. "Watch Howe!" Brad was warned. "He likes to club you with his elbows."

Park remained vigilant and when Howe confronted him, the young Ranger body-checked the veteran cleanly, depositing him on the ice. But then Brad became less vigilant and a few minutes later Howe's stick flashed, cracking into Park's Adam's apple.

For an instant, it appeared as if the blow might have ended his career. Brad fell, unable to swallow, gasping for breath. Ranger trainer Frank Paice dashed across the ice and calmed the kid until he was fully revived and able to skate off the ice under his own steam.

As Brad passed Howe, he turned to his assailant and rasped, "You sonofagun. It could have been my eye. From now on, when you're skating around me, you damn well better keep your head up."

The flak was never heavier than in the spring of 1974 when the Rangers met Philadelphia's ferocious Flyers in the semifinal round of the playoffs. Dave Schultz, number one hitter on the Flyers, made a point of zeroing in on Park early in the third game of the Cup round. First, he bodied Brad heavily in the corner and then, as play swung up-ice, Schultz charged into Park a second time, and knocked him down, straddling the semi-defenseless Ranger and pouring punches at his face.

The Flyers' theory was simplicity itself—beat up on the best Ranger (Park) and Philadelphia would grind out a series victory. "You can't be a hitting team sixty minutes a game," countered Park. "It's exhausting."

But it was just as exhausting for Park, mostly because his Ranger teammates failed to generate as much zest as he did. As a result, the Flyers edged New York, four games to three, and advanced to the Stanley Cup finals.

Because the Rangers failed to win the Stanley Cup during Park's golden years in New York, he became the target of the Madison Square Garden boo birds and eventually was part of one of the biggest trades in NHL history. On November 7, 1975, Park, who was then the Rangers' captain, and Jean Ratelle, the club's foremost playmaker, were traded to the Boston Bruins for Phil Esposito and Carol Vadnais.

Park, who had been openly critical of the Bruins while playing in New York, now found himself in the enemy camp. He made the adjustment with ease and, under coach Don Cherry's guidance, seemed to be a better defenseman in Boston than he had ever been with the Rangers.

Douglas Bradford Park was born July 6, 1948, in Toronto, and learned the game on the city rinks. For many years, Brad's size was against him, but he was also tough. Tough enough to land a spot on the Toronto Junior Marlboros, a club that normally fed gifted stickhandlers to the NHL.

Normally, Park would have been graduated to the Toronto Maple Leafs, but the NHL had instituted a seventeen-year-old draft rule, which enabled the Rangers to land Park. To say the least, Brad was stunned.

When Brad arrived at the Rangers' training camp in September 1968, he was not even remotely considered for a position on the New York varsity. The Rangers had a well-rounded defense and also had been grooming a tall, well-built prospect named Al Hamilton as the fifth defenseman. But with each scrimmage Park out-played Hamilton and the Rangers' braintrust was faced with a dilemma. It was "solved" by sending Park to the minors and keeping Hamilton with the big club. But Brad played too well to be kept down, and Hamilton couldn't cut it with the Rangers so the call went out to Park and he never looked back.

In no time at all, he was being compared favorably to the inimitable Orr. Some observers claimed that Park was better defensively than Orr.

Injuries severely braked the careers of both Park and Orr, but it was the latter who was ultimately forced to retire prematurely while Park, plagued with knee problems, continued to play, although at a more modest pace.

"In some ways," said Don Cherry, "Brad was a better player after all the injuries because he began to pace himself. He wouldn't take as many chances on offense and that meant he was in better position on defense so he was caught out of position much less."

The pain had so troubled Brad that it was freely predicted that he would retire by 1980, but he kept coming back and when the 1981–82 campaign began he was back on the Bruins' blue line playing as smart a game as he ever had in his life.

Unfortunately for him, a number of younger, flashier defensemen such as Denis Potvin of the New York Islanders and Randy Carlyle of the Pittsburgh Penguins were scoring more than Park, although not necessarily playing better defense. The high-scoring defensemen got the accolades and Brad, as he had been during the Orr era, was relegated to the shadows.

But the purists remained appreciative of his skills, particularly his "submarine bodycheck," in which he'd thrust his hip into the path of onrushing attackers, catapulting them upside down to the ice. In 1977 and 1978, Park was one of the primary reasons the Bruins reached the Stanley Cup finals.

It was a case of close, but no cigar; the story of Park's hockey-playing life despite a remarkably efficient career.

The story remained the same as Park became a wealthier man, this time with the Detroit Red Wings with whom he finished his career. Park played adequately despite his failing legs and finally called it a career in 1985. Brad's ill-luck continued after he was named coach of the Red Wings in December 1985. His experience was short-lived. Brad was dropped at the end of the season and spent the immediate future as a television analyst. Brad finally obtained the recognition he deserved in June 1988, when he was elected to the Hockey Hall of Fame.

47

Turk Broda
(1936–1952)

The Turk was fat and funny. And maybe that is the reason why he was often bypassed when the cream of the goalkeeping fraternity was discussed.

Had he been a tragic figure like Terry Sawchuk, a worrier like Glenn Hall, or an eccentric like Jacques Plante, Broda might receive more serious consideration, but the image of Toronto's fabulous fat man always was light and upbeat—except when it came to the big games.

While he is fondly remembered for winning his "Battle of the Bulge" campaign against excess poundage, Broda is also revered by historians for his impeccable ability to excel in the most critical moments.

It, therefore, is not surprising that he twice won the Vezina Trophy for having the best goals against average, was twice a First Team All-Star, once a Second Team All-Star, and played for five Stanley Cup-winning teams.

Broda, along with center Syl Apps, formed the cornerstone of manager Conn Smythe's rebuilding effort when Toronto began its ascent to dizzying heights in the 1940s. The Cup win in 1942 was the first for Broda. Following service in World War II, he returned to help Toronto win an unprecedented three consecutive Cups (1947, 1948, 1949) and still another in 1951.

Turk had the ideal disposition for a goaltender and was a superb team player on a club sprinkled with scintillating characters.

It could be said that Bill Durnan, who starred in goal for Montreal during the same era, was a better textbook goalie than Broda and produced superior averages, but Durnan couldn't match the Turk in Stanley Cups nor longevity. Broda became a big-leaguer before Durnan arrived and outlasted him by two seasons.

The records indicate that Broda's best season—statistically speaking—was 1940–41 when he rang up a 2.06 goals against average. But the vintage Broda appeared during the 1942 playoffs when he starred in the seventh (Cup-winning) game of the finals and in 1947–48 when he powered the Leafs to a first place finish, won the Vezina, and then, surrounded by one of the most formidable teams in history, annexed the Stanley Cup.

Yet, many Torontonians prefer the memory of November 1949 when Smythe demanded that a number of his stars trim their waistlines in a hurry. The antifat edict made headlines throughout North America.

Although Smythe singled out defenseman Garth Boesch and forwards Howie Meeker, Harry Watson, Vic Lynn, and Sid Smith for his blasts, the key target of Smythe's ire was his longtime goaltending stalwart, Broda.

Smythe's opening gun in the "Battle of the Bulge" was a demand that his players reduce their weight to specified limits. Broda, who weighed 197 pounds, was ordered to lose 7 pounds. To underline the seriousness of his offensive, Smythe promptly called up reserve goalie Gil Mayer from his Pittsburgh farm team. It was Tuesday and he was giving Turk until Saturday to fulfill the demand. "I'm taking Broda out of the nets," Smythe said, "and he's not going back until he shows some common sense."

Smythe's outburst reverberated across Canada and parts of the United States, and soon "The Battle of the Bulge" became a cause *célèbre*. Neutral observers regarded Turk's tussle with the scales as a huge joke, win or lose, but to the Toronto boss it was no joke. None of the Leafs were particularly amused either.

After one day of severe dieting, Turk trimmed his weight from 197 to 193, and all of Canada seemed to breathe easier. Smythe had set the final weigh-in for Saturday afternoon, just before the evening match against the New York Rangers at Maple Leaf Gardens. He refused to divulge what specific action he would take against Broda or the other Leafs if they did not pass muster, but he suggested that it would not be lenient. Turk moved forward and gingerly placed his feet on the platform. The numbers finally settled— just under 190 pounds. He had made it! Turk was delighted, and Smythe was doubly enthusiastic because he regarded his goaltender with paternal affection. "There may be better goalies around somewhere," said the manager, "but there's no greater sportsman than the Turkey. If the Rangers score on him tonight, I should walk out and hand him a malted milk, just to show I'm not trying to starve him to death."

That night, Maple Leafs Gardens was packed with 13,359 Turk fans, and when Broda skated out for the opening face-off, the Gardens' regimental band swung into "Happy Days Are Here Again" and followed it with a chorus of "She's Too Fat for Me."

Referee George Gravel dropped the puck to start the game, and the Rangers immediately swarmed in on Broda. This time, however, he was the Turk of old.

Broda's slimmer teammates couldn't beat goalie Chuck Rayner of the Rangers, however, and the first period ended with the teams tied 0–0. It was the same story in the second period, as each team desperately probed for an opening. The Rangers got their big break late in the middle period when Pentti Lund bisected the Toronto defense and moved within easy scoring distance of Broda. Lund found his opening and fired the puck mightily, but somehow Broda thrust his pad in the way and deflected the rubber out of danger. The fans rose and toasted Turk with a standing ovation, and when the second period ended, the contest remained a scoreless deadlock.

Early in the third period, the Leafs were attempting a change in lines when Howie Meeker and Vic Lynn, two of the marked fat men, combined to feed a lead pass to Max Bentley, who normally wouldn't have been on the ice with them. Bentley moved through the Rangers' checkers and unleashed a steaming shot that flew past Rayner. Later in the period another fat man, Harry Watson, skimmed a pass to Bill Ezinicki, who also beat Rayner.

Now all eyes were on the clock as it ticked toward the twenty-minute mark and the end of the game. With only a minute remaining, Broda still had a shutout. The countdown began: ten, nine, eight, seven, six, five…the crowd was roaring as if the Leafs had won the Stanley Cup…four, three, two, one. The game was over; Turk dove for the puck and gathered it in. It was his symbolic trophy for winning the Battle of the Bulge.

Walter Broda was born May 15, 1914, in the wheat country of western Canada. His home town, Brandon, sent many a young hockey player to the professionals, but few appeared less likely to make it than the portly young netminder. Although his skating was poor and his reflexes lacked the spark of a thinner player, Broda earned a spot on the school team—by default. Luckily, his principal began working privately with his student, teaching him the finer points of goaltending, until Broda's game began to improve. He soon caught on with a local club called the Brandon North Stars and played goal for them in a one-game playoff with the Elmwood Millionaires. Broda's club lost 11–1! In 1930–31, he somehow managed to take over the goalkeeping for the Manitoba Hydros, in the Brandon Commercial League. He played so capably in an intermediate league during that time that he was named to its all-star team.

Broda got his break after trying out and failing his audition with the Brandon Native Sons, a top junior entry. Although the manager had rejected him, the Native Sons' boss remembered Turk. He called on Broda that spring when the regular Native Sons' goaltender was ruled overage in a last-minute discovery, and the junior club desperately needed a goaltender.

Amused rather than annoyed at the sudden turnabout by the Native Sons, Turk accepted their offer to take over the goaltending during the Memorial Cup playoffs for the junior championship of Canada.

Brandon swept the series and Broda was at his best, as always would be the case, in the most excruciating moments. It was only a matter of time before he would make his way up to the ranks of the pros. Conn Smythe signed him in 1936 for what turned out to be one of the best moves ever made by one of hockey's most insightful entrepreneurs.

After his playing career, Broda took a number of coaching jobs in both amateur and professional ranks, the last of which was with Quebec in the American Hockey League. He died on October 17, 1972, much too soon, at the age of fifty-eight. The Turk will always be remembered as a happy performer but most of all as a clutch champion.

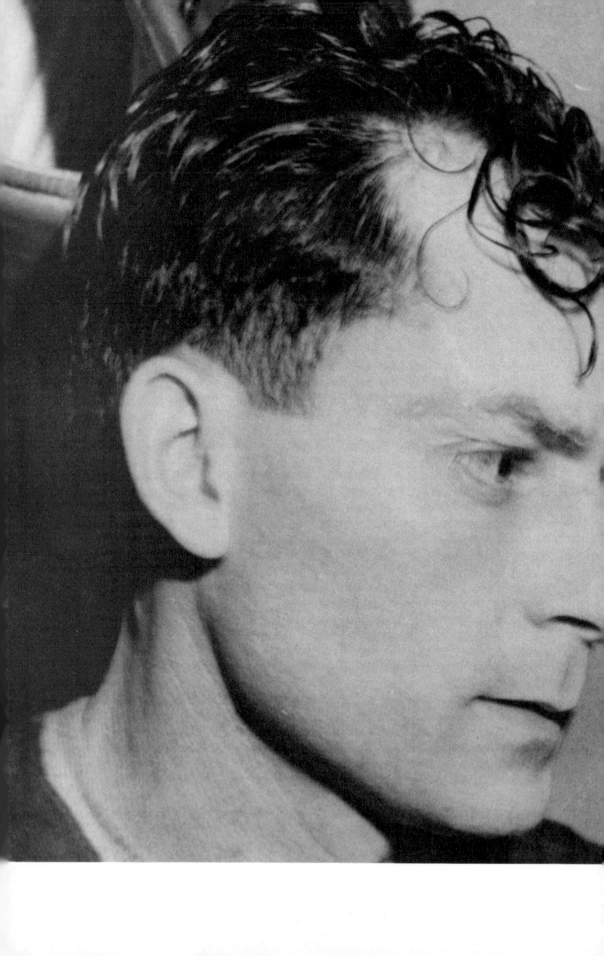

48

Bryan Hextall
(1936–1948)

On the night of April 14, 1940, when Mackenzie King was prime minister of Canada and Franklin Delano Roosevelt was president of the United States, a red light flashed behind goalie Turk Broda of the Toronto Maple Leafs.

The time was 2:07 of the first sudden-death overtime, and the capacity crowd was virtually silent as right wing Bryan Hextall of the New York Rangers waved his stick in the air. He had scored the goal that won the Stanley Cup for the Broadway Blueshirts.

Hextall did not know it at the time, but with each year the goal that gave his Rangers a 3–2 victory over the Maple Leafs has grown in stature until it has become a veritable legend in Manhattan, simply because the Rangers have not won another Stanley Cup since the man called Hex beat the pudgy Toronto goalie. For more than four decades, Rangers fans have had to savor that night; a night that still provides solace for a frustrated Ranger fan's heart.

But Hextall did more than just win a Stanley Cup for the New Yorkers. "He was," said Herb Goren, who covered the Rangers for *The New York Sun*, "the hardest bodychecking forward I had seen in more than forty years of watching hockey."

Hex could hit and he could score. He led the National Hockey League in scoring in 1942, was a First Team All-Star in 1940, 1941, and 1942, made the Second Team in 1943, and played on one first-place team.

The line of Hextall, completed by center Phil Watson and left wing Lynn Patrick, was among the most formidable of its time and might have established itself among the NHL's greatest ever were it not for the outbreak of World War II, the enlistment of Patrick into the armed forces, and the ultimate break up of the unit.

Bryan Aldwyn Hextall was born July 31, 1913, in Grenfell, Saskatchewan. He originally commanded attention during the early 1930s while playing for the Vancouver Lions of the Western Hockey League. The Rangers noticed him after Bryan led the Lions to a first-place finish. Two years later, he was on Broadway at a time when the Rangers' patriarch, Lester Patrick, was dismantling an aging club and rebuilding it with youth. Hextall would soon be teamed with such powerful skaters as Alf Pike, Babe Pratt, Art Coulter, and Alex Shibicky.

When Frank Boucher took over as Rangers' coach in 1940, the Hextall-Patrick-Watson line became the hottest unit in the league, and Hextall was regarded as the best all-round player of the trio.

Unquestionably, Hextall's career was braked by the intrusion of World War II. Many of his teammates returned to the Blueshirts following the cessation of hostilities and discovered that they had lost their touch. Yet, in 1946–47 Bryan managed to crack the then coveted twenty-goal circle. But the following season his production plummeted to only eight goals, and he called it a career in the spring of 1948.

Hextall had accumulated 187 goals and 362 points in 449 games over eleven seasons with the Rangers. "I scored 20 goals for seven straight years," Hextall recalled proudly. "Twenty goals was a big thing then."

He won the NHL scoring title in 1941–42 with twenty-four goals and fifty-six points in forty-eight games. He was league scoring leader and among the top ten scorers on four occasions. And he remembers his Stanley Cup-winning score as if it happened ten minutes ago.

"I took a pass from Dutch Hiller and Phil Watson," Hextall remembered. "The puck came out from behind the net and I took a backhand shot to put it past Broda."

After his retirement, Bryan started a lumberyard and hardware business but his love for hunting inspired him to open a commercial shooting lodge near his home in Poplar Point, Manitoba.

He proudly watched his sons Bryan, Jr. and Dennis, make their way up to the NHL. Each of them had a stint, albeit brief, with the Rangers. Then, hard luck took its toll on the old warrior.

The Hextall name made further impact in the late 1980s when Bryan's grandson, Ron, became a star goalie with the Philadelphia Flyers. But Bryan, Sr. was the original ace of the family and belongs among *Hockey's 100*.

49

Tim Horton
(1952–1974)

Tim Horton had amazing strength. He was a compactly built 5'10", 180 pound man—one of the strongest players in the NHL. In spite of the fact that he was one of the most feared men in the game, his penalties averaged to only one minor penalty in every two games.

Tim was not a dirty player. Horton could hand out thumping bodychecks if the need called for it, but he preferred his own method of leaning on the opposition and steering him (along with the puck) into the closest corner. He would get a strangle-hold on a player, and they'd end up on the ice, their breath squeezed out of them. "I tried him once," Derek Sanderson said, "and he just put the bearhug on me. After a while I heard a cracking noise, and figured it was my ribs going, one by one. Never again." "What Tim was especially good at was breaking up fights," said Bob Haggert, the Toronto Maple Leafs' trainer during the 60s when, with Horton on the rearguard, they won the Stanley Cup four times in six seasons. Horton had only one weakness, according to Punch Imlach, "He hasn't got a mean bone in his body. If he had, they'd have to make a rule against him."

Number 7 of Toronto was a professional. He did not attempt to be sensational. He was so effective because he was taken for granted. He played with no con or showmanship that less talented players must resort to in order to win over fans. He had few peers who possessed his all-around ability. Horton was a superb skater, an adept playmaker with a deadly slapshot, and few players could match him when it came to lugging the puck out of his own territory to ease the pressure.

Swift skater that he was, along with his slapshot, he was awesome at the point. He had, in fact, been a pioneer in utilizing the slapshot in hockey. The coach of the Soviet National Hockey Team saw Horton in 1964 and felt that Tim was the most outstanding player he saw.

In 1965, King Clancy (who coached him at Pittsburgh, and later in Toronto) had this to say about Tim. "We were going nowhere fast. Then Punch Imlach moved Horton from defense to right wing—and the team started to move. I think Horton is as powerful or maybe stronger than Chicago's Bobby Hull."

Horton's accomplishments were many. At the time of his tragic death, he had played in 1,446 games (behind only Gordie Howe with 1,687 and Alex Delvecchio with 1,549). He had scored 115 goals and accumulated 403 assists for 518 total points. He played on four Stanley Cup championship teams, all with Toronto, in 1962, 1963, 1964, and 1967. His totals for sixteen Stanley Cup playoffs (encompassing 126 games) were eleven

goals and thirty-nine assists for a total of fifty points. Tim was elected to the First All-Star Team three times (1963–64, 1967–68, 1968–69) and was an alternate three times (1953–54, 1962–63, 1966–67).

In the playoffs in 1961–62, he set two records with three goals and thirteen assists against the Rangers and Chicago. In 1964, he was runner-up to Pierre Pilote for the Norris Trophy.

It was in 1968–69, however, that Horton had his finest season. He scored eleven goals and had twenty-nine assists and again made the First All-Star Team. He also won the J.P. Bickell Memorial Cup as the Most Valuable Maple Leaf and again finished second in balloting for the Norris Trophy, this time to Bobby Orr.

Horton also holds the all-time NHL regular-season penalty-minute record, having played in 1,446 games (twenty-four seasons) with 1,611 penalty minutes, averaging to only 1.11 minutes penalty time per game. He also holds the club record with Toronto for the longest consecutive game streak spanning from February 11, 1961 to February 4, 1968.

Before the arrival of the great Bobby Orr, Tim was on center stage alone among all of the NHL defensemen. Even at the age of forty-three, while he was a Sabre, he was the only defenseman currently playing (besides Orr) to have scored more than 100 goals. He was also the only other defenseman (besides Orr) to be named to six All-Star teams.

Myles Gilbert Horton was born in Cochrane, Ontario, on January 12, 1930, the eldest of two brothers. He played his early hockey there. In 1945, his family moved to Sudbury. It was there he won a hockey scholarship to St. Michaels in Toronto because of his outstanding play during his high school career. He was a junior "A" player beginning in 1947 for two years while being coached by Joe Primeau (who later became his mentor with Toronto). Tim was a fierce competitor as a teenager playing in the Junior A division of the Ontario Hockey Association, where he oddly enough received 137 minutes in penalties in his first season while also making the All-Star Team.

Undecided if he would turn pro, he made the decision in 1949 to sign a contract with Pittsburgh. At that time, Pittsburgh was a Toronto farm club. During his three seasons with the club, he helped Pittsburgh win one Calder Cup victory, and in the process, earned a berth for himself on the AHL All-Star Team. In 192 games, he had 358 minutes in penalties. Tim spent three seasons with Pittsburgh and was then called up to Toronto.

Toward the end of 1954–55 season, the Maple Leafs were convinced they had found a superstar in Tim Horton. All that changed one night in the Garden, when Bill Gadsby of the New York Rangers body-checked Tim and dumped him to the ice. The end result was a broken tibia and fibula of Tim's right leg and a fractured jaw. The cast wasn't removed until July, and from then until the 1955–56 training camp, he concerned himself with the recuperation process. When Horton finally got back into action, he was not the same player as before. He had no zip or swerve. Horton played in only thirty-five games. The following season he played in sixty-seven games. The next year held promise again, but he suffered a groin injury that cut down on his effectiveness. King Clancy felt that subconsciously Tim was protecting that leg.

It was in 1964, after Horton had been a pro for fourteen seasons that his star began to rise. After years of injuries and warming the bench, being overshadowed by names such as Bob Goldham and Red Kelly, he began to emerge as the leader of the Maple Leafs. Slowly, but surely, Horton became the backbone of the team.

Tim was also involved in many business ventures, including "Tim Horton's Drive-In" and a car business in North Bay that his brother Jerry ran. Tim also saw his doughnut chain grow to thirty-three stores. Because of his success with that franchise, he announced in 1970 that he would be retiring from professional hockey to devote himself full time to his thriving doughnut business.

There was also the matter of money. Tim wanted $85,000. The Leafs felt that they needed him for their chance to make the playoffs but did not want to pay him that amount. They talked him out of that demand for a reported $80,000, and a chunk of money for "certain considerations." However, it was clear that Tim would not figure into the Maple Leafs' long-range plans, which included rebuilding with younger players.

However, the New York Rangers needed someone like Tim Horton. Brad Park and Jim Neilson were injured. A player like Horton could make the difference between winning the Stanley Cup or another year of frustration for the Rangers.

On March 4, 1970, Tim Horton was traded to the Rangers in exchange for "players to be named later." After eighteen years and 1,185 games with Toronto, Tim was no longer a Maple Leaf. However, his statistics spoke for themselves. He had scored 106 goals and 348 assists and missed only seven games with them in his last eight seasons. He made the All-Star Team six times. Tim joined the Rangers on March 4, 1970, against Detroit.

After his departure from the Rangers in 1971, Tim was drafted by the Pittsburgh Penguins, now under his old friend and ex-teammate, Red Kelly. After suffering a broken ankle and separated shoulder in 1972, Tim announced again he would retire, and when Pittsburgh left him off their protected list, the Buffalo Sabres and Imlach purchased him for $40,000. It was Imlach who made the sales pitch that Tim couldn't refuse. The money was right, and Tim felt Imlach was right in feeling that he had one year left.

Tim Horton was one of the most popular of all hockey players. Unfortunately, his career was cut short by a tragic accident. On Thursday, February 21, 1974, Horton was on his way back to Buffalo from Maple Leaf Gardens when he was involved in a one-car crash on Queen Elizabeth Way at St. Catharines. He died instantly. Tim Horton was only forty-four years old.

The hockey world was stunned. Frank Mahovlich, who played ten years with Horton said, "Steady. I never knew a player so steady. No flash, no polish, all hard work."

The Toronto president, Harold Ballard said, "There was never a stronger player in the league, although he never used it to great excess. Hockey has lost a great competitor. He lived as a star and died as a star."

Punch Imlach honored him by saying, "I think Horton, more than any other one player, was the key to those glory days," referring to the great Stanley Cup years of the Maple Leafs.

Every year the Buffalo Sabres Fan Club presents an Unsung Hero Award to the Sabre player who worked the hardest without gaining the recognition of some of the more flamboyant stars. After Tim's death, in honor of his style, never flashy—just hard work, they renamed the award the "Tim Horton Award."

The Buffalo Sabres retired the Number 2 sweater he wore.

One can only guess how much longer this remarkable, robust, and intelligent defenseman might have played. But this much we know. In his twenty-four seasons with the NHL, he was a winner, who more than qualifies for *Hockey's 100*.

50

Art Coulter
(1931–1942)

The last New York Rangers' team to win the Stanley Cup was the 1939–40 edition, and anyone who had the good fortune to watch those Broadway Blueshirts in action would concede that bustling, rawboned Art Coulter, captain of that gloriously gifted club, provided the essential glue that kept it together.

When Rangers' manager Lester Patrick obtained the strapping defenseman from the Chiacgo Black Hawks in exchange for an established favorite, Earl Seibert, the deal surprised the press and dismayed a number of fans. In the months immediately following the deal, it appeared as if Patrick had goofed. Coulter's play was average, at best, and quite often less than that. But Frank Boucher, the Rangers' popular center and Patrick's confidant, had an insight into Coulter's character and requested a meeting with Patrick.

"I asked Lester what was wrong between him and Art," Boucher recalled, "and he said he didn't seem to be able to get through to him. I suggested that Art, being a man of tall pride, should be made captain of the team. If Lester did this and took Art into his confidence I was convinced the change would benefit Coulter psychologically."

Patrick agreed and the move seemed to be a tonic to the new Ranger. In no time at all, Coulter became a mountain of strength behind the New York blue line. He was a Second Team All-Star in 1938, 1939, and 1940. Coulter also was a force behind the Rangers' first place team in 1941–42, the last time the New Yorkers finished atop the National Hockey League.

Tall and muscular, without a trace of fat, Coulter was teamed on defense with Lester Patrick's bruising son, Murray, also known as Muzz. Any forward who attempted to bisect that defense was guaranteed a surplus of black-and-blue marks.

As tough as Coulter and Patrick were on the ice, they were sweethearts in civilian clothes. Both enjoyed the good life of Broadway and Art, in particular, had a reputation as a free spender.

In those days during the Great Depression, it was a rule on the Rangers that the players traveled in groups of four in taxis and one of them was named "cab captain," in charge of the fares. Coulter was one of those "cab captains."

One day, after the Rangers had completed a road trip, Patrick invited all his cab captains into his office so that he could review the various receipts that the players were required to obtain from the taxi drivers. Patrick was unmoved as he noted the receipts ranging from $6.00 to $8.00, but he did a double take when Coulter handed him a chit that totaled $12.75.

"Art," Patrick inquired, "why is your bill so much larger than the others?"

"Well, Lester," Coulter replied, "you've told us that we're in the big leagues now, so I tip like a big-leaguer."

Patrick didn't blink an eyelash. "That's very commendable, Art," he shot back, "but I don't know if the Rangers can afford big tippers like you."

Art chuckled. "Okay, Lester. You have nothing to worry about. I resign my captaincy."

According to journalist Eric Whitehead, who wrote *The Patricks, Hockey's Royal Family*, Coulter retained the captain's "C" on his jersey. This permitted Art to play a part in an extraordinary Rangers conference held the night before the Broadway skaters annexed the Stanley Cup at Maple Leaf Gardens in Toronto.

Whitehead described it thusly: "The Blues had finished three points behind Boston in the league race, had ousted the Bruins in the first playoff round, and now had the Toronto Maple Leafs down three games to two in the final round. The superb goaltending of veteran Davey Kerr and a strong defense anchored by Babe Pratt and Ott Heller had been the principal factors in getting the Blues this far, and now a win in the upcoming sixth game in Toronto with the Leafs would wrap it up."

Frank Boucher, who had become the Rangers' coach, invited his players to the beer parlor of the Ford Hotel. While this may have seemed an unusual place for a team meeting, the gregarious Boucher figured it would set a mellow tone during an anxious time.

"Captain Coulter opened with a toast," wrote Whitehead, "coach Boucher responded by raising his ale glass, there was a rousing 'hear...hear...' from the troops, then a reverent silence as the steins were drained. This, oft repeated, was the extent of the team-meeting agenda, laced, of course, with convivial conversation, the odd burst of ribald laughter, and even an occasionally more or less scholarly reference to the upcoming game against the Leafs."

Clearly, the psychology worked. "It was," said Coulter, "a loosener. The team had been playing great hockey and wanted no part of a seventh game in Toronto. The only danger was that of getting a little uptight, and pressing too hard."

"The next evening," wrote Whitehead, "everybody was beautifully loose and relaxed as the game started. And at the end of the first period the Rangers were down 2–0 after fast goals by Syl Apps and Nick Metz. Lester came into the dressing room, sat down on a bench beside goalie Davey Kerr and said quietly, 'Well, boys, you've had your fun. Now let's get down to business. I've made arrangements for a victory party in the Tudor Room of the Royal York. I'll see you there. Don't let me down.'"

The Rangers rallied to tie the score at 2–2 and then won the deciding game on Bryan Hextall's shot in sudden-death overtime. Understandably, Hextall captured the attention at that stupendous moment in Rangers history, but the bosses, Patrick and Boucher, understood that the New Yorkers would never have gotten that far without the leadership and skill displayed by Coulter.

Arthur Edmund (Art) Coulter was born on May 31, 1909, in Winnipeg, Manitoba. Like so many Rangers, he honed his hockey skills to sharpness on Winnipeg's outdoor rinks before becoming a professional in 1929.

The Black Hawks signed him in 1931 and, ironically, he teamed with onetime Rangers' star, Taffy Abel, on the Windy City blue line. The pair starred on Chicago's first ever Stanley Cup championship team in 1934.

Upon joining the Rangers, he was nicknamed *The Trapper* because he would talk fishing and hunting by the hour. When Boucher, as coach, introduced a revolutionary offensive penalty-killing team in 1939, Coulter was the anchor man with forwards Alex Shibicky and Neil and Mac Colville. So effective was the system that over the season the Rangers outscored their opponents almost two to one when they were shorthanded.

Following the Rangers' first-place finish in 1942, Coulter enlisted in the U.S. Coast Guard at a time when that branch of service had established a hockey team at its base in Curtis Bay (near Baltimore), Maryland. A number of experienced hockey professionals, including Frankie Brimsek of the Boston Bruins and Johnny Mariucci of the Chicago Black Hawks, also joined the Cutters sextet, which played in the Eastern Hockey League. Not surprisingly, Coulter once again was at the helm of a championship team; the Cutters finished atop the Eastern League, and Art was in vintage form.

He retired as an active player at war's end and eventually moved to Florida. One of the Game's genuinely overshadowed heroes, Coulter was elected to the Hockey Hall of Fame in 1974. There were few better at plying the defensive trade.

51

Guy Lafleur
(1971–1984)

"Hockey," said Guy Lafleur, "is like a drug for me. I am hooked. I can't do anything about it." He proved it by trying a comeback with the Rangers in 1988 after being retired for four years.

In fact, Lafleur did a lot about his hockey. He was the predominant National Hockey League player in the 1970s, skating for no less than five Stanley Cup championship teams and, in that span, six first-place teams.

More than any other NHL player, Lafleur both looked like and performed as if he had been trained at the Bolshoi Ballet. If there can be but one descriptive adjective for Lafleur, it is exquisite.

When he was in his prime, Guy skated with a blend of power and grace that was un-matched among his peers. Despite a seemingly frail—by hockey standards—physique, Lafleur was able to generate one of the most dynamically accurate shots in NHL history. A perfect example was an incident in the 1979 semifinals between his Canadiens and the Boston Bruins. With one minute and fourteen seconds remaining in the decisive game, Lafleur raced along the boards at thirty miles per hour. Suddenly, just inside the blue line, he drew back his stick and drove the puck into the far left corner of the net. Bruins' goalie Gilles Gilbert never moved. The goal tied the score. Montreal went on to win in sudden-death overtime, and later, with Lafleur leading the way, the Canadiens took the National Hockey League championship for the fourth straight time.

During the period from 1975 to 1979, when the Canadiens thoroughly dominated the NHL while capturing four consecutive Stanley Cups, Lafleur was their ace in the hole. When the game hung in the balance, the Habs would call Lafleur's number and he would invariably deliver. Time after time, the fleet right-winger would rise to the occasion de-spite everyone in the house knowing that he would often be the target of the opposition's most intense defensive efforts. His ability to play his game in the face of even the most determined checking separates Lafleur from any and all of his competition.

As solid as the Montreal team was in the mid-70s, if you could stop Lafleur, oppo-nents would figure, you could shut down his team. Judging by the success of the Habs, it is apparent how difficult this strategy was to implement.

Lafleur first established himself as an offensive force in the 1974–75 season, when he potted fifty-three goals and added sixty-six assists. The following year marked the first of three consecutive scoring titles for Lafleur, the only Canadien in the history of the orga-nization to accomplish such a feat. His eighty assists in 1976–77 and sixty goals in 1977–78 were league highs for each year and career bests for Lafleur in each category. In

728 NHL contests, Guy Lafleur scored 432 goals and 579 assists, good for fourteenth place on the all-time NHL scoring list. In 104 playoff games, Lafleur garnered 125 points, including fifty-five goals. He led postseason competition in goal scoring twice, assists twice, and total points three times.

Listed at a lithe 6', 175 pounds, the graceful Lafleur, or the "Flower" as his name translates, was subject to numerous tests of physical toughness in his early years in the league. But it was soon evident that roughing him up only served to have him come back twice as hard. Those who considered Lafleur a personification of his nickname were far from accurate. He would not be intimidated. In his ten-year career, Lafleur played fewer than seventy regular-season games only twice.

Lafleur was drafted as the first pick overall in the 1971 amateur draft and was immediately dubbed a "can't miss" prospect with Orr-like potential. Coming off a spectacular junior career with the Quebec Remparts, young Lafleur was envisioned as the heir to the throne of the recently retired Jean Beliveau as leader of the Canadiens. With the stage set for his entrance, Lafleur was expected to display an Oscar-winning performance, nothing less.

With his totals for the first three years reading sixty-four, fifty-five, and fifty-six points, Lafleur was considered a colossal failure by his audience in Montreal. "What happened was very simple," Lafleur remembers. "After my 130-goal season with the Remparts, everybody and his brother took me for some kind of superman. They established Herculean goals for me. The tension wound up crushing me." The ordeal finally came to a head in 1974 when, with his Canadiens' contract expired, Lafleur received an offer from the newly formed Quebec Nordiques of the World Hockey Association.

Returning to the friendly confines of Quebec's *Colisée*, the building that was his home with the Remparts, was an attractive offer indeed to Lafleur, whose flagging fortune in Montreal was taking its toll on his psyche. Later, after signing a new contract with the Canadiens, Lafleur appeared to shed the weight that had hindered his career to that point. With the grief of his first three years now behind him, Lafleur proceeded to tear up the NHL. In the following six seasons, he scored no less than 119 points per year, with a high of 136 points in 1976–77, when he captured the Hart Trophy (league MVP), Art Ross Trophy (scoring title), and Conn Smythe Trophy (playoff MVP). The Flower had finally bloomed.

Guy Damien Lafleur was born September 20, 1951, in the town of Thurso, Quebec. The only boy in a family of five children, his first involvement in the game that would eventually spread his name across the Canadian provinces came when his father joined forces with some neighbors and erected an ice skating rink. It was on that surface that Lafleur took his first strides toward the game he grew to love.

To Lafleur, hockey was more than lacing up his skates for a game. The smell, sounds, and ambiance of the rink were addicting. Arriving early for games and staying late at practice became Lafleur's habits. He would prowl around the arena hours before a game, mingling with the maintenance men and attending to his equipment. On a practice day, he would linger on after his teammates, refining the slapshot that was his trademark.

Streaking down the ice, sliding in on goal, and firing a dart behind the goaltender will be the eternal image of Lafleur's ice capades. He stands as one of the finest pure scorers the game has ever seen. But what put him above the one-dimensional scoring machine was his play in both zones. Along with being a capable defensive forward, Lafleur was a playmaker nonpareil. When carrying the puck into the offensive zone, he could be chased, harassed, and molested and still retain possession long enough to make a nifty pass to a teammate who would be in the clear because of the opposition's overconcentration on Lafleur. As was predicted in his junior years, he had the ability to dominate the ice and control the tempo of a game.

With his angular features and blond mane flying behind him, Montreal's ace earned a spot in the Hockey Hall of Fame. For his dedication to the game and extraordinary performances on the ice, Guy Lafleur is deservingly awarded a permanent place among the rest of hockey's greats here among *Hockey's 100*.

52

Bill Cowley
(1934–1947)

The odds are one in a million that a prospective big-leaguer will be discovered while playing in Paris, France, but such was the good fortune of Bill Cowley who would become the stickhandling master of the Boston Bruins.

In 1934, the twenty-one-year-old center was accompanying the Ottawa Shamrocks on an extended European tour. It was in Paris that he caught the eye of critics and ultimately came away with a professional contract. It didn't hurt that the Shamrocks, with Cowley leading the way, produced thirty-three wins, no losses, and two ties.

Within a decade of that junket, Cowley had accomplished everything a major-leaguer could hope for, and then some. He won the Hart Trophy as the National Hockey League's most valuable player in 1941 and 1943. He led the NHL in scoring in 1941 and was chosen to the First All-Star Team in 1938, 1941, 1943, and 1944. He made the Second All-Star Team in 1945 and was a member of the 1939 and 1941 Stanley Cup championship Bruins.

Cowley's problem—if it can be called a problem—was that he played on the same team with the formidable and infinitely more colorful *Kraut Line* of Milt Schmidt, Bobby Bauer, and Woody Dumart. The trio's exploits frequently overshadowed the effortless grace and subtlety of Cowley who was every bit as good as his more illustrious mates.

During the 1938–39 season, Cowley teamed with Charlie Sands, a smooth-skating wing, and Ray Getliffe, a hard worker who knew how to get the job done. The unit jelled neatly and soon was rated over the Krauts.

The Bruins finished first that year and by playoff time coach Art Ross had made some changes to thwart the New York Rangers, their first-round opponents. Cowley was switched to center for Roy Conacher and Mel Hill.

At the conclusion of regulation time in the opening game the teams were tied, 1–1. Ross divined the Rangers' strategy—stifle Cowley with blanket checking and do the same to Conacher—and summoned Cowley to his side. "We've got to fool them," he said. "They're watching Conacher so carefully it would be better to feed Hill."

Cowley could have been forgiven if he had raised an eyebrow. At that point in time, Hill was regarded as a Grade B shooter, at best, who scored only ten goals all season. Cowley listened to his boss and then decided that Hill would get that puck if he had to present it to him on a lazy Susan.

The sudden death had begun and the teams conducted a series of thrusts and counterthrusts with no result. That they were evenly matched was obvious and it was equally clear that only a very special play would decide the contest. The first twenty minutes of

sudden death ended without result, as did the second overtime period. It appeared that the third sudden death would conclude without result when Cowley took control of the puck with less than a minute remaining.

Cowley crossed into Rangers' territory and lured the big New York defenseman, Murray Patrick, toward him. Patrick couldn't quite get to Cowley in time and the Bruin eluded him, skated into the corner, and fed a perfect pass to Hill who was camped in front of goalie Dave Kerr. Hill deposited the puck behind Kerr at 19:25 of the third overtime. When the red light flashed it was 1:10 a.m.

The second game was virtually a carbon copy of the first. It was 2–2 at the end of regulation time and, once again, Ross employed the same strategy with Cowley—feed Hill. With eight minutes and twenty seconds gone in the first sudden-death period, Cowley charged the Rangers' defense. As the New Yorker braced for his shot, Bill deftly dropped the puck back to Hill who fired a forty-footer into the twine. The time was 8:24 of the first overtime, and the Cowley-Hill combine was the talk of the hockey world.

The Bruins took Game 3, 4–1, in more traditional form, but then it was the Rangers' turn. They won the next three in a row and seemed destined for a major upset as the teams lined up for the seventh and deciding game at Boston Garden.

Again they were deadlocked, this time 1–1 at the end of three periods. Wearied from the heat of an April evening, the teams slogged through one, then a second sudden-death period without producing a score; with more than seven minutes elapsed in the third sudden death the Bruins moved to the attack. Roy Conacher fired the puck at goalie Bert Gardiner, who earlier in the series had replaced Kerr. Gardiner nabbed the rubber in the webbing of his glove and flipped the puck into the corner of the rink, expecting one of his defensemen to retrieve it. But Cowley got there first.

The crafty Boston center continued behind the goal, using the cage as a blocker, viewing the goal area for a possible opportunity. There was Hill, somehow unguarded. Again, Cowley distributed the perfect pass and, before Gardiner could move, Hill sped it home at exactly eight minutes of the third overtime. The Bruins had won the series four games to three.

William Miles Cowley was born June 12, 1912, in Bristol, Quebec. The youngest member of the Cowley clan of four boys and a girl, Bill received his first pair of skates at Christmas, 1924, when he was twelve years old.

Bill launched his youthful playing career as a goalie, gave up a dozen goals in the first period, and was forever a forward after that. He broke into the NHL with the St. Louis Eagles in 1934. When the Eagles folded at the close of the 1934–35 season, Cowley signed with the Bruins.

Cowley played three games on the wing before the veteran defenseman Babe Siebert took the coach aside. "That kid can fly," Siebert said. "Put him at center and he'll rattle in the goals."

In his fourth game with the Bruins—against the Canadiens at Montreal—Cowley was at center. The game was tied in the third period when Bill moved into high gear and sped off on a breakaway with Siebert right behind. As he passed Montreal's blue line, goalie Wilf Cude crouched into position.

"Beat him—it's your play, kid," came Siebert's yell.

Cowley moved right in on goal, wheeled across the goal mouth, and seemed ready to swerve behind the net. Cude was duped by the maneuver and Cowley back handed the puck into the net.

It was the start of a career that spanned eleven years in Boston. Cowley retired after the 1946–47 season, having suffered a broken left hand, a jaw broken in five places, torn knee ligaments, a shoulder separation, and assorted cuts and bruises.

Following his retirement, Cowley coached teams in Renfrew, Ontario, and Vancouver before settling in his native Ottawa. He was elected to the Hockey Hall of Fame in 1968. If there are any doubts that Bill belongs with *Hockey's 100*, just check with Mel "Sudden Death" Hill.

53

Ching Johnson
(1926–1938)

If ever there was a swashbuckling defenseman whose robust play was a perfect metaphor for hard hockey, it was Ching Johnson. And if ever there was a gregarious personality who helped sell the still foreign game of hockey to New Yorkers during the Roaring Twenties, it was Ching.

Johnson was twenty-eight years old when he made his debut on Broadway with the Rangers. It also was the debut for the Blueshirts who were launching their National Hockey League franchise in the 1926–27 season against the powerful Montreal Maroons.

Before the game, Ching suffered doubts about the Rangers' ability to withstand the mighty men from the North. The game itself was billed as the best (Maroons) against the worst (Rangers). Johnson was teamed on the blue line with Taffy Abel. Their names—Taffy and Ching—would soon become bywords to New York sports fans.

Johnson was a big, rawboned hunk of man with a bald head and an extremely positive view of life. "He always wore a grin," said teammate Frank Boucher, "even when heaving some poor soul six feet in the air. He was one of those rare warm people who would break into a smile just saying hello or telling you the time."

Abel was heavier and rounder than Johnson. It was said that when Taffy hit a foe it felt more like being swatted with a fat pillow. When Ching connected, it was like being hit by a train. Ching hit often, but he also was the recipient of many hits and that opening game against the Maroons was a good example of what was to come.

In the first period, the Maroons chose to intimidate the Rangers and Nels Stewart of the visitors went after Johnson, hooking him over the eye with his stick when they clashed along the boards behind the Rangers' net. Although blood was pouring from the cut, Ching nevertheless crashed Stewart to the ice. Referee Lou Marsh gave them both penalties and Ching went to the dressing room where five stitches were placed in the wound. He soon returned to the fray wearing a white patch over the eye. Ching played more effervescently than ever, and the Rangers scored what was considered an upset victory over the Maroons.

Johnson gave New York fans a million bucks worth of entertainment during his career. He was a First All-Star in 1932 and 1933 and made the Second Team in 1931 and 1934. With Ching starring on defense, the Rangers finished first in the American Division and a season later won their first Stanley Cup.

Johnson helped the Rangers to a second Stanley Cup in 1933. "Ching," said Boucher, "loved to deliver a good hoist early in a game because he knew his victim would likely retaliate, and Ching loved body contact. I remember once against the Maroons Ching

caught Hooley Smith with a terrific check right at the start of the game. Hooley's stick flew from his hands and disappeared above the rink lights. He was lifted clean off the ice, and seemed to stay suspended five or six feet above the surface for seconds before finally crashing down on his back. No one could accuse Hooley of lacking guts. From then on, whenever he got the puck, he drove straight for Ching, trying to outmatch him, but each time Ching flattened poor Hooley. Afterwards, grinning in the shower, Ching said he couldn't remember a game he'd enjoyed more."

Ivan Wilfred Johnson was born on December 7, 1897, in Winnipeg, Manitoba. He was nicknamed Ching because he wore a wide grin on his face whenever he body-checked the enemy and when he smiled his eyes gave him an Oriental look; therefore Chink or Ching as in Ching-a-ling-Chinaman.

Johnson was discovered by Conn Smythe, when the hockey entrepreneur was scouting for the Rangers prior to their entry into the NHL. Both Ching and his buddy, Taffy Abel, were playing semipro hockey in Minneapolis. Smythe liked them both but found Johnson a hard bargainer.

"I must have reached agreement with Ching forty times," Smythe recalled. "Each time when I gave him my pen to sign, he'd say, 'I just want to phone my wife.' Then there'd be a hitch and he wouldn't sign. In my final meeting with him I said before we started, 'Ching, I want you to promise that if we make a deal you will sign, and *then* you'll phone your wife.' He promised. We made a deal. He said, 'I've got to phone my wife.' I said, 'You promised!' He said, 'Okay, Connie,' and signed."

Smythe was unloaded by the Rangers before the opening season had begun and was replaced by Lester Patrick.

Johnson played for the Rangers until 1937 and then was dealt to the New York Americans. He completed his NHL career in 1938 but coached briefly in the minors and then turned to officiating. While officiating a game in Washington, D.C., he committed a memorable gaffe.

"I was calling this game," Ching recalled, "when some young forward broke out and raced solo against the goalie. Instinctively, I took this player down with a jarring body-check. Following the game, I apologized to his team. I don't know what made me do it but I did it. I guess it was just the old defenseman's instinct."

Johnson eventually went into the construction business and remained in Washington where he occasionally attended games played by the NHL's Washington Capitals. He was elected to the Hockey Hall of Fame in 1958. Johnson died on June 16, 1979.

Dave Schriner

54

Sweeney Schriner
(1934–1946)

"He was the best left-winger I ever saw. That includes everybody—Frank Mahovlich, Busher Jackson, Bobby Hull, everybody."

The speaker was Conn Smythe, who coached, managed, and studied hockey from the early 1920s through the late 1970s. The subject was Dave "Sweeney" Schriner, who played for the New York Americans and later for Smythe's Toronto Maple Leafs.

They called Schriner *The Great Smoothie* although he could have been tagged *Old Reliable* as well, based upon his knack for producing meaningful goals and assists at critical moments.

Schriner, who melded perfectly on a line with right wing Lorne Carr and center Art Chapman, won the Calder Trophy as rookie of the year in 1935 and led the NHL in scoring in 1936 and 1937. He was First All-Star left wing in 1936 and 1941 and made the Second Team in 1937.

It was Schriner, more than anyone, who lent dignity to an Americans team that often was the butt of twitting sportswriters. Red Dutton, who managed the Amerks during the 1930s, would bust his vest talking about his Sweeney. "What made me so proud," said Dutton, "was that I signed Schriner to his first pro contract. I brought him in along with Art Chapman and Lorne Carr and together they made one of the greatest lines in hockey."

Tall and husky, Schriner had remarkably thin legs for his size. When he won his first scoring championship in 1935–36, goals and assists were at a premium, yet he totaled nineteen red lights and twenty-six assists for a total of forty-five points at a time when the NHL played a forty-eight-game schedule. A year later he topped the league with twenty-one goals and twenty-five assists for forty-six points.

Although the Americans never won the Stanley Cup, they did enjoy a brief moment of glory in the 1938 playoffs when they went up against their hated rivals, the New York Rangers. Schriner and company, always disparaged by their co-tenants in Madison Square Garden, split the first two games with the Blueshirts. The third and decisive match was won by the Amerks when Schriner's pal, Carr, scored at forty seconds of the third overtime period.

Unfortunately, the Great Depression was at its height and the Amerks were hurting like so many professional teams. A number of Dutton's older players were retiring, and he had to wheel and deal to fill their sweaters. Against his will, Dutton traded Schriner to Toronto in one of the NHL's biggest deals. In return, he received Busher Jackson, Murray Armstrong, Buzz Boll, and Doc Romnes.

If Sweeney was superb as an Amerk, he was even better as a Maple Leaf, and his finest hour occurred during the 1942 Stanley Cup finals between the Detroit Red Wings and the Maple Leafs.

The teams were deadlocked at three games apiece with the seventh and final game being played at Maple Leaf Gardens. After two periods, Detroit held a 1–0 lead and appeared capable of nursing it through the final twenty minutes of play. Schriner, who was playing on a line with his old buddy, Carr, and rookie Billy "The Kid" Taylor, sat on his dressing room bench when manager Conn Smythe entered and walked over to the trio.

"I walked over to the corner where they were and gave it to them hard, one at a time and then all three. I'll never forget Sweeney looking up at me with a grin. 'What ya worrying about, boss? We'll get you a couple of goals.'"

Sweeney then made good on his word, scoring with assists from Carr and Taylor. Pete Langelle put the Leafs ahead, 2–1, but the Red Wings pressed for the equalizer. Schriner came back on the ice, accepted passes from Carr and Taylor, and pumped the insurance goal home. The Maple Leafs won the game, 3–1, and the Stanley Cup.

Three years later Schriner helped the Leafs to another Stanley Cup while playing on a line with Carr and Gus Bodnar. That season, his tenth in the NHL, Sweeney scored twenty-two goals.

It was a magnificent last hurrah for Schriner and Carr. Smythe, who was convinced that both warriors were on the verge of decline, hoped his two aces would retire. "I could see it," Smythe said, "yet my toughness never extended to giving the chop to men who had worked hard for me. I talked this over with Schriner and Carr and they decided to retire which I thought was a more honorable way for two great performers to go out, rather than being shipped to the minors."

David Schriner was born on November 30, 1911, in Calgary, Alberta. He was discovered by Red Dutton, a fellow western Canadian, and wasted little time persuading enemy goaltenders that he was for real. Curiously, Sweeney was persuaded to make a comeback in the fall of 1948 with the highly rated Regina Caps, a professional team just a cut below major league level.

"SWEENEY IS FLYING AGAIN WITH REGINA" was the way one headline evaluated his play. Schriner's comeback was remarkable, considering that he had been away from competitive hockey for three years, but he retired from Western Canada Senior League play at the end of the 1948–49 season and turned to coaching.

After trying his hand at coaching, Sweeney eventually returned to his native Calgary, his love of hockey undiminished. He became a regular at Flames NHL games and retained the classy aura that long ago inspired someone to dub him *The Great Smoothie.*

55

Stan Mikita
(1958–1980)

Some years ago, a group of veteran hockey men got together at a banquet and began reminiscing about the sport they had all been associated with for so long. What evolved from their attempts to name the single greatest hockey player was a composite drawn from some of the greats of the past decade or so. This player would have Rocket Richard's accuracy, Gordie Howe's defensive mastery, Bobby Hull's speed and shot, and Jean Beliveau's stickhandling. He would, they agreed, be virtually unstoppable. Listening closely, Chicago Black Hawks' coach Billy Reay stood quietly in amusement. After hearing the selections, Reay suddenly spoke up.

"That's Stan Mikita you're talking about," he said with finality. "He's done more with what he's got than any other player I've seen." And nobody argued. While probably a shade behind those stars in their particular areas of specialty, it was hard to think of any one player who was able to combine all his skills and achieve such a level of proficiency as Mikita. He was the embodiment of the consummate hockey player.

While blessed with a wide assortment of technical skills, Mikita battled every inch of the way to establish himself amongst the National Hockey League's large, often hulking, players. And from the outset, his foes sensed that the pestiferous fellow with the slicked-back black hair was not going to allow himself to be run out of the league by anyone.

During his first six seasons in the NHL, the 5'9", 165-pound centerman was described by one journalist as a "snarling, belligerent, gutter-fighting scamp who thought nothing at all about taking on the whole league." Nicknamed *Le Petit Diable* (The Little Devil) by fans in Montreal, Mikita's truculence earned calls for his blood in rinks throughout the NHL. A fighter he was, but by almost always going up against a larger opponent, he rarely found himself on the long side of the decision. He was, however, fearless in his desire to establish his place in the NHL.

During those early years of Mikita's career, his penalty minute totals often were considerably higher than his scoring numbers, ranging in the low to mid-100s. But between stints in the penalty box, Mikita was still able to spend enough time on the ice in 1961 to help lead the Black Hawks to their first Stanley Cup in twenty-three years. He led all playoff scorers that spring with twenty-one points in twelve games. Where the Hawks had previously been a one-line team with Bobby Hull blazing the way, the development of Mikita and the *Scooter Line* of Mikita, flanked by Ab McDonald and Ken Wharram, gave the Hawks the depth and balance they needed to take the Cup. They were small but aggressive; a tough checking line that managed to get its share of goals also. And Mikita was fast becoming the most dangerous two-way threat in the league.

Stan Mikita

Mikita's point and penalty totals continued to climb in the 1964–65 season when he earned 154 minutes in penalties and led the league in scoring with eighty-seven points. But at the start of the 1965 season, a remarkable transformation took place: the prince of pugnacity had reformed.

It seems as though Mikita's daughter had viewed a Black Hawk game on television and afterwards wondered aloud why her dad was beating a path to the penalty box while everyone else was busy playing on the ice. Unable to answer such a simply logical question, Mikita decided it was time for a change.

Realizing how much more valuable he could be to his team if he spent more time on the ice than in the slammer, Mikita did an abrupt about face. As hell-bent as he had been in establishing his tough-guy image, he was equally as determined to clean up his act. With everyone around the league finding it unbelievable that this was the same little devil that used to terrorize opponents, Mikita became the target of antagonists who wanted to see how much he had actually reformed. Everyone tried to goad him into a fight, but even the stepped-up abuse couldn't change his mind. He was tamer, but effective; aggressive, but lethal.

His penalty marks plummeted, finally hitting a low of twelve minutes in 1966–67. Aided by his new-found temper, Mikita walked away with the scoring championship, MVP, and Lady Byng Trophy that year and repeated his triple crown performance in 1967–68, a feat not accomplished by any player before or since.

Stan Mikita was born May 20, 1940, in Sokolce, Czechoslovakia, to Mr. and Mrs. Stanislas Gvoth. He found his home in St. Catharines, Ontario, through an unusual arrangement between his parents and his aunt and uncle, the Mikitas. Since the Mikitas could have no children of their own, an agreement was made between the two families that would entitle the Mikitas to adopt the Gvoth's second child. During a postwar visit to Czechoslovakia, the Mikitas exercised their option and, in 1948, returned to Canada with their new eight-year-old son, Stanley.

As a youngster, Mikita excelled in every sport he played, finally devoting his energies to hockey. He broke in with the Black Hawks in 1958 and remained with them for the next twenty-two years, finally retiring in 1980. Although always playing in the shadow of Bobby Hull, Mikita himself enjoyed a hugely successful career in Chicago. But to Mikita, there was no second fiddle.

Before the start of the 1972–73 season, rumor flew through the Windy City that Mikita was considering an offer from the Chicago Cougars of the World Hockey Association. After losing Hull to Winnipeg the previous season, the Black Hawks now stood to lose their second superstar in as many years. But when all was said and done, Mikita listened more to his heart than his head. "I had to consider my family and my future," he said, "but when it came down to it, I just wanted to stay with the Black Hawks. Everything doesn't revolve around money. After you play twelve or thirteen years with that Indian head on your jersey, it means something."

And what a main course he was. In his career, Mikita played 1,394 games for the Hawks, piling up 541 goals and 926 assists to rank third on the all-time list behind Gordie Howe and Phil Esposito. Those credentials earned him a First Team All-Star berth six times and Second Team honors twice. He was also the NHL scoring leader four times, two-time MVP, and Lady Byng winner and recipient of the Lester Patrick Trophy for "outstanding service to hockey in the United States" in 1976.

Mikita suffered a serious back injury in 1969 and wore a brace through most of the remainder of his career. Though playing in constant pain, he never let his team down, a testimony to his grit and determination.

When Mikita finally hung up his skates, teammate and goaltender Tony Esposito called it "the end of an era. I always considered myself fortunate to be out there with Stan. I'll probably never play with a greater hockey player."

Agreed.

56

Bullet Joe Simpson
(1925–1931)

No less an authority than Edouard "Newsy" Lalonde, himself a titan of the sport, rated Bullet Joe Simpson "the greatest living hockey player" when they skated against each other in the early part of the century.

Simpson's Mercury-like moves inspired a reporter to tag him with the sobriquet *Bullet Joe* and it stuck for life, although the nickname would have been appropriate for another reason: Simpson performed a number of heroic feats on the battle-scarred Belgian countryside during World War I. Twice wounded, he received the Military Medal as a member of the 43rd Cameron Highlanders.

At the conclusion of hostilites, Simpson returned to Canada and began what was to become a spirited climb to hockey's crest. It began in his home town, Selkirk, Manitoba, continued in Edmonton where he became a cornerstone of the Eskimos' franchise in the Western Canada Hockey League, and concluded in the National Hockey League with the New York Americans.

Organized by bootlegger Big Bill Dwyer in 1925, the Americans—alias the Amerks—moved into Madison Square Garden a year ahead of the Rangers. Thus, it was the Amerks who would sell (or fail to sell) hockey to the New York public. As it happened, the Americans did a remarkable job of winning the hearts of New Yorkers, and Simpson proved to be one of the club's outstanding gate attractions. Bullet Joe was rechristened by Bill McBeth, the Amerk's eager press agent, *The Blue Streak from Saskatoon.*

Simpson and center Billy Burch were among the more galvanic Americans and attracted the most attention from the media. The more the press touted the pair, the more the fans focused on them and demanded more production.

As defensemen went in those days, Simpson was a lightweight at 155 pounds, but he tore into the foe with the confidence of a 200-pounder. Bill Corum, a distinguished columnist of the *New York Journal-American*, described Bullet as "a rollicking, rocking man, flashing down the rink with the puck on the end of his stick."

H.J. Simpson was born August 13, 1893, in Selkirk, Manitoba, and played amateur hockey with the Winnipeg Victorias. He joined Winnipeg's 61st Battalion team and helped them win the Allan Cup, emblematic of senior hockey supremacy in Canada. Following that, he went overseas and ducked bullets in some of the heaviest fighting of a particularly vicious war at the Somme, Passchendaele, and Amiens.

Simpson played for the Americans until 1931 and then managed the team until 1935. He became one of New York's most popular professional athletes and was a close friend of Damon Runyon, Dan Parker, and others among the city's sporting set. Like many of

his teammates, Bullet Joe enjoyed Broadway's night life and once was the butt of an amusing incident at the end of the 1925–26 season.

Those were the days when Big Bill Dwyer's bootleg hooch often would find its way into the Americans' dressing room, with zany results. One such incident took place after an exhibition match with a touring team from Portland, Oregon. The game took place just prior to the arrival of the Ringling Brothers and Barnum and Bailey Circus at the Garden.

As was normally the case, circus officials moved their animals into the menagerie several days before the show opened and in this instance the floating zoo was located about a hundred feet from the team's dressing room toward the rear of the arena.

Following the game with Portland, the Americans were greeted with a case of bootleg booze, which Simpson eagerly poured. After a few hearty rounds, Bullet Joe left the dressing room and headed for Broadway. However, he made a wrong turn and walked straight into the menagerie where he was greeted by a trumpeting elephant and several boisterous lions. Incredulous, Simpson wheeled in his tracks and fled to the dressing room where he grabbed Percy Ryan, the Americans' trainer.

"Where in hell did that bad hooch come from?" Joe demanded. "Christ! I could swear I saw a herd of wild elephants out there!"

Simpson was elected to the Hockey Hall of Fame in 1962 long after he had retired to Florida. He suffered a heart attack in the late 1940s and was close to death when rival hockeyist Art Coulter, NHL President Clarence Campbell, and Simpson's wife, Grace, helped rally him from the brink.

"I was laid up for two years," Simpson recalled. "I was really down when Art took me in. He gave me a job selling skates in his hardware store, four hours a day.

"It may sound funny, selling skates in Florida, but Coral Gables, at that time, had an arena."

Simpson remained a favorite of friend, foe, and the media long after he retired. "Joe," Bill Corum once said, "was the first hockey player I ever knew and remained the favorite of all I have ever known."

Bullet Joe died in December 1973.

57

Yvan Cournoyer
(1963–1979)

Speed and guile always have been essential elements in the composition of Montreal Canadiens teams as far back as the early years of this century. Players like Howie Morenz, *The Stratford Flash*, Maurice Richard, *The Rocket*, and Henri Richard, *The Pocket Rocket*, dazzled the foe with their footwork. So, it was not surprising that, when the Canadiens' fortunes were in decline in the early 1960s, the Habitants' high command once again turned to a skater with a special get up and go.

A right wing like Richard, Cournoyer proved to be just the catalyst required by Les Canadiens. During his sixteen-year career in the National Hockey League, he played for no less than ten Stanley Cup champions and ten first-place teams. He won the Conn Smythe Trophy as the most valuable player in the 1973 playoffs, was a Second All-Star in 1969, 1971, 1972, and 1973, and played for Team Canada when it defeated the Soviet All-Stars during an eight-game tournament in 1972.

Nicknamed *The Roadrunner*, Cournoyer offered an accurate shot to complement his speed. "He was a tremendous shooter," said Joe Daley, who played goal for the Pittsburgh Penguins when Cournoyer was terrorizing the opposition. "His slapshot was awfully hard and he had the ability to put the puck high or low with great accuracy."

A product of the Canadiens' farm system, Cournoyer played junior-level hockey in Montreal and graduated to full-time work in the National Hockey League after a successful tryout the previous year.

At first Cournoyer was burdened with the rap of being a one-way player and was frequently harangued by his martinet coach, Toe Blake. "I was disappointed," said Cournoyer. "At first, when I came into the league, I thought I'd score anywhere from 15 to 20 goals."

The Montreal brass had patience. They were willing to concede some of Yvan's defensive faults as long as he could develop as a power-play ace; and he did. "For a couple of years after Rocket Richard retired," said Sammy Pollock, then the Canadiens' general manager, "our power play wasn't too good. But Yvan worked well and he developed nicely on right wing."

Although Canadiens' captain Jean Beliveau was in the twilight of his career, Cournoyer provided a spiritual and artistic lift to the aging captain. Beliveau recalled a night in Chicago when Yvan faked a shot, noticed the goalie tense up for the drive, but then circled the defense before relaying the puck to Beliveau. By that time the goaltender was drawn so far out of position Beliveau had little trouble finding an opening.

During the 1968 Stanley Cup finals against the St. Louis Blues, Cournoyer put two enemy defensemen out of action with slapshots on the same shift. After both Al Arbour and Barclay Plager were felled by Yvan's bazooka shots, the puck came back to Cournoyer who finally shot it past goalie Glenn Hall.

Yvan Serge Cournoyer was born November 22, 1943, in Drummondville, Quebec. When he was fourteen, his family moved to Montreal and Yvan eventually won a spot on a team in the suburban community of Lachine. During a game between Lachine and Verdun, scouts watched in awe as Yvan orchestrated a rink-length dash culminating in the tying goal with less than a minute remaining in regulation time. When the game went into sudden-death overtime it was Cournoyer who scored the winner.

Cournoyer soon moved up to the powerful Montreal Junior Canadiens where he was coached by Claude Ruel. "Yvan," said Ruel, "had a very special scoring knack. He reminded me in some ways of Maurice Richard, one of the greatest scorers of all time."

The resemblance to Richard was heightened when Cournoyer was promoted to the Canadiens in the 1963–64 season, and he scored a goal in his first game. Lacking the physical stature of a Jean Beliveau or the leadership qualities of a Richard, Cournoyer nevertheless became an essential part of the Habs' attack because of his scoring prowess. In the 1973 Stanley Cup playoffs, for example, he scored fifteen goals in seventeen playoff games and a total of twenty-five points, tops in that series.

As Cournoyer reached maturity as a big-leaguer he was labeled "hockey's most promising scoring superstar of the future." Yvan never quite fulfilled that promise. He never led the NHL in scoring, but he amply demonstrated that a little man with many skills could play as long and as efficiently as the big men. The miniature Stanley Cups on his mantlepiece underline *The Roadrunner*'s qualifications for *Hockey's 100*.

58

Denis Savard
(1980–   )

Like Doug Bentley, a smallish yet, superb Chicago Black Hawk of another era, peripatetic Denis Savard may never see his name on the Stanley Cup. That, however, should not detract from the minuscule center's future entry into the Hockey Hall of Fame. The French-Canadian from the province of Quebec is a throwback to another era.

Denis, in so many ways similar to Doug Bentley, has been the complete hockey showman. His nonpareil skating style has enabled him to do things with a puck that defies even Wayne Gretzky at his finest. A typical Savard masterpiece was authored against the Minnesota North Stars during the 1987–88 season.

It was a play that blended blinding speed with puck wizardry—a combination spin-pirouette-backhand—that thoroughly befuddled Minnesota defenseman Michael Berger and, ultimately, goalie Don Beaupre. "The defenseman got his legs tangled by crossing over," Savard explained, simplifying his genius. "I could see that, so I just turned around him and shot the puck ... all in one motion," Savard's words fail to match the lyricism of his complicated but, oh so quick and effortless movements.

It was a play that set Savard apart from even Gretzky, Glenn Anderson, and Mats Naslund—all speedsters. "What makes Denis so special," said power-skating specialist Laura Stamm, "is the way he's able to speed and change direction well. His skating is so smooth, he looks like he's the only one on fresh ice while everyone else is on a chopped-up pond."

One of Savard's problems, in terms of his public acclaim, has been that he has played on mediocre Chicago clubs for most of his career. The Black Hawks have never been able to get closer to the Stanley Cup than the conference championship during Savard's reign. He has been a lone virtuoso, consistently saddled with a weak supporting cast. But it wasn't always that way. As a youth, Savard learned about winning and losing.

"I was nine years old and we were playing a team called Point Claire," recalled Savard. "If we'd have won the game, we'd have gone on to a tournament in Toronto. That's a big thing when you're a kid. But we lost the game. It's the only thing that I remember about being a kid. I guess I just don't like to lose. I don't like disappointments. I won a lot then, and when you're used to winning, winning, winning, when you lose it marks you."

As a big-leaguer, he has been a marked man, but he has also earned high marks. Edmonton Oilers' coach Glen Sather has compared Denis to Hall-of-Famer Henri "Pocket Rocket" Richard. "I remember seeing Savard play junior hockey in Quebec City," said Sather. "The first thing that came to mind was his similarity to Henri. Savard has the same kind of moves and he's an effortless skater."

Skating became Denis' hallmark, and the "spin-o-rama" his most famous move. "The fastest in the league with the puck," was New York broadcaster Sal Messina's analysis of Denis' ability.

"When Savard gets the puck," said ex-NHL coach Roger Neilson, "he can turn on a dime and drive you crazy. This is how important he is to the Black Hawks; if the other club can't contain him in a game, that will be the difference in winning or losing the game to Chicago."

The Black Hawks were the clear winners in the 1980 "Sign Denis Savard Derby." It had been thought that the Montreal Canadiens, who had a higher pick, would select him in the 1980 draft, but the Habs opted for Doug Wickenheiser—a colossal mistake, as it happened. Denis was drafted third overall, Chicago's first choice in the 1980 Entry Draft, a move the club never regretted.

Denis Joseph Savard was born in Pointe Gatineau, Quebec, August 9, 1963. Montreal was Savard's home for his junior career. He led the Quebec Major Junior League in assists (112) in 1979, was on the QMJHL First All-Star Team in 1980, and won the QMJHL Most Valuable Player in 1980. All of this right under the noses of the Canadiens' high command.

The major concern early in Denis' career was his size. Quebec Nordiques' coach Ron Lapointe, who coached Savard when the ace was in his early teens, remembered the mockery. "Wherever Denis played," Lapointe recalled, "they said he was too small. He became a junior player at the age of 16 and weighed about 135 pounds, but he had a lot of faith in himself and terrific determination. Size didn't really hold him back."

Savard's track record with Chicago has shown his value to the club, and his diminutive stature has no bearing on his size in the record books. During the 1982–83 season, he went 35–86–121 in seventy-eight games and 8–9–17 in thirteen playoff games. His performance that season earned Denis a place on the NHL's Second All-Star Team, a feat he has accomplished only once more since then, when he was selected to the 1987–88 team. In that season, Savard reached the 100-point mark in his fifty-seventh game, the earliest in Chicago history. He set another club mark by scoring 100 points for the fifth time and even had a record seven shorthanded goals.

Even more vivid to Savard-watchers was a truly arresting shorthanded goal he scored at Chicago Stadium against the Oilers. Corraling the puck at center ice, Denis bobbed and weaved his way past *five* Edmonton defenders before firing an off-balance shot past All-Star goalie Grant Fuhr. "It was," exclaimed assistant Chicago coach Darryl Sutter, "one of the greatest exhibitions of stickhandling, skating, and shooting I've ever seen."

Savard boosters will forever be confounded by the question—how good would Denis have been had he played for a super skating club like the Oilers? One can only surmise that his totals would have been in the rarefied Gretzky stratosphere.

Still, Denis Savard has no apologies to make. He has been one of the NHL's premier entertainers, a pure, skilled player whose craftsmanship and numbers qualify him for *Hockey's 100.*

59

Sid Abel
(1938–1943) (1945–1953)

Sid Abel, the artful center of the Detroit Red Wings' famed *Production Line*, along with Gordie Howe and Ted Lindsay, was reflecting on his good fortune and longevity as a big-leaguer. "I kept telling Gloria to pinch me," he said, referring to what he told his wife during the 1948–49 season. "I felt sure that I was going to wake up someday and find that I had been having a wonderful dream." It was no dream; rather, it was the talent of Sid Abel that made everything happen.

He was as creative a center as he was abrasive. His passes were crisp and accurate and his bodychecks were lusty. His durability fooled those who thought he was over-the-hill.

In 1949, at the age of thirty-one, he blasted the winning goal past Turk Broda of the Toronto Maple Leafs one night. After the game, Broda met Abel in the corridor and shook his head, "What's got into you?" Broda asked, "You found the fountain of youth?"

"I don't know," Abel grinned, "but, boy, this is living! Don't ask me what's happening. It just seems that everytime I shoot, I score. And I love it!"

The Abel-Lindsay-Howe line developed into one of the finest lines in hockey history. Abel had the savvy, and Howe and Lindsay had a mixture of style and aggression that intimidated their opponents.

Sid was the backbone of the Red Wings. While he played for Detroit, the powerful team won the Prince of Wales Trophy in 1942–43 and then won it four straight years from 1948–49 to 1951–52. (The trophy is awarded to the team finishing with the most points in the Prince of Wales conference at the end of the regular schedule.)

In 1941–42, Sid was named to the Second All-Star Team at left wing. In 1948–49 and 1949–50, he was named to the First All-Star Team at center. Again in 1950–51, he was named to the Second All-Star Team at center, sharing the honor with Ted Kennedy of the Toronto Maple Leafs. He thusly became the first player ever to win All-Star rating in two different positions.

In 1948–49, while playing in sixty-nine games, Sid was the Individual Goal-Scoring Leader, scoring twenty-eight goals. Most of his goals that year were tying or winning goals, and it was in 1949 that he won the Hart Trophy—emblematic of the player judged to be the most valuable to his team. *Sport Magazine* also bestowed upon him the honor of "Hockey's Man of the Year."

With Sid playing for them, the Red Wings won the Stanley Cup in 1942–43, 1949–50, and 1951–52. They finished first five times, in 1942–43, 1948–49, 1949–50, 1950–51, and 1951–52.

In his thirteen seasons of professional hockey, Sid played in 612 games, scoring 189 goals and 283 assists for a total of 472 points. In ninety-seven playoff games, his statistics were twenty-eight goals and thirty assists for a total of fifty-eight points.

The Red Wings' intimidating *Production Line* was acclaimed as one of the all-time great lines in hockey, and they had the statistics to prove it. In 1948–49, their goal total of sixty-six ranked as the high mark for any line in the league.

To illustrate how powerful a line they were, during the 1949–50 season, Abel scored thirty-four goals (finishing third to Rocket Richard with forty-three and Howe with thirty-five, and *The Production Line* swept to new heights as they finished 1–2–3 in the scoring race. Lindsay won the championship with seventy-eight points, Abel had sixty-nine, and Gordie was third with sixty-eight.

Sid's career was filled with many highlights, including a game against the Boston Bruins. On November 2, 1949, Abel fired three pucks past goalie Jack Gelineau as the Wings beat the Bruins, 5–3. It was the first time he had ever scored a hat trick. "It took me ten years to do it," he cracked, "but it was sure worth the wait."

Sid realized another one of his lifelong ambitions in the 1948–49 season when he scored the 100th goal of his NHL career. It was his eighteenth that year, and the goalie was Turk Broda in a game at Maple Leaf Gardens. Shortly afterwards, at the age of thirty-one, another one of Sid's dreams came true when he had his first twenty-goal season, as he scored twenty-eight goals. That same season, he had a total of fifty-four points, ranking him third in the league.

In the 1949–50 playoffs, the Red Wings had to recover from a 5–0 beating in the first game against Toronto and the loss of the injured Gordie Howe. Sid's leadership finally helped the Red Wings end the Toronto jinx and eliminate the three-time Stanley Cup winners.

It would be Sid's indomitable play that would prove to be the turning point in the championship series with the New York Rangers.

Sidney Gerald Abel was born in Melville, Saskatchewan, on February 22, 1918. Like all of the other youngsters of that area, he played hockey every available moment, wherever there was ice to be found.

Fortunately for Sid, he became the "favorite son" of the postmaster, "Goldie" Smith. Smith was also a scout for the Detroit Red Wings and had helped discover other stars in the NHL, including the great Eddie Shore.

The quality that Abel possessed that caught Smith's eye was his earnest approach to the game. Just like Smith's other protégés, Sid had drive and tenacity of purpose, and this impressed Goldie so much that he invited Abel to visit the Red Wings' training camp in the fall of 1937.

Abel reported to manager Jack Adams. Adams took one look at this slim, 155 pound, 5'11" westerner during an intense practice session. He felt surely that this young man would never stand up under the battering of the pro game. Still, Adams was impressed with Sid. He suggested that Sid stay in Detroit and play in the Michigan-Ontario area. Abel gratefully declined the offer.

He told Adams that he would be going back to his home to play for the Flin Flon team and for Goldie Smith. With that, the young man turned and went back home.

Sid Abel played left wing for the Flin Flon Bombers of Manitoba during the winter of 1937. They enjoyed a fine season and ended up as finalists in the Western Canada playdowns for the Allan Cup. Abel was thought to have been one of the better players on the team, but he felt that his performance that year was only mediocre. Upon his return to Melville, he met a very excited Goldie Smith.

"We're in, Sid," Smith excitedly told Abel, "the Detroit Wings want to sign a contract with you!" Abel was stunned, as he felt that he had not had a good season. "Sign me— what for?" was his reply.

The two men excitedly examined the contract. Then on June 25, 1938, only a few short weeks later, Sid was stunned by the shocking news that his friend Goldie had died. With Goldie gone, Abel suddenly felt alone. Sadly, Sid reported to the Wings' training camp. Goldie had discovered his last star.

In 1938, the Red Wings' camp was in the process of rebuilding. There were almost sixty youngsters, all with hopes that they could make the team. Sid was nervous until he happened to overhear Adams say, "If he can stand up to the rugged going, young Abel is our best bet for the future."

Sid was sent down to the Pittsburgh Hornets that season. He played under Larry Aurie (a former Red Wings' star) and scored twenty-one goals and twenty-four assists for forty-five points. Occasionally during the season, he would be called up to join the Red Wings.

Sid played the next season with the Red Wings. However, he began to think Adams' initial fears might become reality. He was injured smashing into an opponent and broke his shoulder. When he recovered from that injury, he was sent down to the Indianapolis farm team.

But Abel's tenacity on the ice soon had him back on the parent club. It was from that point on that Sid improved his playing ability at left wing and at center ice.

In 1942–43, his natural ability for leadership saw him elected captain of the Red Wings, and Detroit went on to beat the Bruins in four straight games to win the Stanley Cup.

The war was on and Sid saw many of his friends leaving to join the armed forces. At the end of the 1943 season, Sid joined the Royal Canadian Air Force, and in doing so, left a void in the Red Wings' club.

In February 1946, Sid returned to hockey. He was twenty-eight years of age, and he found it was difficult picking up from where he left off. The younger players were fresher than ever, and the game was now so much faster due to the "red-line" pass, a war-time innovation.

In 1946–47, back at center ice, Sid was tried with many wing combinations, but mainly played with Lindsay and Pete Horeck. Abel had to force himself to keep up with the young men's pace. He practiced skating and strategy for long hours until he caught up with the new "modern" game.

Sid again became the spark plug for Detroit. *Old Bootnose* suddenly found himself scoring goals again. That year he scored nineteen goals and twenty-nine assists for forty-eight points. The hours he had spent adjusting to the new style of hockey were well spent. What a comeback he had achieved!

The next season (1949–50), *Old Bootnose* again rose like the phoenix. Skating effortlessly, he swept between Ted and Gordie, passing and scoring as though he were a rookie. In one of the great thrills in sports, captain Sid Abel helped the Red Wings beat the Rangers and brought the Stanley Cup back to the Olympia.

In 1952–53, Sid Abel was released from the Wings to become player-coach of the Chicago Black Hawks. The Black Hawks were a pathetic team, a team that had finished last in five out of six previous seasons. It was yet another challenge for Sid Abel to conquer.

Sid turned the club around. His spirited play at center, along with the incredible goaltending of Al Rollins, helped the Black Hawks into the playoffs. They almost beat the

Canadiens in the semifinal, but lost the series in the seventh and final game.

Abel returned to Detroit, becoming the coach of the Red Wings in January 1958. He remained at that position until 1962–63 when he became the Red Wings' general manager. Despite the fact that Abel and Jack Adams were at odds with each other, Sid remained with Detroit in one way or another through part of the 1970–71 season.

In 1971–72, Sid signed to coach the St. Louis Blues. That was a mistake from the beginning. He was named general manager of the Blues in October 1971 and stayed until April 17, 1973, when he was named general manager of the Kansas City Scouts. As a manager-coach, Sid never really did enjoy the success he had achieved as a player. In 1976, he left hockey to become a broadcaster for Detroit.

Few centers have been more productive than Sid in the vital areas. He was a dogged and creative playmaker, the cog in the wheel with Howe and Lindsay. In 1969, Sid was elected to hockey's Hall of Fame in recognition of all he accomplished during his career.

"Sid," said hockey historian Ed Fitkin, "will go down in the Red Wings' history as the greatest competitor and inspirational force the Red Wings ever had."

60

Johnny Bower
(1953–1970)

He had been called the "ageless wonder." Playing in the goal, the position that is generally thought to be the most dangerous and demanding job in all of sports, Johnny Bower of the Toronto Maple Leafs was well into his forties and was still a first-string goaltender, even though by athletic standards, he should have been well past his prime.

Playing in the nets has driven younger men into early retirement, the demands on their bodies is so great. Physical injuries notwithstanding, the goaltender must also carry the psychological burden of knowing that if he makes a mistake, it often shows up on the scoreboard. Still, Bower continued to play at an age when other men were entering their middle years.

Many felt that without Bower in the nets, the resurgence of the Leafs may never have taken place. He was the key to their success. He joined the club when they were in last place in 1958. Once he took over goalkeeping for them, Toronto was in the playoffs for nine straight years from 1958 to 1967, and again in 1968–69.

Johnny played on a Toronto team with some fine players, including Red Kelly, Tim Horton, Carl Brewer, and Frank Mahovlich, but he was the essential key to their Cup-winning teams.

Bower claimed he was born on November 8, 1924, but there has been a great deal of speculation on that. On three different occasions when he had been hospitalized due to hockey related injuries, he gave three different birthdays. "I've lied about my age so often that I've forgotten how old I really am," he joked.

Regardless of how old he really was, Bower was a wonder in the world of hockey. He was still sprawling to stop shots and kicking deftly at pucks; he was alert and agile. Remarkably enough, he had the reflexes of a much younger man.

Bower would defend his goal with short, desperate moves from side to side, bent in his familiar crouch, bulky and alert. He played every workout and every game like he was playing the seventh game of a Stanley Cup final.

When Bower joined the Leafs, they soared from last place to the playoffs in 1958–59, only to lose in the finals to Montreal. In 1959–60, they again made the finals, again losing to the Flying Frenchmen. In 1961–62, they won the Cup for the first time in eleven years. In fact, while Bower guarded the net for the Leafs, they won the Stanley Cup four times—in 1961–62, 1962–63 (finishing first), 1963–64, and 1966–67.

Bower was such a superb competitor that he never complained about the many injuries he suffered. Injuries would not stop him. He suffered broken ribs when he was shoved into the iron goal posts; a skate blade gashed against his jaw, ripping out a tooth and re-

quiring thirty-two stitches; all of his teeth had been knocked out; and once, while diving for a puck, a stick wedged under his tongue.

Standing 5'9" and weighing 188 pounds, Johnny's face is carved with lines—some curved, some jagged—all healed scars from cuts inflicted by skates, sticks, and pucks. He estimates that he has had over 200 stitches on his face alone just to close the facial cuts he has received.

He enjoyed a fine career, both in the minor leagues and the NHL. At Providence, Johnny's club won the Calder Cup, and he was chosen for the AHL's All-Star Team. He was also named Athlete of the Year, which he considered to be one of the highlights of his career. In fact, he won the AHL's Most Valuable Player Award three times and the Outstanding Goalie Award. He was also named best goalie the one season he played in the WHL.

In 1960–61, he played in fifty-eight games and had two shutouts for a 2.50 average. He was elected to the First Team All-Stars that year and subsequently won the Vezina Trophy.

Bower continued his fine playing in the 1964–65 season when he played in thirty-four games and had three shutouts for a 2.38 average. That year he also won the Vezina Trophy, this time sharing it with his teammate Terry Sawchuk.

Johnny Bower played thirteen seasons in which he played in 552 games and had thirty-seven shutouts for a 2.52 average. His playoff statistics included seventy-four games (five shutouts) for a 2.54 average.

John William Bower was born in Saskatchewan on November 8, 1924. Growing up in the middle of the Depression, Johnny knew what it meant to be poor. His first pair of goalie pads were fashioned from an old mattress, and his stick was cut from a branch with a suitable bend.

Bower received his first pair of skates from a player on a senior team. He was ten years old at the time, and the skates were much too big for him. Glad to even have a pair of skates, he said, "I worshipped those skates even if I couldn't get used to them." Bower ended up playing in the nets because it was the one position in hockey where you didn't have to have skates.

Bower spent two years with the Canadian army during World War II. Receiving a medical discharge in 1943, he returned to Canada. He was still eligible for junior hockey. He played for Prince Albert that season. Other teams in the league questioned how a man who served two years overseas could still be of junior age. But his birth certificate could not be found (and still hasn't been found to this day), and he was allowed to finish the season.

Bower turned pro in 1945, signing with the Cleveland Barons of the American Hockey League. He played well for eight seasons, but in relative obscurity. At that time, there were only six goalie jobs in the NHL, and it was difficult to rise quickly from the minors.

In 1953, Johnny Bower got his chance, as the New York Rangers obtained him. Gump Worsley, then the Rangers' goalie, said, "We thought he was an old man then, and that was nearly fifteen years ago." Worsley had been rookie of the year the season before, but Bower won his job away from him.

The Rangers failed to make the playoffs that year, through no fault of Bower. He gave up only 2.60 goals a game and had five shutouts. Still, the next season Bower was replaced by Worsley, and he was shipped off to Vancouver of the Western Hockey League.

From there he was sent off to Providence of the American League, and finally wound up back in Cleveland in 1957.

Bower might have remained in the minors had it not been for Lady Luck. The Maple Leafs had finished in last place during the 1957–58 season for the first time in the history of the club. Bill Reay, who was the coach at that time, was searching for a new goal-keeper. He was going to sign Al Rollins (who was playing for Calgary in the WHL), but on the night that he was scouting Rollins, Al had an off-night. Reay then decided to sign Bower, who was his second choice. Reay bought Johnny for $10,000 and a junior player.

However, Bower was undecided as to whether or not he wanted to go to Toronto. He was very happy in Cleveland, and he didn't think he could help the Maple Leafs. However, the Leafs offered him a large, two-year contract, and he was persuaded to sign.

Johnny Bower was almost thirty-four years old when he was rescued from the obscurity of the minor leagues. He battled goalie Ed Chadwick for the job for a few months, and then Chadwick was sent to the minors.

Unfortunately, Reay never saw the benefits of his move of signing Bower, as he was fired midway through the season and Punch Imlach took over. Reay's signing of Bower ended up making Imlach look like a genius.

In 1964, Bower once again led the Leafs to championship heights. He had the lowest goals against average in the league (2.12). Bower was unbeatable when tension was at its highest, and he finished up an incredible season by shutting out the Detroit Red Wings, 4–0, in the seventh and deciding game of the Stanley Cup finals.

In 1964, Johnny won the J.P. Bickell Memorial Cup, emblematic of the Maple Leafs' most valuable player. It was the second time he received that honor, having won it in 1960.

In 1964–65, the Maple Leafs obtained Terry Sawchuk from the Detroit Red Wings to share the goaltending chores with Johnny. Most athletes, with their enormous egos, would have been devastated if their team picked up a player of Sawchuk's ability. Johnny Bower didn't resent it, "I just can't play seventy games," he said at the time. "We need two goalies, and Terry is a great one. I'm glad he's with us."

In 1966, Bower played in only twenty-seven games due to injuries, caused mainly by pulled muscles. In 1967, when he was forty-five years old, Bower was still doing work-outs every day. "Of course, I get tired in those two-a-day workouts," he admitted, "but I know if I'm tired then I've been working hard. That's how I stay in shape."

After the 1966–67 season, Bower had to face the threat of being drafted if Toronto did not protect him. But he was not yet ready to retire. The Leafs did in fact keep him, letting Sawchuk go to the Los Angeles Kings.

"When hockey's no longer fun, it's time to quit," Bower once remarked. The fun went out of it for Johnny Bower when constant injuries made him feel "painful muscles I didn't know I had." In 1970, Johnny Bower retired from hockey.

He would join the Leafs' scouting staff as their chief eastern scout and would also coach their goaltenders. Johnny was also a partner in ownership of Waskesiw Lake Hotel in Prince Albert, having bought it with the money he had made from his thriving ham-burger business.

In 1976, this remarkable goaltender was elected to hockey's Hall of Fame. King Clancy remarked, "Of all the people who are in the Hall of Fame, there is none more worthy than Johnny Bower. He is one of the most honest and conscientious hockey players I've ever met. He is in a class by himself as a person. During my fifty-four years of association with the game, I have seen few better hockey players."

Johnny Bower was a fiercely competitive man who often played wracked with pain. He went all-out whether it was a workout, game, or Stanley Cup competition. Bower was agile and ageless, and he enjoyed a career of incredible accomplishments. Whether he was forty-six or fifty when he retired, it did not matter. He belongs in *Hockey's 100*.

61

Ken Dryden
(1971–1973) (1974–1979)

The pose was the person.

More than any of his many dazzling moves in the nets for the Montreal Canadiens, goaltender Ken Dryden will be vividly remembered most for his posture in the crease when the hail of enemy shots had desisted. Big Number 29 would dig the tip of his stick into the ice and fold his arms across the knob, coolly relaxing until the action resumed. Uncharacteristic of the nervous and beleaguered sort that is the stereotypical goalie, Dryden was as cool and confident inside as he appeared on the outside.

In the late 1960s and early 1970s, Montreal was far from a likely setting for a rookie goaltender to make a spectacular entrance; the Canadiens were stockpiled with talent to the envy of the rest of the NHL. It was standard operating procedure with the Habs for freshmen to serve a lengthy apprenticeship on the bench before being thrown into the fray. But after being called up from the Montreal Voyageurs of the American Hockey League in the spring of 1971, Ken Dryden made proponents of the "sit before you skate" theory blush.

After watching his first game from the press box, Dryden played six regular-season games and was impressive in allowing only nine goals. But many hockey people thought the Canadiens were merely throwing Dryden a bone—a couple of games of NHL experience—as they ran through the end of their schedule. The playoffs lurked just around the bend, and veteran Rogie Vachon was expected to tend the twines in the postseason. No one thought they would ever go with a rookie at such a crucial point. No one, that is, except Voyageurs' coach Floyd Curry. He recalled: "I told Sammy Pollock when he took Dryden from us that he had just assured himself of the Stanley Cup. He was that good."

Coach Curry's praises notwithstanding, the Habs' choice to go with their rookie in the opening round of the playoffs against the defending Cup champion Boston Bruins rocked the hockey world. Throwing a twenty-four-year-old rookie against the Orr- and Esposito-led Bruins was likened to sending David with one arm tied behind his back against Goliath. It was not long, however, before it became obvious that this rookie played with the composure and guile of a hardened veteran.

In the see-saw, seven-game series, the Montrealers prevailed, led by Dryden's one spectacular save after another. His performance left the Bruins slamming their sticks against the boards and glancing toward the heavens in hope of some sort of divine intervention.

Propelled by their mammoth upset of the Beantowners, the Canadiens dispatched the Minnesota North Stars in six and the Chicago Black Hawks in seven games to annex the

Cup. And it is hard to believe any of it could have been possible without the standout performance of Dryden. Through twenty playoff games, he compiled a 3.00 goals against average and was awarded the Conn Smythe Trophy as the most valuable player of the playoffs. This, with merely six games of NHL experience under his pads.

Instantly, experts began comparing Dryden to past goaltending greats. At 6'4", Dryden reminded observers of another tall Canadien goalie of the 1940s—the expertly ambidextrous Bill Durnan. "The way Ken gets in front of shots to make impossible saves," said Habs' captain Henri Richard, "he's a lot like Durnan used to be. Dryden murders you with surprise moves from seemingly impossible positions. It's great for a defenseman or a forward to know he's behind you."

As impressive as Dryden's playoff record was in 1971, his 3.00 goals against average was to be the most permissive digit of his career, regular season or playoffs. In 1971–72, the big fellow became the workhorse in the Montreal nets by playing sixty-four games with a 2.24 goals against average, good enough to earn him the Calder Trophy as outstanding rookie of the year. Dryden thus became the first player ever to be named the MVP of the playoffs before proving himself the best rookie in the league.

Dryden became the model of consistency the following season by working fifty-four games between the pipes, compiling a 2.25 goals against average and walking away with his third major award in less than three seasons, this time the Vezina Trophy for the best goals against average.

Although performing at the top of his sport, Ken Dryden was never mistaken for a one-dimensional jock type. Wire-rimmed spectacles, long hair, and a mod style of dress separated the young star from his peers almost as much as his semi-intellectual personality. A graduate of Cornell University and McGill Law School, Dryden was as unpredictable in his career decisions as he was consistent in the nets for the Canadiens.

By 1973, it appeared as though the sky would be the limit for the young netminder. He had reached the peak of his game and seemed a fixture at the Forum. But then he dropped his bombshell. Prior to the 1973–74 season, Dryden announced that, at the age of twenty-six, he was retiring from hockey to accept a job "articling" for the Toronto law firm of Osler, Hoskin, and Harcourt for the sniveling salary of $7,500 a year. At this, the collective jaw of Montreal dropped in amazement.

Dryden had never been secretive of his desires to pursue a career in law and if worse came to worst, would be prepared to sacrifice hockey for the rigors of the courtroom. With the Canadiens, Dryden had been earning a modest salary despite enormous appeal and proven ability. He believed he deserved more money; a salary equal to his standing as one of the best goaltenders in the NHL.

The Canadiens, however, would not budge and Dryden departed. For that season, the Habs struggled with three goaltenders to no avail, being bounced from playoff competition in the first round by the Rangers. A few hundred miles west of the Forum, Dryden worked diligently at his profession and enrolled with an industrial league team where he played defense.

After considerable haggling and finally give and take by both parties, Dryden and the Canadiens came to terms. He rejoined the team for the 1974–75 campaign and found that kicking around the industrial league had done little to keep him on top of his game. He struggled some and wound up with what would be his highest regular season goals against average, 2.69. The Canadiens again did not reach the Cup finals, and the masses buzzed with speculation over the future of their once-prized goaltender.

From the 1975–76 season until his retirement in 1979, Ken Dryden was absolutely outstanding; a goaltender nonpareil in the NHL. His personal statistics, in addition to the fact that the Canadiens earned four consecutive Stanley Cups during that period, is testament to the excellence of both the team and its goaltender.

In the four years of Dryden's dominance, his GA average never climbed higher than 2.30 in 1978–79 and reached its miniscule low of 2.03 in 1975–76. Between those years, he enjoyed his finest season in 1976–77; fifty-six games, ten shutouts, and a 2.14 GA average for the regular season. In the playoffs, fourteen games, four shutouts and an invisible 1.56 GA average.

Kenneth Wayne Dryden was born August 8, 1947, in Hamilton, Ontario. During his career, in addition to the Calder and Smythe Trophies, he received the Vezina one time himself and shared it with Michel Larocque three other times; he was named First Team All-Star five times and Second Team All-Star on one occasion. As an example of Dryden's exceptional ability to handle the puck after making the save, he accumulated nineteen regular season and four playoff assists.

Apparently at the top of his game, Dryden suddenly called it quits—for good this time—after the 1979 season.

In a brief career, Dryden helped the Canadiens to six Stanley Cups. His mettle in the clutch separated Ken Dryden from his peers more than his exceptional size and personality. The combination of all his abilities made him distinctive enough to be ranked here among *Hockey's 100* as one of the finest goaltenders ever to roam a crease in the NHL.

62

Dit Clapper
(1927–1947)

Bobby Orr, Eddie Shore, and Milt Schmidt rank among the most revered of the Boston Bruins, but close behind in the hearts of Hub hockey fans who remember the team prior to World War II is the elegant and versatile Dit Clapper.

Clapper left his imprint in many ways. He was the first National Hockey League player to last in the majors for twenty full seasons—*and all of them with the same team.* He starred as a right wing for the first nine years of his career and then reverted to defense where he proved no less adept with the puck.

As a forward, he was a Second Team All-Star in 1931 and 1935. As a defenseman, he was a First All-Star in 1939, 1940, and 1941 and a Second All-Star in 1944. His championship dossier includes three Stanley Cups and six first-place teams.

Although Clapper preferred the role of pacifist, his temper occasionally boiled out of proportion to his character. His most notorious eruption took place during a game with the Montreal Maroons. An opponent named Dave Trottier jammed the butt end of his stick into Clapper's face. Normally, this would have resulted in a penalty, but referee Clarence Campbell (who eventually became president of the National Hockey League) failed to detect foul play.

Clapper took the law into his own hands and jumped Trottier, whereupon Campbell skated to the scene of the crime. "Clapper," said the referee, "you're a dirty sonofabitch!"

The accusation was doubly surprising to Clapper because everyone in the NHL realized that the distinguished Campbell was a Rhodes Scholar and not given to profanity.

"What did you say?" demanded Clapper.

"I said you're a dirty sonofabitch," he repeated. Instead of leaving bad enough alone, Clapper followed up his tirade with a right cross to Campbell's head, sending the referee staggering back into the arms of the pleased players.

The act of punching out a referee was considered severe enough to warrant a long-term suspension. Instead, NHL President Frank Calder slapped a $100 fine on Clapper and a mild tongue-lashing.

Pressed as to why the punishment was so light, Calder revealed that he had received a report from referee Campbell that tended to shift the blame away from Clapper.

"I was talking loud," Campbell admitted, "when I should have been throwing them into the penalty box."

Clapper is best remembered for his gallant efforts as a forward and defenseman, not to mention his Beau Brummel appearance. With his hair impeccably parted down the middle, Dit dressed meticulously and exuded class. He was the same way on the ice. *The Canadian*

Press in describing Clapper noted that he was "the Jean Beliveau of his day," a reference to the classic Montreal Canadiens' center of the 1950s, 1960s, and early 1970s. Today, Clapper would be compared to Wayne Gretzky.

Aubrey Victor Clapper was born February 9, 1907, in Newmarket, Ontario. After playing amateur hockey in the communities surrounding his home, he showed enough promise to earn a contract with the Bruins in 1927 when Art (Uncle Arthur) Ross was constructing one of the strongest teams to grace NHL ice.

Within two years of his debut, Clapper had outshone virtually every forward in the league. During the 1929–30 campaign—his most productive—Clapper totaled forty-one goals and twenty assists for sixty-one points in a forty-four game schedule. (That was the one season in which the league allowed forward passing from zone to zone.)

Dit, of course, did not work alone. He was fortunate to be aligned with the gifted center Cooney Weiland and left wing Norman "Dutch" Gainor to form what was to become *The Dynamite Trio*, a gallant and effective scoring unit.

Clapper once recalled that his first goal—scored but ten seconds into his first shift—and his 200th goal, which was the winner in a game against Toronto at Maple Leaf Gardens in 1942, were his most memorable.

Many hockey critics regard the 1941 Bruins team, on which Clapper was a defenseman, as one of the most powerful in history. That Boston club won the Stanley Cup with Frankie "Mister Zero" Brimsek in goal and *The Kraut Line* of Milt Schmidt, Woody Dumart, and Bobby Bauer spearheading the attack.

During Clapper's final seasons with the Bruins, he assisted Ross with the coaching chores and then took over as the full-time coach after retiring in 1947. He gave up coaching after two seasons and retired to Peterborough, Ontario, where he made an unsuccessful run as a Liberal candidate in a federal election.

Although he was away from the NHL scene in retirement, Clapper continued to follow the professional game. When Bobby Orr began starring for the Bruins in the late 1960s, comparisons were made by the experts who rated the stars of different eras. When Orr surpassed Clapper's lifetime mark of 228 goals and 248 assists, Dit never pouted but, rather, toasted the lad from Parry Sound, Ontario.

Dit was so enthralled with Orr's Bruins that, in April 1970, he returned to Boston at his own expense to see if the Bruins could win their first Stanley Cup in twenty-nine years.

"I'm looking forward to drinking champagne out of that Cup," Clapper enthused. "It's been such a long time."

The Bruins obliged by winning the Cup, and Dit returned to his home a happy man. The Boston club retired his Number 5 jersey along with his shoulder pads, and, to this day, his name remains one of the most revered in Boston sports. He died January 20, 1978, long after being inducted into the Hockey Hall of Fame.

At the time of Clapper's death, *The Canadian Press*, in a long and glowing obituary, stated that Dit was "one of the NHL's all-time greats." And that he was, on the attack as well as on defense: a worthy member of *Hockey's 100*.

63

Bill Mosienko
(1941–1955)

It has been mistakenly assumed that a truly unique performance on one night in the fourteen-year major league career of Bill Mosienko assured his entrance into the Hockey Hall of Fame.

On the night of March 23, 1952, the man they called *Wee Willie* singlehandedly scored three goals within a space of twenty-one seconds. Nobody is expected to duplicate the feat as long as professional hockey is played.

Yet, Mosienko had more than that one-night stand. He was a remarkably **agile** right wing who played all his hockey for the Chicago Black Hawks and, often, was the sole redeeming feature on an otherwise awful Windy City franchise.

For better or worse, though, all of Mosienko's accomplishments—including his Lady Byng Trophy win in 1945—have been overshadowed by the game, as Mosienko put it, "when I caught lightning in a beer bottle."

Mosienko had twenty-eight goals to his credit prior to the final game of the season against the New York Rangers at Madison Square Garden. In those days, reaching the thirty-goal mark was the equivalent of batting .325 in baseball.

The Black Hawks, who were locked into last place, had little motivation other than professional pride. The Rangers, who were guaranteed a fifth-place finish, simply wanted to end the campaign with a win before the few thousand fans sprinkled throughout the Garden for the finale.

Since the Rangers' regular goalie, Chuck Rayner, had been bedeviled with injuries and New York's back-up netminder, Emile Francis, also was sidelined, the Black Hawks found themselves up against a virtual unknown guarding the home team's goal.

Crew-cut Lorne Anderson had been a varsity netminder for the New York Rovers, the Rangers' farm team in the Eastern League. He had played only two games in the NHL, but was young and promising enough to be given another examination by the Rangers' brass. What better time than the final game—against the subterranean Chicago sextet. "We scored the first goal off him in forty-four seconds but after that for two periods he looked good," said Mosienko.

Mosienko, who was thirty at the time, still had good legs and was skating on a line with two of the few other competents on the team—Gus Bodnar, the center, and George Gee, the left wing. After five minutes of the third period, the Hawks were floundering.

"It looked like we were headed for a beating when our coach, Ebbie Goodfellow, sent our line back on the ice," said Mosienko. "There was a face-off and Bodnar won the draw. He got me the puck in center ice."

The Rangers had Hy Buller on defense. He was a Second Team All-Star, the best the New Yorkers had at the time, but he apparently had concealed an injury in order to play that night.

"When Bodnar got me the puck," said Mosienko, "I took off and went in around Buller. That left me one on one with the goalie. I got off a low wrist shot, along the ice, and it went in on the right side."

As soon as the puck bulged the white twine behind Anderson, the elated Mosienko practically dove into the net after the rubber. The slim crowd was unsure why the visiting player was so anxious to retrieve the puck.

"It was my twenty-ninth goal," Mosienko explained, "and I didn't expect to get another. I figured that since I was so close to a milestone—30 goals—I might as well save the puck. I skated back to the bench and handed it to the coach. The time was 6:09 of the third period.

Goodfellow decided to keep his big line on the ice. It was now 6–3 Rangers, and, who knew, maybe his Hawks would get hot. "Bodnar won the draw again," said Goodfellow, "and sent the puck to Mosie at the blue line. He was really flying."

For the zephyrlike Black Hawk, it was like déjà vu. Once again he was confronted by defenseman Buller, and he outflanked the Ranger as easily as he had the first time and zeroed in on the suddenly beleaguered Anderson.

"I had him all to myself," said Mosienko, "and I figured since I'd been able to beat him on the right side, his glove hand, I'd try it again. So, just like the first time, I slid the puck along the ice. I don't think Anderson was ready for the quick shot and it got by him. The time was 6:20, just eleven seconds after the first goal. Now I had Number 30, so I rushed to retrieve that one, too.

"Anderson was naturally unhappy about what had happened and I'll never forget the look he gave me as I reached into the net for the puck. I took it over to the bench and gave it to Goodfellow."

Neither the coach nor Mosienko even dreamed about his scoring a third goal, nor were they aware of the NHL record of fastest three goals (one minute, fifty-two seconds) set by Carl Liscombe of the Detroit Red Wings in 1938.

"It's funny," said Goodfellow, "but I was thinking of pulling Mosie off the ice after his second goal but I decided to let him stay on for another minute."

This time the scenario differed somewhat. Bodnar won the face-off again, to be sure, but this time the center ladled a pass to the left wing, Gee, rather than Mosienko on the right. The score was now 6–4, and the Black Hawks were hoping to rally for a tie.

"Naturally," said Mosienko, "I was thinking about the hat trick although I wasn't prepared for what actually happened. After all there were more than thirteen minutes left in the game and the Rangers, now only leading by two, figured to tighten their defense."

When Gee got the puck, he moved toward the Rangers' blue line on the left side while Mosienko kept pace along the right alley. As Gee crossed the line into the New York defensive zone, Mosienko streaked goalward from the right.

"George saw me cutting over the line and laid a perfect pass on my stick. Buller was waiting for me but like the first two times I cut around him and went in on Anderson. He'd been burned twice on the right side and this time he moved to the right, figuring I'd try it again."

Mosienko decided to alter his strategy but led Anderson to believe that he was going to shoot the puck along the ice on the right. "Instead," Mosienko recalled, "I pulled him out of the net to the left, then put one over him high into the top right hand corner."

The time was 6:30. Mosienko had scored three goals within twenty-one seconds. It was a new NHL record, but nobody really knew it at that moment. In fact, Mosienko didn't even attempt to obtain the puck a third time around, until Jimmy Peters, one of his teammates, decided Bill should have it. "He had played with the guy who set the old record so he went and got the puck for me and now it's in the Hockey Hall of Fame."

With a break, Mosienko could have made it four goals in sixty-six seconds. Goodfellow kept him out on the ice and, sure enough, the line soon moved into attacking formation, with Mosienko in possession of the puck.

"I was in alone again," said Mosienko, "and faked Anderson out of position. I actually had an open net to hit but I missed the far post by a matter of inches."

The exhausted right wing finally skated past the bench where his coach was waving him off the ice. "When he was in earshot," said Goodfellow, "I said, 'Bill, get off the ice, you're in a slump!'"

Mosienko's three goals reduced the Black Hawks deficit to 5–6. They scored two more and won the game, 7–6. "It was the last game I coached," said Goodfellow, "and one I'll never forget because that's one record that'll never be broken."

William Mosienko was born in hockey-mad Winnipeg, Manitoba, on November 2, 1921. The son of poor parents, Mosienko, growing up during the Great Depression, was delighted when the Black Hawks showed interest in him at the age of eighteen.

When he was nineteen, the Hawks farmed him to Providence and then Kansas City, but his speed was such that the Chicago club finally brought him up to stay and put him on a line with center Max Bentley and left wing Doug Bentley. Thus one of the NHL's most glittering units, *The Pony Line*, was formed.

"The Black Hawks' publicity man, Joe Farrell, came up with the name," said Mosienko. "It was because of our size. The three of us were so small and every time we'd go for the puck we'd give it a little bounce."

The tragedy of Mosienko's fourteen-year NHL career is that despite his 258 goals and 282 assists in 711 games he never sipped champagne from the Stanley Cup, although *The Pony Line* gave the Black Hawks the nucleus of a championship team.

Wee Willie's exceptional speed and guile did not immunize him from injury. He twice tore ligaments in his knees, fractured his toes, suffered a broken collarbone, and broke his nose three times.

Psychologically speaking, Mosienko's worst injury occurred on October 13, 1947, during the first official NHL All-Star Game. Early in the second period, *Wee Willie* was checked into the boards by Toronto Maple Leafs' defenseman Jim Thomson and was carried off the ice on a stretcher with a fractured left ankle.

The player-short Black Hawks were panicked into a trade, dealing Max Bentley to Toronto for five regulars. Superficially, it appeared to be a good deal for the Hawks, but it irrevocably broke up *The Pony Line* and Chicago remained a noncontender for years after.

Mosienko retired from the NHL in 1955 and, with ex-Ranger Alf Pike, helped launch pro hockey in Winnipeg. Their Warriors won the Edinburgh Trophy in their first year and helped lay the groundwork for what eventually would be Winnipeg's entry into the NHL.

Wee Willie eventually gave up coaching the Warriors to operate a twenty-lane bowling alley in Winnipeg. He still appears in oldtimers games and, inevitably, is reminded of that night when he "caught lightning in a beer bottle" with three goals in twenty-one seconds.

"It's a wonderful thing that so many people remember it," said Mosienko. "I'm very proud of what I did."

64

Hobey Baker
(1910–1918)

When the Washington Capitals signed eighteen-year-old Bobby Carpenter to a six-figure contract in September 1981, it was freely predicted by many sportswriters that Carpenter could be the first American-born forward to become a superstar in the Canadian-dominated National Hockey League.

While there have been Americans who have excelled at goaltending (Frankie Brimsek) and defense (Johnny Mariucci), few attackers have been able to attain the level of a Wayne Gretzky, Guy Lafleur, or Bryan Trottier. There was, however, one of Uncle Sam's skaters who was so accomplished that, had he played today, there is little question that he would have been an ace in the Gretzky manner.

His name was Hobey Baker, and the tragedy of it all was that this Pennsylvanian, who might have been the greatest hockey scorer of all time, died the year that the National Hockey League was just getting off the ground.

Like Gretzky, Baker was a natural; a genius at manipulating the puck almost from the very moment he laced on a pair of skates and grasped a hockey stick. His skills as a shooter gained national prominence while Hobey was a student at Princeton University. Incredibly good-looking, Baker captained the Princeton skaters to a pair of intercollegiate championships and immediately captured the attention of professional scouts who sought his services. Baker repeatedly rejected the offers, but that just whet the appetites of the pros even more.

Skating for New York's St. Nicholas hockey club, Baker was the star of an upset victory over a strong Montreal sextet in the Ross Cup series. The fact that an American player could reach Baker's level of proficiency astounded the Canadian critics. One Montreal reporter noted: "Uncle Sam has the cheek to develop a first-class hockey player—who wasn't born in Montreal."

Princetonians were not the least surprised. In a game against Williams College, Baker shredded the enemy defense and scored six goals and three assists. Similar performances against other opponents inevitably resulted in a Hobey Baker mystique and attempts by the enemy to cut down Baker at all costs. During one game, Hobey was slashed across the face but refused to yield.

Hobey gave up hockey after the outbreak of World War I and, typically, enlisted in the most daring fighting group, America's air arm, which had been embraced by the French and called the Lafayette Escadrille. Apparently, air combat offered Baker the same thrills, suspense, and, ultimately, triumph that he found on the ice. According to reports, Baker piloted his aircraft with sheer dedication and skill. He downed three German planes and

was well decorated for his bravery under fire. The French army awarded Hobey its highest military honor, the Croix de Guerre, for exceptional valor.

Having nobly served the Allied cause in victory, Hobey prepared to return to the United States and continue his enormously promising hockey career. On December 21, 1918, the very day he was to return home, Baker told his comrades that he wanted to take one last flight. His crew tried to talk him out of it, fearful of the last flight superstition. Hobey nonchalantly dismissed their protests and took off in a recently repaired aircraft. Once aloft, the plane stalled and Baker was unable to restart the motor. The disabled aircraft plummeted to earth, carrying Hobey to his death.

Hobart Baker was born on January 15, 1892 of wealthy parents at Wissahickon, Pennsylvania. Although he was a product of a genteel suburban Philadelphia upbringing, Hobey liked his sports rough and seemed to thrive on the violence of hockey. But, most of all, he was a craftsman with the puck; his ability the result of endless hours of practice.

He began playing organized hockey at St. Paul's School in Concord, New Hampshire, from where he graduated to Princeton. His feats as a varsity member of Princeton's hockey team turned him into a living legend. Baker's mastery of the puck—and the opposition—was reinforced during his play with the St. Nicholas club.

The tragedy of Hobey Baker is twofold; his death at age twenty-six when he was approaching the prime of his life and the fact that he never fulfilled his hockey destiny in the NHL. Based on the reports of those who viewed stars such as Bill Cook, Frank Nighbor, and Bullet Joe Simpson, Hobey Baker would have been every bit as good as them. Unfortunately, we'll never know for sure.

65

Black Jack Stewart
(1938–1952)

"He wasn't dirty," Hall of Famer King Clancy said, "but he was the roughest sonofagun you ever would want to meet."

The subject was Jack Stewart, a defenseman first with the Detroit Red Wings in the late 1930s and 1940s and later with the Chicago Black Hawks, with whom he concluded his career.

Any forward who attempted to penetrate the Detroit defense of Stewart and his sidekick Jimmy Orlando took his life in his hands. Red Wings' manager Jack Adams, who paired them, boasted one of the most muscular one-two combinations on any blue line.

Apart from being a rough hombre, Stewart (unlike Orlando) was a highly polished defenseman who was named to the First All-Star Team in 1943, 1948, and 1949. He made the Second Team in 1947.

A stickler for conditioning, Stewart would spend the summer on his farm in Manitoba and then report to training camp ready for the season to start. "He would be tougher than a pine knot," recalled Toronto *Star* columnist Milt Dunnell, "dour, dedicated and full of pride. He was fast for a defenseman. In the routine practice races around the rink, few of the forwards could outskate him."

Because of his swarthy appearance he was nicknamed *Black Jack*. He played on two Stanley Cup winners and three first-place clubs.

John Sherratt Stewart was born May 6, 1917, in Pilot Mound, Manitoba. He was discovered by a chap named Gene Houghton who worked in the grain exchange at Winnipeg and was friendly with Red Wings' owner Jim Norris, Sr., who happened to be a grain tycoon as well.

Stewart was as fine a sportsman as he was a hockey player. Toronto hockey historian Ed Fitkin, who once was publicist for the Toronto Maple Leafs, recalled how Stewart could perceive the worth of the opposition even in defeat.

"Jack was always one of the first to congratulate the victors after the Wings participated in a lost cause. Once, when Turk Broda of Toronto won the Vezina Trophy in the last game of the schedule at Olympia Stadium in Detroit, Jack heartily threw his arms around the Turk.

"The two game veterans skated off the ice arm in arm. Thousands in Detroit Olympia stood up to give them thunderous tribute."

Although Stewart's checks have been described as thunderous, Black Jack, the man, was quiet to a fault, except on special occasions. One such occasion was the seventh game of the 1950 Stanley Cup finals against the New York Rangers.

"At our pregame meeting," said Jack Adams, "I warned our forwards they weren't hitting anybody. Rangers had been making them look silly. I tried to tell them they should show some bumping.

"Suddenly, Black Jack jumped in. I don't think he ever opened his mouth at a club meeting before—unless he was asked a question. This time, he said: 'You bums get out there and hit somebody. If you don't, I'll be hitting you.' That night we got some bodychecking."

And with Stewart providing airtight defense, the Red Wings won the Cup in the second sudden-death overtime on Pete Babando's screened shot.

As much as he revered Stewart, Adams realized that his thumping warrior was approaching the end of his career. Less than five months after the defeat of the Rangers, Adams included Stewart along with goalie Harry Lumley, defenseman Al Dewsbury, and forwards Pete Babando and Don Morrison in a blockbuster deal with the Chicago Black Hawks. The Red Wings received goalie Jim Henry, forwards Metro Prystai and Gaye Stewart, and defenseman Bob Goldham in return.

Black Jack was playing capably for Chicago when he suffered a ruptured spinal disk. Doctors wrote him off as a hockey player. He was thirty-four and they said he should be grateful if he could walk again, without a cane or crutch.

Stewart accepted their advice, applied some of his own willpower, and returned to the Black Hawks' lineup. He did, after all, have a job to do. Unfortunately, the fickle finger of fate was working against him. During a game against the Rangers, Stewart and Clare Martin were paired on defense. They liked to line up an onrushing forward and put him in a human vise as the enemy tried to split their defense. On this night, the eel-like Edgar Laprade moved into the Black Hawks' zone. But Laprade fooled them and Martin rammed his partner to the ice, as one observer noted, "colder than a mackerel."

Black Jack was hospitalized and required twenty-one stitches to close his wounds. After spending two weeks in the hospital, he announced his retirement. Then, to the amazement of all, he returned to the ice and played two more games for Chicago.

He concluded his career after the 1951–52 season and 566 regular-season games. He then went into coaching, starting with Chatham in the Ontario Hockey Association's Senior League. He then coached two years on the junior level with Kitchener before moving up to the high pro ranks with Pittsburgh of the American League. He gave up coaching for good in 1963 but remained active as a horse racing steward. His love for racing began in his native Pilot Mound, Manitoba, where his father staged race meetings.

Black Jack was as pure as any bodychecking defenseman could be; respected by friend and foe alike, a natural for *Hockey's 100*.

66

Cooney Weiland
(1926–1939)

Any discussion of the golden age of hockey in Boston would have to include the name of Cooney Weiland. He launched his career in Beantown in 1928 and played for the Bruins until 1932, returning again in 1935. He concluded his National Hockey League career as a Bruin in 1939.

By any standard of comparison, Weiland was a superlative center. He was the balance wheel on Boston's *Dynamite Trio*, playing between Dit Clapper and Dutch Gainor when the Bruins won their first Stanley Cup in 1929. He scored forty-three goals in forty-four games that year.

Cooney led the National Hockey League in scoring in 1930 with the Bruins, but two years later he was dealt to the Ottawa Senators and then the Detroit Red Wings.

"Weiland," said former goalie and author S. Kip Farrington, Jr. "was a great face-off man, one of the best I've ever seen. He also was—like Hooley Smith and Frank Nighbor—an excellent three-way stick checker. He was a master of the poke, sweep and hook checks."

He played well for Detroit, but the feeling was that Weiland would be at his best back in Boston. One night, in 1935, the Bruins' manager Frank Patrick met with his Detroit counterpart, Jack Adams.

"If I had Cooney Weiland," Patrick said, "Boston would be able to make the finals."

"If I had Marty Barry," Adams retorted in reference to Boston's big, dour center, "Detroit would win the Stanley Cup."

That did it, and a trade was made that, literally, helped both teams. Cooney moved between Gainor and Clapper, while Barry was inserted between Larry Aurie and Herbie Lewis to form the set of forwards chiefly responsible for Detroit's first Stanley Cup triumph in 1935–36. Weiland guided the Bruins to a pair of first-place finishes and another Stanley Cup in 1939.

Ralph Weiland was born November 5, 1904, in Seaforth, Ontario. He turned pro with the Minneapolis Millers and then graduated to the Bruins. In his book, *Skates, Sticks and Men*, Farrington noted that Weiland had a vast repertoire of ice skills.

"Cooney was outstanding at breaking up power plays and getting the puck in breakaways out of the end zone when the Bruins were playing shorthanded," wrote Farrington. "I believe his greatest night was January 1, 1931 in Madison Square Garden in a game against the Rangers. The Bruins and the Rangers were tied 3–3 in the third period, with about ten minutes to play, when Cooney was tripped from behind while he was going in alone to shoot against John Roach.

"Cooney slid headfirst into the boards and was knocked cold. By the time he was revived, the game was eight minutes into overtime and the Bruins were playing not one but two men short. Cooney returned to the ice and a minute later broke away and started in toward the goal in a duplication of his play in the third period. Only this time he scored the winning goal *before* he fell and slid into the boards again. Momentarily, Cooney was out again, but he had won the game, 4–3."

Weiland produced a 100 percent effort whether he was with a winner or loser. During his one full season with the Ottawa Senators, he was the leading scorer for the last-place club. Yet, it was his precision of handling the subtle skills of the game that caught the attention of experts.

"The finest individual face-off that I can recall, and the most important in a terrible spot, occurred in the Stanley Cup semifinals between Boston and Toronto in April 1939," said Farrington.

"There was a rule that year that if anyone other than the goalie fell on the puck in his defensive zone, there was a face-off. Weiland faced off with Bingo Kampman, the tough defenseman and the Maple Leafs' best face-off man. The puck was square in front of the net, the Bruins were leading by one goal, and there were about five minutes to play. The referee blew his whistle, the puck dropped—away it went, and wound up across the Toronto blue line into their zone. Nobody was able to touch it on the way back. I will never forget it."

Following the Bruins' 1939 Stanley Cup victory, Weiland retired to become coach of the Boston sextet. They finished first in 1939–40 and 1940–41 and also won the Stanley Cup in the latter season. Surprisingly, Weiland achieved even more acclaim as a collegiate coach than he did in the majors. He was recommended for the Harvard coaching job in 1950 by Farrington and turned the Crimson team into an Ivy League power. Between 1950 and his retirement in 1971, Weiland was named the New England Coach of the Year in 1955, 1957, 1961, and 1962—and the American Hockey Coaches Association Coach of the Year in 1957 and 1971. He retired as Harvard hockey coach in 1971 and that same year was voted into the Hockey Hall of Fame. A year later, he received the Lester Patrick Trophy for his outstanding service to amateur hockey in the United States.

67

Dave Keon
(1960–1982)

When Lou Fontinato cruised and bruised his way around Madison Square Garden for the Rangers in the late 1950s, he abided by a simple personal philosophy: "*You* gotta hit first, or they'll run you out of the league." That line of reasoning remains the rule more than the exception as much today as thirty years ago. But there is, and has been since 1960, one small (5'9", 167 pound) nonobserver of that rule who outlasted Fontinato and the rest of his ilk: a speedy little center named Dave Keon.

"It's a good theory," Keon once said of Fontinato's rules of the ice. "Good in the sense that there's some truth to it. But it doesn't apply to *everybody*. I know I don't have to go around hitting to stay up here."

The only thing Keon needed to hit was the enemy net, which he did well enough to keep him around the NHL for the better part of two decades. But Keon was more than a goal scorer. He always has been respected as a tenacious checker and a leader.

In his own way, Keon was as tough and aggressive as his larger opponents. The difference was Dave's preference for playing within the rules. It would have been easier for Keon to compensate for his lack of size with an illegal stick here or a grab there, but that was not Dave Keon. Between 1960 and 1981, he served a total of 111 minutes in penalties, a figure many players eclipse in a year. But for Dave, it was easy since he had been Mister Clean since his early amateur hockey days in Canada.

Keon attended St. Michael's College in Toronto on a scholarship from the Maple Leafs, who then sponsored the school's hockey program. It was there that Keon developed his inimitable style while under the guidance of Father David Bauer, his coach.

When Keon left St. Michael's and jumped directly to the Leafs without wasting a minute in the minors, he found himself playing for Punch Imlach, who endorsed the hockey maxim, "If you can't beat 'em in the alley, you can't beat 'em on the ice." A happy marriage between the impudent Imlach and choirboy Keon seemed unlikely, to say the least.

So when Keon hit the ice in 1960, all eyes focused on the lithe youngster to see if he could handle the rough going in the pros. In his third game, Keon pumped in his first NHL goal, and by season's end he had scored twenty which, in those days, was the equivalent of a .300 batting average in baseball. Keon's play earned him the Calder Trophy as rookie of the year and prompted Imlach to concede that "in time, Keon may be as good as Henri Richard of Montreal." That was high praise indeed.

As Keon's career in Toronto progressed, it became obvious that comparisons were irrelevant. He distinguished himself among his teammates as a leader; a catalyst. He didn't wait for things to happen, he made them happen. The ultimate team player, Keon was the spark that ignited the Maple Leaf's diverse mixture of talent. In his second season with the club, Keon helped lead the Leafs to their first Stanley Cup in eleven years, totaling twenty-six goals and thirty-five assists during the regular season and eight points in twelve contests in postseason play.

Toronto went on to annex the Cup the following two years as well and then again in 1966–67, when Keon was voted the most valuable playoff performer. Keon, while establishing himself as one of the most dangerous two-way players in the league, played on four Cup-winning teams in his first seven seasons in the NHL, a feat rarely accomplished by many professionals in their entire careers.

David Michael Keon was born March 22, 1940, in the mining village of Noranda, in northwestern Quebec. As a means of avoiding a lifetime in the copper mines, which was the destiny of most youngsters in his home town, Keon turned to hockey. Laboring in obscurity both on the ice and under the ground, at the age of fifteen, opportunity approached Dave Keon.

Vince Thompson, geologist and part-time Maple Leafs' scout, happened to see the young lad playing a hockey game in Noranda. After watching him play, Thompson composed a short but urgent letter to Maple Leaf Gardens. "Come get this boy," implored Thompson. "If you don't, another team will hurt you with him some day." With that, the Leafs' scout Bob Davidson was immediately dispatched to the scene and Keon's career was under way.

In addition to the Calder Trophy in 1960–61, Keon also captured the Lady Byng Trophy in 1961–62 and 1962–63, along with the Conn Smythe Trophy as the most valuable player in the playoffs of 1966–67. A two-time Second Team All-Star at center, Keon toiled fifteen seasons for the blue and white, scoring 365 goals and 493 assists. And, remarkably, he never received more than twelve penalty minutes in any season.

In 1975, Keon signed a contract worth approximately $300,000 with the Minnesota Fighting Saints of the newly formed World Hockey Association. The Leafs' captain at the time, Keon was not anxious to abandon his old club and there was more than money behind his motivation. The Leafs, undergoing one of their many housecleaning periods, had let it be known that veterans such as Keon and Norm Ullman were expendable. It was Keon's feeling that had he signed anew with the Maple Leafs, he would have been traded. He did not foresee himself a Leaf in the future and by accepting the Saints' offer, simply wished to control his future. And, as Minnesota's coach Harry Neale so aptly put it, "Dave's strength has always been the things he can do when he *doesn't* have the puck."

Keon played with the Fighting Saints, Indianapolis Racers, and New England Whalers of the WHA before finally returning to the NHL when the New England entry was absorbed as the Hartford Whalers in the league's expansion movement in 1979–80. During his WHA career, Keon netted 102 goals to go along with 189 assists.

In the fall of 1981, at the ripe old age of forty-one, Keon opened yet another NHL season as captain of the Whalers and, while possibly having lost a half-stride, gathered no cobwebs. His diligence with the puck, moxie, and leadership qualities made him an invaluable asset to his young squad.

He plugged as hard as the first day he appeared as a crew-cut rookie in Toronto. Keon soon retired. His career was summed up best by his former teammate and Hall of Fame goaltender, Jacques Plante: "Keon was proof that it's not the size of the body but the size of the heart that counts in this game."

The Davey among the Goliaths of the NHL, he is honorably awarded his hard-earned place here among *Hockey's 100*.

68

Babe Pratt
(1935–1947)

Babe Pratt had a certain *joie de vivre* that reminded oldtimers of another Babe from a different sport and an earlier era, that being Babe Ruth. Both indulged in the good life, often to excess, yet they were capable of Promethean accomplishments.

Pratt was a defenseman who could rush the puck and score goals in the manner of latter-day blueliners such as Bobby Orr and Denis Potvin. He had a flair for the dramatic and the ability to satisfactorily conclude a project he had begun. The Babe was architect of one of the most dramatic winning goals in Stanley Cup history. This was in the seventh game of the 1945 Stanley Cup finals against the Red Wings. With the score tied, 1–1, late in the game, Pratt fired the puck behind goalie Harry Lumley and the Leafs triumphed, 2–1.

By all rights, Pratt should have been a New York Ranger at the time. He had come up through the Ranger system and was a star playing for Lester Patrick's team, but Patrick must have had second thoughts about Babe's off-ice deportment. Conn Smythe, the Toronto manager, had been watching Pratt for years and dealt for him when he got the chance.

"I remember once," said Smythe, "when Pratt was with the Rangers and we were tied late in the game. A good Ranger forward got hurt and Pratt was moved up to a wing. I thought,'Aha, here's our chance to win.' Who got the winning goal? Pratt, playing forward."

The Babe won the Hart Trophy as the National Hockey League's most valuable player in 1944 and was a First All-Star that same year. A season later, he was voted to the Second All-Star Team.

"If he'd looked after himself he could have played until he was fifty," said Conn Smythe in his memoirs, *If You Can't Beat 'em In The Alley.* "But he was as big a drinker and all-around playboy as he was a hockey player."

Walter Pratt was born January 7, 1916, in Stony Mountain, Manitoba, but grew up in the city of Winnipeg. His hero was National Hockey League star, Frank Frederickson, who lived near the Pratt home.

Babe played his early hockey on Winnipeg's numerous outdoor rinks in temperatures as low as forty degrees below zero Fahrenheit. When he was fifteen, he moved up to the junior level and began demonstrating the moves that soon would attract the attention of major-league scouts. Al Ritchie, a New York Rangers bird dog, took a look at Pratt and reported back favorably to Rangers' manager Lester Patrick. The Babe was invited to the

Rangers' camp in 1934 and played well enough to win a professional offer, but he chose to return to the amateur ranks for another year.

A year later he returned to the Rangers' base and was signed to a contract. Babe was farmed out to Philadelphia at first but soon was recalled by Patrick as part of a dynasty-in-the-making. Here is what Pratt told me about the club in an interview:

"By the end of the thirties, Patrick had really developed a powerful hockey club; we could play terrifically, offensively as well as defensively. Conn Smythe, who was then running the Toronto Maple Leafs, said that the 1940 Rangers were the greatest hockey club he'd ever seen. In those days, whenever we came to Toronto, Smythe would advertise us as 'The Broadway Blues, Hockey's Classiest Team.'

"Our club was so well-balanced that our first line scored 38 goals, the second, 37, and the third line, 36, over the season.

"On that Ranger team we had three great centermen—Clint Smith, Phil Watson, and Neil Colville—plus so many good wingmen that we were able to put the pressure on the other team when we were a man short. Our power play was so strong that once the Toronto Maple Leafs took a penalty we kept the puck in their end of the rink for the entire two minutes—and scored two goals.

"It was a different kind of game then. Today, they stress boardchecking and checking from behind, both unheard of when we played. We'd hit a man standing right up and now the players don't seem to want to take that kind of check. The only check they want is on the first and fifteenth of the month.

"Sure, we played a tough game but we also had a million laughs. There was a newspaperman from *The New York World-Telegram* named Jim Burchard who liked to drink, tell stories, and do wild things like swim across the Hudson River. Once, we had Ukulele Ike traveling with us and, naturally, Burchard had his own uklele which he played every night we were in a Stanley Cup round. We also had quite a few jokers on the team. Ching Johnson was one; he was also one of the finest players when it came to working with rookies. Ching was from Winnipeg too, and he sort of took me under his wing."

It also probably helped speed Pratt's exit from New York. When the Rangers traded the Babe, they accepted an untried rookie, Red Garrett (who was killed during World War II) and a mediocre forward, Hank Goldup. Babe stabilized the Toronto backline and personally delivered a Stanley Cup in 1945. But the Maple Leafs floundered the following year and Smythe decided to go with youth.

Pratt was traded to the Boston Bruins, played one season with them, and then was sent to the minors. Instead of quitting, he played for the Hershey Bears, Cleveland Barons, and New Westminster Royals before calling it a career in 1952 after skating for the Tacoma Rockets.

Those who knew and loved the Babe were delighted when the Vancouver Canucks signed him as a goodwill ambassador when they entered the NHL in 1970. There were few big-leaguers with as much goodwill as Pratt and even fewer with his talent.

69

Charlie Gardiner

(1927–1934)

Only his relatively brief career prevented Charlie (Chuck) Gardiner from receiving a higher place among *Hockey's 100*. Certainly, there have been few better goaltenders during any of the game's epochs.

Before illness cut short his career, Gardiner played seven years with the Chicago Black Hawks, produced forty-two shutouts, and had a remarkable 2.13 goals against average. He won the Vezina Trophy (best goalie) in 1932 and repeated it in 1934. Thrice (1931, 1932, 1934) he was voted to the First All-Star Team and in 1933 made the Second Team.

The Black Hawks had never won a Stanley Cup championship until 1934, and it was then, thanks to Gardiner's efforts, that they prevailed. He permitted only twelve goals in eight playoff games for a 1.50 average.

Gardiner was one of the first of a legion of Windy City hockey heros and Chuck, few could dispute, helped plant the seed of hockey interest in that city. A cocky Scotsman, he nevertheless distracted fans from an abysmally weak Black Hawks team.

Charles Robert Gardiner was born December 31, 1904, in Edinburgh, Scotland, and arrived in Canada with his family in 1911. He grew up in hockey-mad Winnipeg during the 1920s and was discovered in 1925 while playing for a team in Selkirk, Manitoba.

Signed by the Winnipeg Maroons, he played through the 1926–27 season unaware that the Black Hawks were scouting him. He was signed by Chicago owner Major Frederick McLaughlin and played poorly in his first four games with the Black Hawks. Shortly thereafter he turned it around and was enroute to permanent stardom.

One could fill a volume detailing Gardiner's exploits. A game against the powerful Boston Bruins is a case in point. Eddie Shore, the premier defenseman of the Bruins, was zooming in on Gardiner for a shot when the Black Hawk goalie edged out of his crease to meet him. In this way, Gardiner trimmed down the shooter's angle and forced Shore to shoot wide of the target. Undaunted, Shore pursued the puck behind the net, but Gardiner wheeled around and tripped the big Bruin.

In those days, the NHL awarded one-minute penalties to goalies, and Gardiner was ordered off the ice. While he sat out his foul, teammate Wentworth moved into the nets without the benefit of goaltender's equipment and managed to blunt the Bruins' attack.

Meanwhile, the impatient Gardiner was leaning on the boards awaiting the moment when he would finally spring from the penalty box. When his sentence expired, he leaped over the wooden boards and dashed headlong for the goal.

At the moment Gardiner was released, Boston defenseman George Owen captured the

puck. He carefully aimed for the four-by-six-foot opening and drilled the rubber for what appeared to be a goal. But it never went in. Charlie had made the save.

By 1929, Gardiner had improved so much that he finished second to the immortal George Hainsworth of the Montreal Canadiens in the race for the Vezina Trophy. In 1932, he would finally win the coveted prize and be named to the All-Star Team. Charlie was the one piece of pure gold on the roster and the lever that could catapult the Hawks to the heights of greatness.

In 1932–33, the Black Hawks finished fourth—out of the playoffs. The following year, they rallied and launched their most serious assault on first place. That they failed by seven points and finished second to Detroit was no fault of Gardiner's. His goaltending reached new degrees of perfection. He allowed only eighty-three goals in forty-eight games and registered ten shutouts. In fourteen other games, he permitted just one goal.

But astute Gardiner watchers perceived that there was something unusual about the goalie's deportment, and they couldn't figure out just what it was. Gardiner had lost his jovial manner and appeared to be melancholy.

Unknown to everyone, Gardiner was suffering from a chronic tonsil infection. The disease had spread and had begun to cause uremic convulsions. However, the goaltender pressed on. Winning the Stanley Cup became an obsession with him, and the Black Hawks responded by defeating first the Canadiens and then the Montreal Maroons. This put them in the Cup finals against the awesome Detroit Red Wings.

The best-of-five series opened in Detroit and the Black Hawks won the first game, 2–1, in double overtime. In the second, also at Detroit's Olympia Stadium, the Hawks ran away with the game, 4–1. When the teams returned to Chicago for the third, and what appeared to be the final game, all hands were ready to concede the Stanley Cup to the Black Hawks.

But it was not to be Charlie Gardiner's night. His body was wracked with pain, and he prayed that he might recapture his physical condition of seasons past. Charlie moved between the pipes for two periods, but the relentless Detroit attack overcame him in the third. Detroit won the game, 5–2.

Gardiner collapsed on a bench in the dressing room minutes after the final buzzer but recovered quickly enough to realize that, psychologically, the Black Hawks were collapsing with him. Summoning all the strength at his command, Charlie peered across the room and said: "Look, all I want is one goal next game. Just one goal and I'll take care of the other guys."

On April 10, 1934, Gardiner returned to the crease, hunched his shoulders, tapped his pads, and prepared for battle. His body was numb from fatigue, but he was determined to overcome the pain and play his game.

For two periods, Gardiner was never better. He held the Detroiters scoreless, but the Black Hawks were also unable to score. Even as it drained him of energy, Gardiner screamed encouragement to his players, but it was to no avail. The red-shirted Detroiters' counterattack developed new intensity, and Charlie did all he could to keep them at bay. He did and the game went into sudden-death overtime.

There were those who doubted that Gardiner could sustain both the physical and mental strain much longer, yet when the overtime began he was smiling and even waved his stick to the crowd. For another twenty minutes, he blunted the best shots the enemy could hurl at him, but his teammates could do no better and a second sudden-death period was required.

Charlie could no longer smile. Flames of pain burned his insides as he tried to concentrate on the black rubber disk. The overtime had begun again, and for ten minutes there was no resolution. Suddenly, little Mush March of the Black Hawks took command, skating into Detroit ice. He cracked his wrist and the puck took off and sailed past Wilf Cude and into the net. The time was 10:05 when the Black Hawks had annexed their first Stanley Cup.

Gardiner hurled his stick in the air and then just barely made it back to the dressing room under the backslaps of his teammates.

The roar of the crowd had hardly subsided when Charlie was taken to the hospital. He underwent brain surgery and following the operation died on June 13, 1934.

Those who watched Gardiner in action on a regular basis suggest that he was the greatest of all time. Certainly, in seven years of NHL play he demonstrated an uncanny puck-stopping ability. However, his career was too short to permit inclusion on a higher plane, although this, in no way, diminishes Gardiner's accomplishments.

70

Syd Howe
(1929–1946)

Midway in the 1981–82 season, when Wayne Gretzky began dominating the hockey scene at the tender age of twenty, someone asked Hall of Famer Gordie Howe whether he got as much acclaim at age twenty as Gretzky was obtaining.

"Hell," said Gordie, "the only thing people ever asked me when I was twenty was whether I was related to *Syd Howe*."

In the 1940s, it was considered an honor to be related to Syd Howe. He wasn't the greatest of the Detroit Red Wings, but he ranked among the most versatile shooters ever to torment an enemy goaltender. Syd could play virtually any position but was used mostly as a left wing or center.

He was named to the Second All-Star Team as a left wing in 1945, but, by far, his most notable accomplishment took place a year earlier; on the night of February 3, 1944, to be exact. The Red Wings were at home to the New York Rangers on that night, and at 11:27 of the first period, Howe launched what was to become known as one of the most impressive individual performances in history.

Taking a pass from Don "The Count" Grosso, he beat Ken "Tubby" McAuley in the Rangers' net. Just eighteen seconds later, Howe scored again. The score was 3–0 for Detroit late in the second period when defenseman Cully Simon delivered a pass to Howe and he beat goalie McAuley at 17:52, giving him a hat trick. Exactly sixty-two seconds later, Grosso spotted a free Howe, dispatched the pass, and still another red light went on for Syd. It was 5–0 for the Red Wings, and Howe already had four goals.

For eight minutes of the third period, the Rangers stymied him, but then his linemates Grosso and Modere "Mud" Bruneteau moved rapidly into the Rangers' zone. Howe was in position and whipped the rubber home at 8:17.

By now, Detroit coach Jack Adams knew he had the game in the bag—it was 8–0 for the Red Wings—so he gave his top line as much ice as possible and, sure enough, less than a minute later Bruneteau and Grosso collaborated once more, fed Howe, and just like that he had *his sixth goal of the game.*

"They left me out there on the ice to try and get more goals," Howe remembered. "I had a good chance to break the all-time record (Joe Malone scored seven goals for the Quebec Bulldogs in 1920) but I couldn't do it."

Over the years, Howe has played down the importance of the six-goal game. "I got a lot more satisfaction out of two other nights," he said.

In one of them, he set a league record for the then fastest overtime playoff goal,

twenty-five seconds after the start of the extra period. It happened on March 19, 1940, against the New York Americans.

"The score was 0–0," Syd recalled, "and I was playing on a line with Bruneteau and [Carl] Liscombe. I went down the left side and sent a low shot into the corner. The other time I'll never forget is the 'night' Detroit fans gave me toward the end of my career. I got a lot of gifts, including a piano.

"You know how it is when they give you a 'night'. It usually turns out that the team gets beat and you can't come close to scoring. I was a lot luckier. We beat the Black Hawks, 2–0, and I scored both goals."

Sydney Harris Howe was born September 18, 1911, in Ottawa, Ontario. He broke into the National Hockey League with his home town team, the Senators, during the 1929–30 season and a year later was with the Philadelphia Quakers before returning to the Senators in 1932. He was transferred to the St. Louis Eagles in 1934 and came to Detroit in 1935 along with defenseman Ralph "Scotty" Bowman in a deal said to involve $50,000, which was big money in those days of the Great Depression. It was one of Detroit's best deals, for Howe emerged as a versatile forward who could play virtually any position, and play it well.

Point-wise, Syd's best season was 1943–44 when he scored thirty-two goals and twenty-eight assists for sixty points in forty games. He played for three Stanley Cup winners and three first-place teams.

It is noteworthy that Howe pinpointed the turnabout in hockey's attacking style as taking place during the 1942 Stanley Cup finals between the Red Wings and the Toronto Maple Leafs. "Up until that time," Syd explained, "the attacks and counterattacks were more or less straight up and down, with the puck either carried or passed back and forth into the enemy zone. But in the 1942 series Detroit started the 'new' way of *shooting* the puck into the opposition's zone and *chasing* after it."

Syd remained a Red Wing through the 1945–46 season and then retired just before Gordie Howe came on to the scene. After retirement, Syd Howe returned to his native Ottawa and would be reminded of his six-goal accomplishment whenever another NHLer came close to matching his feat. In the early 1960s, he was attending a gathering at the home of his friends in Ottawa. On that night, word got around that Bobby Rousseau had scored five goals. "The people at the party," said Howe, "were more worried than I was about Rousseau breaking the record."

In time, Red Berenson of the St. Louis Blues would equal Howe's modern mark but nobody has ever surpassed it. Howe was elected to the Hockey Hall of Fame in 1965. In a sense, it is unfortunate that his skill has been overshadowed by the *other* Howe, the greatest player of all time.

71

Dick Irvin
(1915–1929)

Were it not for a fractured skull suffered while he was playing for the Chicago Black Hawks, Dick Irvin very likely would have written an even more glorious chapter in National Hockey League history than already has been transcribed. But when Red Dutton of the Montreal Maroons flattened Irvin, Dutton inadvertently launched one of the most accomplished of NHL coaching careers. As time unfolded, Irvin's name became synonymous with coaching excellence while his extraordinary feats as a player faded from memory.

Those who remember Irvin as a young professional in western Canada invariably mention his prowess as a scorer and his courage under the cruelest conditions. Once, while playing for Regina, Irvin was deliberately hooked under the chin by a notorious foe named Spunk Sparrow.

Irvin had a habit of playing with his tongue between his teeth and the blow of Sparrow's stick was so severe that Dick bit right through his tongue. Instead of heading to the infirmary for repairs, Irvin insisted upon continuing. He won the face-off, wheeled past the penalty bench where Sparrow was incarcerated, and walloped his adversary so hard that Sparrow required sixteen stitches to close the wound. Only *then* did Irvin head for the dressing room where the doctor sewed up his tongue, which was hanging by a shred.

Throughout most of his playing career, Irvin was eclipsed by only the very best. While playing for the Portland Rosebuds, for example, Irvin finished second in scoring to Bill Cook of Saskatoon, who was regarded as the finest right wing of his time.

Coincidentally, in Irvin's rookie year in the National Hockey League he finished runner-up to the scoring champion—Bill Cook.

James Dickenson Irvin was born July 19, 1892, in Limestone Ridge, Ontario, just outside the city of Hamilton. His family moved to Winnipeg in 1899, and it was while living there that Dick learned to skate on the Red River.

In time, he became well-known throughout Winnipeg amateur hockey circles. One night, while watching a game at Winnipeg Amphitheater, Dick was a witness while Dolly Gray of the Winnipeg Monarchs broke his shoulder. Irvin was asked to replace the injured Gray and obliged by scoring five goals in an 8–3 win over Winnipeg Varsity. From that point on Dick never looked back.

Playing for the Monarchs against the Toronto Rugby and Athletic Association team in 1914, Irvin scored *all* of his team's goals in a 9–1 victory. The nine-goal effort earned Dick a place in Robert Ripley's "Believe it or Not" syndicated newspaper feature.

Irvin turned pro with Portland in 1914 and played one full season before enlisting in the Canadian army. He served for three years, returning to Canada where he resumed his hockey career with Regina. Following two years with Regina, Irvin moved west to Portland during the golden era of western hockey.

Irvin was an instant hit skating for the Rosebuds in Portland and undoubtedly would have remained there for several seasons were it not for the fact that the Western League could not weather its financial crisis and finally packed it in. The NHL, meanwhile, was expanding throughout the United States, and Chicago, among other cities, obtained a franchise.

The Chicago Black Hawks' owner, Major Frederick McLaughlin, decided to purchase the entire Portland Rosebud hockey club, and in 1926, Irvin made his debut in the Windy City. Coach Pete Muldoon named Dick captain of the new entry and Irvin responded by leading the Black Hawks in scoring.

It was early in his second year as a Black Hawk when Irvin was flattened by Red Dutton and hospitalized with a fractured skull. After his release from the hospital, Dick was refused permission to play for the remainder of the season. He returned the following year, played a few games, and then was appointed coach of the Chicago sextet.

The conclusion of Irvin's playing career marked the start of a twenty-six-year career as an NHL coach. He remained behind the Black Hawks' bench until 1931 when he switched to the Toronto Maple Leafs. He stayed in Toronto, working under manager Conn Smythe until 1940.

He led the Maple Leafs to their first Stanley Cup championship in 1932, but his halcyon years as a coach were spent in Montreal during the 1940s and early 1950s. He won Stanley Cups with Les Canadiens in 1944, 1946, and 1953.

As a coach, he became increasingly truculent behind the bench as he aged. Irvin was considered a terrific stimulant for Canadiens super-scorer Maurice "The Rocket" Richard during *The Rocket*'s early years, but in the early 1950s, some critics believed that Irvin prodded Richard into tempestuous combat too often and this, in turn, led to innumerable penalties for Richard. Frank Selke, Sr., a great friend and booster of Irvin, was managing director of the Canadiens at the time and finally decided that Irvin was having a negative effect on Richard. Irvin resigned from the Canadiens in 1955 and took the job as head coach of the Chicago Black Hawks for the 1955–56 season.

Those close to Irvin realized that he already was suffering from a terminal ailment and, as the season progressed, Dick's condition worsened. Gamecock that he was, Irvin remained at the helm until the end of the campaign and even considered a return for the 1956–57 season. He finally acknowledged the depth of his illness and retired at the start of the new campaign. The NHL immediately named him to the position of goodwill ambassador, and Dick worked when he could. He died in May 1957 and was elected to the Hockey Hall of Fame a year later.

72

Dale Hawerchuk
(1981–   )

It never helps to be called *The Next Gretzky*, and it certainly was no asset to Dale Hawerchuk when he was drafted by the Winnipeg Jets in 1981. Not only was the Toronto native being compared with hockey's greatest star, but he would have to face him on a regular basis in the Smythe Division.

Since there has been only one other *next Gretzky*—the incomparable Mario Lemieux—it is hardly surprising that Hawerchuk has appeared to be somewhat short of marvelous. But neither Jets' general manager John Ferguson nor any Winnipeg hockey fan has any complaints about Dale's production. He has consistently ranked among the NHL's top ten scorers and has virtually carried the Jets' franchise ever since he won the Calder Trophy as the rookie of the year in 1982. Yet, Hawerchuk has managed to remain out of the media mainstream for most of his career.

The 5'11", 195 pound center, whose nickname is *Ducky*, has often been ignored for three reasons. First, he's been buried in Winnipeg, hardly the media capital of the NHL; second, he lacks Lemieux's charisma; and third, unlike Gretzky, he has been wary of the media throughout the years.

Dale's distancing from the press has cost him All-Star votes and the attention he deserved. "Definitely, I've noticed the difference," lamented Hawerchuk, "especially from the media centers in the east. Players in the west...the guys in the east don't see them often enough to make a good judgment." Yet, Hawerchuk has always been a top producer. He led his junior team, the Cornwall Royals, to back-to-back Memorial Cup championships and was one of the stars of the *Rendez-Vous '87* NHL-USSR series.

Hawerchuk has matured as a player in the NHL. He has transformed his style of play from that of a player who would not go into the corners to a bumping and grinding all-around player. "That's what I thought that I had to do for us to win," he explained. "As you get older you realize that it's not necessary to get two or three points in a game. You learn to win instead of just putting numbers up."

Learning how to win was something that *Ducky* did well. As the youngest player ever to win the rookie of the year award (he was just nineteen), he "lived up to the expectations right from his first year," said Jets' scout Tom Savage. "He's more or less carried the load, year after year after year. But in the east, you didn't hear much about any of the players in Winnipeg. The rest of the country had yet to be convinced."

His point production soared only three seasons after Dale's arrival in the NHL. In 1984–85, he recorded a career-high 130 points, including fifty-three goals. He was third in overall scoring and led the Jets to a second place finish in the division. "He's the leader,

he's the captain of this hockey club and he sets the tempo for this team," said Winnipeg coach Dan Maloney.

Skating ability is what allows Dale to perform in the fast lane. He has excellent lateral movement and a tremendous stride that enables him to get anywhere on the ice he has to go. As one NHL official analyzed: "Next to Gretzky, Hawerchuk has the best lateral moves of any skater in the league. He can make moves at any speed and in any direction, and he has good one-step quickness that starts him on his way instantly."

Dale Hawerchuk was born in Toronto, Ontario, on April 4, 1963. As a fifteen-year-old, he played his Junior B hockey at Oshawa under coach Mike Keenan who later would be Dale's Canada Cup coach. Curiously, Keenan hardly recognized Hawerchuk at the start of the tourney, but after sitting for most of the first few games, Hawerchuk then got major amounts of ice time and he responded. Scoring on a slapshot midway into the second period of the semifinal game against Czechoslovakia, he led his team to a win and final berth against the Russians. In the third and final game, a *Ducky* goal gave Team Canada the lead for good. To those who recall Hawerchuk's teen years, the NHL stardom was no surprise.

In 1981, he won the Player of the Year award from the Quebec Major Junior Hockey League as well as the Canadian Major Junior Player of the Year Trophy. One of the Jets' scouts followed Dale's junior career very closely and remembers hearing his wife say, "The Kid, The Kid, that's all I ever hear about." Well, now everybody has heard of "The Kid."

Accolades followed Hawerchuk everywhere he went during his last year in the Quebec Junior League. Drafted in the shadow of American-born Bobby Carpenter, *Ducky* managed to grab his share of the spotlight. "The things that he did as a 17-year-old you didn't really see other players at that age do," scout Savage recalled. "When a player is in a class by himself, it makes [scouting] easier."

Hawerchuk has all the qualifications of a superstar, although he has never skated for an NHL championship team. He scores frequently and with ease, stickhandles adroitly, and is an able captain. That he is not *The Next Gretzky* is certainly not Dale Hawerchuk's fault. He has remained a vital part of the Winnipeg organization, leading them into the playoffs every season since draft day 1981. His accomplishments qualify him for *Hockey's 100.*

73

Frank Brimsek
(1938–1950)

Mr Zero.

There was never one before, and there will never be one again. Frank Brimsek was the original, and after him they threw away the mold. One would be hard pressed to find an American-born player who made a more emphatic impact on "The Game." And were it not for a World War II stint in the United States Coast Guard—which significantly disturbed his future—Brimsek might well have emerged as the greatest exponent of goaltending we have even known.

As it was, his career featured a number of truly sensational chapters from the moment it was announced that he would depose the remarkable Tiny Thompson in the Boston Bruins' net.

In Frankie's rookie season of 1939, he won both the Calder Trophy as the best newcomer in the league and the Vezina Trophy for his outstanding play in the nets, the only American player ever to accomplish that achievement. That year, Frankie was voted to the First All-Star Team. He repeated as the Vezina winner in 1942 and was the First All-Star Team goalie that year. Brimsek was named to the Second All-Star Team six times during his Boston career. With Frankie in the nets, the Bruins won the Stanley Cup twice and three times finished first.

He was an American legend in hockey. In 1966, Frankie Brimsek, born and raised in Eveleth, Minnesota, became the first United States player of professional hockey elected to the Hockey Hall of Fame. He was also inducted into the U.S. Hockey Hall of Fame.

Brimsek had quite a sensational break in the majors. In 1937, he had been assigned to Boston's American League farm club, the Providence Reds. Boston's goaltender was none other than Tiny Thompson, known to the hockey world as "the goalie without a weakness." Thompson was the best in the business, a four-time Vezina Trophy winner. Prospects didn't look good for the American kid buried in the minors.

It was quite by accident that Brimsek got his first chance to play in a big-league game. Thompson developed an eye infection, and Art Ross, the general manager and coach of Boston, sent for Brimsek. Frank was nervous. It was tough enough to fill in for any goalie, but the pressure was colossal considering the kid was being asked to fill the nets for the great Tiny Thompson.

Frank's jitters vanished once the game started. Frankie, then only twenty-three years old, won his NHL debut by a score of 3–2. Three nights later, with Brimsek in the nets, the Bruins beat the Detroit Red Wings.

Thompson recovered, and Frankie was sent back to Providence. But Ross had liked what he had seen. He now had a dilemma on his hands. Popular with the fans, Thompson was great and had been Boston's solid rock for ten years. At thirty-three, he would have several more outstanding seasons.

Trading Thompson would not go over well with the multitude of Bruin supporters, especially if Tiny's replacement failed. Ross journeyed to Providence to take another look at Frankie, who turned in a couple of shutouts while Ross scouted him. On November 28, 1938, Tiny Thompson was dealt to the Red Wings for $15,000.

On December 1, 1938, in a game against the Montreal Canadiens, Frankie Brimsek went into the nets not as the replacement for an injured Thompson, but as the regular goalie for the Bruins. Although the game was played at the Montreal Forum, Brimsek was aware there were critical eyes watching his every move.

The evening turned into a disaster. Montreal, who had won only once in their eight previous contests, beat Boston 2–0. In Detroit, the exiled Thompson beat Chicago 4–1. It left little reason to doubt that Ross had made a mistake.

Frankie Brimsek was down but not out. It took only the next seven games for him to become a hockey legend. Playing the next game against the Chicago Black Hawks, Brimsek recorded his first ever NHL shutout, as Boston beat Chicago by a score of 5–0.

However, the fans were not yet warming to him, and Frankie did little to improve his image. He had an idiosyncrasy of wearing red hockey pants instead of the team's then gold, brown, and white colors, and his footwork left much to be desired. But his glove was quick and his confidence was enormous. The Boston fans would be in for a surprise.

Two nights later, the same teams met in Boston. It was Frankie's first appearance before the hostile Bruins fans. Brimsek claimed he could feel the coolness from the crowd.

Frankie's next game was against the New York Rangers. Although the Rangers belted him with thirty-three shots on goal, Frankie stopped them all, as he earned his third straight shutout by a score of 3–0. He had 192 minutes and 40 seconds of scoreless goaltending. Thompson's modern record of 224 minutes and 47 seconds was in reach.

By now, even the Boston fans were wildly supporting Brimsek. The Bruins were so confident of Frankie's ability that they often sent five men into enemy territory, leaving Brimsek to fend for himself. The next game was against Montreal at the Boston Garden. Boston jumped to a 2–0 lead in the first period, while Frank held Montreal scoreless. The amazing string of scoreless goaltending ran to 212 minutes and 40 seconds.

At the 12:00 minute mark of the second period, the tension in the Garden grew. At 12:08, the arena went wild! Brimsek, in only his fifth game as the Bruins' regular goalie, had erased Tiny Thompson's scoreless record. However, with less than a minute to go in the second period, four Bruins were caught down ice, and Herb Cain took a pass from George Brown and dumped the puck in the Boston goal. Brimsek's marvelous streak had ended at 231 minutes and 54 seconds. Boston went on to win the game 3–2.

Thanks largely to the talents of the young American goalie, Boston was now in first place. Brimsek next shut out Montreal 1–0. Next were the Detroit Red Wings, and the first face-to-face meeting with Thompson. Both goalies played well, but Boston won 2–0. Frankie cut down the New York Americans next, by a score of 3–0. It was his third straight shutout, and his sixth in seven games.

Brimsek went after his own record in the next game against the Rangers. He held New York scoreless during the first period. During the second period, Phil Watson put the puck in the net for the first goal on Brimsek in 220 minutes and 24 seconds of hockey. When Frankie reached down to retrieve the puck, the fans gave him a standing ovation.

Frankie Brimsek had done the impossible—he had won over the Boston fans and made them forget Tiny Thompson.

Francis Charles Brimsek was born on September 26, 1915, in Eveleth, Minnesota. His interest in hockey, oddly enough, was accidental. His older brother John was the second-string goaltender on the Eveleth High School team, but what he really wanted to be was a defensemen. John moved up to the blue line, and brother Frank took over in the nets.

After playing at Eveleth High, he goaltended for a short time at St. Cloud Teachers College. He decided to give the pros a shot, and in 1935, Frankie traveled to Baltimore for a tryout with Baltimore of the Eastern Amateur Hockey League. He failed.

Hitchhiking back home to Minnesota, depressed and disappointed, Frank was about to land in hockey by accident once more. Running out of cash while he was in Pittsburgh, Frankie stopped off at the old Duquesne Arena to see if he could borrow money for food. Lady Luck shined again on the Minnesota native, as the Pittsburgh team in the Eastern League, the Yellow Jackets, needed a goaltender. Frankie got the job. For two years, Brimsek was that club's goalie.

In the fall of 1937, Ross signed Brimsek to a pro contract. He had never even seen the young man play. Assigned to the Providence Reds, Boston's American League farm club, Frankie waited in the minors. In 1938, Brimsek, barely one year out of the amateurs, was Boston's goalie.

Looking back on that rookie season, Frankie said, "Tiny was such a great goaltender. I had to be good or they would have chased me right out of Boston."

During that spectacular rookie season, Brimsek finished with a brilliant 1.59 average and had ten shutouts. He had given up only seventy goals in forty-four games. Rightfully he was awarded both the Calder Trophy and the Vezina Trophy.

Frankie played for Boston for five sparkling seasons, winning the Vezina Trophy again in 1942. At the end of the 1942–43 season, he enlisted in the United States Coast Guard, and for the next two years, he served aboard a patrol craft in the Pacific.

After the war, Frankie gave the National Hockey League another try. He returned to Boston for four seasons, but his comeback was a great disappointment. He had lost his edge. The Bruins kept waiting and hoping for the magic to come back. It never did. Boston traded Frankie to the dismal Chicago Black Hawks in 1949. There, Brimsek bombed terribly, and he retired after one season.

Frank had retired at the relatively young age of thirty-four. He had been the best, and he had been unique, an American-born, American-developed goaltender, excelling at his skill. He had played on Stanley Cup winners. He had stood alone on the mountaintop, the finest in his profession. The war had caused him to lose his skill, and Brimsek had little choice but to retire.

After he retired, Frankie settled in Virginia, Minnesota, a small town only five miles from Eveleth. He became an engineer for the Canadian National Railroad, guiding freight trains between the various cities in Canada.

His goaltending for the prewar Boston Bruins will forever be cited by hockey's *cognescenti* as the definitive work of its time. Frankie Brimsek proved beyond a doubt that an American could make it in the Canadian-laden National Hockey League.

74

Duke Keats
(1916–1929)

For sheer smarts as a hockey player, few could equal and nobody could top Duke Keats. Frank Patrick, a Hall of Famer and himself one of the most astute judges of hockey talent, once observed of Keats: "Duke is the possessor of more hockey grey matter than any man who ever played the game. He is the most unselfish superstar in hockey. I have watched him innumerable times. In one game, I specially checked up on his play. He gave his wingmen thirty chances to score by perfectly placed passes. He's the brainiest pivot that ever pulled on a skate, because he can organize plays and make passes every time he starts."

Keats originally made his mark with the Toronto Arenas in 1916, and then the Edmonton Eskimos of the Western Canada Hockey League, operated by Frank and Lester Patrick. It was a splendid league, the equal of the National Hockey League. Keats' Edmonton teammates included aces such as Barney Stanley and Bullet Joe Simpson, each of whom is in the Hockey Hall of Fame.

By the early 1920s, *The Duke* reigned as one of the most popular and accomplished players in western Canada. "He was the hero of Edmonton," wrote Canadian journalist Ken McConnell, "and undoubtedly one of the greatest center-ice men who ever laced up a skate."

Gordon Keats was born March 1, 1895, in Montreal, but learned his hockey in North Bay, Ontario. He joined the McKinlay-Darragh mine team in the old Cobalt Mining League when he was fourteen. Two years later, when he was only sixteen, he joined the Toronto Arenas.

One night in 1916, Keats scored two goals in twenty seconds for the Toronto club against Quebec City. "He is the one hockey player who will always remain my superstar," said McConnell.

While playing for the Arenas—also known as the Blue Shirts—Duke enlisted in the 228th Sportsmen's Battalion of Toronto, which entered a team in the NHA for the 1916–17 season, when wartime spirit was reaching its peak.

From time to time, the schedule called for the Arenas to play the Battalion sextet. By no small coincidence, Duke's sergeant made a point of assigning him to guard duty on those occasions. This piqued several Blue Shirts' fans, who were worried that *The Duke* would be absent from the match between the 228th and Toronto on January 20, 1917.

Word of Keats's impending guard duty was leaked to the Toronto newspapers, and public sentiment was militantly against the sergeant's shenanigans. "Keats," said Ken McConnell, "was thrown into the guardhouse but was released the day of the game after every newspaper in Toronto had printed the story. He was allowed to play against his battalion mates."

For some time, the army regretted its decision. Early in the third period, Toronto's goaltender, Billy Nicholson, was penalized. In that era, goaltenders had to serve their penalties in the penalty box, so a replacement for Nicholson was needed. *The Duke* himself strapped on the goalie pads and took his position in front of the nets. "He played the remaining twenty minutes," according to the NHL history, "without allowing a goal."

Further controversy about Keats's right to play for Toronto was ended on February 10, 1917, when the 228th Battalion received orders to go overseas. Duke, of course, was with them. When he returned from active duty, Keats signed with Edmonton of the Western Canada Hockey League. According to Babe Donnelly, he was a better hockey player than ever.

Keats led the Western Canada Hockey League in scoring in 1922–23 and steered Edmonton to the league championship and a match-up against the Ottawa Senators in a battle for the Stanley Cup. But the easterners prevailed, although Duke had made a very favorable impression on NHL types. This was significant because the WCHL was in the process of disintegrating and the Patricks, Frank and Lester, had decided to sell their best players to the expanding National Hockey League.

The Duke was plucked by manager Art Ross of the Boston Bruins who, in turn, dealt him to the Detroit Cougars during the 1926–27 season. The following season, the Cougars dispatched Duke to the Chicago Black Hawks. He concluded his big-league career in 1928–29, returned to western Canada, but remained close to the hockey scene.

He was elected to the Hockey Hall of Fame in 1958 and died January 16, 1972.

"In all sports," wrote Ken McConnell, "there is an outstanding figure and Duke Keats, the grand old center-ice man of the West, was just such an individual."

75

Billy Smith
(1971–   )

It is no coincidence that in the decade spanning 1975–85 the New York Islanders were one of the NHL's premier teams and that Bill Smith blossomed into one of the most memorable goaltenders on the continent. His renown is due to a distillation of artistry and durability and an unquenchable thirst for victory.

"In the 30 years I've played and coached pro hockey," said Don Cherry, now a commentator for *Hockey Night in Canada,* "there's never been a player who's wanted to win as bad as Smitty. That's why you won't find a better money goalie. And that goes for the great ones like Terry Sawchuk and Glenn Hall. And if you don't believe it, look at the record."

The arithmetic makes a better case for Smith's invincibility than attorneys F. Lee Bailey and Edward Bennett Williams ever could. Smith has accumulated four Stanley Cups championship rings since his playoff debut in 1975, when he orchestrated the Islanders to an arresting opening-round upset over the Rangers. Furthermore, *Bad Billy*, as he is known to the foe, has totaled eighty-eight playoff wins (Terry Sawchuk had fifty-four and Glenn Hall had forty-nine); won the Conn Smythe Trophy (playoff MVP, 1983), the Vezina Trophy (best goaltender, 1982), and the All-Star Game MVP Award (1982); shared the Jennings Trophy (best goals against average, 1983) with then-teammate Roland Melanson; and had an All-Star berth (1982). "I'm a money goalie," he says, with a combination of candor and simplicity that is his trademark.

No one could have guessed that there were such accolades in store for the 5'10", 185 pound native of Perth, Ontario. Born December 12, 1950, Bill was the youngest son of Joe and Annie Smith, and since his older brothers had begun skating and playing long before he did, Billy became the family goaltender by default. "They were a lot better than I was," recalled Smith of his siblings. "That meant that they'd do the shooting and whether I liked it or not, I had to go in the net and stop them."

However, the youngster played well enough for the Cornwall Royals in 1969–70 to attract the attention of the NHL's Los Angeles Kings. The Kings handed him a contract and dispatched Smith to Springfield of the American League. In two seasons, he totaled fifty-five penalty minutes, a figure that inspired Bill Torrey, who was putting the new Islanders franchise together, to scout the kid. Torrey was impressed and drafted Smith in June 1972 for the original Islanders team. The rest is for the record books.

To those who viewed Smith in twenty enemy rinks around the NHL, the husky son of Joe and Annie Smith was no less than Darth Vadar on skates, a misanthrope who would

think nothing of crippling Wayne Gretzky or removing Lindy Ruff's eye. Superficially, at least, this would appear to be the case if one peeks at Smith's scrapbook.

Bad Billy twice ignited international incidents by wreaking havoc with pretty-boy Gretzky. He feuded with such behemoths as Dave Semenko, Paul Holmgren, and Terry O'Reilly, not to mention a smaller terror named Tiger Williams. Since turning pro in 1971, Smith has often accumulated more penalties than some of his defensemen, and in 1978–79 he reached a career high of fifty-four penalty minutes.

Pinpointing the most egregious of Smith's transgressions is a matter of endless debate among the Society for the Prevention of Cruelty to Crease-Crowders, but the assault on Lindy Ruff serves as an example of the divided views concerning the goalie's ethical standards. During the 1980 playoff between the Islanders and the Buffalo Sabres, several enemy forwards trespassed Smith's inviolable crease—the area in front of the net that is technically off limits to enemy attackers. As so often is the case, the referee either did not see, or did not choose to see, the infractions committed in the four-by-eight-foot rectangle.

The Islanders' goalie, however, took careful note of each incursion, and when Sabres' rookie Lindy Ruff threatened to be yet another interloper during a match at Nassau Coliseum, it was only natural that Smith should raise his right arm, the one carrying the goalie stick, in the direction of his onrushing foe. The top of the stick shaft jolted Ruff in the eye, sending him to the ice contorted with pain. From the Sabres' viewpoint, it was an outrageous cheap shot, unprovoked, unnecessary, and, though Ruff was not seriously hurt, grounds for severe punishment. The way Smith remembered it, though, it was Ruff who should have used more discretion and a better road map.

"Ruff deserved what he got," said Smith afterwards. "He wanted to be a hero, but he was a sucker instead. He was trying to run [charge] me, though he would never admit it. He skated up from behind and came this close [Smith held up two fingers an inch apart] to hitting me. Now, why would a guy have come within inches of my shoulder if he wasn't trying to run me? He had the whole ice to go up and down—the whole ice. So why did he have to come right on top of me? He didn't have to; that's the point. All I did was put my stick up to protect myself; I didn't go to hit him. In that situation if I really wanted to hurt him, I could have crucified the guy."

It was Smith who was subsequently crucified over *L'Affaire Ruff*, as well as his contretemps with the Great Gretzky. During an Oilers-Islanders match at Nassau Coliseum in 1981, the first shot in what evolved into an ongoing Smith-Gretzky serial was fired by *Bad Bill*. It started when the angular Edmonton ace loped behind the Islanders' net, attempting either to deliver a pass or circle in front and fire point-blank at Smith. To cope with such forays, Smith had refined a neat gambit introduced in the 1940s by another eruptive goalie named Bill "Legs" Fraser. As his foe would deploy behind the net, Fraser would whirl his stick boomerang-style over and behind the net with such speed that his startled opponent would be shocked into losing the puck.

Smith added a clever fillip to the Fraser plan. Instead of looping his stick over the net, Bill curled it around the right side with virtually the same results. In theory, the maneuver of trying to dislodge the puck from the enemy is no different for a goaltender than when a forward or defenseman attempts to annex the rubber; the difference being that the goaltender wields a larger club than his challengers.

In this instance, on the night of October 27, 1981, Gretzky crumbled like a toothpick behind the Islanders' net when Smith's stick made contact with *The Great One*'s leg. The contact was no more severe than that inflicted hundreds of other times by others checking the skinny center. Nevertheless, Gretzky was escorted from the ice never to return that evening. One might have thought that Gretzky was finished for the season, but in fact, he returned the next night to give one of his virtuoso performances as the Oilers trounced the New York Rangers. Nevertheless, the incident elicited so much invective from the media that NHL Vice-President Brian O'Neill, the league's minister of misconduct, reviewed films of the collision and not only exonerated Smith but added an off-the-cuff wrist-slapping for the media-types who had been trying to make a mountain out of an unorthodox backcheck.

Unfortunately, Smith's bluster and occasional blockbusting often beclouded the artistic part of his goaltending. He was as much a part of the Islanders' four-straight Stanley Cup dynasty as anyone and underlined his worth by remaining a pivotal part of the team through the 1987–88 season. When the Islanders won the Patrick Division regular season title on April 2, 1988, Smith could take pride in the fact that he had played thirty-eight games, allowing only 133 goals against for a respectable 3.22 goals against average—and this at age thirty-seven. That same season, Smith's name was etched into the record book when he tied Turk Broda's record for 302 all-time career wins.

Smitty could never be placed on a plateau with Glenn Hall, Terry Sawchuk, or Georges Vezina as one of "the very best" goaltenders because there are shortcomings in the technical aspects of his game. But William John Smith has more than overcome those defects and has become eminently qualified to be included in *Hockey's 100*.

76

Peter Stastny
(1980–   )

In a between-periods interview at Nassau Coliseum during the 1987–88 season, Peter Stastny was momentarily dumbfounded when the broadcaster suggested that someday he would certainly be voted into the Hockey Hall of Fame. "I'm flattered," said Stastny. "I had never thought about it before." Yet, many others have given it considerable thought. And for good reason. To begin with, Stastny won the Calder Trophy as NHL rookie of the year in 1980 and set records for the most points and assists by a rookie that season. From that point on, he virtually carried the Nordiques along with kid brother Anton—and briefly, elder brother Marian—through the 1987–88 campaign.

Though frequently the target of NHL hatchet men, Peter proved to be as consistent as he was productive. From the 109 points he scored in his rookie year, Stastny reached 139 the next season and totaled 124, 119, 100, 122, 77, and 111 the following years. Not bad for a native of Czechoslovakia who made an exquisitely smooth transition to NHL hockey.

"The play here is harder," said Peter of the change of pace. "The quality average of the league is better. All the teams have very good players. They are strong, they can skate and they have good shots. In Czechoslovakia, there are four or five very good teams that can represent the country, but there are only eight teams that have only a very few good players."

If Stastny could be compared, style-wise, to any other NHL superstar it would be Bryan Trottier of the New York Islanders. Each has been creative with the puck, industrious to a fault, and able to score goals as well. That Stastny was able to instantly acclimatize himself to NHL hockey without breaking stride merely magnifies his accomplishments.

No less amazing was the manner in which Peter and Anton arrived in Quebec via their native province of Slovakia (in eastern Czechoslovakia). The script was suitable for a James Bond thriller. It was the stuff from which spy and counterspy legends are woven, only this time the winners were the Quebec Nordiques, in particular, and the National Hockey League in general.

The plot started simply. As a unit, the Stastnys were the best attacking formation in Czechoslovakia during the 1970s and one of the finest forward lines in the world. But, Peter, Anton, and Marian had had their fill of European hockey and wanted to try their skills in North America. *Les Nordiques* desperately wanted to sign the brothers. The Quebec sextet began developing plans to expedite the Stastnys' exit.

There was one mountainous problem: Czechoslovakia is a Communist country and

had no desire to allow any of its world-class hockey players to emigrate. And that is where this cloak-and-dagger story began.

A precedent had earlier been set for smuggling a hockey player out from behind the Iron Curtain. In 1974, Vaclav Nedomansky, then regarded as *The Bobby Hull of Bratislava*, defected and was spirited to Canada where he signed with the World Hockey Association's Toronto Toros. Angry over the humiliation, Czech authorities vowed that nothing of the kind would ever happen again, but they didn't bargain for Gilles Leger. His title was "Director of Player Personnel" for *Les Nordiques*, but Leger might well have been working for the Central Intelligence Agency. It was Leger who helped spirit Nedomansky across the border, and it was Leger who began making inquiries about the Stastnys when his bosses in Quebec asserted that they wanted to build a team that would equal their provincial rivals, the Canadiens, in talent.

In 1979, Leger launched the NHL's version of *Mission Impossible*. He snooped around tournaments in which the Czech National Team was playing and made discreet inquiries about the Stastnys. Leger's appearance did not go unnoticed by the Czech authorities, but they did not know that the Nordiques emissary had made contact with a secret agent, known as "007," who had an "in" with the Stastnys.

By the time that the 1980 Olympic hockey tournament had started, the Nordiques had begun their attempted coup in earnest, even dubbing it their "European Project." They hoped contact with the Stastnys, skating for the Czech national team in the Olympics, would be made at Lake Placid, New York.

Enough preliminary contacts had been made for the brothers to be aware of the Nordiques' intentions. Despite a high level of security cordoning off the Czech team, a Nordiques intermediary was able to break through and once again broach the subject to the skaters. "Each brother was not prepared to say, 'Forget the family and forget the house. Forget my popularity, forget my country, my nation, my language, all those things and leave.' They were not prepared to do it," recalled Marcel Aubut, president of the Nordiques.

In time, however, the Stastnys' attitude would change. Peter and Anton were vacationing at Innsbruck, Austria, when they finally placed a call to Quebec City. Aubut was on the other end of the line and began smiling when he was told that Peter and Anton were, in fact, interested in coming to Canada. Leger was contacted by his boss Aubut as soon as Aubut hung up the phone. Within hours, the two club officials were airborne for Europe and a meeting with the brothers.

The eldest brother, Marian Stastny, who had been studying to be a lawyer, accompanied Anton and Peter, although Marian had made it clear that he was not prepared to make a move—at least not yet. Aubut conferred with the younger pair, but they did not come to terms quickly. They seemed to have an acute awareness of their value and were not anxious to sell themselves cheap. After protracted contract negotiations, the three hammered out an agreement, which Marian perused and approved. Both Anton and Peter would receive more than $200,000 a year for six years.

Aubut reminded Marian that he was welcome to join the Nordiques at his pleasure, but the elder Stastny gratefully declined, adding that he would try to make the move at a later day, with the Czechs' approval—assuming that were possible. Marian returned to his native Bratislavia without his brothers, wondering whether they would succeed in the notoriously tough NHL. He also wondered whether the escape would succeed.

Peter, who was accompanied by his pregnant wife, Darnia, and Marian had made elaborate plans with Aubut and Leger, as well as the mysterious "007." The Nordiques officials would drive Peter and Anton to Vienna, while Darnia made the trip in another car with "007."

That chapter in the adventure worked out according to the blueprints. Once in Vienna, the Czechs were hidden in a hotel room under Aubut's name, while the Nordiques pair went to the Canadian embassy to obtain safe passage for the players and Darnia. Secret Czech security police spotted them and tried to head them off, but they made it to the Canadian compound and arrangements were made for a team of Austrian policemen to herd the Stastnys to a plane bound for Montreal.

The brothers and Darnia eluded the Czech security and reached the plane for Canada. It arrived on August 25 in Montreal, where a relieved Aubut wiped the perspiration off his brow. "Had I known the dangers I never would have done it," he said. "Had I known that I'd be risking my life and the lives of others, I never would have done it."

With Peter and Anton in the lineup, the Nordiques emerged as a formidable NHL club although never a champion. In 1982, Quebec advanced past Boston to play the vaunted New York Islanders in the Wales Conference championship. Although the Nordiques were beaten in four straight games, the Stastnys—particularly Peter—were outstanding. It was the portent of things to come. Peter has consistently been among the league scoring leaders and ranks among the elite scorers of all-time. Only four other players—Wayne Gretzky, Phil Esposito, Mike Bossy, and Mario Lemieux—have been able to better his single season scoring total of 139 points. And for that, is he is one of *Hockey's 100*. A checking Czech who also can score!

77

Babe Dye
(1919–1929)

Long before the slapshot or curved stick made their debut in National Hockey League rinks, the powerful drives of Babe Dye were giving goaltenders ulcers throughout the NHL.

Dye's mighty and accurate shot won him scoring championships in 1923 and 1925, and the right wing's name became a household word in Toronto, Hamilton, Chicago, and New York during his hockey career in the NHL.

Playing ten seasons of hockey, Dye had a great career in the game. Thanks largely to their high-scoring right wing, the Toronto St. Pats finished in first at the end of the 1920–21 season. In the 1921–22 season, the St. Pats won the Stanley Cup. Awarded the Art Ross Trophy in 1923 and 1925, Babe was well deserving as he led the league in scoring points. In 1923, he had twenty-six goals and eleven assists for thirty-seven points, and in 1925, he did even better, with thirty-eight goals and six assists for forty-four points.

Among players with 200 or more goals, Dye is third on the all-time list of the highest goals-per-game average, as he scored 200 goals in 271 games, for an outstanding average of .738. In 1921, the Babe's goals-per-game average was an amazing 1.46, good enough for sixth place on the all-time list. He was honored for his outstanding play in 1970, when he was inducted into the Hockey Hall of Fame.

"Babe could shoot the puck from any length or from any spot on the rink," said Canadian author Ron McAllister. "He could score with his back turned, or from any side at all." As a testimony to Dye's scoring ability, twice in his career with Toronto he scored five goals in a single game.

Dye was a small but strong right wing with limitless potential. He was unique among the long list of athletes who had learned their sport in the famous Jesse Ketchum School playground in Toronto, for unlike the others, Dye had lost his father only a year after he was born, and it had been his mother, Esther Dye, who had vowed her son would have an athletic background. Essie proceeded to instruct him herself.

Cecil Henry "Babe" Dye was born in Hamilton, Ontario, on May 13, 1898. An all-around athlete, Babe played all sports. He eventually joined the Hillcrest Seniors in the Toronto Senior Hockey League, starting as a right-winger.

In 1917, Babe joined the De La Salle Hockey Club, and that year the team won the championship. At nineteen, Dye joined the artillery, and soon found himself playing on the hockey and baseball teams. Victory was near, and soon the army hockey players were

in civilian clothes. In 1918, Charlie Querrie, manager of the Toronto St. Pats of the Senior League, contacted the players of the army squad.

Babe made himself a household word, as he played brilliantly. Dye scored thirty goals in twenty-four games to tie for the league lead with Harry Broadbent of Ottawa. Unfortunately, Toronto finished second behind the arch-rivals, but the St. Pats were to get another shot at them on March 11, 1922, before 8,000 screaming fans in Mutual Street Arena.

Rookie goaltender John Ross Roach complemented the Babe's offensive artistry. A nervous goalie, Roach held the Senators to four goals while Toronto scored five to take a surprising one-game lead. The two-game total-goals series moved to Ottawa, and all the home team needed was a two-goal lead to beat the upstart Toronto team.

The defending champs could not get one past Roach, although his defenses were crumbling around him. Roach held tight, and Toronto managed to hold the powerful Senators to a 0–0 tie, good for a 5–4 total goals advantage, and the right to meet Vancouver for the Stanley Cup.

In the playoffs, Babe did not fully assert himself until the Stanley Cup finals reached the second game. Vancouver, with Lester Patrick behind the bench, edged the St. Pats 4–3 in the first contest. Babe scored a goal at 4:40 in sudden-death overtime to give Toronto a 2–1 win in the second game. Vancouver went ahead for the last time in the series with a 3–0 win in the third game.

Now on the brink of elimination, the St. Pats showed their mettle in the fourth game, beating Vancouver by a score of 6–0. Dye was impressive, as he led the rout with a pair of goals.

The fifth and final game took place on March 28, 1922, at Mutual Street Arena. Hockey critics agreed that for two periods the final game between Vancouver and Toronto was a Stanley Cup classic. With the St. Pats holding a 2–1 lead in the third period, Babe scored his memorable "mystery goal." Dye's blast, hit with such ease and speed, made the flight from stick to cage so quickly that Lehman, the goalie, waited crouching for it—long after it had left Dye's stick.

"No one but Dye knew where the puck was," McAllister said, "the crowd finally roared and pointed to the Vancouver net. There was the puck! Then, the light was flashed on and the goal registered." Totally blown away, Vancouver gave up two more goals. Toronto won 5–1 and became the Stanley Cup champions.

Dye's sparkling hockey play continued as he starred in Toronto's colors. Scoring seventeen goals in nineteen games in the 1923–24 season, Babe had not even reached his athletic peak.

In the 1924–25 year, Toronto finished a close second to Hamilton, thanks to their offensive weapon, Babe Dye. He had scored thirty-eight goals in twenty-nine games. League arrangements dictated that second-place Toronto would meet the third-place Canadiens for the right to play Hamilton in the NHL finals. Demanding more money, the Hamilton players staged a surprise strike. League President Frank Calder angrily rejected the demands and ordered the winner of the Toronto-Montreal series to be the league champions.

Dye was overshadowed by a new star on the NHL horizon—Howie Morenz—a spectacularly speedy center who overwhelmed every skater on Toronto. He led Montreal to a 3–2 win and then a 2–0 victory. Babe was held scoreless in the series, and Toronto lost possession of the Stanley Cup.

Dye played one more season for the St. Pats. Although he scored eighteen goals in the 1925–26 year, the team slipped to sixth place in a seven-team league. He was traded to the Chicago Black Hawks the following season, where he scored twenty-five goals.

In a preseason practice with Chicago in 1927, Dye broke his leg. The injury hastened the end of his career. His swan song came one year later, during the 1928–29 season, as Babe played briefly and ingloriously for the New York Americans. It was the end of Babe Dye's illustrious hockey career.

After his retirement from the sport he loved so much, Dye lived in Chicago where he worked for a large construction company. Cecil Henry "Babe" Dye passed away January 3, 1962. Hockey had lost one of its most spectacular players.

From the start of his magnificent career, straight to the very end, Babe credited his mother for his hockey development. Such an immense talent as the high scoring and powerful shooting of Babe Dye is not seen often in hockey. Babe's remarkable goal-scoring abilities and his sensational achievements mark him as one of hockey's all-time finest.

78

Ray Bourque
(1979–   )

In much the same manner that Denis Potvin was overshadowed for years by another gifted defenseman Bobby Orr, so too was Ray Bourque burned by Paul Coffey's press clippings. It wasn't until the 1986–87 season that the French-Canadian blueliner became the top banana of the NHL backline bunch.

"Bourque was the stalwart of the NHL team's rear guard in the two-game 'Rendez-vous 87' series against the national team of the Soviet Union and the kingpin for Team Canada in the six-nation Canada Cup international tournament," recalls Frank Orr of *The Toronto Star*. "Now at the peak of his career, Bourque could maintain a stranglehold on the Norris for the next few seasons."

Ray not only annexed the 1987 and 1988 Norris Trophies but also demonstrated that many of Bobby Orr's qualities, which captured the imagination of Boston Garden fans in the early 1970s, are evident in him.

"He reminds me so much of Bobby Orr," said Bruins' general manager Harry Sinden. "Ray is so shy and innocent like Orr was when he came up. He has so much poise it's incredible; so much hockey sense. I get goose bumps from watching him."

On "Phil Esposito Night" at Boston Garden, December 3, 1987, Bourque stole the show with a display of class and dignity. He surprised the Garden crowd by giving up his Number 7 jersey in favor of 77. It was the same move that Esposito, himself, made when he moved from the Bruins to the New York Rangers in 1975. "I gave Phil back his number. He worked so hard here and he deserved it," said Bourque. "This is something that I was involved in and that feels great. It's his night, but it was a great thrill for me."

Bourque has enjoyed dozens of special nights since becoming a Bruin in 1979. And the comparisons to Orr do have a certain validity. Certainly, Bourque's biggest asset on the ice is his skating ability. He has speed and agility that is almost unmatched in the NHL. "I use my speed when the club is on a two-on-two or three-on-three rush," Bourque explained. "If I can get up into the play, then it's an odd-rush in our favor." His puckhandling ability is on par with his skating skill. Ray is just as liable to skate the puck out of the zone as he is to pass it.

Nor does his shot suffer any lack of potency because of his other talents. "Bourque is dangerous anywhere he has the puck and he can put the puck anywhere he wants," explains Michael Berger, editor of *Goal Magazine*. "He can shoot pucks from his goal line, through the air, and hit the opposition net dead center. His shot is hard, even from that distance, and lands in the net as if it were fired from a gun."

He demonstrated that during Game 1 of the Wales Conference championship against the New Jersey Devils. With the score tied 3–3 in the third period, Bourque snared a loose puck inside the Jersey blue line and blasted a shot past goalie Bob Sauve for the game-winner.

Bourque can also play the physical game with the best of the NHL backliners. He is not afraid to use the body, and his play in the corners is often fearsome. Bourque's upper body strength is what allows him to fire a rocket from the point, as well as pin a man along the boards.

Raymond Jean Bourque was born on December 28, 1960, in Montreal, Quebec. His sparkling career began with Verdun of the Quebec Major Junior Hockey League. "Ray is the best defenseman to come out of the QMJHL," said Rodrique Lemoine, owner of Bourque's junior team, the Verdun Blackhawks. "He is…a second Bobby Orr. He is even bigger and stronger than Orr.

Drafted first overall in the 1979 entry draft by Boston, Bourque was touted as the turn-around player of the Bruins' defense corps. "The future of the Boston Bruins on defense has been turned around pretty good in the last couple of hours," chortled Sinden at the time of the draft. "Bourque has all the talents. He's a good skater, an exceptional shot, a fine playmaker, a team leader." The praise was well-deserved. He won the rookie of the year award in 1980, as well as making the NHL First All-Star Team. He's been a member of the team four times since and has also earned spots on the Second All-Star Team three times.

Until the mid-1980s, Bourque betrayed a woeful lack of leadership and often seemed quite willing to sacrifice offense for defense. But maturity has changed his attitude and his style.

In 1987, he won the James Norris Memorial Trophy for best defenseman in the league. He captured fifty-two of fifty-four possible first-place votes and was one of the most impressive winners of the trophy since Bobby Orr won unanimously in 1970. He led all defensemen in scoring that season, posting a career-high seventy-two assists and ninety-five points in seventy-eight games.

"I would have been very disappointed if I had not won it [The Norris Trophy] that season because I felt I had a really good year," said Bourque. "Over the years I haven't said anything when I didn't get it. But I said to myself that once and for all I had to get my hands on that trophy."

He has also logged his share of international ice time. Bourque has played on three Canada Cup teams (1981, 1984, and 1987) and in *Rendez-Vous '87,* which has stepped up the level of his play.

"For me, the most important part of it is, when you reach a certain level in your play, you need some place to check it out," expressed Bourque. "Playing with so many great players on an NHL All-Star Team or Team Canada and against a team as good as the Soviets is the best place to do it. I'm certain every player in the NHL feels that way, no matter what you hear."

Bourque's value to the Bruins was underlined during that 1987–88 season. He paced Boston to a strong second place finish in the Adams Division and playoff triumphs over the Buffalo Sabres, Montreal Canadiens, and New Jersey Devils. Because of his skill and durability, Bourque has frequently been asked by coach Terry O'Reilly to log extra ice time. Thus it is hardly surprising for Ray to play twenty-five to thirty minutes per game. Eventually, fatigue does set in, and Bourque seemed tired and less than effective in the Bruins' 1988 Stanley Cup final loss to Edmonton.

There's very little that Ray Bourque can't do, and even less that he can't do well. He is surely the most dangerous player on the Boston Bruins, and one of the best blueliners in the NHL.

79

Red Dutton
(1926–1936)

By all odds, Red Dutton did not figure to enjoy a decade-long National Hockey League career and then further honors as a club owner and president of the NHL. The hard-bitten son of a wealthy Canadian, Dutton had fought with Canada's legendary Princess Pats regiment in World War I and nearly lost both legs when an artillery shell exploded a few feet away from him.

At first doctors were prepared to amputate but decided against such a measure. Dutton recovered sufficiently to be shipped back to Canada and, despite the early medical report to the contrary, was eventually back on skates. By the early 1920s, he was playing for the Calgary Tigers in the old (but top-grade) Western Canada Hockey League alongside such high-quality players as Eddie Shore, Bill and Bun Cook, and Frank Boucher.

A defenseman with flaming red hair, Dutton teamed with Herb Gardiner and became so proficient that the leg wounds suffered in the battle of Vimy Ridge were forgotten as was the seven-hours-a-day training regimen that enabled Dutton to achieve big-league condition. When the WHCL went under, Red was signed by the Montreal Maroons of the NHL and played four seasons with them until he was obtained by the New York Americans, who sought him above all for his combative nature.

Above all, Dutton was renowned as a scrapper. Playing for Calgary, he originally made his mark during the 1924 Stanley Cup finals against the Montreal Canadiens. The Habitants had a defenseman named Sprague Cleghorn, whose vicious play had earned him a reputation as the scourge of big-league hockey.

Dutton was unimpressed. When Cleghorn butt-ended him with a stick, Red turned around and belted the Canadien in kind. "Cleghorn is remembered to this day as one of the meanest men who ever played the game," said Toronto *Sun* columnist Trent Frayne, "but there was nothing surreptitious about Dutton's responses; he simply threw down his stick, tossed off his gloves and sailed into Cleghorn. Blood flowed like wine."

Red was no less courageous as a Maroon. He teamed up with Reg Noble, and the way Dutton would tell it, just sitting next to Noble in the dressing room should have qualified him for the Victoria Cross. "Reg," said Dutton, "would drink a case of beer the day of a game. His breath would knock you down."

An incident that best symbolizes Dutton's approach to hockey took place at the Forum in Montreal. The Maroons and Canadiens had become arch-rivals, and they were lined up, on this night, preparing for the opening face-off. For some reason, the referee was unable to find a puck with which to launch the game. The official skated over to the timekeeper's table, but there was none there so he asked someone to obtain a puck from

the dressing room. Dutton was so frustrated and so anxious to get the fray going that he shouted: *"Never mind the damn puck. Let's start the game!"*

Dutton's truculence was translated into penalty minutes that usually reached three figures. Although the NHL only played a forty-four-game schedule at the time, Red set what was then a record of 139 minutes for a season. His coach Eddie Gerard eventually tired of Dutton's excessive penalties and finally benched him for three games.

Gerard actually admired Dutton. When the former was named general manager of the New York Americans, he went out of his way to deal for Red. It was a fortuitous move. Long after Gerard had departed the Manhattan scene, Dutton had established himself as one of the city's most popular sports figures.

Red played splendidly on defense for the Amerks who, unfortunately, were suffering financial woes. At one point, Dutton loaned owner Big Bill Dwyer (New York's most notorious bootlegger) $20,000. When Dwyer's fortunes collapsed, the NHL took over the Americans and placed Dutton in charge. He played through the 1935–36 season and then became owner-coach.

Dutton was as crafty on the bench and in the front office as he had been on the ice. Lacking a farm team, he still managed to ice a respectable and, occasionally, contending team. His finest hour as a coach came in the spring of 1938. The Amerks finished second in the NHL's Canadian Division and then whipped the Rangers in the opening playoff round. They came within a whisker of beating the Chicago Black Hawks in the next playdown before being eliminated.

Mervyn A. Dutton was born July 23, 1898, in Russell, Manitoba. His father had a construction business and, before he entered pro hockey, Red worked on one of his dad's railway construction projects.

He enlisted in the Canadian army at the outbreak of World War I and was in the midst of the action when a hunk of high explosive nearly killed him. The shrapnel hit him in the buttocks and ripped open his thigh and calf. He was only eighteen when it happened, having lied about his age to get into the service to begin with. It was his twentieth month at the front line when he was felled. When he got back to Canada in 1919, he was determined to play hockey.

And he did. Not with the dexterity of an Eddie Shore but with a verve that endeared him to all but his victims.

After retirement, Dutton carried the Americans, financially and otherwise, until the 1942 season when the decimation of the lineup caused by World War II forced abandonment of the team. When NHL President Frank Calder died, Dutton was asked to replace him. He remained president until 1946 when he opted for the construction business and turned the gavel over to Clarence Campbell. Dutton was asked to drop the first puck at the Stampede Corral in 1980 when the Calgary Flames made their NHL debut. He was one of a kind—a man you would want on *your* hockey team.

80

Chuck Rayner
(1940–1953)

It is mind-boggling to imagine what dizzying heights Chuck Rayner might have reached if he had enjoyed the luxury of playing for a genuinely powerful hockey team. But such was not *Bonnie Prince Charlie*'s good fortune. The bushy-browed goaltender made his debut with the subterranean New York (Brooklyn) Americans and finished his valorous puck-blocking career with a rather pathetic New York Rangers aggregation.

In between, he demonstrated that he was either the very best or certainly among the top three goalies in the world, despite the fact that he never had a first place team or a Stanley Cup championship to show for it, but his hard-fought reputation spoke for itself.

Rayner nonetheless made a permanent impression on the NHL and earned his way into the Hockey Hall of Fame. He is the only goaltender ever to have scored a goal by skating the length of the rink in an organized hockey game (although not in the NHL).

He was also among the very first to participate in what was then a revolutionary two-goalie experiment, along with his long-time sidekick and pal, James "Sugar Jim" Henry.

The 1949–50 season was in many ways the high point of Rayner's career, as he singlehandedly led the Rangers to the Stanley Cup finals.

It is a measure of Rayner's ability that he won the Hart Trophy—only the second goaltender in history at that time—as the NHL's most valuable player in the 1949–50 season.

Playing for a mediocre Ranger team that never finished higher than fourth, *Bonnie Prince Charlie* led the Rangers to upset the Canadiens in the 1950 playoffs. They went on to the final round against the Detroit Red Wings. Playing not one home game, they surprised the entire NHL with their strong bid, only to lose the seventh game in dramatic fashion—in an electrifying, double-overtime affair.

Rayner became the first goaltender ever to score a goal. During World War II, while he was playing for the all-star Royal Canadian Army team, Chuck was guarding the goal when a ten-man scramble occurred behind his net. He saw the puck squirt free, with no one between him and it. The temptation was too much for him to resist.

He left his net and charged down the ice. His opponents were so surprised that they simply stopped in their tracks. Rayner skated within a few feet of the goal and shot. The opposing goaltender was dumbfounded and lunged, but the puck sailed right into the net.

When he won the Hart Trophy in 1950, it was one of the most popular announcements in the annals of the game, as he was one of the nicest guys in the sport. Oddly enough, the year he won the Hart Trophy he placed only fourth in the standings for the Vezina Trophy.

It was his remarkable and sensational performance in the 1950 playoffs that compensated for this. He was incredible during the series, as he stopped virtually impossible shots. Although the Rangers' quest for the Stanley Cup was stopped, the results of the voting for the Hart Trophy was a credit to the sportsmanship of hockey when the tall goaltender's name was announced.

He was only the second goaltender at that time to win the Hart Trophy. Rayner received thirty-six out of a possible fifty-four points for a thirteen-point lead over Ted Kennedy of the Toronto Maple Leafs. The great Maurice Richard of the Montreal Canadiens finished third in the balloting with eighteen points.

Chuck made the Second Team All-Stars three times, in 1948–49, 1949–50, and 1950–51. In his eight seasons with the New York Rangers, encompassing 424 games, he had twenty-four shutouts, plus one shutout in the playoffs.

Rayner won the West Side Association Trophy as the Rangers' most valuable player during the years 1945–46 and 1946–47 and shared it in 1948–49 with Edgar Laprade.

In August 1973, *Bonnie Prince Charlie* was inducted into hockey's Hall of Fame, in honor of his contributions to his sport.

Claude Earl Rayner was born in the small town of Sutherland, Saskatchewan, on August 11, 1920. Like all of the youngsters of that locale, he went down to the local skating rinks to play the national pastime. Chuck always wanted to be a goaltender. In 1936, when Chuck was sixteen years old, he played goal when the Saskatoon Wesleys reached the junior playoffs against the Winnipeg Monarchs. He then went into the goal for the Kenora Thistles in 1936.

At the end of the 1939–40 season, Chuck went down to the New York Americans' farm club, the Springfield Indians. Rayner had only played seven games for the Indians when Earl Robertson of the Americans suffered a head injury, leaving open a berth in the nets.

Rayner was called up to take over Robertson's place and so, in 1940, the young man from Sutherland was playing in the NHL.

Rayner played in the goal for the Americans throughout the 1942 season. He then went home and joined the Royal Canadian Armed Forces. Discharged from the service in 1945, Chuck returned to hockey to discover that the New York Americans had disbanded, and that all members of the team were to be part of a raffle for the other NHL teams.

Chuck Rayner's name was pulled out by Lester Patrick of the New York Rangers. And thus began one of the oddest stories in sport. Patrick had already hired a goalie, Sugar Jim Henry. Chuck finally won the Ranger goalkeeping job permanently.

Rayner had to retire after the 1952–53 season. He had damaged the cartilage in his knee. An operation temporarily held the knee up, but again, the knee weakened to the point where he felt he couldn't do the job anymore.

Chuck suffered through many injuries, and there's no telling how long he could have played if he had a mask and an alternate goalkeeper.

After his retirement as a player, Chuck returned to western Canada where he coached the Nelson Leafs. After two years he then went to Alberta and coached the Edmonton Flyers. He then did some work for the Rangers, and then for the Detroit Red Wing organization with his friend Sid Abel.

By the mid-sixties, he had been coaching nine years, but he didn't enjoy it. Chuck didn't like having to tell a kid that he was traded.

Bonnie Prince Charlie left the sport completely. By 1979, he had been away from hockey for almost ten years.

Chuck was a courageous man who often played black-and-blue. He was the kind of man who played when a lesser man would have sat out. It was tragic that such a nice guy with his capabilities never played on a Stanley Cup championship winner. However, no one will ever forget the heroics that Rayner accomplished during the exciting 1950 play-offs with the Cinderella Rangers, and he is well-deserving of his spot in *Hockey's 100*.

81

Bob Gainey
(1973–   )

To this day, there is no doubt that many hockey observers will raise skeptical eyebrows at the suggestion that Bob Gainey, the long-striding Canadiens left wing, should be mentioned in the same breath as a Lemieux or a Gretzky. But for more than a decade, hockey purists have recognized that, despite his modest scoring totals, Gainey stands among the NHL's *crème de la crème*. And the fact that he won the Selke Trophy as the best defensive forward the first four years it was awarded (1978–81) is testimony to his prowess.

"He [Gainey] is technically the best hockey player in the world," said Viktor Tikhonov, coach of the Soviet national team that beat the NHL All-Stars in the 1979 Challenge Cup series.

Gainey's comprehensive game was virtually flawless—unless one was looking for a fifty-goal scorer—from the start of his NHL career in 1973–74. Born September 13, 1953, in Peterborough, Ontario, Bob was Montreal's first-round draft pick in 1973, after an excellent tour of duty with the Peterborough Petes of the OHA. Briefly placed with Montreal's farm team in Nova Scotia, Gainey was elevated to the big club in short order, where his natural stride combined with enormous strength (6'1" and 200 pounds) and on-ice savvy enabled him to become a threat on offense, while acting as a third defenseman against enemy assaults. A linchpin on Montreal's four-straight Cup-winning machine (1976–79), Gainey peaked in 1979 when he was voted the Conn Smythe Trophy as the most valuable player of the Stanley Cup playoffs.

"Gainey won the trophy as much for his defensive contributions as his scoring output," said Mary Flannery of the *New York Daily News*. "If Gainey weren't a hockey player, he'd be a farmer. He appears to have the temperament, the stolid nature. He keeps plowing, working his wing with steady dependability that eventually pays off...Gainey has been a respected but anonymous toiler on the star-studded Canadien lineup."

Not that Gainey's play slipped during the 1980s. Late in the 1987–88 season, Bob received a remarkably long standing ovation at the Forum following the first hat trick of his career. However, the truly golden Gainey years ran from the mid-1970s through the end of the decade. It was then that the Scotty Bowman-coached dynasty dominated hockey play, and Gainey was regarded as the ultimate clutch player.

Well before the Montreal Canadiens marched to their fourth consecutive Stanley Cup in 1979, and weeks before it was known who would be named the most valuable player in the championship round, *The Montreal Star* went out on a limb in discussing the subject.

There on page one of its first news page, *The Montreal Star* ran a full color photograph of the man who the newspaper figured to be the playoff hero. It wasn't Guy Lafleur, Serge Savard, or Jacques Lemaire. Bob Gainey was the player in question, and there, in a four-column headline, *The Montreal Star* asserted: GAINEY SHINES IN PLAYOFFS—HIS TYPE OF GAME.

The description that followed was exquisitely accurate: "It starts from the moment he gathers the puck in the graceful curve of his stick. Head up, eyes blazing like hot little coals, he gets beyond one man...then another, and by now there is no longer a crowd in the Montreal Forum, but a noise engulfing it. This is Bob Gainey. He evokes this noisy reaction from Canadiens' fans when he has the puck, and an even greater one when he doesn't, because playoff hockey is Gainey's type of game."

Tough, unobtrusive hockey was the hallmark for the Gainey game. That is why he was the first recipient of the Frank J. Selke Trophy in 1978.

"If I had to pick one man for his consistency and value to his team," said Serge Savard, then a Canadiens' All-Star defenseman and now the team's general manager, "especially during the playoffs, it would be Gainey."

On a team laden with superstars, from the front line to the goalmouth, Gainey was recognized—if not by the fans—as the backbone of the club.

"Bob," said former goalie Ken Dryden, "is the guts of this team. Everything you see on the ice is Bob Gainey off the ice, too. The same intensity and drive marks Bob Gainey the person as Bob Gainey the hockey player."

One of the most outstanding contributions made by Gainey developed during the 1979 Stanley Cup finals against an upstart New York Rangers team that stunned the defending champions by winning Game 1 of the series on the sacred Forum ice. The Rangers scurried to win that contest and the next one at Madison Square Garden.

Then, in Game 4, with Montreal leading the series two games to one, Gainey outraced Ron Greschner for a loose puck behind the Rangers' net and fed Rejean Houle for the Canadiens' first goal. Late in the third period, with the Canadiens trailing by a goal, Bob produced a vintage goal that says more about his style than anything else.

Pursuing the puck, Gainey crumbled New York defenseman Dave Maloney along the boards to the left of the Rangers' net. "He left the Ranger captain for dead on the ice," commented *New York Times* columnist Dave Anderson. Bob seized the puck, skated to within shooting distance of the net and flung a devastating shot past goalie John Davidson. That tied the score, enabling Montreal to win the match in overtime. "The Stanley Cup final," noted Anderson, "turned on Gainey's goal."

Gainey set a personal record in that playoff year, scoring a point a game (six goals, ten assists, and sixteen points in sixteen games) and justifiably garnered the Conn Smythe Trophy as the series' most valuable player.

The Canadiens, with Gainey still the catalyst, won another Stanley Cup in 1986, but began a downward spiral, playoff-wise, since then. The trend paralleled the aging of Gainey and his loss of speed. Yet, Gainey was still as revered as he had been almost a decade earlier—only now the fans knew as well as his teammates that Bob was unobtrusive yet invaluable. The words of long-time teammate Larry Robinson were just as valid in 1988 as they were when originally uttered in 1979: "He works so hard and he sets the tome of almost every game. You're going to get a good game from him every time."

If the NHL had a prize for "Unsung Hero of a Decade," it would undoubtedly belong to Bob Gainey.

82

Tom Johnson
(1947–1965)

There were few more durable or intelligent defensemen in the National Hockey League than Tom Johnson. Although he played in the shadow of the great Doug Harvey during much of his NHL career, Johnson proved as capable at his profession as any defenseman. Playing on the dynastic Montreal Canadiens for thirteen seasons, he played on six Stanley Cup championship teams and six first-place clubs, which merely serves to emphasize the point.

Johnson was exceptionally durable, playing in 978 games, and might have played a full twenty years of big-league hockey had he not been felled by a serious leg injury. He finished first in the balloting for the Norris Trophy as the National Hockey League's best defenseman in 1959 and was named to the First All-Star Team that year. In 1956, he had been a Second All-Star Team member.

During the 1958–59 season, when Harvey was injured, Tom became the new team leader. He baffled the opposition with his inimitable but unheralded double-back play. As an opponent would speed in, Tom would lunge at the puck.

Lynn Patrick, the Boston Bruins' general manager, said, "I'd always been a great admirer of Tom Johnson. I'll never forget the year we were leading Montreal in the playoffs while he was out with an injury. Well…he returned to the lineup and that was the end of us. He's been one of the game's outstanding competitors for a long time."

That was the kind of athlete Tom Johnson was—talented, hard-working, and unrecognized. Playing next to Harvey, the best defenseman of his time, and perhaps the greatest ever, Johnson's hockey contributions went unnoticed. "It's simple," Emile Francis, then the general manager of the New York Rangers, said, "Johnson's trouble was playing on the most colorful team in hockey history. With guys like Maurice Richard, Boom Boom Geoffrion, Jacques Plante, and Jean Beliveau in the lineup, nobody ever noticed Johnson. But he was the *real* worker on the team."

When Johnson won the Norris Trophy in 1959, he interrupted what would have been an eight-year ownership of that award by Harvey. "That was the year Doug was hurt," Tom good-naturedly said. "The Norris Trophy and the time the Canadiens won their fourth straight Stanley Cup championship were the biggest satisfactions for me," Tom stated.

Much to his own amazement, Tom Johnson was elected to hockey's Hall of Fame in 1970. If Johnson was surprised, then the Hall of Famer Eddie Shore was outraged. So upset with Johnson's entry into the Hall was Shore that he offered to buy back his own induction.

Johnson looked back at his banner year of 1959 with pride, but he put it in perspective. "I didn't really consider it my best year. It just happened that year I got a lot of scoring points [10 goals, 29 assists]. It seems that's what a lot of the voters look for, even in defensemen. I thought any year between 1955 and 1960 I played the game about the same."

Although Tom returned to hockey following a serious eye injury, the Montreal brass later questioned the quality of the vision in his right eye. Johnson never again reached his former level of play, and when he continued to miss his checks and began to cost the Canadiens goals, the Forum fans turned on him. Eventually Montreal left Tom unprotected in the draft, and the Bruins claimed him for $30,000 in 1963.

Thomas Christian Johnson was born February 18, 1928, in Baldur, Manitoba. Young Johnson knew early on what he wanted to be. "When I was in the third grade," Tom said, "the teacher asked us to write down what we wanted to do when we grew up. I wrote 'professional hockey player.' That was the first time I'd ever thought about it."

When Johnson was seventeen, he tried out for the Winnipeg Monarchs. "I wasn't much of a skater, and I didn't think I'd make the team." When the coach went over to Tom, he prepared for the worst and expected to take his skates packing. Instead the coach said, "Johnson, where do you want to play, forward or defense?"

After training with Winnipeg, the Montreal Royals, and the Buffalo Bisons for a few seasons, Johnson, a gawky but determined youngster, moved up to Montreal in 1950. Teammate Ken Mosdell recalled, "Everybody said Tom was a bad skater, and that might have been. But, dammit, nobody could catch him. He could move."

Tom also gained the reputation that he could hit. In his first game at Detroit, Johnson banged with notable toughs Gordie Howe and Ted Lindsay. "He's a villain," accused former goalie John Ross Roach, "one of the cruder woodchoppers to appear here in some time." Not an all-time dirty player, Johnson nevertheless was well known for his physical style of play. Stan Mikita, the Chicago Black Hawks' all-star center, once said, "Johnson's on my black list. He liked to hit you from behind. When he got into a fight he never dropped his stick. Instead of using his fists, he used his stick for protection."

Andy Bathgate, then the New York Rangers' leading scorer, believed Johnson was one of the five most notorious spearing specialists in the NHL. "Spearing is the most savage, sneaky trick in hockey," he said, "and the most lethal. It's going to kill somebody."

Johnson felt Bathgate was being unfair in his criticism. "When Bathgate made that crack about my spearing, I didn't have a *single* spearing penalty in my entire career. His remarks were in poor taste. Not so much for me, but for hockey in general. I don't like to see people knock the game." However, the underrated defenseman never apologized for his fighting. "Fighting is a necessary part of the game. If you're challenged, you've got to stand up to the guy and fight. But on skates, and with all the equipment, fighting takes a lot out of you. After one or two minutes, you're exhausted." Tom, muscular and strong at 5'11" and 190 pounds, could certainly hold his tough ice attitude responsible for getting him into fights, although he admitted he'd lost more fights than he'd won.

While most hockey players married early, saved their dollars, and led simple lives, Tom Johnson proved to be the exception. The flashy, well-dressed Johnson remained single, spent freely, owned race horses, and indulged in the finer things of life. While his teammates dined at club quarters in Manhattan's Picadilly Hotel, Tom dined at the Americana Hotel. "Tom's first class all the way," Harvey said. "I can remember Tom cracking up a Thunderbird after he had only seventy miles on it. The old boy didn't blink an eye. Just went out and bought another. He's more conservative now—he only buys one new convertible a year."

Playing for Boston during the 1964–65 season in a game against Chicago, forward Chico Maki's skate slashed the motor nerve in Johnson's left leg, ending his playing career. He had played fifteen big-league seasons, and probably would have played in five more if not for the crippling injury. There was an emergency three-and-a half hour operation to patch Johnson's leg back together, but he would never again play in the National Hockey League.

"Nobody—nobody—tried harder to make it back as a player than Tom Johnson," said Bruins' board chairman Weston Adams. "He worked like mad, but he just couldn't make it."

Following the leg injury, which ended his playing career and gave him a permanent limp, Johnson remained with Boston and became head coach in 1970. His club won the Stanley Cup in 1972, and he remained behind the bench one more season. He then became assistant to general manager Harry Sinden. Johnson has remained Sinden's first-lieutenant and troubleshooter to this day. His affable, cigar-plugged-in-mouth appearance has cheered all twenty-one press rooms around the NHL. The unsung player of the dynastic Canadiens still remains in the background, but, as always, he gets the job done. On artistry and longevity, Tom Johnson is a deserved member of *Hockey's 100*.

83

Bill Quackenbush
(1942–1956)

One of the ironies of major-league hockey is that some of the toughest, most blood-thirsty teams down through the years also have been graced with calm, cerebral, discreet players who have been the antithesis of their team's image.

Bill Quackenbush, a defenseman with both the Detroit Red Wings and Boston Bruins, was just such a gentleman. Like Red Kelly, another decorous Red Wings' defenseman, Quackenbush was clean enough and competent enough to win the Lady Byng Trophy in 1949, while playing for a Detroit club notorious for such sluggers as Terrible Ted Lindsay and Black Jack Stewart.

Although the temptation to join the brawlers always was quite apparent, Quackenbush resisted the lure and played a pure defense. In so doing, he made a greater impact on the game than some of his more violent teammates.

More than anything, Quackenbush was an extraordinary practitioner of his art. He was named to the National Hockey League's First All-Star Team in 1948, 1949, and 1951, during an era when the NHL was oozing with top-notch backliners. Bill made the Second Team in 1947 and 1953.

It is a measure of the influence of Quackenbush that some hockey writers have suggested that the NHL name a trophy in his honor to be given to the league's best defensive defenseman.

Along with winning the Lady Byng Trophy in 1949, quite an accomplishment for a defenseman, he once went a span of 137 games (over three different seasons) without taking a penalty.

Bill Quackenbush played with some of the all-time greats of the sport and was a regular when a kid by the name of Howe came to Detroit.

"He came in when he was seventeen and anyone looking at him could tell he had talent. It was just a matter of time before he became the kind of hockey player he was. He was one of the best all-around hockey players I've ever played with."

Hubert George Quackenbush was born March 2, 1922, in Toronto, Ontario. He played his hockey on the city's innumerable outdoor rinks during the Great Depression and was ready for the big time shortly after the outbreak of World War II.

Quackenbush played on the Red Wings' 1943 Stanley Cup-winning team and played on two first-place teams. When the Red Wings finished first at the conclusion of the 1948–49 season, there was no hint that Bill would be traded, but Jack Adams stunned the hockey world by dealing Bill to the Boston Bruins.

For Quackenbush, it was a comedown in more ways than one. Not that life in Detroit was all glamour. Adams ran a spartan ship at Olympia Stadium, but conditions in Boston Garden were even worse.

In the spring of 1952, the Boston Bruins took on the powerhouse Montreal Canadiens in the Stanley Cup semifinals. Bill Quackenbush, normally known for his sturdy, inconspicuous, mistake-free play, was involved in one of the most famous hockey episodes in Stanley Cup history. The series had gone seven games with Montreal winning the first three games and Boston winning the next three.

Early in the seventh game, Maurice "The Rocket" Richard was knocked flying by a vicious check from burly Leo Labine. As *The Rocket* lay on the ice, motionless, speculation was that he was through for the series, if not longer.

The game was tied late in the third period, 1–1. The Bruins, with steady Bill Quackenbush on his right-defense position, had just killed off four minutes of penalties.

All of a sudden, *The Rocket* was on the ice, and the puck was on his stick. With a quick motion, he dug his blades into the ice and turned toward Quackenbush's side of the ice.

"I was on the left side just then, normally I played the right side, when the Rocket started coming down towards me. I chased him into the corner, and I thought I'd closed him off, but he made a quick turn and was moving out in front of our net. My partner on defense was a rookie and from lack of experience he neglected to come out and cut off the Rocket, who swiftly put the puck behind Sugar Jim Henry. That made it 2–1, and eventually we lost 3–1 on an open-net goal.

"The Rocket just made a super play. He was one of the greatest, if not the greatest goal-scorers ever to play the game."

The play is one of the all-time greats in hockey lore, and though Quackenbush boasts, "It's the only time in fourteen years the Rocket beat me," Richard made this type of play a common element in his arsenal against rival teams and shell-shocked goalies.

At the conclusion of the 1955–56 season, Bill Quackenbush hung up his skates for good, opting to return to school. For seven years, he attended Northwestern University in Massachusetts at night while working as a manufacturer's agent during the day. He also raised three sons after retiring from the NHL, while at the same time earning an associate's degree in engineering.

"After about twelve years out of hockey I decided I'd like to get back into it, so I talked to Herb Gallager at Northeastern, and went to work there as assistant coach."

In the mid-sixties, Princeton was looking for a quality coach for their men's ice hockey team. Bill Quackenbush applied and was accepted. For six years, he coached the team, lending his vast knowledge and great understanding of the game to the young men of the Princeton University hockey team. When, after his sixth year, the team began failing to win, Quackenbush stepped down as coach, but was soon back coaching a different kind of ice hockey.

"Eventually they got a girl's team here and they needed a coach. They asked me to volunteer. I felt that anything I can do to help them learn the game would be a pleasure for me. The girls were very receptive, they really wanted to learn. When I tell them things, even now, they thank me. It's a lot of fun."

Aside from coaching the women's hockey team, Quackenbush also coached the varsity golf team. Always, he remained the same gentleman and scholar he was when he originally signed a contract with crusty Jack Adams in 1942.

There have been better defensemen than Bill Quackenbush, but none who was classier, on or off the ice. His career proves that there *is* credibility to the line that nice guys can survive in the war games on ice.

84

Roy Worters
(1926–1937)

The dream of every hockey scout in search of a goaltender is to find a man who is agile, but tall and wide so that he can fill as much of the six-feet-wide by four-feet-high entrance to the net as possible. Some of the greatest netminders, from Georges Vezina to Ken Dryden, were big men who filled much of the air space leading to the net. All of which helps explain why Roy Worters was such a marvel at his profession.

Worters was a goalie who measured only 5'3" and 130 pounds, yet his stature compared to other notables who guarded the twine remains immense to this day. And the fact that he generally played for inferior clubs such as the New York Americans merely adds to his glitter.

His drawbacks notwithstanding, Roy was the Hart Trophy winner in 1929 as the National Hockey League's most valuable player, the Vezina Trophy (best goalie) winner in 1931, and was twice voted to the Second All-Star Team (1932 and 1934).

Worters is best remembered for his heroic performances with the Americans, but he actually broke into the majors as a member of the Pittsburgh Pirates, which joined the NHL in the fall of 1925. After a salary dispute with the Pirates, Worters was traded to the Amerks for the then unheard of sum of $25,000 plus two players.

The deal was the bane of Worters' hockey life at first. Hard-nosed galleryites at Madison Square Garden taunted him with catcalls. "So, you're worth twenty-five grand, eh? Worters, you're not worth twenty-five cents!"

At first, the goalie, who, inevitably, had become known as *Shrimp*, was distressed by the insults, but gradually he pulled his game together and captured the imagination of Madison Square Garden spectators. After one match he received a standing ovation.

Shortly thereafter, Worters had the distinction of losing a game to the Montreal Canadiens *without a goal being scored against him*. It was a 0–0 tie late in the match when Howie Morenz of the Canadiens broke into the clear for a shot at Worters. Roy stopped the blistering drive, deflecting it into the corner. But, as Morenz unleashed his shot, Bullet Joe Simpson of the Americans tossed his stick at Morenz. In those days, the stick-throwing foul was punishable with an automatic goal. Montreal won the game, 1–0.

"Although Roy never saw the Stanley Cup awarded to his team," said Ron McAllister, "he won every individual honor that a goalkeeper could possibly earn, and more. The thought of what he might have achieved with a winning team before him, makes him a man of mystery in the record books."

Worters could have gained entrance to the Hockey Hall of Fame on guts alone. He suffered 216 stitches *in his face alone* and continued playing despite the pain of cracked

ribs, a broken kneecap, three broken toes, and countless lesser injuries, including the loss of eight teeth.

Roy Worters was born October 19, 1900, in Toronto, Ontario, the son of a trolley car motorman. When he was old enough to carry a load, Roy began delivering milk for his uncle's dairy. In return, Roy received free milk. "The future goalkeeper knew the lesson of work before he learned the meaning of life," said a friend.

He began his hockey career as a forward and remained up front until he was seventeen when the goal-weak Toronto Riverdales searched for someone to tend the twine. Roy volunteered and the Riverdales suddenly began winning games. Eventually, he moved up the junior ranks to the Toronto Canoe Club.

The Canoe Club, with Worters performing uncanny feats in goal, marched to the Memorial Cup, symbol of junior hockey supremacy in Canada. One of Roy's most formidable opponents was a young whiz named Howie Morenz, who later would ripen as a superstar with the Montreal Canadiens. "Morenz," Worters once said, "is some wild wind, that number 7 of Canadiens. To me, he's just a blur—77777!"

To Morenz, Worters was like a wall in front of the uprights, despite his miniscule size. Over a span of 488 games, Worters' goals-allowed average was 2.36; uncanny considering the feeble defense in front of him.

Worters also was an innovator. He was the first netminder to direct rebounds into the corners of the rink with the back of his gloves, and, needless to say, demonstrated that a Lilliputian goalie could be as good as a big man with the pads.

At the age of thirty-seven, he was still blocking shots for the Amerks when he suffered a severe hernia and was hospitalized. Red Dutton, who had become manager of the team, believed that Roy was capable of a comeback and offered Worters a sizable sum to return to the wars, but the goalie declined and returned to his native Toronto.

"When Roy quit the game," said Ron McAllister, "few players or fans remained untouched by his tremendous contribution to the game."

A foe, who had been frustrated by Worters for several seasons, said later: "For years after Roy left the game it was hard to realize that he had been gone from the NHL for good."

He stayed close to the sport he loved so well and worked with the NHL Oldtimers Association, as well as local charities. He was inducted into the Hockey Hall of Fame in 1969, twelve years after he had died of throat cancer. He was a David among Goliaths.

85

Roger Crozier
(1963–1977)

Roger Crozier was one of the great stylists of goaltending. Small for a goalie, he never-theless played fourteen seasons in the National Hockey League. Unfortunately for Roger, he played most of his hockey career on mediocre teams, playing for the Detroit Red Wings, the Buffalo Sabres, and later the Washington Capitals. Equally unfortunate were the stomach and pancreas problems that plagued Roger throughout his career.

A compulsive worrier, Crozier developed an ulcer at age seventeen. Many times he could not eat before a game, or afterwards. Despite the many troubles that faced Roger—the illness, the nerves, or the mediocre clubs that he played on—he was an outstanding goaltender during his long career.

Roger followed a line of great Detroit goaltenders, beginning with Johnny Mowers, Harry Lumley, and Terry Sawchuk, and he was more than capable of continuing the tradition. Crozier broke into the National Hockey League in the 1964–65 season, when he was only twenty-two years old. *The Dodger* played extremely well and won the Calder Trophy as the best newcomer in the league. Detroit finished in first that year with him in the nets.

Crozier was the goalie for the First All-Star Team in 1965, an honor he richly de-served. In the 1966 Stanley Cup finals, Roger won the Conn Smythe Trophy as the most valuable player for his team in the playoffs, even though Detroit lost the final to the Montreal Canadiens, after a two games to zero Red Wing lead in the series.

Hockey critics weren't fans of Crozier, who was small at 5'8" and 155 pounds, and they doubted that his sprawling style would succeed in the NHL. Crozier had spent his 1963–64 season in Pittsburgh, but Detroit coach Sid Abel had faith in him.

During the 1966 playoffs, Roger virtually singlehandedly defeated the powerful Mon-trealers in the first two games. His play inspired even his rivals to toast Roger's excel-lence. Jacques Laperriere, the fine Canadien defenseman, remembered it like this. "We were just as good, maybe better. What won those first two games for them was their goalie, Roger Crozier. He was making all the saves, and it looked like we could never get the puck past him."

Montreal took the next two games from Detroit on the Red Wings' home ice, and then took the fifth game at Montreal. Leading three games to two in the series, Montreal went back to Detroit to try and wrap it up.

The Canadiens got started when Jean Beliveau scored a goal in the first period. In the second, Montreal's Leon Rochefort put the puck past Roger, and Norm Ullman scored for

Detroit to make it 2–1. Floyd Smith tied it in the third period, and the game went into overtime.

With two minutes into the overtime, a rush was mounted toward the Detroit goal, with Henri Richard heading for the slot. Just as Henri tried to get his stick on the puck, Detroit defenseman Gary Bergman knocked him to the ice.

Laperriere said, "Richard fell to the ice on his stomach and I remember him sliding. I don't know how many feet, toward the goal, the puck against his arm or his body. Crozier was hugging the post as Richard slid toward him. It looked like he had it covered. But somehow the puck slid with Richard and as he went past the post, the puck slid past Crozier—there couldn't have been more than four inches of opening—and across the goal line. There it stopped."

An unusual ending, and Montreal had won the Stanley Cup. The most valuable player? Roger Crozier, whose play had been sparkling as he held off the Chicago Black Hawks, and played so well against Montreal.

Roger got his ulcer when he was seventeen, playing junior hockey in St. Catharines, and he was never again 100 percent healthy. The years of pro hockey only made him more nervous and neurotic. However, nerves were not his only ailment. One morning Roger woke up with a massive pain in his stomach. He was rushed to the hospital, where doctors diagnosed his condition as pancreatitis. The infection of the pancreas gave him only a 50–50 chance for survival. For four days, Roger hovered near death as he was treated with drugs and fed intravenously. Roger recovered, but when he reported to training camp for the 1965–66 season, his weight had dropped twenty pounds, and his skin coloring had a yellowish hue.

Traded to Buffalo in 1970, Roger played several seasons, but missed many games due to his illness. He had five pancreas attacks that put him in the hospital for over nine months. When Crozier came back to Buffalo after almost a year of illness, he was scheduled to start against Toronto. During the warm-ups, he was hit on the right side of his neck, just above the collarbone by a drive off the stick of defenseman Jerry Korab. That area is just about the only spot on a goaltender's body that is not protected by a pad or a mask. Roger was knocked unconscious by the powerful shot.

Because of his constant illness, even when Roger returned to action, he was still not in the best of health. On a bad day, he felt weak and nauseated. And even on the good days, he wasn't feeling well. Roger said, "I never feel one hundred percent, and I never will again. I just have to accept it."

Roger Allan Crozier was born March 16, 1942, in Bracebridge, Ontario. Born to a family of fourteen children, Roger began playing goal at six years of age. When he was fourteen, he was still in the nets; by this time he was playing goal on an intermediate team with men twice his age. It was then that Bob Wilson, the scout who discovered Bobby Hull, spotted Roger. The only difference was that Wilson knew immediately that Hull would be a star, and with Crozier he figured he was too small to ever make it to the National Hockey League. But the Black Hawks were in desperate need of a goalie for their junior team in St. Catharines, so Wilson signed Crozier.

Crozier's next step up was to the St. Louis squad of the Central Pro League for the 1962–63 season. Roger figured that was as high as he could ever hope to aspire. "I never even thought about the NHL then," he said later.

Little did Roger Crozier know what would lie in his hockey future. The antics of defenseman Howie Young had been grating to the Detroit Red Wings, and they decided to unload him—for any offer. They sent Young to Chicago for Crozier and a minor league defenseman. Roger then spent the 1963–64 season playing for Pittsburgh and doing such a good job that Detroit's general manager Sid Abel decided he belonged in the NHL.

Crozier made good on Abel's faith with his outstanding play in his rookie season. He was the only goaltender in the NHL to play all of his team's games, playing in seventy, and allowing an average of just 2.42 goals per game. Roger led the NHL in shutouts that year with six. The Detroit Red Wings finished in first place, and the excellent goaltending by Crozier was largely responsible for it. He made the First All-Star Team and won the Calder Trophy for the best rookie of the year. He lost the battle for the Vezina Trophy on the final day of the season to the Toronto duo of Terry Sawchuk and Johnny Bower.

Roger went home that year with $9000 of bonus money and the proof that he belonged in the National Hockey League. Although by now his self-confidence should have been growing, he worried more than ever. "The only time I really forget about my problems is after a game when we've won," Roger said. "But by the next morning I'll be worrying again."

Roger was one of the first modern goalies—he perfected the butterfly style. He was a great stylist and was an interesting goalie to watch. To think that his minor-league coaches had tried to "cure him" of his habit of sprawling! Had they been successful, it would surely have been hockey's loss.

Roger Crozier, all-star fretter, recollected on life as a National Hockey League goaltender. "I like everything about hockey, the traveling, the friends I've met, the interviews. Everything but the games. They're pure torture."

In 1974, when Roger was with Buffalo, he demanded his release from the club. He had a three-year, $250,000 contract, but he had been shipped to the minors after his continuous illness. In 1977, he was sent to the Washington Capitals. After his retirement, Roger remained with the Capitals' organization as the assistant general manager.

Roger Crozier, worrier *extraordinaire*, was a fine goaltender who finished his career with a respectable goals against average of 3.04 and had a lifetime thirty shutouts. He was a gutsy man who was plagued by nerves, stomach problems, and a pancreas infection, but Crozier never let those handicaps stand in the way of competing. Despite his recurring illness, Roger played in 518 pro games. One of his finest assets was that Crozier had the ability to keep his wits when the going was the toughest. Even if Roger Crozier sometimes let his own worrying create problems, he was always a more than capable goaltender.

86

Carl Brewer
(1957–1980)

In a sport that treats iconoclasts like lepers, Carl Brewer was regarded by some hockey conservatives as an unmanageable kook who would have been better suited for the ministry or lighthouse work.

His clashes with Toronto Maple Leafs' general manager-coach Punch Imlach became legend and set the tone for Brewer's later challenges to the hockey establishment. It was Carl, as much as any other player, who was responsible for the ascendency of the NHL's first and only union leader, Alan Eagleson.

None of this would have been possible unless Brewer had been one of the best players of his era; and that he was. Carl played defense for three Stanley Cup-winning Toronto sextets and one first-place team. He was First Team All-Star in 1963 and made the Second Team in 1962, 1965, and 1970.

A lyrical skater who obtained the most out of every stride, Brewer possessed an excellent poke check and was as capable of organizing a rush as he was in clearing his defensive area of attackers. In some quarters, he was considered a "bad man," but this was more a function of Brewer's bluster than an actual mean streak.

Brewer epitomized the thinking man's hockey player. Teamed with rugged Bob Baun on the Toronto backline, Carl worked splendidly with his hard-hitting buddy. Together, they formed one of the best defensive duets the NHL has ever known.

For a time, it seemed that Brewer and Baun would go on indefinitely, keeping the Maple Leafs in contention for the Stanley Cup. But suddenly, at the end of the 1964–65 season, during which he led the NHL in penalties, Brewer announced that he was quitting professional hockey to study at the University of Toronto.

From then on his career took one bizarre turn after another. Although he was in the prime of his playing life, Brewer chose to coach in the grade B International Hockey League; play hockey in Finland; skate for the Canadian National Team; and return to the NHL—first with the Detroit Red Wings, then the St. Louis Blues, and finally, the Maple Leafs.

Carl Thomas Brewer was born October 21, 1938, in Toronto, Ontario. Like so many of his teammates on the championship Maple Leafs teams, Brewer made his way to the top through the labyrinth of Toronto amateur leagues, until he finally won a tryout with the Maple Leafs in the 1957–58 season.

A year later, he was a Maple Leaf regular and, along with Baun, helped execute one of the most amazing comebacks in hockey. The Toronto club trailed the New York Rangers by nine points with only two weeks remaining in the 1958–59 season. With Brewer playing like a ten-year veteran, the Leafs caught the Rangers on the final day of the season and, ultimately, beat them out for a playoff berth.

At the time, Carl was a happy-go-lucky kid, quite willing to accommodate the martinet Punch Imlach. But as the years progressed, Brewer became increasingly disenchanted and more rebellious.

The Brewer-Imlach controversy had widespread implications in terms of management-player relations. Those in the pro-Imlach camp charged that Brewer was disturbing the status quo that had worked so well. They also emphasized that Brewer was challenging one of hockey's most successful men, based on the number of Stanley Cups Imlach had won.

A major cause of Brewer's problems with Imlach was Carl's liaison with Eagleson. "There was no doubt in my mind at the time that Eagleson was destined for big things in many areas. He was the type of person who made things fall into place. Thanks to the Eagle, I believe I was the first hockey player to earn a six-figure salary, and take satisfaction in that. Today people wonder whether the kids coming to the NHL are worth the kind of big money they are being paid. My answer is that the hockey establishment had dictated that the kids are worth six figures. The media plays a part in it, too. Someone else, not the kids, created this situation. I also think it came about because such stars as Ted Lindsay and Doug Harvey—the original players who tried to organize a union—had been underpaid and they made so much of what eventually happened with the Players' Association possible."

Although the Brewer-Eagleson liaison could have proven destructive to both player and attorney, it proved just the opposite. Eagleson's power increased by the season, until it reached a point where he dealt with the NHL power structure on an equal footing.

Brewer, although he had made several enemies around the league, established himself in business and made a number of friends in Europe, especially with those connected with the Finnish hockey leagues.

What puzzled those who knew the man was whether or not his thirst for competition would be satisfied by playing—or coaching, for that matter—on a level below that of his innate talents.

For several years, he seemed capable of rationalizing his moves but, by the end of the 1960s, he appeared to be in need of major-league action once more.

His problem was his difficulties with Imlach. The Maple Leafs' boss, who could be vindictive at times, was in a position to blacklist Brewer. Instead, he included Carl in a trade with the Detroit Red Wings.

After being away from the NHL scene for five years, Brewer returned—as a member of the Detroit Red Wings— in 1969–70 and was a major reason why the Red Wings enjoyed a renaissance. "In seventy-six games we had 40 wins, 21 losses and 15 ties. For me it was a fascinating experience because this had been a team that was down; yet it had a lot of poised veterans like Gordie Howe and, to my way of thinking, it was the best team in the NHL."

For Brewer, skating as a teammate of the inimitable Gordie Howe was an experience that produced mixed emotions. As a kid growing up in Toronto, he had admired Howe as a superstar. As an opponent of Howe when Carl was with the Maple Leafs, Brewer deplored what he considered Howe's indiscriminate use of his hockey stick to injure opponents. Now he was viewing Gordie from still another perspective. "As a person, I considered him an ordinary guy. As a superstar, he was extraordinary. He could change the complexion of the game with just his presence on the ice. His opponents, many of whom were kids when he was already a star, were awed by Howe. They would play ten minutes and then spend the rest of the game watching him."

After only a season in the Motor City, Brewer was dispatched to St. Louis where he was signed by the Blues' owners, Sid Salomon, Jr., and his son, Sid Salomon III. It had been said that the Salomons were too involved in their hockey club and that they did not allow the hockey men to run the operation. Whatever the case, Brewer seemed pleased to be a member of the Blues.

When Brewer left the Blues following the 1971–72 season, it was believed to be his NHL swan song. He disappeared from the big-league scene and concentrated on a number of business ventures. But during the 1979–80 campaign, when the Maple Leafs were undergoing a rejuvenation—under Imlach, of all people—Brewer asked his old adversary for permission to attempt a comeback. Imlach agreed and Carl played twenty games for his alma mater. He collected five assists and didn't look the least bit out of place.

That, however, was enough, and when the 1979–80 season had ended, Brewer called it quits—for good. He was a rare individual, kept the pot boiling at all times and, most of all, was a superb defenseman. That, unfortunately, was overlooked in all the turmoil he created.

87

Guy Lapointe
(1968–1984)

Virtually lost in the crowd during an era when Bobby Orr, Brad Park, Denis Potvin, and Larry Robinson were the predominant defensemen, sloe-eyed Guy Lapointe nevertheless was consistently among the best.

"He's such a nice guy," former Boston Bruins' coach Don Cherry once said of him, "that I can't get mad at Lapointe even when he is killing my team."

Compared to other aces, Lapointe has always been a Mister Inbetween. He lacked the élan of an Orr, the stickhandling skills of a Park, or the muscle of a Potvin, yet he invariably got the job done for the Montreal Canadiens.

Lapointe was named to the First All-Star Team in 1973 and the Second Team in 1975, 1976, and 1977. During a seven-season period, from 1973 through 1979, he skated for five Stanley Cup winners and played on a total of seven first-place teams.

As calm and deliberate off ice as he is on, Lapointe was able to adjust to a variety of coaches, from Claude Ruel to Scotty Bowman to Bob Berry, and maintained a high standard of excellence into the 1980s, while never dominating in the manner of an Orr or Potvin.

Guy Gerard Lapointe was born March 18, 1948, in Montreal. His father was a captain in the Montreal fire department and his older brother, Andre, was a Montreal cop. At age eighteen, Guy seriously considered following in the family tradition of public service and filled out an application with the Montreal police department. However, some splendid play for the Montreal Junior Canadiens attracted the eyes of the parent club, and Lapointe was dissuaded from pounding a beat. Instead, he began pounding opponents on the Canadiens' blue line. By the early 1970s, he had become a regular and emerged as one the league's best backliners.

It was in the spring of 1973 that Guy was named to the NHL's First All-Star Team, and not coincidentally the Canadiens won their eighteenth Stanley Cup championship. Combining bruising bodychecks with nimble puck-carrying, Guy quarterbacked the Canadiens' attack. In a typical attack, Guy would circle the net driving his legs like pistons en route to the enemy goal. The opposing team was confounded by Lapointe's versatile activities, particularly his hard shot from the point or his radar-sharp passes that had the Canadiens' "Head-Man-The-Puck" trademark.

Until the 1972–73 season, Lapointe had been known as a defenseman with modest offensive abilities. He scored fifteen goals and eleven goals in the 1970–71 and 1971–72 seasons respectively, before bursting out with nineteen goals in 1972–73. It was then that coach Scotty Bowman decided to place Guy on the potent Montreal power play. The result—the Canadiens improved their scoring on the man-advantage situation.

Early in his career, the Canadiens had dispatched the youngster to their Houston farm club in the Central League. Lapointe, who had never lived any place other than the province of Quebec and spoke only French, had difficulty stickhandling the English language.

Mastering English was only one of many problems for Guy in Houston. An attack of viral pneumonia threatened to end his career before it had peaked. But he licked the ailment and, a season later, skated for the Canadiens' Montreal Voyageurs farm club. That was a time he savored.

Guy scored eight goals from his defense position and displayed enough talent to win a spot on the parent club during the last, hectic, unfortunate days of the 1969–70 season. On the season's final night, Montreal was eliminated from a playoff berth and the Forum was shrouded in gloom. It was the first time in thirty years that the proud Habitants had failed to make the playoffs!

Although the team was down, Lapointe was on the way up and nobody could stop him. On the ice, the Canadiens looked like a brand-new team as the ebullient Lapointe orchestrated defense and offense en route to the 1971 Stanley Cup championship. Lapointe's 107 penalty minutes correctly suggest that the Canadiens had a stickhandler who wasn't afraid to battle, yet was prudent enough not to fight at the drop of a puck.

A fractured cheekbone ruined the 1971–72 season for Lapointe. Even after it had healed, Guy appeared hesitant and hardly the musketeer of old.

But by 1972–73 his health was A-1 again and so were the Canadiens. The point was demonstrated most vividly in the third game of the Stanley Cup quarterfinal series with the pesky Buffalo Sabres. Trailing 2–0, the Frenchmen appeared grounded after one period of action. Guy, who had developed into a formidable leader, tongue-lashed his teammates during the intermission. The Canadiens responded to Lapointe's bilingual blast and went from a collection of Clark Kents to Supermen. They disposed of Buffalo, and then Philadelphia and Chicago on the way to their eighteenth Stanley Cup triumph.

Lapointe, thus, followed a long and distinguished tradition set by Montreal all-star defensemen Doug Harvey, Tom Johnson, Butch Bouchard, and Lapointe's former teammate Jacques Laperriere.

None of them, however, combined the strongest elements of offense with defense in the manner of Lapointe, the total fireman-cop-on-ice! However, at the start of the 1980s Lapointe's craftsmanship began to suffer. He played only thirty-three games during the 1980–81 season, appearing in but one playoff game; for him an all-time low. At first, under new coach Bob Berry, Guy appeared to be springier and infinitely more effective during the early part of the 1981–82 competition and indicated that he was not quite ready for the scrap heap. But the Canadiens disagreed and dealt him to the St. Louis Blues late in the season.

Guy concluded his career with the Bruins and then became an assistant coach with the Quebec Nordiques. Lapointe can rest assured that he will be long remembered for his solid, if unspectacular, contributions to one of the most glorious periods in the Canadiens' long and rich history.

88

Kevin Lowe
(1979–   )

"For more than a couple of years," said Detroit Red Wings' coach Jacques Demers, "there's been one player—and only one—who I would say can be called 'The Most Underrated in the NHL' and that's Kevin Lowe of the Edmonton Oilers."

The fact that Lowe has been overshadowed over the years on a team sprinkled with flamboyant characters such as Wayne Gretzky, Mark Messier, and Glenn Anderson is hardly surprising. For most of his NHL career in Edmonton, Lowe's coolly efficient defense play was upstaged by the dynamically-rushing Paul Coffey, a Norris Trophy-winner and one of the most exciting players of the decade.

"What you have to remember about Kevin," added his long-time general manager and coach Glen Sather, "is that he gave a tremendous effort every time he stepped on the ice. As he proved when we won the Stanley Cup in 1987, he can score goals and play strong offense but, more important, he's as good as any defenseman we've ever had."

Lowe's problem—if it can be called a problem—was the Oilers' hellbent-for-goals style during the 1980–87 Gretzky-Coffey era. "This meant that an even greater amount of pressure was put on Lowe," said New Jersey Devils' defenseman Ken Daneyko, "but Kevin always has been the type of player who rose to the challenge. You can bet that Edmonton would not have won four Cups in five years if Lowe wasn't holding up that defense."

Unlike Coffey, Ray Bourque, and other Bobby Orr-type defensemen, Lowe has always been a keep-my-own-end-clean brand of backliner ever since he made his NHL debut in 1979. There has always been a bite to his bodychecks and a mean streak that seems to go hand-in-hand with greatness in defensemen.

"Lowe's toughness is like all the other parts of his game," added Daneyko. "It has been overlooked because offense has always been the Oilers' strong suit. But among the pros, Kevin is known as 'the Defenseman's Defenseman.'"

Nothing underlined the signifcance of Lowe to the Oilers' success more than his performance during the tumultuous 1987–88 season. Before the regular schedule began, a dispute between Coffey and Sather erupted into an all-out conflict that ultimately resulted in Coffey walking out on the team.

Sather emphatically refused to cave in to Coffey's demands and, ultimately, placed him on the trading block. Where once the defense revolved around Coffey's attacking forays, the backliners now had to adapt to a more conservative mode.

"We knew as soon as Paul left the team that our defense would have a different role," Lowe replied. "For the first time we would place tremendous emphasis on our ability to

keep the scores low rather than run up as many goals as we possibly could. I knew that this would place much more emphasis on my abilities and, to tell the truth, I was delighted."

Lowe anchored a defense that featured relatively inexperienced big-leaguers such as Jeff Beukeboom, Chris Joseph, and Craig Muni, yet he imbued his teammates with confidence and performed more forcefully than ever before in his career. "Kevin," said Gretzky, "is the kind of performer who's more appreciated by his teammates than the fans. He's as important off the ice—especially in the dressing room—as he is during the crunch period of a game."

Lowe's importance to the Oilers' Cup crusade was never more evident than it was during the 1987–88 season. He played the best defense of his life following the Coffey trade but suffered a serious arm injury during the homestretch and, according to most medical sources, would be unable to return for the 1988 playoffs. Undaunted, Lowe made plans to somehow rejoin the team.

"What I had failed to find out was whether there was a cast I could wear that would give me enough protection yet provide me with some mobility," Lowe recalled. "We did a lot of research and finally found a program that would work."

Few athletes in any sport would have displayed the true grit that was evident in Lowe when he returned to the Edmonton lineup *before* the 1988 playoffs began. Bedeviled with a cast and limited in his range because of the injury, Kevin nevertheless became an inspiration for the Oilers. With each playoff round—first Winnipeg, then Calgary, Detroit, and finally, Boston—Lowe raised the level of his game a notch, although he was still suffering from his unhealed wound.

"We had a job to do—to win that fourth Cup—and I didn't plan to sit on the sidelines if I could help it," Kevin asserted.

When the Oilers defeated Boston, 6–3, on May 26, 1988, to annex their fourth Stanley Cup in five years, the triumph was as much a tribute to Lowe's defensive work as it was to the scoring of Gretzky, Messier, and Anderson. Rather than lose its effectiveness with the loss of Coffey, the Oilers' defense improved under Lowe's leadership.

Kevin Lowe was born April 15, 1959, in Lachute, Quebec, a French-speaking town north of Montreal. His parents ran a dairy business—Lowe's Dairy is still well-known throughout the area—and Kevin went off to play junior hockey for the Quebec Remparts in the late 1970s.

The first player ever drafted by the Oilers, he was selected twenty-first overall in the 1979 NHL entry draft and gained a varsity berth during the 1979–80 season, his rookie year and the Oilers first in the NHL (previously, Edmonton had been in the World Hockey Association).

Kevin's improvement paralleled the Oilers' growth, and when Edmonton won its first Stanley Cup in 1984, defeating the New York Islanders, Lowe enjoyed his best season in the big league.

He also became one of the NHL's foremost goodwill ambassadors. Bilingual, Lowe frequently appears on French-language telecasts and has long been a favorite of French-speaking reporters. The NHL's renaissance man, Lowe writes a regular column for the *Edmonton Sun* and also has had a radio program on an Edmonton station.

"Kevin is a credit to that hockey team," said Jacques Demers, "and a credit to hockey as well."

Unfortunately, the lack of flamboyance in his play has tended to limit the attention he merited throughout the 1980s. "But," as Gretzky noted, "I'd hate to think where the Edmonton Oilers would be without Kevin Lowe."

89

Grant Fuhr
(1981–   )

It is a measure of Grant Fuhr's excellence that he has become fully recognized as the pre-eminent goaltender of the late 1980s, despite the fact that he is not a media darling and has been overshadowed by Wayne Gretzky, Mark Messier, Kevin Lowe, and numerous other present and past Edmonton aces over the years.

Fuhr's awards speak more eloquently than the netminder himself. He has played on four Stanley Cup championship teams and has thrice been a member of the NHL First All-Star Team, including an appearance in *Rendez-Vous '87*.

When the Oilers wiped out the favored Calgary Flames in a four-straight division sweep in the 1988 playoffs, the difference was goaltending. Fuhr was near-flawless. The Calgary goaltending was atrocious.

In the 1988 finals against the Boston Bruins, Fuhr again repelled the enemy when it counted, and he was as much responsible for his club's fourth Cup win in five years as his scoring brethren.

This hardly surprised those who had scouted Grant as a teenager. Perhaps the definitive word on Fuhr was provided by the Oilers' oft-praised scout Barry Fraser. He persuaded Oilers' general manager Glen Sather that Fuhr should be Edmonton's first selection in the 1981 entry draft and Sather has never regretted the move. "I expected Grant to be as good as he is," says Sather. "But I didn't expect him to become so successful so quickly."

Those who saw Grant play junior hockey in Victoria were not surprised. One of his teammates was Barry Pederson, a center who jumped right into a Boston Bruin jersey when Fuhr moved up to the Oilers. "Even as a junior," said Pederson, "Grant was very intelligent, very confident, very poised on the ice. You'd never see him make a dumb mistake. If anyone was going to make it big in the NHL, it was going to be Grant."

In many ways, Fuhr was special. The fact that he was the NHL's first black goalie certainly was a cause of discussion. Los Angeles Kings' general manager Rogatien Vachon put it another way: "When people around the league talk about Fuhr they talk about 'that goaltender from Edmonton,' not 'that black goaltender from Edmonton.'"

The color of Fuhr's skin, nevertheless, has been a factor in some of the precincts visited by the Oilers, particularly New York City with its enormous black population. "We really wanted Fuhr," recalled former New York Rangers' general manager Craig Patrick. The Broadway Blueshirts attempted to make a deal so that they could pick ahead of the Oilers in the 1981 draft, but the ploy never materialized. Still, when Fuhr arrived in New York with the Edmonton sextet, he was billed not so much as a hot rookie but as the

NHL's first black goalie. Naturally, the questions inevitably touched on Jackie Robinson and Fuhr's emotional kinship with the black who broke the baseball barrier.

"I've never felt any extra pressure because of race," said Fuhr. "I've never experienced any sort of discrimination. Race has never been an issue."

Raised in the upper-middle class Edmonton suburb of Spruce Grove, Fuhr was adopted by white parents who owned a large Ford dealership in the Edmonton area. He began playing hockey when he was five and gravitated toward goaltending "because it was a position I liked and it was fun."

By the time he had reached his teens, Fuhr was regarded as exceptional enough to play in fast junior amateur leagues, culminating with the Victoria Cougars of the Western Hockey League. Vancouver Canucks' scout George Wood, himself a former goalie, was impressed with Fuhr's calm under fire as was Jack Shupe, the Cougars' coach.

"He had a really good temperament to be a goaltender," said Shupe. "He was always easy-going and nothing seemed to upset Grant. You could score on him and he didn't change outwardly whatsoever. I always felt that he played better and tougher if he let in a soft goal. He'd really bear down then."

The hoopla notwithstanding, Fuhr still had to prove himself against the NHL's big guns. Other junior goalies who had been drafted high in other years proved disappointing under fire. In 1972, Michel Larocque was drafted sixth by the Montreal Canadiens with much the same "guarantees" that accompanied Fuhr's delivery to Edmonton. Larocque proved to be an abject disappointment. A year later, John Davidson was drafted fifth, and he, too, was merely a modest success, at best.

Unlike those busts, Fuhr displayed a consistency born of excellent reflexes, a superb glove hand, and ballet-like kicks. Grant revealed these assets on his first tour of the NHL. He was particularly impressive at Madison Square Garden, where he defeated the Rangers 5–3 on two occasions. Fuhr's teammate Wayne Gretzky praised his padded pal. "I've never seen a goalkeeper at his age with so much composure," said Gretzky. "He just stands there making save after save."

As much as they admired his talents, the reporters took a dim view of Fuhr's low-key, often inaudible—and occasionally non-existent—answers to their questions. After his two New York conquests, Fuhr opened the pages of the *Daily News* where he read Frank Brown's review: "Fuhr is as blasé as a player can be about his remarkable start."

Fuhr: "It was just another game and we got two points out of it. I haven't got over being in the NHL yet. I'm just trying to make it with this team."

Fuhr made it as well as any goaltender of the 1980s. For several years, he shared goaltending duties with Andy Moog, but Fuhr invariably got the nod in big playoff games. In the fall of 1987, Moog opted to play for the Canadian Olympic team, and Fuhr was burdened with the heaviest workload of his life. He played in a record seventy-five games and produced a 3.43 average. In the playoffs, Grant was in goal for every one of Edmonton's eighteen games as the Oilers marched to their fourth Cup triumph in five years.

It is said that goaltenders are a strange breed and are often ostracized by their teammates. But this has never been the case for Fuhr.

"He's well liked by the guys, which helps because they want to play well in front of him," said Gretzky. "They respect him because he's not cocky."

It is conceivable that Fuhr could retain his level of excellence through the early 1990s. But even if his game suffers a sharp decline, it would not detract from the fact that he has been one of the premier goalies of contemporary times.

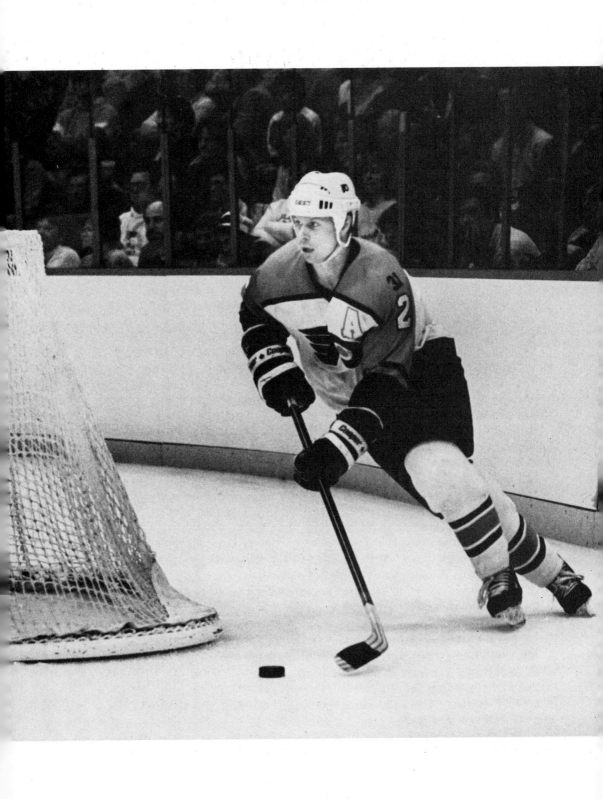

90

Mark Howe

(1979–   )

There has only been one thing "wrong" with this speedy, deft-passing defenseman who comes from Detroit, Michigan—his last name is spelled H–O–W–E.

Had Mark Howe been anyone but the son of the inimitable Gordie Howe, he would have been acknowledged as a genuinely superior hockey player in his own right and a future Hall of Famer.

"But," said former NHLer Aldo Guidolin, "there's no way that Mark can win because he's Gordie's son. Fans will always be comparing him with The Old Man. That, as it happens, is like comparing a mere mortal to God."

Yet when perused carefully, Mark Howe's credentials—dating back to his teen days in Detroit—have been impeccable.

At the age of fourteen, Mark was a leading member of the 1969–70 U.S. National Junior Champion Detroit Red Wings. At sixteen, he was a member of the 1972 silver medal winning U.S. Olympic team. At seventeen, he starred for the Toronto Marlboros, winners of the 1973 Memorial Cup. At eighteen, and again at nineteen, Mark starred alongside his father and brother Marty as a member of the Avco-World Trophy-winning Houston Aeros of the World Hockey Association.

Mark was the first NHL defenseman to score two shorthanded goals in a single period (October 9, 1980 at St. Louis), and the second defenseman in the NHL to score three goals in one period (Ian Turnbull was first in 1976–77). Mark also holds the Whalers' record of points in twenty-one straight games set in 1978–79.

Although Mark has never played for a Stanley Cup champion, he did help the Philadelphia Flyers to the Cup finals both in 1985 and 1987. Like Paul Coffey, Mark accents offense while still doing a laudable job behind the blue line. His best season, numerically, was 1985–86, when he totaled twenty-four goals and fifty-eight assists for eighty-two points. Does that impress him? Actually, Mark will tell you that he is grateful for any points he obtains. The reason is quite simple: Howe was nearly killed during a hockey game early in his career. As it happened, he "escaped" with a severe injury.

The Whalers were playing the Islanders on December 27, 1980, at the Hartford Civic Center. Cross-checked by defenseman Bob Lorimer, Howe crashed into the sidepost of the net and then fell into the cage itself. With the impact, the net rose off its mounting and tilted back, leaving the base of its bayonet-like center prong sticking up. Howe, sliding uncontrollably, pitched onto it.

Six inches of metal plunged into Mark's lower back and buttock, slicing through fat, touching the wall of the rectum, and grazing the sphincter muscle—which controls continence and elimination—and then twisted toward his hip. It wouldn't have been worse had he been bayoneted on the battlefield.

What followed is a combination of miracle and nightmare.

As Howe pulled himself off the prong, he began to bleed heavily. He didn't know if the makeshift spear had touched his spine or sliced through organs. All he could tell those crowding around him was that he had been stabbed. The full extent of the injury was masked by his equipment.

There was no ambulance at the Civic Center and no first-aid equipment to deal with shock and heavy bleeding. Once an ambulance did arrive, Howe was rushed to the hospital where he lay in the emergency room. The bleeding was stopped, but it was an hour before Dr. John DeMaio, the family's physician-surgeon arrived.

He had only been told that Howe had suffered a "laceration." Later he confessed to Colleen Howe, Mark's mother, that had he known the gravity of the injury, he would have insisted treatment begin immediately. "God had Mark in His arms at that moment," said Colleen, "but our blessing is that He went in there with Mark, and Mark survived with his career and his body."

Howe's recuperative powers were so strong that he only missed seventeen games that season and finished with nineteen goals and forty-six assists, an accomplishment for any backliner.

Significantly, the injury inspired a major design change in the traditional Art Ross-type hockey net. The bayonet-like centerpiece was removed, and the net was placed on super magnets to give it flexibility in case of collision.

Howe has endured several traumas since that night in Hartford. He was traded to the Flyers in August 1982 with the Whalers' third-round choice for Ken Linseman, Greg Adams, and Philadelphia's first- and third-round choices in the 1983 entry draft. Howe has become a permanent member of the Broad Street Bullies, although he has invariably put the accent on finesse and has proved to be one of the best advertisements the Flyers ever had.

As a four-time member of the NHL First All-Star Team (1983, 1986, 1987, and 1988), he has established himself as one of the most impressive contemporary defensemen, accenting style while providing substance.

"I've been very proud of Mark's accomplishments," concluded Gordie Howe. "He's had a wonderful career." In short, Mark has carried the family name well. His quality of play, level of dedication, and drive to win put him in a class above the average NHL defenseman and qualify him to be one of *Hockey's 100*.

91

Rod Langway
(1978–   )

Whether the story is apocryphal or not, a tale has been circulated among Capitals watchers about a young player on the team who foolishly disobeyed the rules established by coach Bryan Murray and, therefore, cost the club points in the standings.

As the yarn goes, Langway was so incensed by the kid's breach of protocol that he closed the dressing room door behind the team one day and so withered the lad with invective that the rule-breaker would have felt considerably more comfortable had he been wasted by a laser beam. The young man got the message and proceeded to shape up.

If nothing else, the vignette symbolized precisely what Rod Langway stood for on the Washington hockey team. He not only was the chief-shaper-upper, the leader-with-words-and-deeds, but a commanding figure like few others in big-league professional hockey.

On top of that, at one point, Rod Langway was the best defenseman in the NHL. Despite the fact that he was known as a defensive defenseman, Langway was able to outpoint Paul Coffey and Ray Bourque for the Norris Trophy in 1983 and 1984.

"There's no doubt about who's better—it's Langway," said then Bruins' defenseman Mike Milbury. "If I had to pick between them, I would rather have had Langway because he had a better approach to the game. He was more of a team player with a lot more character. And that's the thing you want most of all on a hockey team."

Detroit Red Wings' coach Jacques Demers added, "Rod plays from 35 to 40 minutes a game sometimes. He's the key to the blue line and the reason why Washington's goals against average has usually been so low."

Take Langway out of the lineup, and the Caps are in trouble. It happened in the 1988 playoffs, Rod was injured early in the Devils-Caps series, and the Caps went down the tubes.

Few hockey players have earned the title "majestic" and perhaps only one Hall of Famer, Jean Beliveau, comes immediately to mind when the term is mentioned. Even fewer players can legitimately be called "franchise-savers" in the true sense of the word. But when one talks about Langway, it is not stretching the point to suggest that what we have here is a "majestic franchise-saver," or, as they say on Capitol Hill, "a class act."

When the towering defenseman joined the Washington Capitals in 1982, the club had never made the Stanley Cup playoffs. But with Langway leading the way, the Caps have enjoyed post-season action every year since then. He has also been at the forefront of the U.S. hockey movement, captaining Team USA's entry in the Canada Cup tournament.

But the Langway years have not been without hardship and controversy. His Caps have been tagged with the "choke" label, and team captain Langway has lived through his

share of the controversy, including the notorious Bobby Carpenter-Bryan Murray feud and a money-oriented trade demand that took him from Montreal to Washington.

The most remarkable aspect of Langway's development was his transformation from a relatively obscure backliner with the Montreal Canadiens (1978–82) to a franchise-maker with the Capitals. Rod was the centerpiece of an amazingly provocative deal in 1982. Then Canadiens' general manager Irving Grundman sent Rod, Doug Jarvis, Craig Laughlin, and Brian Engblom to the Caps for Rick Green and Ryan Walter. The deal eventually cost Grundman his job, partially because Langway blossomed into a superstar with the Capitals.

Rod Correy Langway was born on May 3, 1957, in Formosa, Taiwan. Coming from a family of nine, Rod found his niche early in his upbringing.

Throughout his early years, Langway demonstrated leadership potential. He began his pro career with the Birmingham Bulls of the now-defunct World Hockey Association. He moved to the NHL in 1978–79 with the Canadiens and they won the Stanley Cup that same season.

When he came to Washington, he emerged as the most visible player on the franchise and a respected member of the Capital district sports community.

Despite the accolades, Langway has had one major cross to bear during his Capitals' career. And that is Washington's failure to make any noticeable dent at playoff time. Nevertheless, any man who can save a franchise single-handedly deserves to be placed in the Pantheon. No one deserves it more than Langway.

92

Gerry Cheevers
(1961–1980)

An interesting blend of healthy truculence, daring inventiveness, superior intelligence, and amazing agility (even when he appeared overweight in his declining years) made Gerry Cheevers unusual and several cuts above most of his goaltending peers.

Pugnacious almost to a fault, Cheevers more than anything was a winner. He shared the goaltending—with Eddie Johnston—on the Boston Bruins last two Stanley Cup championship teams in 1970 and 1972. In 1973, he was voted the best goaltender in the World Hockey Association. He was the number one goalie for Team Canada in 1974 during the series against the Soviet All-Stars and was durable enough to span two decades as a professional.

Few could match Cheevers's competitive zeal. His policy was strict and honest: when you lose it's like being shot on the battlefield and don't go shaking the hand of the enemy for that! Such was the case in 1971 when goalie Ken Dryden and the Montreal Canadiens upset Cheevers's Bruins. At game's end, the teams lined up for the traditional handshaking ceremonies, but Cheevers had already made a quick exit to his dressing room.

"I wanted to tell Dryden when it was all over that he'd done a big, big, job, but I didn't," said Cheevers. "When the teams met in a straggly line at center and shook hands, I wasn't among those present. I've never congratulated a guy for beating me. I sure as hell didn't feel like gripping Mahovlich's paw, and Harper's and Lemaire's. They put lumps on me and took my money; why should I applaud them?"

Later, Cheevers called over Jacques Beauchamp, a Montreal journalist who was heading to the plane that would carry the victorious Canadiens—and Dryden—back to Montreal. "Jacques," he said, "when you get on the plane, tell that giraffe [Dryden] he had one hell of a series. Tell him congratulations for me, Jacques."

The congratulations had enveloped Cheevers many times during a career that included 418 regular-season National Hockey League games and eighty-eight playoff matches. His goals against average was 2.89 for the regular campaigns and 2.69 for the playoffs.

In a sense, the figures were deceptive because Gerry goaled for a Bruins club that invariably accented offense—Phil Esposito, Bobby Orr, and Ken Hodge were the big guns—and ignored defense. Which meant that Cheevers was pretty much on his own.

Nicknamed *Chessie*, Cheevers set an NHL record during the 1971–72 season, when he played goal through thirty-two unbeaten games. "He was one of the all-time greats when it came to money games," said Phil Esposito, a long-time teammate.

Gerald Michael Cheevers was born December 7, 1940, in St. Catharines, Ontario, and seemed destined for a career with the Toronto Maple Leafs, which owned his rights during the early 1960s. He was obtained by the Bruins in 1965 and, after a few trips to the minors, made it to stay in the NHL in 1967, at a time when Boston's fortunes were on the rise.

In time, fans were hanging banners over the Boston Garden balcony: "WE'RE BELIEVERS IN GERRY CHEEVERS."

After the Bruins won the Stanley Cup in 1972, Cheevers jumped to the Cleveland Crusaders of the World Hockey Association and remained in the WHA until 1976, when he returned to the Hub sextet. It was no coincidence that Cheevers's return marked another upturn in the Bruins' fortunes. His habit of pursuing and stickhandling the puck delighted Boston Garden fans, and his goaltending still had a snap of sharpness.

Gerry remained a Bruins goalie until his retirement after the 1979–80 campaign, when he was named Boston coach. The transition from the nets to the bench was not an easy one. "It was," said Cheevers, "a tremendous learning experience."

But coaching did not agree with Cheevers. In time, he was released by the Bruins and became a TV hockey analyst for the Hartford Whalers. Still, he is remembered as a championship goalie.

93

Hap Day
(1924–1938)

It could legitimately be said that Hap Day was as effective a coach as he was a player—and he was very good at both occupations.

An aspiring pharmacist, Day wound up starring for the Toronto Maple Leafs' 1932 Stanley Cup-winning team. Exactly ten years later, he coached the Maple Leafs to another Cup triumph and followed that with an unprecedented run of three consecutive Stanley Cups in 1947, 1948, and 1949.

Throughout his career, Day was closely linked with Maple Leafs' founder, Conn Smythe, both as a business partner—Smythe had a very successful sand and gravel company in Toronto—player, and coach. Smythe admired Day's durability and dedication as a defenseman and his insights and iron-fisted rule as a coach.

"When I named Hap coach in 1940," Smythe once recalled, "he was everything I wanted. He could do things I couldn't: fire people; bench them; live always on what a man could do today, not what he had done a few years ago."

Day's dependability as a player was never more evident than on the night of April 2, 1932, at Maple Leaf Gardens, when the Leafs faced-off against the Montreal Maroons. This was the second of a two-game total-goals series. The first game had ended in a 1–1 tie.

In Game 2, the Maroons built up a 2–1 lead on goals by Hooley Smith and Jimmy Ward while Red Horner scored Toronto's lone goal. The third period was nearing conclusion, and Maroons' goalie James "Flat" Walsh was repelling the Maple Leafs' most dangerous thrusts. It remained for Day, who was team captain, to deliver his finest moment as a player.

He gathered the puck on his stick deep in Toronto territory and proceeded to pick his way through the Montreal defense like a pinball making its way down the machine. He outmaneuvered Nels Stewart and "deked" Lionel Conacher and then Archie Wilcox, until he was face to face with goalie Walsh.

Day's shot was described by one reporter as "whizzing and bounding," but whatever it did, it slithered past Walsh to tie the game and force a sudden-death overtime. Late in the first overtime period, Bob Gracie scored for the Maple Leafs who advanced to the Stanley Cup finals whereupon they routed the Rangers.

Clarence Henry Day was born June 14, 1901, in Owen Sound, Ontario. Like so many stars of the 1920s and 1930s, Day learned his hockey under severe conditions. At times, he would plod miles through the snow to find a place to play hockey, and he eventually became a leader with the Midland Juniors.

Hap's courage and ability enabled him to climb the long, hard hockey ladder in Ontario. He moved from the Midland Juniors to the intermediate sextet and then to Hamilton's Tigers. Hockey was not the only subject on his mind; Day wanted very much to be a pharmacist, and he enrolled at the University of Toronto, from which he eventually obtained a degree. While attending the university, he played for the varsity hockey club, was discovered by Toronto hockey entrepreneur Charlie Querrie, and was persuaded to turn pro.

At the time, Toronto's major-league team was known as the St. Pats. The name was changed to the Maple Leafs when Smythe bought the team and obtained all the former St. Pats players. "Day and Ace Bailey," Smythe remembered, "were about the only two real hockey players we got in the deal."

Apart from his significant contributions to the Maple Leafs on the ice, Day was a marvelous team player and one who infused considerable humor into the team's dressing room. The Toronto club of the early 1930s was known as *The Gashouse Gang of Hockey* because of the *joie de vivre* exuded by Day and his cohorts.

Day was strong and fearless. He could bodycheck with the best of them, but he was not averse to using his arms to envelop the foe. "Some other teams didn't like him being such a heavy lover on the ice," said Smythe. "He'd have those arms around a guy and never let go. He was a 'what we have, we hold' man, all the way."

Smythe released Day after the 1936–37 season whereupon he signed for one year with the New York Americans, and then retired. He returned to Toronto and was hired by Smythe to coach the Maple Leafs in 1940.

Day was at the helm in the spring of 1942 when the Maple Leafs authored the most extraordinary comeback in the history of any major sports world championship. Down three games to none in the Stanley Cup finals with the Detroit Red Wings, *the Maple Leafs then won the next four straight games and the Stanley Cup.*

In 1945, the same teams met in the finals. This time the Maple Leafs won three in a row. Detroit rebounded to take Games 4, 5, and 6, setting the stage for the pulsating seventh match. Again, Day's strategy prevailed and Toronto triumphed.

Never was a coach more exceptional than in the late 1940s when Day engineered the first ever three-year parlay. Toronto annexed the Cups in 1947, 1948, and 1949.

Following the 1949–50 season, Day retired as coach. He liked to tell this story about how fame is fleeting, although he was regarded as one of the greatest coaches of all time. "It was 1951 and I was on a scouting trip out west for the Leafs. I was in a rail seat in the Edmonton rink when the Edmonton and Saskatoon teams came on the ice.

"One of the Saskatoon players was leaning on the boards near me, and I recognized him as Reg Bentley, brother of Max and Doug. I had known Reg from a few years before when the Chicago Black Hawks gave him an NHL tryout.

"So I called, 'Hi, Reg!' He looked so puzzled that I decided to help him out. I leaned forward and said, 'Happy Day.'

"'Thanks, and the same to you,' answered Reg, as he smiled politely and skated away."

After coaching, Day was promoted to manager of the Maple Leafs, but the club faltered—through no fault of his—and Day ultimately became embroiled in a dispute with Stafford Smythe, Conn's son, who was taking over the operation of Maple Leaf Gardens.

Bitter about the manner in which he was being treated, Day resigned and returned to private business. His relationship with Conn Smythe was injured but eventually repaired, and the pair remained friends until Smythe's death in 1980.

They were a grand pair and Day, almost as much as Smythe, helped develop the Maple Leafs into one of the most formidable teams in professional sports.

94

Andy Bathgate
(1953–1971)

For about five years in the late 1950s and early 1960s, there existed in New York City a cult of hockey fans the members of which were quite content to do very little else but visit Madison Square Garden simply to see Andy Bathgate in action on right wing for the Rangers.

"Watching Andy play a good game," said Joseph Breu, who then covered the NHL for United Press International," was no less enjoyable than watching Jason Robards starring in *Long Days Journey Into Night* down the block on Broadway."

Like Robards, Bathgate was the consummate performer. He combined the art of stick-handling and shooting to near perfection. His shot, which he endlessly practiced, became so devastating that it was favorably compared with the mighty blasts of Bobby Hull and Bernie "Boom Boom" Geoffrion, both of whom were his contemporaries.

Bathgate wasn't quite as flashy as Hull nor as blessed with all-star teammates as Geoffrion, but he was good enough to win the Hart Trophy as the NHL's most valuable player in 1959 and was voted to the First All-Star Team at right wing in 1959 and 1962, as well as the Second Team in 1958 and 1963.

The Bathgate bloc could recite a litany of beauteous plays executed by their hero. One that qualifies among his best was a one-on-one play—Bathgate vs. the goaltender.

Perhaps his most difficult move was delivered against Glenn Hall of the Chicago Black Hawks. At the time, Hall, alias *Mister Goalie*, was the best netminder in the business. On this occasion, Bathgate received the pass directly in front of Hall but more to the right of the net. Rather than simply shoot the puck, Andy performed a 180 degree pirouette, culminating with the puck on his stick at the left side of the cage. Hall remained with Bathgate until Andy then completely reversed the move with another pirouette, this time winding up precisely where he had begun. By this time, Hall's body was so contorted he was literally unable to move whereupon Bathgate deposited the rubber in the empty right corner for a goal. It was vintage Bathgate and a play that few, if any, could duplicate.

Andy had been tabbed a future big-leaguer when he was still a teenager playing for the Guelph (Ontario) Biltmores in the Ontario Hockey Association's Junior A division. When Guelph won the Memorial Cup, emblematic of junior hockey supremacy in Canada, a number of the Biltmores were earmarked for the Rangers.

Under Phil Watson's coaching, the Rangers made the playoffs three straight years (1955–56, 1956–57, and 1957–58). In March 1958, the club finished second, the highest for a New York club since 1942.

Bathgate earned acclaim as one of the most threatening shooters in the game. "I worked on my shooting at least fifteen minutes every single day. To my mind shooting practice is one of the most overlooked aspects of the game. I see coaches emphasizing skating all the time but, to me, the most important thing is shooting the puck. When you shoot the puck it's not how straight it is that counts, it's the quickness of the release, and that's what I kept working on when I was a Ranger."

Unlike many of his contemporaries, Bathgate was extremely scrupulous about conditioning. "In my entire life I've never had a drink or a cigarette and it made me feel good as a player. Some nights I'd go out on the ice and I'd know just by looking at the opposition that I was in much better shape than him and it was to my advantage, both physically and mentally."

Bathgate was also a cut above the average player in terms of his intellect. He was thoughtful and sensitive to the needs of his teammates. When a core of NHL players began laying the groundwork of a union, Bathgate was one of the organizers. He believes that his participation in developing a players' association inspired the Rangers to deal him to Toronto at the very apex of his popularity as a Ranger.

It was no secret that Bathgate's success in Toronto would vitally hinge on his relationship with the boss, Punch Imlach. At first, all went well. Imlach was more than pleased with Bathgate's efforts in February, March, and April 1964. "Andy did," said Imlach, "exactly what I'd had in mind when I made the deal."

The 1964 Cup win marked the high-water level of the Bathgate-Imlach relationship. From then on, it was all a decrescendo, marked by bitterness and an eventual trade. The feud came to a head in the spring of 1965, when Montreal eliminated the Maple Leafs in six games of the Stanley Cup semifinals. "He was a different Bathgate from the guy who had said being traded to Toronto was the biggest break of his life." charged Imlach.

In no time at all, Imlach traded Bathgate, Billy Harris, and Gary Jarrett to the Red Wings for Marcel Pronovost, Ed Joyal, Larry Jeffrey, Lowell MacDonald, and Autry Erickson. "Frankly," Bathgate explained, "I didn't enjoy Punch's methods of training. By my second season in Toronto I just wasn't enjoying playing so I spoke to Punch and I had to give him a reason to get me out of Toronto. So, I said something to one of the reporters; Punch overemphasized it and I wound up in Detroit."

Andrew James Bathgate was born August 28, 1932, in Winnipeg, Manitoba. He followed his older brother, Frank, east to play first-class amateur hockey in Ontario.

As much as anyone, Andy helped develop the hockey renaissance in New York City during the 1950s, and it seemed almost heretical for the Rangers to trade him to Toronto. After his feuds with Imlach, Andy began to lose his touch. He was drafted by the Pittsburgh Penguins when the Steel City sextet entered the NHL in 1967.

While still displaying flashes of the old brilliance, Andy no longer had the legs to enable him to keep up with the play. He later quit the NHL and played briefly in Switzerland. When the World Hockey Association planted a franchise in Vancouver, he returned to the ice wars as coach, although an eye injury suffered in a home accident in 1973 limited his vision by 80 percent in his right eye.

Nevertheless, Andy returned to action once more in 1974 with the Vancouver Blazers and actually was a dominant factor for the seven games in which he played, but a contract dispute with management finally inspired him to pack it in once and for all.

Bathgate returned to Toronto where he went into the golf business and also became involved with agricultural investments. He never did get completely away from the rinks. He soon joined the Toronto edition of the NHL Old-timers. Late in the summer of 1981,

Andy took part in a hockey tourney with members of the original six NHL teams. "He looked like he could have stepped right back into the NHL today," said tourney director Gerry Patterson, "and been a superstar."

Class was Andy Bathgate's hallmark—as a teenager, as a big-leaguer, and as an NHL old-timer. If ever a man was a credit to the game, Bathgate was it.

95

Alex Connell
(1924–1937)

Ottawa, the capital of Canada, spawned many an exceptional hockey player, but few were better than Alex Connell, who tended goal for the Ottawa Senators, Detroit Falcons, and, finally, the Montreal Canadiens in a National Hockey League career spanning thirteen years.

Playing for Ottawa in 1927–28, he set a league record of *six consecutive shutouts*. Like his Ottawa neighbor, Clint Benedict, he played on Stanley Cup-winning teams in two different cities—for the Ottawa Senators and the Montreal Maroons.

Connell's career record, 1.99 goals against average, is astonishing under any set of circumstances. After helping the Senators win the Stanley Cup in 1927, he amassed fifteen shutouts the following season, as well as a remarkable goals against average of 1.30. Connell had permitted but fifty-seven goals in forty-four games. His record-breaking shutout run spanned 446 minutes and 9 seconds.

Alex Connell was born February 8, 1902, in Ottawa, and seemed destined for a career as either a lacrosse or baseball player. He turned to professional hockey with the Senators in 1924 and played for Ottawa until 1932, when he had a brief fling with the Detroit Falcons. It was during that stint that he became famous for yet another reason. "Alex," said Bill Roche, "was the only hockey player to cause the police riot squad to be called out in New York City."

The episode took place in 1932 at the old Madison Square Garden on Eighth Avenue and Fiftieth Street in New York when the Americans were hosting the Detroit Falcons in a game that would decide whether or not the Amerks would go into the playoffs later that spring. At the time, the Amerks were owned by the infamous Bill Dwyer, reputed mob boss, and undisputed King of the Bootleggers in New York, as well as several other states.

The game was tied at the end of regulation time, 1–1, and the two teams went into a ten-minute overtime period. With about five minutes left in the period, Detroit received a penalty, giving the Amerks the much-needed advantage in manpower. The New York players realized it was their opportuntity to take the initiative and win the game. It was a must situation.

The red-, white-, and blue-clad Americans bore down and administered intense pressure on the Falcons. Red Dutton, then a battling defenseman for New York, took a blistering shot that, according to the goal judge, eluded Connell and ricocheted in and—just as quickly—out of the net. The red light went on, and the Amerks celebrated their "win."

But trouble was brewing: the referee, George Mallinson, disallowed the goal. He claimed he had perfect view of the play, and the puck never went in. Connell agreed.

During the melee that ensued, the goal judge berated the shocked goaltender with a string of the vilest profanities Connell had ever heard. Connell was not about to stand for any more of that kind of abuse. He skated around back of the net and, taking advantage of the man's nose, which was sticking through the mesh, bopped the goal judge directly and resoundingly on his protruding proboscis. This sent the surprised and infuriated goal judge reeling in his own blood and started a panic among the security force at the Garden who knew the man to be a "high official in Bill Dwyer's mob."

Alex Connell had unknowingly put his own life in grave danger with one well-placed, ill-timed punch. But Connell was more concerned with the game, and after play was resumed (the goal was not allowed), he held the Americans scoreless and the game ended in a 1–1 deadlock.

As Alex Connell left the ice, he noticed for the first time that there were policemen lining the walkway. Everywhere he looked he saw the boys in blue in great force blocking the spectators from approaching the players. When he got into the dressing room and began peeling off his sweaty uniform, two plainclothes detectives walked up, identified themselves to him, and then stood on either side of him, with their guns drawn. It was explained to him that the man he had punched out was Dwyer's right-hand man, and that there might be some serious ramifications if proper precautions were not taken.

Quickly, after he had finished dressing, Connell was shuffled into a waiting taxi and driven, along with his police escort, to the hotel where the team was staying. The cops combed the lobby for suspicious looking characters before bringing in the befuddled Alex Connell. He was then given strict instructions not to leave his room for the remainder of the evening.

Connell recalls how the rest of the evening went: "An old friend was visiting with me that night and after we had talked about the strange goings-on, we decided to leave the hotel to get some sandwiches before I went to bed.

"We went out the front door and had only walked about ten feet when I remembered the cop's warning. Then I noticed there were some people standing around us, one big mean-looking guy looked right at me and came towards us. We ducked into a diner and seated ourselves at separate counters. The large man came in and ordered me to go over to him for questioning. I paid no attention to him, so he repeated his order, adding that if I knew what was good for me I'd do what I was told.

"Then I walked over to him. He demanded, 'Aren't you Alex Connell, goalkeeper with the Detroit Falcons?' I replied that I not only did not know who Alex Connell was, but that I'd never heard of any Detroit Falcons.

"After a couple of minutes of him repeating the question and me repeating my answer, he apologized for bothering me and left."

When the cops heard about the incident from the hotel night manager, they decided to stand guard outside Connell's room for the rest of the night.

The next day, Connell learned that his quick thinking and fast talking had probably saved him from a one way "ride" with the gunslinging hoodlums.

Connell finished his career in 1937 with the Maroons. Even then, at the age of thirty-six, he was able to produce a nifty 2.37 goals against average. He then retired, and died May 10, 1958.

96

Allan Stanley
(1948–1969)

Allan Herbert Stanley holds the dubious distinction of being booed out of his NHL home in New York not once but *twice*. No other member of hockey's Hall of Fame can make that statement.

Few who applauded the debonair defenseman in September 1981 at the induction ceremonies in Toronto recalled that Stanley holds the world's record for vilification of a professional athlete. Nor did they realize that his ascent to stardom despite such adversity is as much a reason for his induction as was Stanley's pure defensive ability.

If *Big Allan*, as we knew him, had told anyone in 1954 that someday he would make it to the Hall of Fame, New York City's Tactical Patrol Force would have rushed him to the Bellevue Hospital psychiatric ward in a straightjacket.

At the time, Stanley was a member of the New York Rangers and happened to be the unwilling recipient of the biggest buildup of any hockey player in the Blueshirts' history.

The men responsible for the torrent of ink were Frank Boucher, general manager of the Rangers, and Stan Saplin, the club's creative press agent. Together in the fall of 1948, they created the myth of Stanley's invincibility.

"One night," said Saplin, "Allan was a minor-leaguer in Providence, enjoying a postgame glass of beer with a few teammates at midnight. The next noon he was in Leone's restaurant and being acclaimed, in effect, as the savior of the downtrodden Rangers."

Rangers' fans, who had savored the luxury of but one playoff team in seven years, delighted in Stanley's buildup but could not tolerate the letdown that followed. They had expected a combination of Superman and the Incredible Hulk. Instead, they got a defenseman who played D–E–F–E–N–S–E.

To obtain Stanley, the Rangers dispatched three pro players, cash, and the rights held by the Rangers to the services of an amateur. The value was estimated at the time to be about $70,000. By today's fiscal standards, it would be close to $1,000,000.

In no time at all, the "$70,000 Rookie" was being chided as the "$70,000 Beauty," and then the "$70,000 Lemon." None of this would have happened had the Blueshirts been winners, but they hovered between mediocrity and melancholy.

Boucher, who had brought Stanley to New York, appreciated Allan's talents more than most and was upset by the fans' reaction. He decided to spare Stanley any more hurt by playing him only in away games, but that just left the Rangers with a rusty defenseman, and further increased the fans' hostility.

"They'd boo every time I touched the puck. Then they began to boo every time I got on the ice. Why, even the few games when I sat on the bench, they'd yell at me."

The agony endured for six years, with one brief break when the Blueshirts took the Detroit Red Wings to the seventh game of the 1950 Stanley Cup finals before losing. Lynn Patrick was the New York coach at the time and called Stanley his most valuable Ranger.

"Every summer," Stanley once recalled, "I'd think about improving my play the next year and winning the fans over to my side. I was always hoping that I'd play like Superman."

And so Stanley's agony went on, seemingly interminable, until a cool Wednesday in 1954, when Allan's agony was stilled.

Boucher raced into the Ranger press office and announced with a mixture of anger and relief that he had traded Stanley and forward Nick Mickoski to the Chicago Black Hawks for Bill Gadsby, a high-quality defenseman, and Pete Conacher, a forward.

The trade was as sensational as the original deal for Stanley, since Gadsby was also considered a potential star. (As it happened, Gadsby played twenty years in the NHL, never skated for a Cup winner, and was named to the Hall of Fame in 1970.)

Big Allan played two seasons in Chicago with little hint of martyrdom. In the fall of 1956, the Black Hawks gave up and general manager Tommy Ivan prepared to send him to the Hawks' minor-league affiliate in Buffalo.

Lynn Patrick, who had moved on to Boston quickly grabbed the "$70,000 Beauty" for less than $15,000, and the Bruins were off and running.

Needless to say, Stanley played some of his best games against the Rangers at Madison Square Garden. He played two seasons in Boston, and when the Bruins figured *Big Allan* had had it, Punch Imlach gladly interceded and signed the old geezer for his Toronto Maple Leafs. It was the kind of move that helped brand Imlach a genius.

Stanley skated just as deliberately in Toronto as he had with the Rangers. The difference was that he was now playing before a sophisticated Maple Leaf Gardens audience who appreciated his defensive gifts as much as his boss, Imlach.

It was no coincidence that the Leafs annexed four Stanley Cups with the big guy snowshoeing behind the blue line. Stanley's play had a blend of majesty and intelligence that was both hard and clean. Textbook defense, you might say, the kind that is as rare today as a nickel cup of coffee.

Could *Big Allan* have achieved the same distinction as a Ranger? Under the circumstances, it would have been a 50–1 shot.

The inescapable problem in New York was frustrated fans who would not—or could not—get off his back.

"There is always a nucleus of fans," said Saplin, "who pay their way in whether their team is a winner or not. They need an outlet, though, for the bitterness that grows within them as failure piles upon failure."

In the eyes of the Ranger faithful, Stanley was an abject failure, a skater who never fulfilled his notices, who would never cut it on Broadway, and, needless to say, would never make it to hockey's Hall of Fame.

Welcome, now, to the distinguished company among *Hockey's 100*, *Big Allan*. Nobody ever beat bigger odds than you.

97

Gump Worsley
(1952–1974)

He looked more like a beer salesman—who enjoyed tasting his product—than a hockey goaltender. His pot belly made it seem like a Herculean task for him to even wave at, let alone nab, the swiftly flying rubber puck. His lack of height gave one the impression that he never could see the shooters what with the bigger men blocking the view in front of him. Nevertheless, Gump Worsley proved to be one of the best at his trade—blocking pucks—and one of the most courageous, as well as one of the most unorthodox.

Nothing says it more for Worsley's courage than the fact that he was the very last of quality goalies to play between the pipes without a protective face mask. Nothing says it more for his ability than the fact that he was winner of the Calder Trophy as rookie of the year in 1953 and the Vezina Trophy as top goaltender in 1966 and 1968 (the latter of which was shared with Charlie Hodge). He was named to the First All-Star Team in 1968 and the Second Team in 1966. Gump was formally inducted into the Hockey Hall of Fame in September 1980.

There have been few first-rate netminders more durable than Worsley. He turned pro in 1952 when the National Hockey League embraced but six teams and retired more than two decades later when there were more than twice that number. He was goalie on four Stanley Cup-winning Montreal Canadiens sextets, yet he is best known for his escapades as a member of the New York Rangers between 1952 and 1963.

The Rangers often seemed mired in a subterranean section of the NHL, yet Worsley always seemed to be performing like Horatio at the bridge. New York fans appreciated the roly-poly goalie, but his coach, the volatile Phil Watson, was less enthused. Watson constantly singled out Worsley for criticism in one form or another. Despite Watson's harangues, Worsley played splendid goal for the Rangers in the late 1950s, but then the team began to decline.

In his autobiography, *They Call Me Gump*, Worsley admitted that he turned to the bottle to ease the anguish. "I was using the bottle to chase all of those bad games and bad goals. I used to feel like a duck in a shooting gallery."

Worsley's Manhattan miseries ended on June 4, 1963, when he was traded to the Montreal Canadiens. As Gump succinctly put it, "That was the day I got out of the Ranger jailhouse."

Playing for the Canadiens was not exactly utopia for Worsley, at least not at first, but there was no question that he would be an asset. He proved it in the spring of 1965 during the Stanley Cup finals against the Chicago Black Hawks.

After playing the first two games of the series, Gump tore a thigh muscle in Game 3

and had to be replaced. The series went down to a seventh and final game with the teams tied at three wins apiece. Gump had been taking injections for his injury and was improving but doubted that he would play in the seventh match.

Prior to the game, Worsley was sitting in the Forum lounge when Larry Aubut, the Canadiens' trainer, walked in and told him he *was* playing. "I glanced at my wife, Doreen, as she ordered a rye and ginger ale—for herself. I could have used one, too, but instead I headed for our dressing room to get ready for the game. Was I nervous? Here I'd been playing pro hockey for fifteen years and finally was getting the big opportunity. This was it. The final game for the Stanley Cup championship. You bet your ass I was nervous."

Almost immediately, Camille Henry of the Black Hawks skated in alone on Worsley. "My legs were knocking," Worsley admitted. But he made the save and went on to blank the Black Hawks 4–0.

"Nothing," said Worsley, "has ever matched that thrill. The first Cup victory is always the biggest moment in a hockey player's life. I was the luckiest guy in the world."

Lorne Worsley was born May 14, 1929, in Montreal. As a kid, Worsley liked Davey Kerr, hero of the Rangers' 1940 Stanley Cup championship team. He got his first break after winning a tryout with the Verdun Cyclones, a junior team from a Montreal suburb, while playing for a second commercial-league club.

In 1949, Worsley was invited to the Rangers' training camp and was assigned to the Rangers' farm team, the New York Rovers of the old Eastern League. He played well and drank well. "We ran from bar to bar in those days," Worsley confessed, "and you know how many bars there are in New York. About 10,000. After most games we'd go out drinking and stay out until the joints closed at four in the morning. We were always there for the last call."

Nevertheless, Worsley continued the upward climb: from the Rovers to the New Haven Ramblers of the American League, with stopovers at St. Paul and Saskatoon, before reaching the Rangers.

Although Worsley won the rookie of the year prize in 1953, the Rangers had bought Johnny Bower, a highly regarded minor-leaguer, and installed him in the net the following season ahead of Gump. But Worsley returned to stay the following year and remained a New Yorker until he was dealt to the Canadiens. After a squabble with the Canadiens in 1970, he was picked up by the Minnesota North Stars and concluded his career in April 1974.

Nicknamed *Gump* because, as a kid, he resembled the cartoon character Andy Gump, Worsley played his 860th regular-season NHL game against the Philadelphia Flyers on April 2, 1974. The final goal—he allowed 2,432 in his NHL career—was scored by Dave Schultz, who was born the year Worsley played his first pro game in 1949.

"That made me feel old," said Worsley. "Too old to consider another comeback."

He retired and became a scout for the Minnesota North Stars, a position he retained until recently. The Gump never did look like much, but he did know how to stop the puck, and his longevity and championship rings attest to the fact that he did his job better than most.

98

Murray Murdoch
(1926–1937)

If ever the Hockey Hall of Fame selection committee was guilty of a miscarriage of justice, it was in its failure to nominate Murray Murdoch to its ice Pantheon. If for no other reason than the fact that Murdoch was the National Hockey League's first iron-man, he rated entry. But he was more than that. As a New York Rangers left wing, he epitomized the work ethic, was a guiding force on Stanley Cup-winning teams in 1928 and 1933, and later became one of the most respected collegiate coaches in North America.

"Murdoch gave his all to the game," wrote S. Kip Farrington, Jr. in his book *Skates, Sticks and Men.* "He literally ate, slept and breathed hockey. He gave the sport all he had, but he would be the first to admit that hockey has given him a multitude of satisfying rewards in return."

One of those, quite naturally, was his iron-man mark. *Murray never missed a Ranger game for eleven successive seasons,* which amounted to 508 NHL regular-season games and fifty-five Stanley Cup playoff matches.

When the original Rangers team was being organized by Conn Smythe in 1926—Smythe was fired before the season started and replaced by Lester Patrick—Murdoch had just graduated from the University of Manitoba. Smythe liked what he saw of the lad, although he couldn't have imagined how durable he would be. Murdoch was in Winnipeg when Smythe was signing other would-be Rangers in Duluth.

Murdoch, who was a newlywed, received a telegram from Smythe: MEET ME HERE IN DULUTH STOP ALL EXPENSES PAID.

To that, Murdoch wired back: IF YOU WANT TO SEE ME COME TO WINNIPEG.

Decades later, Murdoch recalled the fateful rendezvous. "Smythe came to Winnipeg, we talked and he offered me a $1,500 signing bonus and a $5,000 salary. I remember sitting in the lobby of the Fort Garry Hotel, thinking it over, and I was just about to say no when Conn leaned over a coffee table and slowly counted out $1,500 in $100 bills. That clinched it. For a young guy just married and with a summer job selling insurance, that looked like an awful lot of money."

Despite the agreement with Smythe, Murdoch was less than enamored of the man who was designated to lead the New York sextet. But when Lester Patrick took over as manager and coach, Murdoch became one of the most valuable Rangers. Patrick played him on a line with Billy Boyd and Paul Thompson. It was the New Yorkers' checking line and one of the best there was.

"Murray didn't get the buildup that the modern players receive, but he was a superstar in his own right," said Kip Farrington. "His iron-man record stood as a tribute to his durability and desire."

John Murray Murdoch was born May 19, 1904, in Lucknow, Ontario, and was skating shortly after he learned to walk. He first made his name in the sport while attending the University of Manitoba.

Following the Rangers' 1933 Stanley Cup championship—their second in seven years—Murdoch and other members of the old guard began to falter, although Murray played capably through the 1936–37 season, the last for himself and defenseman Ching Johnson. Shortly thereafter, General John Reed Kilpatrick, himself an alumnus of Yale, recommended Murdoch for the job of head coach of the Eli hockey team.

From that point on, Murdoch became something of a hockey legend on the collegiate coaching level. "Murray brought to Yale a quiet dignity and professionalism," said Farrington. "The ruddy-faced Canadian, once a handsome, blond-haired centerman, helped popularize the sport at Yale."

Murdoch coached at Yale for twenty-eight years before retiring in 1966. One of Murray's players, Bill Hildebrand, captain of the 1963 squad, said this of his coach: "Murray was one of the greatest college coaches who ever lived, if just from the standpoint of his knowledge of hockey. He knows the game inside out but, most of all, the players respect him because he's a real man in every way."

In 1974, Murdoch was awarded the Lester Patrick Trophy for service to hockey in the United States. He deserved it as much as he deserves to be in the Hockey Hall of Fame.

99

Alex Delvecchio
(1950–1974)

When the Detroit Red Wings' *Production Line* is mentioned as one of the most accomplished offensive trios of all time, Sid Abel is invariably noted as the center between Gordie Howe on right wing and Ted Lindsay on the left. And while this was true for a significant period of time, the fact remains that Alex "Fats" Delvecchio was as relevant, if not more so, than his predecessor.

Less abrasive than Abel, Delvecchio nevertheless was a stylist in the clean, competent manner of such respected centermen as Syl Apps and Jean Beliveau.

Delvecchio was a three-time winner of the Lady Byng Trophy (1959, 1966, and 1969) and was voted to the Second All-Star Team in 1953. He was also one of the few players to gain All-Star acclaim at two different positions, being named to the All-Star squad as a left wing in 1959.

There was good reason why Fats never made the First Team—during his twenty-three-year National Hockey League career he played mostly in the shadow of such classic centers as Beliveau, Stan Mikita, and Henri Richard. Nevertheless, Delvecchio's credentials are evident. He played on three Stanley Cup championship teams and seven first-place clubs. He became captain of the Red Wings in 1961 and scored twenty or more goals in thirteen of his seasons.

Delvecchio was polished, both on and off the ice. "Respect; that's the word," said Canadian journalist Earl McRae. "It's not hard to respect Fats Delvecchio." In his twenty-three seasons with the Wings, Delvecchio was widely known as one of the classiest players around.

He also had durability, missing only forty-three games in twenty-two full seasons. And from 1957 to 1964, Fats played in 490 consecutive games.

Bruce MacGregor, Delvecchio's Red Wings teammate during the late 1960s, also remembers big Number 10's easy and graceful approach to the game. "Alex was a natural athlete," MacGregor said. "His biggest assets were his skating and passing; a fluid skater with an effortless style. I remember him centering for big Frank Mahovlich. Frank had that big, sweeping stride, and it was tough for centers to judge where he'd be for a pass. But Alex would hit him almost every time, right on the money."

Born December 4, 1931, in Fort William, Ontario, Peter Alexander Delvecchio broke onto the Red Wings' squad at the tender age of nineteen and contributed fifteen goals in his rookie campaign as the Wings swept to the Stanley Cup championship. Alex went on to roll up some very impressive statistics in his career, placing himself second to

Gordie Howe on the all-time NHL lists for regular season games (1,549), points (1,281), and assists (825).

His calm but firm demeanor eventually made Fats one of the most suitable candidates to take over the chores behind the bench of a struggling Red Wings team in 1973, and in November of that year, Alex Delvecchio was officially named coach of the 2-9-1 club. His controlled discipline, laced with a healthy respect for his players as individuals, made Fats successful at his new craft, raising the comatose Detroiters to a level of respectability, and at the same time making life pleasurable for his troops. He was not averse to picking up some cold cuts and beer after a game, or taking the team out to dinner after a practice. But rather than being taken advantage of because of his good naturedness, Delvecchio gained the respect of his entire team, allowing them to simply go out and do what they were paid to do: play hockey.

A man of skill, honor, and respect, Alex Delvecchio was a realist as well. A poem that hung on the wall of his office during his term as Red Wings' coach summarized the precarious nature of the NHL coach and player:

The Indispensable Man

Sometimes when you're feeling important
Sometimes when your ego's in bloom
Sometimes when you take it for granted
You're the best qualified in the room
Take a bucket and fill it with water
Put your hand in it up to the wrist
Pull it out and the hole that's remaining
Is a measure of how much you'll be missed.

Although as dispensable as any other mortal, Alex Delvecchio and the greatness that earned him his rank in *Hockey's 100* will nonetheless be missed.

Larry Robinson
(1972–   )

Chatting with a friend during a summer dinner party at the Concord Hotel in 1987, Larry Robinson confided that the "politics" that had permeated the Montreal Canadiens' dressing room was getting him down. There was more than a hint in the big defenseman's voice that he was ready to pack it in after more than a decade-and-a-half of high-quality play.

In fact, few thought that Robinson would show up at the Forum in 1987–88. A freak polo injury later that year resulted in hospitalization and a leg damaged enough to cause rumor-mongers to suggest that, yes, this time Montreal's blue line leader was history. Yet, the indefatigable defenseman endured painful therapy and returned to the roster not long after the campaign began. To just about everyone's surprise—with the exception of Larry Robinson— he appeared to be in mint condition.

"I've always taken pride in the fact that I've worked hard at whatever I did," said Robinson. "From my earliest days, growing up on the farm, I never looked at life as something that came very easy and I translated it as a challenge for Larry Robinson to make the team. No matter what may have been written, I never looked at it as though I had a spot made and, believe me, that helped."

It helped in 1987–88. When Robinson returned to the Canadiens' lineup, the Habs were floundering. He lifted their game and the *bleu, blanc, et rouge* took over first place in the Adams Division for the rest of the campaign. Nevertheless, it remained a season of turmoil for Robinson.

The "politics" of which he had spoken privately at the Concord during his Catskill mountain vacation had now become a public issue in Montreal. Robinson became a vocal critic of controversial coach Jean Perron along with several other Canadiens. In May 1988, Robinson was still around Ste. Catherine Street, but Perron was forced out of his job. But by August, Robinson's agent, Don Cape, was talking about moving Larry to another NHL team.

Coach-busting was not normally a job associated with the low-key, articulate Robinson. "I don't want to be remembered for that," said Larry. "I want to be remembered as a team player; one who sacrificed personal goals for the hockey club. Also, as one of the best defensemen of my era. I always strived to be the best at what I did."

Usually, he succeeded. Robinson was an integral part of the Canadiens' glorious run of four consecutive Stanley Cups (1976–79), and, despite his advanced age, he played a major role in the Habs' surprise Cup win in 1986. "That last one," Robinson recalled, "was the most satisfying to me and the most fun simply because we weren't supposed to win.

"Having played on six Stanley Cup-winning teams, starting way back in 1973, and coming all the way up to 1986—that's a span of 13 years—is not bad. I'm proud of that and of my longevity. The fact that I outlasted almost all the draft picks higher than myself—with the exception of Marcel Dionne—is, in my mind, a great accomplishment."

Sportsmanship—an element sorely lacking in big-league athletics—was always a part of Robinson's game, and, in that respect, he has always been one of the most respected players in the NHL. "I've tried to be a role model for the kids," he explained, "and wherever I've gone, I've tried to promote hockey in the NHL in a positive way."

Until the 1974–75 season, the only fame defenseman Larry Robinson attained was from an incident on February 17, 1974. That was when he clipped the wings—and the ego—of Philadelphia Flyers' brawler Dave Schultz before a delighted Montreal Forum crowd and a national television audience. Most Canadiens fans who had witnessed the fight came away convinced that head-knocking was Larry Robinson's destiny—being a policeman on the ice. But what was not as obvious at the time was that this big fellow was quite a talented as well as rugged defenseman and would soon become the cornerstone of the impenetrable defense of the Canadiens' teams that captured five Stanley Cups in the 1970s.

Robinson, at 6'3", 210 pounds, was exactly what the stylistic Canadiens needed. With the majority of their personnel being more artistic than overtly physical, the Habs needed a tough, no-nonsense type of rearguard; someone who could force the opposition to think twice before trying any intimidation tactics on their mitelike forwards and keep the Canadiens' crease clear of belligerent types who might make life a bit too difficult for Kenny Dryden. After the Schultz incident, Robinson's reputation had been established. He would no longer have to drop his gloves to prove his point. He could now concentrate on the physical but clean game that was his natural style and spend more time on the ice than in the sin bin, thus helping his team's cause to the maximum.

Though not the prolific scorer that some of his contemporaries were, Robinson established his ability as a strong, rushing puck carrier. And his ability to lug the rubber and engineer the offense in clutch situations made his offensive contributions most timely. "He took quite a few games and broke them open with an end-to-end rush," said ex-Bruins' defenseman Mike Milbury. In time, Robinson reached NHL maturity and ranked with Denis Potvin, Kevin Lowe, and Rod Langway as one of his decade's best defensemen.

Virtually assured a place in the Hockey Hall of Fame, Robinson played as intensely in his seventeenth pro season (1987–88) as he had in his rookie year. "Skating always was my most valuable asset," he explained, "and it's been that way for a long time. The fact that I've been able to combine my size with my skating has made a difference, particularly when you consider that there have been a lot of guys in the NHL who were big but didn't have the quickness or anticipation that I had. To be over six feet and more than 200 pounds and still be a mobile defenseman are qualities that have helped me stay around for a long time."

Sometimes it seemed, only "politics" could stop Larry Robinson. And though last on the list of Hockey's 100, he most certainly is not the least.

The Honor Roll

Jack Adams
George Armstrong
Irvine "Ace" Bailey
Donald "Don" Bain
Marty Barry
Bobby Baun
Clint Benedict
Red Berenson
Dickie Boon
Emile "Butch" Bouchard
George "Buck" Boucher
Russel Bowie
Harry "Punch" Broadbent
John Bucyk
Billy Burch
Harry Cameron
Sprague Cleghorn
Neil Colville
Samuel "Rusty" Crawford
Jack Darragh
Allan "Scotty" Davidson
Cy Denneny
Gordie Drillon
Charles Drinkwater
Thomas Dunderdale
Tony Esposito
Arthur Farrell
Frank Foyston
Herb Gardiner
Jimmy Gardner
Eddie Gerard
Rod Gilbert
Hamilton "Billy" Gilmour
Frank "Moose" Goheen
Mike Grant

Wilfred "Shorty" Green
Silas Griffis
George Hainsworth
Joseph Hall
George Hay
William "Riley" Hern
Hap Holmes
George "Tom" Hooper
George "Red" Horner
Henry "Harry" Howell
John "Bouse" Hutton
Harry Hyland
Ernest "Moose" Jackson
Harvey "Busher" Jackson
Elmer Lach
Newsy Lalonde
Jacques Laperriere
Jean "Jack" Laviolette
Hugh Lehman
Jacques Lemaire
Percy LeSeur
Harry Lumley
Joe Malone
Sylvio Mantha
Jack Marshall
Frank McGee
Billy McGimsie
Duncan "Mickey" McKay
George McNamara
Patrick "Paddy" Moran
Frank Nighbor
Edward "Reg" Noble
Harry Oliver
Joseph Lynn Patrick
Tommy Phillips

Pierre Pilote
Didier Pitre
Harvey Pulford
Frank Rankin
Jean Ratelle
Ken Reardon
George Richardson
Gordon Roberts
Arthur Ross
Blair Russell
Ernest Russel
J.D. "Jack" Ruttan
Serge Savard
Fred Scanlan
Earl Siebert
Oliver Siebert
Albert "Babe" Siebert
Darryl Sittler
Alfred Smith
Reginald "Hooley" Smith
Thomas Smith
Russell "Barney" Stanley
Bruce Stuart
Hod Stuart
Cyclone Taylor
Cecil "Tiny" Thompson
Colonel Harry Trihey
Norm Ullman
Jack Walker
Marty Walsh
Harry Watson
Harry Westwick
Fred Whitcroft
Gordon "Phat" Wilson

The Ten Best Playoff Performers

1. **Maurice Richard:** *The Rocket*'s red glare was invariably more evident in the playoffs than at any time during the season.
2. **Gordie Howe:** Some have disparaged Howe for his failure to score big goals during the Stanley Cup rounds, but Gordie was the leading playoff scorer *no less than six times in his career*.
3. **Dickie Moore:** Twice the leading playoff scorer, Moore had his last hurrah with the St. Louis Blues after twice retiring and, despite gimpy legs, still produced an astonishing seven goals and seven assists in eighteen games.
4. **Jacques Plante:** There never would have been a Canadiens playoff dynasty without the peerless goalkeeping of Plante. He produced the best goals against average from the 1956 playoff through the 1960 round.
5. **Bobby Orr:** The Bruins' extraordinary defenseman scored the Cup-winning goal in the 1970 clincher against St. Louis and was equally dominating for Boston when the Bruins won the Cup again in 1972.
6. **Ted Kennedy:** When the Maple Leafs were in a jam during the halcyon years of the late 1940s, Kennedy could be counted upon to produce the big play. He played on five Stanley Cup winners.
7. **Nels Stewart:** When the Montreal Maroons won the Stanley Cup in 1926, Stewart scored six goals. *No other player scored more than one. Ole Poison* always was a threat in the postseason tourney.
8. **Syl Apps:** The stalwart Maple Leafs' captain was chiefly responsible for the ultimate playoff comeback—Toronto won four straight from Detroit after being down three games to none—in 1942, and led the Leafs to Cup wins in 1947 and 1948.
9. **Tim Horton:** Admired for his defensive consistency throughout the Maple Leafs' Cup reign in the early 1960s, Horton also produced a mighty offensive effort in 1962 finishing second in scoring with sixteen points in twelve games as Toronto won the Cup.
10. **Pentti Lund:** The most unsung of all playoff aces, Lund emerged as a hero in 1950. The New York Rangers' left wing was assigned to check Maurice Richard. Lund not only snuffed out Richard but went on to become the leading scorer in the entire playoff round.

The Ten Best Clutch Scorers

1. **Maurice Richard:** The one shooter any coach would ever want on the ice in sudden-death overtime would be *The Rocket*. His flair for the dramatic has never been matched.
2. **Mel "Sudden Death" Hill:** A modest scorer for the Boston Bruins during the 1938–39 season, Hill scored a pair of sudden-death goals against the Rangers early in the playoff series and the overtime winner in the seventh game.
3. **Modere "Mud" Bruneteau:** The Detroit Red Wings and Montreal Canadiens played the longest game ever on March 24, 1936. Bruneteau scored the winner for Detroit four minutes and forty-six seconds after the ninth period began.
4. **Ken Doraty:** Prior to Bruneteau's classic, Toronto Maple Leafs' forward Ken Doraty settled what then was the longest game (April 3, 1933) with a goal against Boston at four minutes and forty-six seconds of the sixth overtime.
5. **Howie Morenz:** *The Stratford Streak* was the Maurice Richard of his era and generally conceded to be the hardest player in the league to stop.
6. **Frank Boucher:** Ever reliable, Boucher paced the New York Rangers to their first Stanley Cup in 1928 with the only goals in a 2–0 win over the Montreal Maroons in the decisive game.
7. **Nels Stewart:** *Ole Poison* was *the* man for the Montreal Maroons; a shooter of consummate accuracy and one whose clutch skills were underestimated.
8. **Max Bentley:** The manifold skills of *The Dipsy Doodle Dandy* were amply demonstrated in 1947, 1948, 1949, 1950, and 1951 when the Toronto Maple Leafs were the class of the NHL.
9. **Bryan Hextall:** The foremost Rangers' shooter in the late 1930s and early 1940s, Hextall won the last Stanley Cup for the Blueshirts with a sudden-death goal against the Maple Leafs in April 1940.
10. **Leo Reise Jr.:** Basically a defensive defenseman with limited scoring talents, Reise emerged as an incredible clutch shooter in the bitter and bloody 1950 Stanley Cup semifinal between the Red Wings and the Maple Leafs. With Detroit trailing two games to one, Reise scored a sudden-death goal in the second overtime of Game 3. He won the series with another overtime goal in the seventh match.

The Ten Best Defensive Forwards

1. **Claude Provost:** The eminently clean guardian of the likes of Bobby Hull and other big guns, Provost played on *nine* Montreal Canadiens Stanley Cup winners. They couldn't have done it without him.
2. **Joe Klukay:** Known as *The Duke of Paducah*, Klukay labored on the Toronto Maple Leafs' late 1940s Cup winners in the shadow of Syl Apps, et al., but his defensive work and penalty-killing was flawless.
3. **Ed Westfall:** When Bobby Orr and the Big, Bad Bruins were winning Stanley Cups in 1970 and 1972, Westfall was neutralizing the enemy aces with mangnificent aplomb while managing to score a few himself.
4. **Marty Pavelich:** Complementing *The Production Line* on the awesome Detroit Red Wings of the 1950s was this slithering center who tormented the foe with his tenacious checking.
5. **Bob Gainey:** The NHL struck the Frank J. Selke Trophy for the best defensive forward in 1978, and Bob Gainey of the Montreal Canadiens won it for the next four consecutive seasons—and continued to sparkle through 1987–88.
6. **Bob Nevin:** During the Toronto Maple Leafs' playoff-winning reign of the early 1960s, Bob Nevin's work on right wing went unheralded by the masses but not unnoticed by general manager-coach Punch Imlach.
7. **Nick Metz:** Joe Klukay's alter ego for several years in Toronto, Metz preceded the Duke, playing on Cup winners in 1942 and 1945 before the late 1940s dynasty gave him a smidgen of prominence.
8. **Tony Leswick:** So effective was Leswick, the New York Ranger, against Gordie Howe that the Detroit Red Wings dealt for him to get him off Howe's back. With Tony on their side, the Wings won three Stanley Cups.
9. **Red Kelly:** Having been an all-star defenseman, Kelly was superbly equipped to play defensive center as he did after being dealt from the Red Wings to the Maple Leafs.
10. **Steve Kasper:** During the 1980–81 and 1981–82 seasons, when Wayne Gretzky was breaking all existing scoring records, one center was able to consistently neutralize Gretzky. Kasper, the Boston Bruins' defensive ace, was that thinking young man and was rewarded with the Frank J. Selke Trophy. By 1987–88, he added offense to his defense totaling twenty-six goals, forty-four assists, and seventy points.

The Ten Best General Managers

1. **Frank Selke, Sr.:** At the close of World War II, Selke moved from the Toronto Maple Leafs to the Montreal Canadiens and constructed the foremost dynasty the sport has known.
2. **Conn Smythe:** Selke's mentor, Smythe organized the original New York Rangers and then built the Maple Leafs into a winner. His signal accomplishment was the design of the Stanley Cup winners in 1947, 1948, 1949, and 1951.
3. **Bill Torrey:** At a time when the World Hockey Association had decimated NHL rosters, the New York Islanders were born. Torrey patiently designed the club around brilliant draft choices such as Denis Potvin and Bryan Trottier and produced four straight Stanley Cup championships in 1980, 1981, 1982, and 1983.
4. **Sam Pollock:** Although the Canadiens' machine might have faltered after Selke's retirement, Pollock redesigned it, assuring that Montreal would remain a major contender throughout the 1970s.
5. **Tommy Gorman:** Never has a general manager been successful with more different teams than Gorman. He managed three different Stanley Cup winners (the Ottawa Senators, Chicago Black Hawks, and Montreal Canadiens) and also provided the New York Americans with a few moments of glory.
6. **Glen Sather:** Like Torrey, *Slats* took over a young team under difficult circumstances and produced four Stanley Cup winners (1984, 1985, 1987, 1988) in a remarkably short time.
7. **Jack Adams:** The Detroit Red Wings during the 1930s and 1940s were among the NHL's most consistently dominating teams. Adams created the farm system that delivered Gordie Howe, et al., to Detroit.
8. **Art Ross:** One the most creative hockey thinkers, Ross developed an endless series of aces, starting with Eddie Shore and culminating with the Boston Bruins' renowned *Kraut Line*.
9. **Tommy Ivan:** A crumbling Chicago Black Hawks franchise was saved from complete destruction by Ivan, who rebuilt a farm system that led to the Windy City's last Stanley Cup in 1961.
10. **Punch Imlach:** The retirement of Conn Smythe left the Maple Leafs aimlessly fluttering in the 1950s. Imlach resurrected the club and produced four Stanley Cup winners in the 1960s.

The Ten Best Coaches

1. **Hector "Toe" Blake:** It is enough to say that Blake guided the Montreal Canadiens to *eight* Stanley Cup championships, including a run of five straight from 1956 through 1960.
2. **Hap Day:** The man who engineered the greatest comeback in Cup history (1942 vs. the Detroit Red Wings), Day coached five Stanley Cup winners, including a then unprecedented run of three in a row in the late 1940s.
3. **Al Arbour:** When Arbour took control of the New York Islanders, they were at a subterranean level. He patiently guided them to a position of eminence and respect while winning four consecutive Stanley Cups.
4. **Lester Patrick:** Patrick's name is etched on three Stanley Cups; once with the Victoria Cougars and twice with the New York Rangers. He was innovative and inspiring.
5. **Dick Irvin:** After coaching the Maple Leafs to a Stanley Cup in 1932, Irvin later won three Cups for the Canadiens. He harnessed Maurice Richard and produced magnificently exciting "firewagon-style" teams.
6. **Glen Sather:** Both general manager *and* coach of the Oilers, he had to develop a youthful corps including Wayne Gretzky, Mark Messier, and Kevin Lowe. He did it to the tune of four Stanley Cups in five years (1984–1988), which was a commendable feat.
7. **Tommy Ivan:** When Jack Adams molded the Red Wings into a contender in the early 1950s, it was Ivan who masterminded Stanley Cup wins in 1950, 1952, and 1954.
8. **Punch Imlach:** Carrying the dual title of general manager and coach never bothered Imlach. Apart from his four Stanley Cups, he demonstrated that older skaters could be resurrected and turned into big winners.
9. **Anatoli Tarasov:** The "father of Soviet hockey," Tarasov demonstrated to the North Americans that European creativity could be used to an advantage in the NHL. His teams were among the first to persuade both Canadian and American fans that the best hockey was not necessarily played on this side of the Atlantic.
10. **Scotty Bowman:** Brilliant at times, Bowman won four straight Stanley Cups (1976, 1977, 1978, and 1979) for the Canadiens but could not rekindle his spark after taking over the Buffalo Sabres. Still, his accomplishments cannot be overlooked.

The Ten Best Defensive Defensemen

1. **Doug Harvey:** Best known for his total ice generalship, Harvey was the center-piece of the successful Montreal Canadiens club in the 1950s because of his defensive excellence.
2. **Tim Horton:** Somewhat less creative than Harvey, Horton nevertheless patrolled his side with diligence and power during the Toronto Maple Leafs' golden era of the early 1960s.
3. **Eddie Shore:** Shore's versatility as a rushing defenseman with the Boston Bruins beclouded his crunching play behind the blue line.
4. **Ching Johnson:** The towering New York Ranger spent little time rushing when there was so much bodychecking to be done. He was the best Manhattan has ever seen.
5. **Hap Day:** A vastly superior intelligence (in relation to most other defensemen) gave Day an advantage, which he exploited to the fullest on the Maple Leafs of the early 1930s.
6. **Emile Bouchard:** Overshadowed by *The Punch Line*, "Butch" Bouchard was the first of the grand post-World War II Canadiens' defensemen who made life infinitely easier for Vezina-winner Bill Durnan.
7. **Jack Stewart:** There were few stronger men or more emphatic hitters or diligent defense players than Black Jack. The Detroit Red Wings would have been impotent without him.
8. **Dit Clapper:** The Bruins' defense centered around this stately and thoughtful athlete who was quite willing to use his body as well as his head.
9. **Jim Thomson:** When the Toronto Maple Leafs won three straight Stanley Cups (1947, 1948, and 1949), the defense of Thomson and Gus Mortson was impenetrable. Mortson rushed more often. Thomson quietly did the defensive work.
10. **Allan Stanley:** The quintessential defensive defenseman, Stanley was pivotal—along with Horton—during the Toronto reign of the early 1960s.

The Ten Best Little Men

1. **King Clancy:** There was never a more resilient defenseman who managed to distill humor and courage with his artistry. The fact that he never won a fight during his lengthy NHL career never tempered his pugnacity.
2. **Roy "Shrimp" Worters:** Although the goaltending theory has always been "the more net filled the better," Worters amply demonstrated that a tiny man with catlike moves could play as well—or better— than the best of the big ones. Worters was the best of the little men and, in the opinion of some, the best of them all.
3. **Ted Lindsay:** Notorious for his vicious use of the stick, Lindsay nevertheless could handle his dukes and was one of the most dangerous offensive left wings in the game. *Old Scarface* was never hampered by his size.
4. **Henri Richard:** A French-Canadian version of Lindsay, *The Pocket Rocket* was every inch as tough as his brother Maurice and a remarkable playmaker to boot. The mind boggles at the thought of Henri Richard's ability inside Jean Beliveau's body.
5. **Yvan Cournoyer:** Never one to raise a fist in anger, *The Roadrunner* exploited speed above all. His pacifism never proved to be a deterrent.
6. **Denis Savard:** This slippery little Chicago Black Hawks' centerman effectively dodged all determined efforts by opposing checkers to tally eighty-seven assists and 119 points in the 1981–82 season, his second in the NHL. Along with his scoring skills, Savard proved sufficiently quick and tough enough to play all eighty regular-season games and averaged better than a point per game while leading the Black Hawks to their best playoff performance in almost a decade. He continued starring through the 80s, and in 1987–88 he recorded 44–87–141, his best season so far in the NHL.
7. **Pat "Whitey" Stapleton:** Remarkably agile, this Chicago Black Hawks' defenseman pressed plenty of muscle into his miniframe. He was an unsung hero during Chicago's golden hockey era of the early 1960s.
8. **Aurel Joliat:** A ferocious 5'6" and 135 pounds, Joliat earned the nickname *Mighty Mite* with his amazingly tough, physical style. A marvelous stickhandler and passer, as well as a lethal shot, Aurel combined finesse and feistiness to become one of the most respected players of his time.
9. **Buddy O'Connor:** A one-time member of the Montreal Canadiens' *Razzle-Dazzle Line*, this slightly-built center became an NHL hero after being traded to the New York Rangers. He went on to miss the scoring title by a single point, but captured both the Hart and Lady Byng trophies during the 1947–48 campaign.
10. **Harold "Mush" March:** A fifteen-year veteran of the Chicago Black Hawks, March is best remembered for a shot he fired at Detroit goalkeeper Wilf Cude on April 10, 1934. The score was tied at the time when Marsh dented the twine at 10:05 of the second overtime period to give the Black Hawks their first Stanley Cup championship.

The Ten Best Hockey Arenas

1. **Boston Garden:** Reeking with nostalgia and never modernized in the manner of the Montreal Forum or Maple Leaf Gardens, the Bruins' home is the Ebbets Field of the NHL and, hopefully, will remain that way.
2. **Maple Leaf Gardens:** The jewel of the Canadian arenas. "The House That Conn Smythe Built" has retained much of the flavor of opening night in 1931. Introduction of organ music has diminished its appeal.
3. **Montreal Forum:** Like its Toronto counterpart, the Forum remains a shrine. Its lobby is graced with bronze castings of the Canadiens' top heroes. Post-World War II improvements have not hurt a bit.
4. **Chicago Stadium:** Despite its location in a seedy part of Chicago, the Stadium—like Boston Garden—oozes with history. The cavernous interior still echoes with cheers for the Bentleys and Bobby Hull.
5. **Detroit Olympia:** Gone but not forgotten, the showcase "theater" for Gordie Howe, Ted Lindsay, and Sid Abel, Olympia is also remembered for Pete Cusimano, the octopus-thrower at Red Wings games.
6. **Old Madison Square Garden:** Located at Forty-ninth Street and Eighth Avenue, a block from Times Square, the old Garden had terrible sight lines from the side balcony, but a magnificent ambiance that made one love New York hockey.
7. **Quebec Colisée:** "The House That Jean Beliveau Built" has been enlarged since *Le Gros Bill* played for the Quebec (Junior) Citadelles. The 100 percent Gallic crowd is unmatched throughout the league.
8. **St. Louis Arena:** Although it has been completely refurbished, the St. Louis Arena dates back to 1929. Its loaf-of-bread center and two adjacent towers make it unique.
9. **The Spectrum:** One of the least-flawed hockey rinks, the Spectrum is equally appreciated by fans and media alike. There is good seating for all. Rooters, they say, will boo the loser of a wheelchair race.
10. **Nassau Coliseum:** Not only are even the cheapest seats obstruction-free but the sky boxes and press areas provide the best views possible. While relatively new, the Coliseum has the good feel of a venerable arena.

The Ten Best Referees
of All Time

1. **John Ashley:** Invariably calm and always in complete command of the ice, Ashley was both distinguished in appearance and performance. The fact that he had been a professional defenseman for many years added to his insights.
2. **Mickey Ion:** When this man told a colleague, in a rink jammed with 15,000 frenzied fans, "There are only two sane people here—you and me," he was betraying the good sense that made him a superior whistle-blower.
3. **Bill Chadwick:** Although sightless in one eye, this courageous New York-born official saw more than most refs. He backed down from no one and made some of the most difficult calls in critical situations of any of his ilk. When Detroit owner Jim Norris tried to have him fired, it proved he was a winner.
4. **King Clancy:** Like Ashley, Clancy had been a defenseman who could translate his playing experience to hockey's penal system. His ebullience and humor gave him an edge over his more serious brethren.
5. **Bobby Hewitson:** Remarkably, this gentle, perceptive fellow was the sports editor of the *Toronto Telegram*, while a full-time NHL referee. He handled a whistle as well as he did an editorial pencil.
6. **Red Storey:** A flame-haired, towering referee, Storey imported his knowledge as both a football and hockey star to the rinks. Controversial to a fault, Storey cut short his own career, resigning in protest over an "off the record" critique made by NHL President Clarence Campbell.
7. **Jack Mehlenbacher:** *The Sleeper* of referees, Mehlenbacher did his job so quietly, effectively, and efficiently, that no one ever bothered to acknowledge his superiority, other than the players, who respected his work.
8. **Mike Rodden:** It is no accident that this referee from hockey's earlier era is in the Hall of Fame. Curiously, Rodden, like Bobby Hewitson, also was a sports editor for a Canadian daily.
9. **Cooper Smeaton:** An official who saw things clearly and saw them whole, Smeaton was so distinguished a referee that he was later named a trustee of the Stanley Cup.
10. **Frank Udvari:** An absolutely abysmal (even he'd admit that) whistle-blower in his early years, Udvari eventually ripened into one of the very best. Long after his retirement, he was summoned from the stands at Nassau Coliseum to pinch-hit for an injured referee. Although wearing his suit pants and borrowed skates, Udvari proceeded to officiate one of the best games ever refereed in the building.

Photograph Credits